# Sunset
# Cook Book for Entertaining

*Sunset*
# Cook Book for

LANE MAGAZINE & BOOK COMPANY

# *Entertaining*

By the Editors of Sunset Books and Sunset Magazine

MENLO PARK, CALIFORNIA

# Contents

**9 SPECIAL MEALS FOR SPECIAL OCCASIONS**

*Menus and party plans for a variety of events, from simple get-togethers to exotic and challenging affairs*

10 Authentic Indian Curry Dinner
12 Finnish Coffee Smörgåsbord
13 A Patio Buffet
13 Spanish Paella Dinner
14 Patio Luau
16 An Elegant Duckling Dinner
   How to Have a Wine-Tasting—page 16
17 A Wine-Tasting Party
18 Turkish Meze
21 Oriental Meal Cooked at the Table
22 Fruit and Cheese Snack Tray
   Good Morning Breakfasts for Guests—Page 23
24 Build-Your-Own-Salad Lunch
25 French Peasant Aïoli
26 Scandinavian Buffet
28 Champagne Party
29 Barbecued Ham Buffet
   Planning the Perfect Menu—Page 29
30 Mexican Tamalada
32 Greek Buffet
33 Shellfish on Ice
34 The Chinese "Hot Pot"
36 A Waffle Party
   How to Serve Unexpected Guests—Page 37
38 Japanese Sushi Picnic
40 Portuguese Country Dinner
41 Nouveau Riche Hamburgers
42 Wintertime Buffet
   Have an Old-Fashioned Taffy Pull—Page 42
43 Supper Beside the Fire
44 The Fondue Party
47 Picnic for Patrons of the Arts
48 Italian Fritter Meal
48 Cold Salmon Buffet
49 Tahitian Party

**51 APPEALING APPETIZERS**

*Recipes for tempting hot and cold snacks, as well as sit-down treats to serve before a special meal*

52 Dips, Spreads, Tidbits
Simple but Special Appetizers—Page 54
A Guide to Caviar—Page 57
63 First-Course Dishes
Icy Ideas for Presenting Appetizers—Page 64

**69 SOUPS AND SALADS**

*Recipes for both light and hearty, cold and hot soups, as well as new and imaginatively different salads*

70 Soups
Garnish Ideas for Soups—Page 73
Dressing up Green Salads—Page 76
77 Salads
Folded Napkins and Custom Touches—Page 83

**89 DISTINCTIVE ENTRÉES**

*Recipes ranging from simple to complex, for informal or elegant occasions, including main-dish salads and soups*

90 Beef and Veal
Garnishing the Entrée—Page 92
Steak—A Favorite Party Entrée—Page 95
98 Lamb
Presenting the Pleasures of Wine—Page 101
Cooking with Wine—Page 104
105 Pork
111 Poultry
How to Use Chafing Dishes—Page 116
The Art of the Small Dinner Party—Page 119
Shopper's Guide to Wine Labeling—Page 121
124 Seafood
Cooking and Saucing Fish—Page 128
The Versatile Omelet—Page 131
133 Varied Entrées
138 Soup or Salad Meals
Crisp and Crunchy Breads—Page 140

**145 ACCOMPANIMENTS AND SIDE DISHES**

*Recipes for vegetables, rice, pasta, and breads—to serve with the entrée or as a separate course*

146 Vegetables
Flavored-Butter Seasonings—Page 149
A Guide to Serving Cheeses—Page 156
161 Pastas and Cereals
Wine Age and Vintage—Page 163
164 Breads
Even Butter Can Be Beautiful—Page 165
Fancy Shapes for Dinner Rolls—Page 169

**173 DISTINGUISHED DESSERTS**

*Recipes for a sweet finale or for a special refreshment— all of which can be partially or entirely made in advance*

Elegant Ice Cream Finales—Page 176
Two Beautiful Dessert Garnishes—Page 180
Bombes for a Burst of Compliments—Page 185
Easy Fresh Fruit Desserts—Page 191

**195 HOT AND COLD DRINKS**

*Recipes for cool fruit and milk drinks, sophisticated adult concoctions, cold and hot punches*

Icy Ways to Serve Drinks—Page 199
Coffees from Around the World—Page 201
Cool Drinks with Coconut Milk—Page 203

**204 SUBJECT AND RECIPE INDEX**

*Quick and handy reference to all foods, drinks, menus, tips, and ideas for entertaining throughout the book*

ILLUSTRATIONS BY FRANK L. LANZA

COVER PHOTOGRAPH: Danish Chicken and Meatballs au Gratin, see page 113.
PHOTOGRAPHERS: Glenn Christiansen—Cover, 50, 99, 125, 135, 144, 194.
Bruce Harlow—172. Darrow Watt—8, 61, 68, 79, 88, 107, 114, 153, 166, 179, 188.

This book was produced in California. Printing and binding by Peninsula Lithograph Company,
from lithograph film by Balzer-Shopes Lithoplate Company, Inc. The type is Palatino
and Helvetica, composed by Spartan Typographers. Paper is Mountie Handmade, furnished
by Northwest Paper Company, Cloquet, Minnesota.

# Foods for Entertaining

THIS BOOK IS DEDICATED to providing the ultimate in dining delight for your guests and the maximum of leisure and pleasure for you, the hostess.

Three main features are aimed at helping you prepare a wide variety of sumptuous foods with a minimum of worry and fluster:

- Tested menus and party plans suitable for many different occasions.
- Recipes unique enough to be appropriate for special entertaining, but also sufficiently easy and convenient to make.
- Guides and tips for adding those perfecting touches and embellishments which transform an ordinary get-together into a memorable event.

The menus and party plans on pages 9 through 49 range from very simple and informal get-togethers to bountiful and elegant affairs. You may follow these plans exactly, modify them by making the suggested substitutions, or use the menus to inspire your own ideas.

To plan your own menus, you may select from the large and varied individual recipes on pages 51 through 203. Each recipe is accompanied by valuable information you need to make a wise choice—the number of servings it produces, a description of how the dish will look or taste, instructions for serving and garnishing, and notes telling how far ahead preparation may take place. Most of these dishes are much easier to make than the glamorous results indicate, and many may be made entirely in advance.

Numerous "tips" and helpful guides appear throughout the book. Some contain information useful for planning a party or for purchasing foods; others are devoted to garnish or serving ideas. Still others are collections of simple recipes suitable for impromptu entertaining or for balancing a menu of more complicated dishes.

Each menu and recipe in this book has been prepared and tested by the home economics department of *Sunset Magazine*.

# Special Meals for Special Occasions

THE MENUS AND PARTY PLANS offered in this chapter are not great in number, but they are varied. Some are very simple and easy to arrange; a few are exotic enough to challenge the confident and experimental cook. Some are intended for posh occasions, others for very informal get-togethers, perhaps out-of-doors. Some are definitely for adults; others are suitable for groups of all ages, or young people.

Different ways of entertaining are represented. Most involve full meals: those planned around one important main dish, those of several courses served at the table, those presented buffet-style, and those served out-of-doors. Others are ways to entertain without a complete meal—snacks, beverage parties, teas, and informal occasions where the guests may pitch in to help make what they eat. These informal party ideas are particularly useful for the younger set, but most will also have appeal for adults.

In every case possible, a menu appears with a description of each dish. Then tips are given on how to arrange or decorate the party and how to time preparation of the food. Whenever a recipe would generally be used *only* for this particular kind of event, it is printed following the tips. However, the recipes for all-purpose dishes you might serve with many kinds of meals are *not* with the menu, but are printed in the main recipe section of the book, beginning on page 50. (This is done so these all-purpose recipes may be considered for the menus you plan yourself.) Nevertheless, a good description of such all-purpose dishes is in the menu, *plus* the number of the page in the recipe section where the recipe appears. You can tell from the menu description whether the dish appeals to you and then easily turn to the recipe.

In many of the menus, alternates are suggested. In some cases, you may choose between several dishes to make with recipes in this book. Or the choice offered may be between something you make and something you buy ready-made. This feature should let you adapt the menus to your taste or to the time and effort you want to spend.

# Authentic Indian Curry Dinner

*FOR SIX TO EIGHT PEOPLE*

**PODINA CHUTNEY**

Mint and onion chutney

**CHANA MASALA**

Garbanzo beans with ginger, chiles, and coriander

**KEEMA CURRY**

Spiced ground lamb and green peas

**BHINDI MASALA**

Spice-stuffed okra sautéed in butter

**GULAB JAMANS**

Fried pastries in cardamom-flavored syrup

If you enjoy a good Indian curry dinner, you can duplicate an authentic meal more simply than you may imagine. With ground spices and the frozen, canned, and packaged foods available in markets, it is easier to prepare many Indian foods here than in India.

## PODINA CHUTNEY

Using an electric blender, you can whirl this chutney together in a minute. Indians usually add some hot seasoning, but you may prefer to keep it cool to contrast with the curry. Most people like it mildly spiced, with about 2 canned green chiles.

1 medium-sized onion, sliced
1 clove garlic
1 teaspoon chopped fresh ginger (or ¼ teaspoon ground ginger)
1 pint fresh mint leaves or ½ cup dried mint (or 2 bunches fresh coriander)
3 tablespoons lemon juice
½ teaspoon salt
Fresh California green chile pepper or canned green chiles, to taste (optional)

Put the onion, garlic, and ginger into the blender jar and whirl until finely chopped. Add the mint (simmer dried mint in boiling water 2 minutes, drain), lemon juice, and salt and blend into a smooth sauce. To make this sauce a little hot, blend in green chile pepper, starting with 1 chile. Cover and refrigerate several hours or longer. Makes about 1 cup.

## CHANA MASALA

This is a particularly easy recipe to prepare; it uses canned garbanzos.

2 tablespoons butter or margarine
1 large onion, chopped
2 cloves garlic, minced or mashed
1 teaspoon chopped fresh ginger (or ¼ teaspoon ground ginger)
1 large tomato, peeled and chopped
2 small, dried hot chile peppers, seeded and crushed (or ¼ teaspoon cayenne)
½ teaspoon <u>each</u> salt and pepper
3 teaspoons ground coriander
½ teaspoon <u>each</u> cinnamon and ground cumin
¼ teaspoon ground cloves
2 cans (15 oz. <u>each</u>) garbanzo beans
2 tablespoons chopped parsley

In frying pan, heat the butter; add the onion, garlic, and ginger and sauté until the onion is lightly browned, about 5 minutes. Add the tomato, chile peppers, salt, pepper, and spices; cover and cook, stirring often, about 3 minutes. Drain the beans, reserving liquid. Add beans to hot sauce; cook about 5 minutes, adding a little of the bean liquid, if needed. Top with parsley.

## KEEMA CURRY

Frozen peas are added to this quick-cooking curry at the last minute so they retain their attractive bright green color; total cooking time is about 20 to 25 minutes. Taste the curry while it is cooking, and add cayenne or liquid hot-pepper seasoning to raise the heat level to your taste—¾ teaspoon cayenne in addition to the 2 dried hot chile peppers called for in the recipe might be a good amount. Or for milder flavor, omit the chile peppers and add chile powder.

2 tablespoons each butter and salad oil
2 medium-sized onions, chopped
2 cloves garlic, minced or mashed
2 teaspoons chopped fresh ginger (or ½ teaspoon ground ginger)
　About 2 small, dried hot chile peppers, seeded and crushed
2 teaspoons turmeric
3 teaspoons salt
1 medium-sized tomato, peeled and diced
2 pounds ground lean lamb
1 package (10 oz.) frozen peas, partly defrosted
1 teaspoon ground coriander
¼ teaspoon pepper
　Dash each of cinnamon, ground cumin, and cloves
　About 1 tablespoon minced fresh coriander or parsley

Heat the butter and salad oil in a large heavy frying pan (one with a lid); add the onion, garlic, and ginger; sauté until onion is lightly browned. Add the chile peppers, turmeric, salt, and tomato; stir and cook about 5 minutes. Add the lamb and cook, stirring, until the meat has lost its pinkness, about 10 minutes. Stir in the peas, ground coriander, pepper, and mixed spices. Cover, and simmer 4 to 5 minutes.

　Spoon into a warm serving dish, sprinkle with fresh coriander or parsley.

## BHINDI MASALA

This okra is stuffed with spices, then sautéed quickly in butter; it retains bright color and crispness.

2 packages (10 oz. each) frozen okra
2 tablespoons ground coriander
1 teaspoon salt
1½ teaspoons ground turmeric
½ teaspoon each pepper and ground cumin
　About 3 tablespoons each butter and shortening or salad oil
1 can (1 lb.) small white onions (optional)

Allow the okra to defrost at room temperature; wipe each dry with paper towels. With the tip of a small sharp knife, cut a slit in the side of each okra. Combine the coriander, salt, turmeric, pepper, and cumin; with a small spoon put about ¼ teaspoon (or a little less) of the spice mixture in each okra (you should have about one quarter of the mixture left). This much of the preparation can be done as much as 3 hours ahead; refrigerate okra until cooking time.

　Just before serving, heat about 2 tablespoons *each* butter and shortening in a frying pan over medium-high heat; add the okra and stir-fry about 7 to 8 minutes, or until tender, adding more butter and shortening as needed. Spoon okra into a warm serving dish.

　If onions are used, stir the remaining spice mixture into butter remaining in the pan, add the drained onions, and stir until lightly browned and heated through. Add to the okra in the serving dish.

## GULAB JAMANS

Instant dry milk powder and prepared biscuit mix greatly simplify the preparation of this traditional Indian dessert. You make it a day ahead.

2 cups sugar
4 cups water
4 whole cardamom pods (or 6 whole cloves, or 2 sticks cinnamon)
1⅓ cups instant dry milk powder
⅔ cup biscuit mix
⅛ teaspoon soda
3 tablespoons butter or margarine
½ cup milk
　About ¼ cup sliced almonds (optional)
　About 1½ pounds (or 3 cups) shortening or salad oil for frying

Combine the sugar and water in a pan. With a sharp knife, make a slit in the ends of each whole cardamom pod, if used; drop spice into sugar mixture. Bring to a boil, stirring until sugar is dissolved. Boil until reduced by about half; turn heat to low.

　Meanwhile, combine the dry milk powder, biscuit mix, and soda. Add the butter and cut in with a pastry blender until well distributed. Stir in the milk, then turn out on a lightly floured board and knead thoroughly for about 15 minutes, or until smooth and elastic. Break off pieces of dough and roll into balls about the size of cherries, rolling a slice of almond inside each, if you wish. Drop the balls, a few at a time, into deep fat heated to 340°. Fry until deep brown, turning to brown evenly. Remove from fat with a slotted spoon and drop into the hot syrup.

　You can do this much a day ahead, letting the syrup and sweet balls stand at room temperature. Immediately before serving put back over heat just until heated through. Serve warm, with syrup spooned over the balls.

# Finnish Coffee Smörgåsbord

*FOR TWELVE TO EIGHTEEN PEOPLE*

### FINNISH COFFEE BREAD
Cardamom-flavored braided loaf
Recipe on page 171

### POUND CAKE DUSTED WITH POWDERED SUGAR
From the bakery or made from your favorite recipe

### OLD TIMES CAKE
Pastry layers filled with strawberries and whipped cream
Recipe on page 189

### ORANGE TORTE COOKIES
Almond-filled loaf sliced into cookies
Recipe on page 192

### THREE FINNISH COOKIES
Raspberry Strip Cookies, chocolate-tipped Horseshoes, and
Cinnamon Half-Moons—all made from one basic dough
Recipes on page 193

### HOT COFFEE
With lump sugar and cream

For a pleasant change from the usual tea, try this Scandinavian "coffee." You eat seven baked sweets and sip at least four cups of coffee if you're having Coffee Smörgåsbord the Finnish way. A Finnish coffee table can serve a variety of occasions, evening or daytime: a gathering of neighbors, dessert party, club meeting, open house, or tea.

To serve the authentic foods, set aside one grand day of baking before the party and prepare the bread, cakes, and cookies suggested here. All the recipes are simple, and three kinds of cookies are made from one basic dough.

Or, you can entertain in the same manner with less effort if you make just one or two of the seven sweets and buy kinds similar to the rest.

In Finland no two coffee tables are alike. Each homemaker serves her own combination of favorites to suit the occasion and her mood. Still, certain traditions are always observed that give almost an air of ritual.

Three main attractions appear: a sweet yeast bread, an un-iced pound cake, and a fancy filled or decorated cake. Four kinds of cookies are added to make the traditional total of seven sweets.

The coffee table is served in three courses: the first consists of the sweet yeast bread and a cooky or two; the second is the un-iced cake, also with a few cookies; and the third is the fancy cake. (In Finland, it's considered a breach of etiquette if you don't sample a little of each course.)

Guests have at least one cup of coffee with each course. (Finnish coffee cups are about one-fourth smaller than ours.) Difficult to master, but also part of the ritual, is drinking the last cup of coffee through a lump of sugar which you hold between your teeth.

The Finnish bread, cake, and cookies, which can be baked ahead, are rich with eggs and butter; that's why they keep fresh so long. The eggy pound cake is prettiest if baked in a tube pan, dusted with powdered sugar, and decorated with fresh blossoms in the center. But a loaf-shaped bakery cake can be attractively decorated. Make coffee by your standard method, but brew it less strong than usual.

# A Patio Buffet

*FOR EIGHT PEOPLE*

### HERBED LEG OF LAMB WITH ROASTED POTATOES

Seasoned with lemon juice, mustard, thyme, and rosemary
Recipe on page 103

### COLD BROCCOLI WITH CASHEWS

Seasoned with olive oil, lemon, and chervil
Recipe on page 150

### FRESH CUCUMBER MOLD

Puréed cucumbers in gelatin with whipped and sour cream
Recipe on page 85

### CROISSANTS

From the bakery, served warm if desired

### ORANGE CHEDDAR CHEESECAKE

A refreshing variation on traditional cheesecake
Recipe on page 190

Except for the roasting of the leg of lamb and potatoes together in the oven, last-minute preparation is almost eliminated. Everything is served cold except the entrée.

# Spanish Paella

*FOR EIGHT PEOPLE*

### SPANISH OLIVES, SALTED ROASTED ALMONDS, PICKLED ARTICHOKES

### STUFFED EGGS

To serve as appetizers with dry Sherry

### PAELLA

Saffron-flavored rice with meats and seafood
Recipe on page 133

### MIXED LETTUCES WITH OIL AND VINEGAR

### NATILLUS

The Spanish version of Floating Island
Recipe on page 182

The classic Spanish dish of saffron rice, studded with meats and seafood, is hearty enough to serve as a main dish and varied enough to need little accompaniment. Pork, chicken, sausages, shrimp, and lobster with bits of pimiento are the principal ingredients.

# Patio Luau

QUANTITIES MAY BE ADJUSTED TO SERVE FROM FOUR TO TWENTY-FOUR PEOPLE

**COCONUT CHIPS AND SALTED NUTS**

**ROAST PORK, HAWAIIAN-STYLE**
Baked with leaves and bananas, for authentic flavoring

**BAKED SWEET POTATOES**
Cooked with the roast pork

**LOMI-SALMON-STUFFED TOMATOES**
Salty salmon with chopped green onions and tomatoes

**POI (OPTIONAL)**
Hawaiian taro-root "dip," purchased in cans

**MIXED SALAD GREENS WITH AVOCADO
AND PAPAYA**

**CHOCOLATE-MACADAMIA NUT SUNDAES**
Served in coconut shells

For small parties, Hawaiian hostesses often roast the traditional *kalua* roast pig in the oven instead of in an *imu* (pit dug in the ground). A pork roast, either a pork butt or a fresh leg of pork, has a satisfactorily authentic flavor when roasted in the oven with ti leaves (or lettuce) and bananas.

This simplified version of the Hawaiian luau is good for casual summer entertaining. The menu is flexible in variety and quantity and can be prepared with a minimum of work and time. Although the pork and poi are traditionally eaten with the fingers, regular eating utensils will be needed for the other foods.

If you want to provide a Hawaiian setting for your party, use arrangements of fruits, flowers, potted plants, and ferns. You can decorate the table with pineapples, papayas, mangoes, coconuts, tropical blossoms (plumerias, gardenias, and hibiscus are popular ones in the Islands), or other garden flowers. Ti leaves, available at most florist shops, add greenery to the table decorations and the serving platters. If light is needed, use candles, hurricane lamps, or patio torches.

This luau is most easily served buffet-style. The guests serve themselves, then sit down to a gaily decorated table on the patio or in the dining room. Cover the table with tapa cloth or paper, fish net, straw mats, or plain white cloth or paper. Use wooden bowls and trays for serving (monkeypod wood is especially suitable). Paper plates are appropriate, often used for luaus in the Islands now. Some of

your guests may want to try eating with their fingers, so be sure to provide plenty of napkins.

Individual bowls of poi and a serving dish with rock salt are the only foods served on the dining table. Red rock salt is traditional and readily available in Hawaii. You can substitute white ice cream rock salt, which you'll find in most food stores. (This salt is much coarser than what the Hawaiians use, so crush it before serving.) You may also use Kosher salt.

When a whole pig is roasted in an imu, the meat is juicy, and flavored with the fruits and vegetables that are cooked with it, the leaves that cover it, and the rock salt that is packed in and around the pig. Here these same flavors are captured in a roast cooked in the oven. To simulate the high heat of the imu, which gradually cools as the pig cooks, start the roast at high temperature, later turn heat down.

## ROAST PORK, HAWAIIAN-STYLE

Pork butt or fresh leg of pork (allow ½ to
   ¾ pound meat with bone per person)
1  teaspoon <u>each</u> rock salt (red or white),
   liquid smoke flavoring, and soy sauce
   per pound of meat
About 4 unpeeled bananas
Medium-sized sweet potatoes (scrubbed,
   not peeled). Allow 1 for each person
4  to 6 ti leaves (or lettuce leaves)
2  tablespoons water per pound of meat

Place meat on a large piece of heavy foil. Sprinkle
with salt, smoke flavoring, and soy sauce. Arrange
bananas and sweet potatoes around the roast. (The
bananas are used for flavor only, and should be dis-
carded when the roast is cooked.) Pull the foil up
around the meat, bananas, and potatoes; cover the
meat with ti leaves, and add the water.

Finish wrapping the meat in the foil, using several
sheets if necessary to seal it tightly. Let the package
stand several hours or overnight in the refrigerator
in a large shallow pan, turning it several times to
distribute the juices and let the flavors penetrate the
meat. Roast the meat with the fat side up for maximum juiciness. (Mark the package, so you'll know
which side has more fat.)

Put the pan and the meat package in a 500° oven
for 1 hour; then lower the oven temperature to 400°,
and roast 3 more hours for a 3-pound roast, and then
an additional 20 minutes for each pound of weight
above 3 pounds.


## LOMI-SALMON-STUFFED TOMATOES

Because salty lomi salmon is not easy to obtain outside Hawaii, here is an easy way to make your own.
This process should be started a day ahead.

1  pound fresh salmon fillets
½  cup rock salt (red or white)
   Juice of 1 lemon
12  medium-sized tomatoes
½  cup chopped green onions

Cut salmon into small pieces and place in a bowl.
Cover with rock salt. Squeeze the lemon juice over
the fish and mix gently.

Cover and refrigerate about 12 hours or overnight,
stirring occasionally to distribute the salt and lemon
juice. The fish will become very firm and salty.

On the day of the party, rinse the fish and soak it
in cold water for 2 hours, changing the water several
times. Drain salmon and shred with your fingers.

Hollow out tomatoes. Chop the pulp and mix it
with the shredded fish and green onions. Use this
mixture to fill the tomato shells. Makes 12 servings.


## POI (OPTIONAL)

Traditionally, poi is served with the roast pork. It is
available in many stores, either canned or frozen.
Don't look upon poi as a food to be eaten alone for
its own flavor. It is a starchy accompaniment of mild
flavor much like rice, potatoes, or bread in its use.

The canned variety is quite thick when you buy it
and needs to be thinned before it is served. Pour the
poi into the top of a double boiler; add 2 to 3 tablespoons water per 1-pound can and salt to taste. Heat
over boiling water, stirring until smooth; then whirl
in a blender or beat with a wooden spoon until the
poi is very smooth.

Frozen poi should be prepared according to the
package directions.

Serve poi in individual bowls (¼ to ½ cup per
person) and pass finely crushed rock salt or serve salt
in little individual dishes. Poi should be at room
temperature or slightly chilled.


## CHOCOLATE-MACADAMIA NUT SUNDAES

Although this dessert differs from the traditional coconut pudding *(haupia)* or pineapple, this chocolate-nut
sundae, using macadamia nuts, is sure to be popular
with your guests.

Vanilla ice cream
Coconut shell bowls (optional—see
  instructions)
Chocolate sauce
Chopped macadamia nuts

Place a large scoop of ice cream in each coconut shell
bowl, paper bowl, or plate. Top the ice cream with
chocolate sauce and macadamia nuts. Decorate each
plate with a flower.

For the coconut shell bowls, drain fresh coconuts
and cut each in half with a power saw. Each shell
should be thoroughly washed and the bottom sanded
to make a flat base.

Leave the coconut meat in the shell—your guests
may want to spoon out a bit to eat with the ice
cream or later take the shells home with them.

# An Elegant Duckling Dinner

### FOR FOUR PEOPLE (RECIPES EASILY DOUBLED TO SERVE EIGHT)

**ROAST DUCKLING WITH ORANGE SAUCE**

Served with steamed rice
Recipe on page 123

**HOT FRESH PINEAPPLE AND PAPAYA SLICES**

**GREEN BEANS WITH WATER CHESTNUTS**

Recipe on page 148
Or use frozen Chinese pea pods with water chestnuts

**RASPBERRY TORTE**

Meringue with ladyfingers and fresh or frozen berries
Recipe on page 177

**DRY RED WINE**

Such as Zinfandel or Cabernet Sauvignon

A well-roasted duck makes one of the most glamorous and appreciated company entrées. Yet many hostesses hesitate to prepare it, fearing that it may turn out too fatty. The method of roasting in this recipe guarantees you will have a crisp-skinned, succulent bird with juicy, lean meat.

## HOW TO HAVE A WINE-TASTING

At a wine-tasting party, the wine not only is the beverage but the entertainment as well. Nearly everyone is curious about wines and delighted to have a chance to try new kinds. A tasting provides a good setting for mixing people who do not know each other. The wines give reason for striking up a conversation, and people must mill about if the bottles are set up on different tables.

The most simple tasting, with four to six kinds of wine to try, may be accompanied by an assortment of cheeses and crackers or good bread. (See "A Guide to Serving Cheeses," page 156. You may want to combine a cheese-tasting with the wine-tasting.) Allow a minimum of a half bottle of wine *total* per guest.

A more sophisticated tasting may offer an array of appetizers designed to complement the wines offered. Seafood and vegetable appetizers may be served with white wines; pâtés, meats, and stronger cheeses with the reds. Although being too much of a purist about foods served with wine at most meals is not advisable, you should choose those for a tasting which let the wines shine.

Vinegar, heavy spice, asparagus, citrus fruits, strong or salty dips, and strong fish are best avoided.

Obviously a wine-tasting may be a complete meal—at the table or buffet-style. For a buffet tasting, arrange wines and accompanying foods in order on a long table, or set up each course on a separate table.

The choice of wines for comparison at tastings may be made several ways. You might choose to have two appetizer wines, two whites, two reds, and two dessert wines so that comparison can be made at each stage. But there is no reason why a tasting cannot be devoted solely to whites, reds, or Sherry if you would like to get to know one type in depth. You could make your tasting even more narrow, sampling various brands of California Burgundies made from just the Pinot Noir grape. Or you can make comparisons between California and European wines of the same type.

"A Shopper's Guide to Wine Labeling" on page 121 gives much information and hints about how various wines might be compared.

# A Wine-Tasting

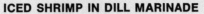

**MELON OR PAPAYA WITH PROSCIUTTO OR HAM**

**APPETIZER WINE**

---

**ICED SHRIMP IN DILL MARINADE**

Recipe on page 59

**RYE WAFER BREAD**

**WHITE WINE**

---

**SLICED TOMATOES WITH CAPERS**

**ROSÉ WINE**

---

**PASTA A PESTO**

Noodles with basil sauce—recipe on page 163

**COLD ROAST BEEF**

**RED WINE**

---

**BEL PAESE CHEESE, CRUSTY BREAD, FRUIT**

**DESSERT WINE**

Have all the food ready before guests are due, and the wines at the prescribed temperature. The dessert course of cheese, bread, and fruit can be in place on the buffet as decoration through the meal. Bring on the other foods, wines, and glasses (chilled if to be served with chilled wine) in order of eating. Have the table or tables set with individual places.

For the appetizer wine, serve either sweet or dry Vermouth (a blended wine flavored with herbs) over ice.

For the white wine to accompany the iced shrimp, select dry, tart Rhine wine; serve well chilled. Among Rhine types are Johannisberg and White Riesling.

The light pink rosé, with fruity flavor, should be served chilled. If made from the Grenache grape, this wine will be labeled Grenache Rosé.

The red dinner wine to accompany the pasta should be a ruby-colored Claret served at cool room temperature or very lightly chilled. Good wines in the Claret category may be labelled Zinfandel or Cabernet Sauvignon.

The dessert wine may be one of the sweet wines made from muscat grapes, such as Muscat de Frontignan, Light Sweet Muscat, or Black Muscat. All these retain some of the flavor of the grape; they may be served chilled or at room temperature. If muscat wines are not available, you may substitute Port.

One bottle of each kind of wine is sufficient per 6 to 8 people.

For the appetizer, top slender wedges of chilled Crenshaw melon or papaya with paper-thin slices of prosciutto (cured ham available in Italian delicatessens). If not readily available, substitute very thinly sliced pastrami, plain baked ham, or Westphalian ham.

To prepare tomatoes for 8 people, select about 4 large tomatoes and peel if desired. Cut in thick slices and arrange on a tray with 3 or 4 hard-cooked eggs, cut in wedges. Garnish with tender lettuce leaves. Sprinkle liberally with coarsely chopped capers (about 1½ tablespoons) and drizzle with olive oil (about 2 tablespoons). Sprinkle very lightly with salt, and grind black pepper over the vegetables.

You may roast your own beef or buy slices from a delicatessen.

# Turkish Meze

*BUFFET FOR A FEW PEOPLE OR A VERY LARGE GROUP*

**ASSORTED CHEESES, PICKLES, NUTS, COLD
MEATS, AND FISH**

**TOMATO SALAD WITH MINT OR DILL**

Sliced tomatoes sprinkled with chopped fresh herbs

**SHREDDED CARROT, RADISH, AND CABBAGE SALAD**

Dressed with olive oil and lemon juice

**BLACK OLIVES AND ANCHOVY-STUFFED
GREEN OLIVES**

Marinated in olive oil with lemon slices

**MARINATED SHRIMP OR LOBSTER**

Cold seafood simply seasoned

**BROILED EGGPLANT SALAD**

Whole eggplant is charred for smoky flavor, then peeled and
puréed, with oil and lemon juice seasoning

**WHITE BEAN SALAD**

Beans cooked with onion, diced vegetables, and garlic—served
cold with garnish

**CIRCASSIAN CHICKEN**

Slivered cold chicken with creamy walnut-flavored sauce

**FRENCH BREAD**

**FRESH FRUIT**

---

If you have had the idea that Turkish food is spicy and exotic, put the impression out of mind before considering this buffet meal. These particular dishes are simple, made of foods almost everyone likes, and have been immediately appreciated by many Americans completely unacquainted with Turkish food. They do not taste "foreign" at all, yet are completely authentic.

The name *meze* (pronounced "meh-zeh") may sound exotic, but is just a word designating foods which whet the appetite. The most ordinary Turkish meal may begin with a few meze foods. Often, for parties a great many dishes are spread out, either on the dining table or on a buffet, producing a Middle Eastern smörgåsbord.

Meze is especially suited to Western informal entertaining, for most of the dishes are served at room temperature, are best made in advance, and are portable. You could even adapt your menu to a picnic, as is done in Turkey.

Many of the dishes are just salted nuts, bread, pickles, cheeses, and cold cuts you buy at your market. Others, like the olives and salads, take very little preparation. Only two of these meze dishes require much advance planning and cooking. Just the Circassian Chicken would be difficult to make in Turkey;

but even this has been made easy with the use of canned chicken and a blender.

You'll notice great variety in the meze foods, but one ingredient, olive oil, reappears frequently. It's essential to the flavor, so don't substitute other cooking oils. Buy a good quality oil. Even if you haven't cared for olive oil, you'll probably discover that you like it in Turkish cooking, because its heaviness is always cut with such pungent flavors as lemon or onion.

A meze party does not call for special dishes or table decorations. Cover your table with a colorful cloth and use any pottery, copper, or brass serving dishes you have. Because fresh fruit is the most suitable and authentic dessert to follow a meze meal, you might arrange a large, handsome bowl as the centerpiece. Add candles and flowers (carnations or tulips are most typical in Turkey) to further decorate your table.

Whatever dishes you use, include several plates per person, and encourage your guests to try a few foods at a time rather than heaping different foods on top of one another on the same plate. Each of these dishes has its special flavors that are best enjoyed independently of the others.

The quantities given in the recipes that follow, with the addition of some of the purchased meze foods, should serve about 8 people a full meal. You can adjust quantities for larger groups by doubling recipes and increasing either quantitiy or variety of purchased foods.

If you want to add a hot dish, the recipe for Stuffed Grape Leaves or Cabbage with lemon sauce on page 94 will serve 8 to 10 people amply. The leaf rolls, which may be made as much as a day ahead, are authentically Turkish.

You could also use this menu as part of a shish kebab barbecue. A recipe for *Arni Souvlakia,* Greek shish kebab, is on page 103.

## MEZE FOODS YOU CAN BUY

Select your favorites from the list that follows, and be sure to accompany your meze meal with plenty of sliced French bread or a comparable bread.

**Cheese.** Turks use a white cheese similar to Greek *feta* and a yellow cheese similar to Greek *kasera,* both obtainable at many delicatessens and cheese shops. Gruyère, jack, Cheddar, fontina, or any cheese you prefer would be suitable, too.

**Pickles.** Any non-sweet cucumber pickles, pickled peppers, or pickled cabbage (available in Oriental markets).

**Nuts.** Salted and toasted nuts, such as walnuts, almonds, filberts, or pistachios.

**Meats.** Pepperoni, salami, tongue, pastrami, or other cold cuts.

**Fish.** Sardines, anchovy fillets, herring, any smoked fish, or caviar.

## TOMATO SALAD WITH MINT OR DILL

**Tomatoes**
**Fresh dill weed or mint (or dried dill weed**
 **and fresh parsley)**
**Olive oil**
**Lemons**

Arrange slices of tomatoes attractively on serving plate. Sprinkle generously with chopped fresh dill or fresh mint (or you might use half dried dill weed with fresh chopped parsley). Dress with olive oil and lemon juice.

## CARROT, RADISH, AND CABBAGE SALAD

**Lettuce**
**Carrots**
**Large white radishes or turnips**
**White or red cabbage**
**Olive oil**
**Olives, red radishes, or parsley**
**Lemon wedges**

Arrange lettuce on a platter. Shred carrots and white radishes or turnips. Finely shred cabbage. Arrange separate mounds of the vegetables on the plate. Sprinkle olive oil over each mound. Garnish the plate with olives, red radishes, or parsley. Have lemon wedges on the plate to squeeze over when served.

## OLIVES

In Turkey, the favorite olive is a dried black kind. Many delicatessens sell these, usually called Greek olives. They're called for in one of these recipes; the other uses Spanish-style green olives.

**Black Olives.** Pour boiling water over Greek-type olives and let stand until the water cools. Drain and pat dry. Pack olives in pint jars, each with a slice of lemon. Cover with olive oil. Marinate several days.

*(continued on next page)*

**Green Olives.** Use Spanish-type olives stuffed with anchovy, or buy pitted green olives and a can of anchovy fillets and stuff your own. Put a small piece of pimiento over the anchovy stuffing to make the olives more colorful. Pack the drained olives into pint jars, add a lemon slice or two to each, and cover with olive oil. Marinate at least 3 days.

## MARINATED SHRIMP OR LOBSTER

2 pounds lobster tails or large shrimp
1 quart boiling water
2 bay leaves
1 teaspoon salt
½ cup olive oil
½ teaspoon dry mustard
3 tablespoons lemon juice
   Chopped fresh dill or fresh parsley

Drop lobster or shrimp into boiling water with bay leaves and salt; simmer about 5 minutes, or until flesh loses its translucent look.

Drain and cool. Shell and cut lobster meat into bite-sized pieces. Shell shrimp, split lengthwise, removing the sand veins. Marinate 1 to 2 hours in olive oil, dry mustard, and lemon juice. Arrange pieces on a serving platter and pour some of the marinade over top. Garnish with chopped fresh dill or fresh parsley.

## BROILED EGGPLANT SALAD

4 pounds eggplant (Japanese variety or
   small regular ones)
   Lemon juice
⅓ cup olive oil
4 teaspoons wine vinegar
5 teaspoons lemon juice
¾ teaspoon salt
   Lettuce
   Green pepper rings and olives

Pierce the skin of each eggplant with a fork and arrange on baking pan. Place about 4 inches below a preheated broiler and broil, turning several times, until the skin is charred and the flesh is very soft. Remove and when cool enough to handle, peel off all the skin. Cut open and remove seedy pocket (not necessary to remove all seeds); moisten with a little lemon juice.

Drain in a strainer about 30 minutes. Put eggplant into a blender with olive oil, vinegar, 5 teaspoons lemon juice, and salt. Whirl until smooth (or mash with a fork until blended). Serve in a bowl lined with lettuce. Garnish with pepper rings and olives.

## WHITE BEAN SALAD

1 pound dried white beans
   Water
1 large onion, chopped
1 cup olive oil
1 medium-sized potato, peeled and diced
1 large carrot, sliced or diced
5 cloves garlic, minced
1½ teaspoons <u>each</u> sugar and salt
   Chopped parsley
   Lemon wedges

Soak beans overnight in water to cover (or cover beans with water, bring to a boil, boil 2 minutes, let stand 1 hour). In a large heavy pan, sauté onion in olive oil until soft, but not browned. Add the beans, including soaking water, potato, carrot, garlic, sugar, and salt.

Cover and simmer until beans are tender but still hold their shape, about 1 hour. Add water, if needed, to just cover the beans. Cool in the pan. Serve at room temperature with the pan juices and sprinkle chopped parsley over the top. Garnish with lemon wedges, if desired.

## CIRCASSIAN CHICKEN

1 can (about 3 lbs., 4 oz.) whole chicken,
   or 3 whole chicken breasts
1 slice white bread
   Water
1 cup walnut meats
½ small onion
1 teaspoon paprika
½ teaspoon salt
¾ to 1 cup chicken stock or liquid from
   canned chicken
¼ cup olive oil
2 teaspoons paprika

If chicken breasts are used, cook until tender in salted water, flavored with an herb bouquet of parsley, bay leaf, and thyme. If canned chicken is used, remove skin and bones.

Shred meat into small pieces, arrange on a serving plate; save the stock or liquid from can. Mask the chicken meat with a sauce made as follows:

Remove crusts from bread, soak in water, then press out the water. Put bread in blender with walnut meats, onion, 1 teaspoon paprika, salt, and chicken stock or liquid from canned chicken (should be consistency of thickened gravy); whirl until smooth.

To garnish, combine olive oil with 2 teaspoons paprika, let stand a few minutes, then strain through a paper napkin to remove paprika grains. Drip the red oil over the masked chicken meat. If you make this dish ahead, refrigerate it, but let it come to room temperature to serve.

# Oriental Meal Cooked at the Table

*FOR FOUR PEOPLE*

## CUCUMBER AND CRAB SALADS

Thinly sliced cucumbers and chunks of seafood dressed with oil
and white vinegar. Or see suggested recipe for Japanese
Cucumber Salad on page 80

## ALTERNATE 1: CASHEW CHICKEN

Cooked in electric frying pan—Chinese-style with vegetables
and mushrooms
Recipe on page 115

## ALTERNATE 2: JAVANESE SATÉS

Cooked on hibachi over charcoal—skewered teriyaki steak, rolled
in toasted sesame seed, served with hot fresh fruit
Recipe on page 91

## HOT STEAMED RICE

## GINGER ICE CREAM SUNDAES

Vanilla ice cream topped with sauce of candied ginger
Sauce recipe on page 176

Guests enjoy an intimate supper party when the main dish is cooked right at the table. But the hostess probably enjoys it most because she needn't spend any of her time in the kitchen. Such a meal seems to go best when you limit the number of diners to four, or six at most.

With the preceding menu, you have a choice of main dishes, depending on your tastes and the method of cooking you prefer. The Cashew Chicken takes only 5 minutes to cook in an electric frying pan, which nearly everyone has on hand. If you have a table-size hibachi and want to go to the trouble of lighting charcoal, you may prefer the Javanese Satés, which cook in about 10 minutes each.

The simple cucumber and crab salads may be marinated ahead. Serve the salads first, in individual bowls, so the guests will have something to whet their appetites while the main dish is cooking. The candied ginger sauce for the ice cream also is made ahead. Before dinner time, all you have to do is cook the rice.

# Fruit and Cheese Snack Tray

## POMEGRANATE CHEESE LOAF

Blended cream, Roquefort, and Cheddar cheeses (studded with pomegranate seeds if fruits are in season)

## MELBA TOAST OR CRISP CRACKERS

## CRÈME DE MENTHE GRAPES

Frosted with powdered sugar

## PISTACHIO PINEAPPLE FINGERS

Fruit spears dipped in chopped nuts

## HONEYED FIGS

Chilled in honey and Port

Too often now, it seems, hostesses feel obligated to entertain with a full-scale party or dinner. Informal entertaining, where guests drop over for an hour or two in late afternoon or after dinner, should be done more often. This fruit and cheese tray can serve as a snack for such get-togethers at almost any time of day.

Everything is a finger food, but be sure to have plenty of small paper napkins handy for eating the juicy figs. Everything can be served on one large tray. Many kinds of beverages can be served with this snack, including a special coffee (see page 201), spiced tea, fruit juice, punch, carbonated beverages, Sherry, Port, or Vermouth.

## POMEGRANATE CHEESE LOAF

1 package (8 oz.) cream cheese (at room temperature)
⅛ pound Roquefort cheese
½ pound Cheddar cheese spread or Cheddar, shredded
Pomegranate seeds (optional)

Blend cheeses together until smooth. Chill thoroughly, then shape into a loaf or ball. Dot surface with pomegranate seeds and chill until ready to serve.

You can make the cheese mixture several days before shaping and serving.

## CRÈME DE MENTHE GRAPES

Divide a medium-sized bunch of seedless grapes into small clusters; wash and drain thoroughly. Dip each cluster into a small amount of crème de menthe. Dust grapes generously with powdered sugar, place on a baking sheet, and set in the freezer or freezing com-partment of your refrigerator for 25 to 30 minutes. Then refrigerate until ready to serve. Arrange grapes on tray and sprinkle lightly with powdered sugar, if desired. Instead of crème de menthe, you can dip the grapes in egg white, slightly beaten, then sprinkle with powdered sugar.

## PISTACHIO PINEAPPLE FINGERS

Cut fresh pineapple into small fingers, or use canned spears. Dip one end of each piece in finely chopped pistachios. Arrange on tray, or chill until ready to use.

## HONEYED FIGS

Choose well-shaped, dried light (Calimyrna) figs, and chill for 2 or 3 hours in a mixture of half honey, half Port. Serve figs in a small dish of the honey and Port on the cheese tray.

# GOOD MORNING BREAKFASTS FOR GUESTS

Usually you have time to plan ahead for breakfast guests, but not always. Sometimes they are people you invite to stay overnight after a late party, out-of-town visitors who breeze in unannounced, or good friends you suddenly decide to join for a fishing or ski trip.

Breakfast menus are fairly standard—usually fruit or juice, eggs, breakfast meats, and bread or pastry, often with some sweetness. When you can plan in advance for a special breakfast, it is possible to bake sweet breads or do something a little different with meat. However, for impromptu occasions your best bet is to dress up the eggs in some fashion and make a favorite kind of pancake. If time is short or the larder bare, French toast may be the quickest elegant emergency solution.

Following are easy ways to make eggs with a company touch (some even include the breakfast meat), plus some French toast variations.

**Baked Eggs and Sausages.** For each serving, butter 1 custard cup and add a sprinkle of chervil or summer savory to each. Carefully crack 1 egg into each cup and top with 1 teaspoon light cream. Sprinkle with salt and paprika. Arrange 2 precooked tiny link sausages in each cup. Bake in a 350° oven for 12 to 15 minutes, or until whites are just firm.

**Baked Eggs in Tomato Shells.** Scoop out the pulp and drain 4 medium-sized tomatoes (save the pulp and juice for use later in a sauce). Sprinkle the inside of each tomato shell with a dash of salt, pepper, and basil. Break 4 eggs, one at a time, into a small dish and gently slip one into each tomato. Bake in a 350° oven for about 20 minutes, or until eggs are almost set to the degree of doneness you prefer. Sprinkle each with 1 teaspoon grated Parmesan cheese and place under the broiler until cheese is just bubbly. Garnish with a sprig of parsley.

**Scotch Eggs.** Hard-cook 8 small or medium eggs and remove shells. With your hands, flatten 1¼ pounds pork sausage meat on a floured board, and cut into eight pieces. Mold meat around each egg, rolling it around with your hands until the egg is completely covered. Dip sausage-covered eggs in 1 egg, slightly beaten, then in fine dry bread crumbs (about ¾ cup), and deep fry in moderately hot fat (about 370°) for 4 to 5 minutes, or until sausage is deep brown.

**Corned Beef Hash and Egg Cups.** Spoon canned corned beef hash into buttered custard cups, or cups shaped from heavy foil. Make a hollow in the center; drop in an egg, dot with butter, sprinkle with salt and pepper, and add 1 teaspoon whipping cream. Bake in a 375° oven for 15 to 20 minutes, or until whites are just firm. A 1-pound can of corned beef hash will make about 6 servings.

**Pimiento Egg Cups.** Open canned whole pimientos (there are about 4 in a 4-oz. can) and use one to line each custard cup or muffin tin. Drop an egg in each cup and season with salt and pepper. Pour 1 tablespoon of whipping cream on each egg and bake in a 350° oven for 12 to 15 minutes or until whites are just firm. To make sauce for 4 to 6 eggs, use 1 cup canned white sauce; add 3 tablespoons shredded sharp cheese and heat until cheese has melted. Use spoon to lift out baked pimiento cups and place on toast; top with sauce. Serve immediately.

**Apricot French Toast.** Beat 2 eggs with ¾ cup canned apricot nectar and ¼ teaspoon salt until blended. Crush 3 cups presweetened corn flakes to make about 1 cup coarse crumbs. Dip 8 slices of firm French bread, 1 at a time, into egg mixture to coat both sides well. Then coat with the corn flake crumbs.

Using a total of ¼ cup butter or margarine, heat about 1 tablespoon at a time in a frying pan until bubbly (add more butter as you fry additional slices). Fry prepared bread, 2 or 3 slices at a time, over medium heat until lightly browned on both sides; turn only once. Serve hot with honey or syrup. Makes 4 servings.

**Sesame French Toast.** Dip the bread in an egg-milk mixture (¼ cup milk and a pinch of salt per beaten egg), then sprinkle one side thickly with sesame seed. Melt butter in frying pan; using a wide spatula, place bread in pan with sesame seed side down. Sprinkle top with sesame seed before turning. When brown on both sides, transfer to a hot platter, top each slice with a curl of crisp bacon.

# Build-Your-Own-Salad Lunch

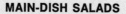

*FOR A SMALL OR LARGE GROUP*

### MAIN-DISH SALADS

Guests make their own from a choice of ingredients

### MINESTRONE

See instructions following for dressing up purchased soups with
wine and sausages
Or prepare rich Minestrone, North Beach Style,
from recipe on page 139

### REFRIGERATOR BISCUITS, TOASTED
### ENGLISH MUFFINS

### CHILLED WATERMELON

The charm of this salad buffet is that each person concocts his own main dish. The elements are a big bowl of salad greens, several dressings, a variety of cooked and raw vegetables, cold meats, fish, cheeses, and relishes. Small dishes of some of the salad ingredients, plus dressings, may be placed on a lazy Susan for added convenience. You may serve the soup before the salads or after, as preferred. The hot soup may be omitted if you prefer a lighter meal.

**Suggested Salad Ingredients.** You can choose from torn lettuce or romaine; sliced tomatoes and cucumbers; chilled cooked peas, beans, carrots, or beets; ham, roast beef, crisp bacon, chicken or turkey, and salami cut in cubes or strips; cubed Swiss, Cheddar, jack, or blue cheeses; hard-cooked eggs; shrimp, tuna, or crab; drained kidney beans or garbanzos; artichoke hearts, olives, onion rings, and canned whole mushrooms (or fresh ones, sliced).

French, garlic, and blue cheese dressings provide a good choice. If you wish, set out a cruet of olive oil, a selection of vinegars, a pepper mill, and lemon wedges.

**Minestrone Suggestions.** You can dress up canned soup or packaged mix with wine and sausages.

If you use thick minestrone (1 large can, 2½ lb.), add ½ cup dry red wine and 2 sliced garlic sausages; heat as directed. If you use the condensed kind, buy 2 cans (about 10 oz. *each*), add 1½ cans water and ½ can dry red wine; stir in 2 sliced garlic sausages and heat as directed.

For each 3⅛-ounce envelope of dry minestrone, substitute ½ cup wine for an equal amount of the water called for; add 2 sliced sausages and heat.

Whichever preceding method you use for the soups you buy, you will have enough for 4 to 6 servings.

# French Peasant Aïoli

## AÏOLI SAUCE

Garlic mayonnaise to eat with the following:

### HOT OR COLD SEAFOOD, VEGETABLES, EGGS

### FRENCH BREAD

The people of Provence on the southeastern coastal area of France make a whole meal of crusty bread, seafood, vegetables, and a garlic mayonnaise sauce called Aïoli (pronounced "eye-*o*-lee"). This golden sauce *reeks* of garlic. But its flavor is an exciting experience once one gets past the aroma, and an enhancement to plain accompaniments.

Indications are that Aïoli Sauce came from the Greeks, who still have a similar garlic sauce by that name, thickened with bread crumbs, walnuts, or potatoes, rather than egg as the French version is. The transfer of name as well as flavor to France probably occurred in the dim past when Greek colonists populated the French southern coast. Or it may have happened when the Romans, who prized Greek cooking and its civilized refinements, moved in later.

**To Prepare an Aïoli Meal.** The array you present as Aïoli can be freely chosen from locally available fish, shellfish, and vegetables—but no meat.

Since the meal is typically peasant-style and help-yourself, you have great latitude in presenting the food. If you serve it from the center of a big roomy table, with knives and cutting boards handy to all, you can leave the foods whole and handsome, letting guests break or cut them up to eat. For buffet service, dishing up is simplified if the larger pieces of vegetables and fish are precut, then reassembled to preserve their appearance. For individual service, you can arrange an assortment of Aïoli ingredients like a still life picture, on a plate.

The cooked foods that Aïoli Sauce complements might include the following:

**Hot boiled new potatoes**
**Hot or cold cooked green beans and artichokes**
**Cold cooked shrimp and lobster (remove lobster meat, cut, and return to shell)**
**Hot or cold poached halibut, lingcod, or other lean white fish (served whole if possible)**
**Hard-cooked eggs**

The following raw vegetables are suitable:

**Fennel (also called sweet anise or finocchio)**
**Red or white cabbage (cut or to be cut in wedges)**
**Cherry tomatoes or regular tomatoes (to be cut in wedges)**
**Mushrooms**
**Turnips and zucchini (sliced partly through to snap apart)**
**Cauliflower**
**Green peppers (seeded if desired)**
**Belgian endive**
**Smaller inner romaine leaves**

## AÏOLI SAUCE

6 to 8 medium-sized or 4 large garlic cloves
1½ tablespoons lemon juice
½ teaspoon salt
3 egg yolks
½ cup salad oil
½ cup olive oil
1 to 2 tablespoons water

Force garlic through a garlic press and combine in a bowl with lemon juice, salt, and egg yolks. Beat with a rotary beater or wire whip until blended. Add oil a few drops at a time, beating rapidly and constantly. When sauce thickens, you can add more oil, but no faster than it can be easily mixed in. Thin with water if needed.

Chill sauce, covered, for at least several hours to mellow flavor. Makes 1¾ cups.

# Scandinavian Buffet for Fifty People

### SCANDINAVIAN LIVER PÂTÉ

With pumpernickel bread and Danish Fried Onions

### DANISH MEATBALLS

Tender beef and pork balls served from chafing dish

### MACARONI SALAD

With nippy horseradish dressing

### PICKLED BEETS

### AGURKESALAT

Cucumber salad with dill

### CRÈME ROYAL VIKING

Chilled pudding with apricot and chocolate topping

Serving a large group requires a tested menu and party plan. The dishes must be easily prepared so that more than one cook can work on the meal, and the expense of ingredients should be kept low, particularly if the meal should be a fund-raising enterprise. Usually a buffet-style service works best for a group. This adaptation of a Scandinavian smörgåsbord fits all these requirements for such large-scale entertaining.

Because the recipes are for such large quantities and seldom would be used for another purpose, all of them are included here, rather than in the recipe section of this book.

At one end of your buffet table, arrange slices of the liver pâté on a platter, garnished with lettuce. Have thinly sliced buttered pumpernickel or dark rye bread nearby, and a large bowl of the Danish Fried Onions.

The meatballs can be made ahead, then placed in chafing dishes. The very unusual macaroni salad, soft and creamy in texture with a sharp horseradish dressing, is dished into lettuce cups with an ice-cream scoop for individual servings.

Use a large, institution-size can (about 6½ pounds) of small whole pickled beets. (One can should be sufficient, but just to make sure, look on the label for the "count"—the number of beets in the can.) Drain beets well before placing in bowl.

The dessert is made ahead, complete with topping and garnish. You put it in small plastic or paper dishes, arrange on cooky sheets, and refrigerate or freeze. If you freeze it, remember to remove from the freezer about a half hour before serving time.

### SCANDINAVIAN LIVER PÂTÉ

1   pound chicken livers
1   pound fresh pork fat
6   ounces lean fresh pork
4   anchovy fillets
1   large onion
1   egg, beaten
1   pint half-and-half (light cream)
1   tablespoon salt
½   teaspoon pepper
½   teaspoon thyme
1   cup flour
½   pound sliced bacon

Scald the chicken livers by putting them in a wire strainer and pouring boiling water over them. Combine with the pork fat and pork, anchovies, and onion cut in chunks. Using the fine blade of your food chopper, grind the mixture three times. Add the egg, cream, salt, pepper, thyme, and flour, and mix well. Line the bottoms and sides of 2 loaf pans (9 by 5 inches) with the bacon slices and fill pans with mixture; put pans in a larger pan of hot water, and bake in 350° oven 1 hour. Cool 10 minutes, turn out.

## DANISH FRIED ONIONS

10 pounds yellow onions
   About 2 cups shortening
   Salad oil for deep frying
   Salt

Peel and slice onions. Using several frying pans, fry the onions very slowly in shortening until soft and beginning to brown. Stir to keep from sticking. When much of the moisture has cooked out, fry the onions a few at a time in deep fat, heated to 370°, until they are brown and very crisp. Drain on paper towels, and sprinkle with salt.

## DANISH MEATBALLS

  7 pounds lean beef
  5 pounds fresh pork
12 eggs
  6 cups fresh bread crumbs
  6 cups milk
  2 pounds finely minced onions
  2 tablespoons salt
  2 teaspoons pepper
1½ teaspoons ground allspice
  1 quart warm milk
   About ½ pound (1 cup) butter
   About 1 cup salad oil
   Flour
  4 cans (10½ oz. each) consommé (optional)

Have the meat ground three times. Combine with eggs, bread crumbs, 6 cups milk, onion, salt, pepper, and allspice; beat together well. (The beating may have to be done in two or three batches; an electric mixer helps.) Add the warm milk gradually and beat until smooth. Chill thoroughly, then form into small balls and brown in a mixture of half butter and half salad oil. Because the mixture will still be quite soft, you may find it easier to spoon it into small balls directly into the heated fat in the frying pan. When browned on all sides, remove meatballs from frying pan, drain on paper towels, and dust lightly with flour. If you make the meatballs ahead, reheat them in chafing dishes in consommé.

## MACARONI SALAD

  3 pounds elbow macaroni, cooked
  1 quart mayonnaise
  1 quart sour cream
  1 cup cream, whipped
  1 cup vinegar
  1 cup grated fresh horseradish, or about 2
    cups prepared horseradish
¼ cup sugar
  2 teaspoons salt
50 lettuce cups
   Paprika

Turn the cooked and drained macaroni into large bowls. Then mix together the mayonnaise, sour cream, whipped cream, vinegar, horseradish, sugar, and salt; blend together with the macaroni. Chill thoroughly. Serve with an ice cream scoop into lettuce cups, and sprinkle each serving with a little paprika.

## AGURKESALAT

12 long, thin cucumbers
  2 tablespoons salt
½ cup white vinegar
½ cup water
¼ cup sugar
¼ cup dill weed or minced fresh dill

Slice cucumbers as thinly as possible. (If they are waxed, peel them.) Sprinkle with 2 tablespoons salt, and refrigerate for at least 2 hours. Drain. Combine vinegar, ½ cup water, sugar, and dill weed. Mix well and again refrigerate until well chilled. Serve without garnish.

## CRÈME ROYAL VIKING

  7 cups milk
  5 cups sugar
  1 tablespoon salt
28 egg yolks
  6 envelopes unflavored gelatin
  2 cups cold water
  7 cups whipping cream
  2 tablespoons vanilla
  1 pound dried apricots
  1 quart water
  1 cup sugar
½ pound sweet chocolate

Heat the milk with sugar and salt, stirring until the sugar is dissolved. Beat the egg yolks well, and beat them gradually into the hot milk. Cook over hot water until thickened. Soak gelatin in the cold water, then add to the hot egg mixture, stirring until dissolved. Cool, but do not allow to set. Whip the cream and fold into egg mixture. Add vanilla.

*Note: Unused egg whites may be frozen and later used for angel food cakes or meringues.*

Pour into individual serving dishes. If 5-ounce paper dishes are used, it will fill 50 of them more than half full. Allow to set. Spread with apricot topping (see following instructions), sprinkle with chocolate curls, and chill.

**Topping.** Cook apricots in water until soft, add sugar, and force through a wire strainer; cool. To make chocolate curls, shave bar of chocolate with a vegetable peeler.

# Champagne Party

**HOT HAM-FILLED MUSHROOM CAPS**

Stuffed with ground ham, sour cream, and ripe olives
Recipe on page 60

**HOT SHRIMP TOAST CANAPÉS**

Minced shrimp, green onion, and water chestnuts on toast
Recipe on page 60

**MOLDED CHICKEN LIVER PÂTÉ**

Rich pâté with peak of amber jellied consommé
Recipe on page 62

**EDAM CHEESE BALLS**

Served in waxy, red, hollowed-out cheese shell

**FRESH PAPAYA OR MELON AND PROSCIUTTO**

**CELERY OR FENNEL AND GIANT RIPE OLIVES
IN ICE RING WITH GARNISH**

**CHAMPAGNE OR CHAMPAGNE FRUIT PUNCH**

Punch of Champagne, white wine, grapefruit soda,
and whole fresh strawberries
Punch recipe on page 202

The food for a Champagne party should be delicate, bite-size, and unusually attractive. One or more kinds of hot tidbits passed on trays are particularly welcome. Presenting such a party without catering or serving help is not easy, but it is possible to offer this selection of appetizers with no more than one member of the family being away briefly for last-minute attention to the hot foods.

The mushroom caps may be baked a little ahead, covered, and kept warm. The shrimp canapés can be assembled ahead, broiled briefly just before serving. If you set up a buffet service for the cold items to which guests may help themselves at first, you can slip away after everyone has arrived to bring in the hot foods.

The molded pâté, topped with amber aspic, can be made a day ahead. With it serve small, thin triangles of dark bread, and provide butter knives for spreading. Cut the top off a red Edam cheese and use a melon-ball cutter to scoop balls out of the center. Smooth out the inside of the waxy red shell, and fill it with the balls; provide toothpicks. Cut papaya or melon into bite-size pieces and wrap each with a

paper-thin sliver of prosciutto or smoked ham; fasten with a pick and arrange on trays.

Use a ring mold to make a ring of ice (see instructions on page 199); you may mold cucumber slices, olives, or leaves of the celery or fennel inside it. Place the ice ring on a platter or in a shallow bowl (sufficient to contain water from melting). Fill the ring with the largest pitted ripe olives you can find and small pieces of celery or fennel cut fan-shape.

Serving punch rather than plain Champagne will be simpler. No one need be occupied with opening bottles and pouring during the party, as guests can help themselves at the punch bowl. The cost is less because the punch also contains still wine and sparkling soda.

# Barbecued Ham Buffet

*FOR EIGHT TO TEN PEOPLE*

### SPARKLING CRANBERRY-MINT COCKTAIL

Recipe on page 196

### CHARCOAL-BARBECUED HONEYED HAM

Cooked out-of-doors in smoke cooker or on covered grill
Recipe on page 109

### HOT CARROT-ASPARAGUS PLATTER

Gingered carrots and Parmesan-topped asparagus
bordered with mashed potatoes
Recipe on page 155

### GRAPEFRUIT-AVOCADO SALAD

Prepared by your favorite recipe or according to suggested
recipe on page 78

### HOT CRESCENT ROLLS

### PINEAPPLE SHERBET

Purchased ready-made or prepared by recipe on page 174

noteworthy features: The ham is barbecued on a covered grill, and
ombined on a special platter that's both attractive and easy to serve.
which can be prepared in advance, would be excellent for Easter dinner.

## THE PERFECT MENU

st as
ing.
the
stic
ers

in
an-
ite.
Color is important.

Another element artists consider is texture. The perfect
menu contains variety in this respect—some things are
soft, smooth, spongy, or liquid; others are firm, chewy,
flaky, crunchy, or crisp.

Artists also consider variety and harmony. The predomi-

nate flavors in the dishes served should rarely be the
same, but they should be compatible. There should also be
variety and contrast in other areas—consider both fresh
or raw foods and cooked, aged, or dried foods; temperature variety (ranging from frozen through piping hot); both
simple dishes and complex ones.

Other considerations in menu planning are practical, not
artistic. You should estimate carefully the proper amount
of food to prepare for your guests and the types of food
pleasing to their tastes and diets. Select dishes which can
mostly be made ahead. If last-minute cooking or baking
is required, check that sufficient cooking units are available on top of the range and that oven space is sufficient.

The perfect menu is rarely an accident, but it is always
a supreme pleasure to encounter.

# Mexican Tamalada

*TAMALE-MAKING PARTY FOR AS MANY AS FORTY PEOPLE*

**TURKEY TAMALES**
Made by the guests

**RIPE OLIVES, GREEN ONIONS, RED RADISHES**

**FRIJOLES**
Refried beans from the can, heated

**HOT, SOFT TORTILLAS**
Corn or flour type

**SLICED ORANGE, AVOCADO, AND PAPAYA SALAD**
On lettuce with French dressing

**JACK CHEESE WITH QUINCE OR GUAVA PASTE**
Squares of cheese topped with thin slices of fruit paste
(or substitute moist-pack dried fruits)

In Mexico tamales are a feature of fiesta time, and their preparation is an important part of the celebration. Although not difficult to make, they take time; but the minutes pass in a hurry when there are many hands to make light work. Then, when the tamales are hot and ready to eat, the party gets under way in earnest, with eating, dancing, and games — all part of a *Tamalada*.

In the West, where good homemade tamales are very popular but hard to find, a Tamalada is a fine way to provide an ample supply of this Mexican specialty for a congenial group of tamale devotees and have a party at the same time. Assemble your guests, make a big batch of tamales, and serve all you can eat. Divide what is left to freeze at home.

At the Tamalada, the tamale makers spread a *masa* mixture on corn husks — this is made from Mexican masa flour (sometimes called corn tamale or tortilla flour). In the center they place cooked turkey meat and chile sauce, a pitted ripe olive half, and several raisins. The corn husk is folded over the filling and tied with strip of another husk. Then, the tamales are steamed on a rack above simmering water in a steamer or pressure cooker for about an hour. By the time all the tamales are made, one or more batches of tamales will be hot and ready to eat.

You will need to go to a Mexican store or gourmet shop for certain ingredients — the masa flour, two kinds of dried chiles for the sauce, dried corn husks, tortillas, and the guava or quince paste.

Prepare the masa mixture, turkey meat, chile sauce, and corn husks ahead. Complete instructions follow for all of this, including items needed for making the tamales, folding and steaming them. These recipes will make about 200 tamales.

## TURKEY TAMALES

2  **pounds cleaned corn husks (instructions follow)**
    **Prepared masa (recipe follows)**
    **Turkey meat (recipe follows)**
    **Chile Sauce (recipe follows)**
3  **cans (about 7 oz. each) pitted large ripe olives (optional)**
1  **pound seeded raisins (optional)**

You need knives or spatulas (putty knives are good); scissors; 2 tablespoons for each tamale maker; and 1 large or several smaller steamers, or a pressure cooker, for the tamale cooking. Steamers may be improvised from any large lidded kettle; just place a rack in the bottom (on jar lids to raise it if necessary) and water *below* the rack.

Select a wide pliable husk and lay it flat on the table, the tip toward your right. (Note: Sometimes one husk is not wide enough to make a good tamale. If that is the case, put 2 or 3 narrow husks together, overlapping them about an inch, and "paste" together with masa. If they don't close completely over the filling with a good overlap, spread another husk with masa and put it, masa side down, over the opening.)

Spread husk with about 2 tablespoons prepared masa, covering a space in the center about 4 inches wide and 5 inches long, and about 3 or 4 inches from the bottom of the husk at your left. Let the masa come completely to bottom edge and about ½ inch from top edge.

Now put about 2 rounded tablespoons of the turkey-chile filling in the middle of the masa. Top with half a pitted ripe olive, split the long way, and 2 raisins, to give a very Mexican flavor.

Turn husk so the point is toward the back of the table. Fold husk over the filling, first the side spread completely to the edge, then the other side. Now gently turn up the bottom, fold the pointed top down over it, and tie in the middle with a strip of husk. Trim the pointed end and clip ends of tie.

When enough tamales have been made to fill the steamer, arrange them carefully on a rack (stack them in layers if you wish) and steam for 30 minutes if they are to be frozen and reheated, 45 minutes to 1 hour if to be eaten at once. (To reheat frozen tamales, steam for 30 to 40 minutes.)

**The Husks.** You will need 2 pounds top-quality dried corn husks. Separate leaves and discard silk and any dried fauna that may be in the interstices. Cover husks with warm water and soak at least 2 hours, preferably overnight. Keep damp until ready to use.

**The Masa.** Be sure to use authentic masa flour and lard. Make no substitutes.

24   cups (about 7 pounds) dehydrated masa flour (sometimes called corn tamale or tortilla flour)
15   cups (3¾ quarts) turkey stock (or water, plus ⅓ cup chicken stock concentrate)
2   tablespoons salt (more if stock is not salted)
7   cups (3½ pounds) lard

Combine masa flour, warm turkey stock (or water and concentrate), and salt. Divide into 4 parts for easier handling. Beat ¼ of the lard (1¾ cups) until fluffy, add 1 part of the masa, and beat as long as possible. If you have a heavy-duty mixer, use it. An ordinary electric mixer can be used if the mixture is done in 8 batches. When all has been prepared, cover with a damp cloth and keep cool.

**The Turkey.** If turkey is frozen, thaw in refrigerator.

18   to 20-pound tom turkey
    Salt
    Water

Remove neck and giblets (do not use liver); cover remaining giblets with water and simmer to make stock. (The meat may be chopped and added to other turkey meat, if desired.) Sprinkle turkey inside and out with salt, wrap in heavy foil, and seal. Place in a large roaster and bake in a 400° oven 4 hours, or until a meat thermometer, inserted in heavy part of thigh, registers 180°. Save all pan juices, cool turkey, and remove meat from bones. There should be about 8 pounds of boneless meat. Cut it into pieces as for a salad. Do not grind or chop. Break carcass, put in a large pot, cover with water, and simmer until a good rich stock is produced. Combine stock with juices and giblet stock. Give 2 quarts of it to the person making the sauce, the remainder (if any) to the masa makers. Take cut-up turkey to the Tamalada and add to the chile sauce.

**Chile Sauce.** If you wish, make an extra half-batch of the sauce to serve separately over the tamales. Heat this sauce very slowly, taking care not to scorch it.

1   pound dried Mexican chiles (chiles pasillas)
1   pound dried California chiles
9   cups water
4   large onions
4   large cloves garlic
¼   cup lard or turkey fat
1   cup dehydrated masa flour
2   quarts turkey stock
2   tablespoons vinegar
3   tablespoons salt

Do not wash the dried chiles. Toast them in a heavy ungreased skillet, on a griddle, or in a 400° oven until they have an aroma like that of toasting nuts. This takes about 2 minutes. Do not scorch, or the sauce will be bitter. Cool; remove and discard stems, seeds, and dried pink pithy part. Wash well. Cover with 9 cups water and soak for an hour or two, then whirl, a few at a time, in an electric blender (or mash in a mortar). Strain. There should be 2 quarts of purée; if there isn't, add enough water to make up that amount.

Chop the onions, mince garlic very fine (or press it), and cook in the lard or turkey fat until the onion is transparent. Add the dehydrated masa flour, stir smooth, then pour in turkey stock. Cook until thick; add the vinegar. If the turkey stock is salted, add half the salt, taste, and add remainder if needed. Combine with chile purée. Before the tamale making starts, add the turkey meat to this sauce.

# Greek Buffet

*FOR EIGHT PEOPLE*

**GREEK COUNTRY SALAD**

Sliced tomatoes and cucumbers with cheese and olives
Recipe on page 82

**RICE-STUFFED GRAPE LEAVES (OPTIONAL)**

**ALTERNATE 1: MOLDED EGGPLANT MOUSSAKA**

Meat filling molded inside glossy eggplant skins,
served with tomato sauce
Recipe on page 102

**ALTERNATE 2: PASTITSIO**

Meat and macaroni baked in custard sauce
Recipe on page 134

**KOULOURA OR SWEET FRENCH BREAD**

**SWEET LEMON-YOGURT CAKE**

Light, un-iced cake made with yogurt and flavored with lemon peel
Recipe on page 192

**FRESH FRUIT**

Here is a menu of Greek dishes that gives you a choice of entrées to prepare. The Molded Eggplant Moussaka is a showpiece dish, moderately difficult to make. A meat filling is enclosed in a mold of glossy eggplant skins with beautiful result. If you want an easier and more foolproof dish, select the Pastitsio. Most of the preparation for either dish may be done well ahead. The other dishes on the menu require no last-minute attention. The salad should be made several hours ahead in order to marinate.

If you have access to a Greek shop or well-stocked gourmet store, you may want to pick up some authentic accompaniments—*feta* cheese and Greek black olives for the salad; the doughnut-shaped bread, *kouloura;* and canned stuffed grape vine leaves. However, none of these things is necessary. Blue cheese and American ripe olives may be used in the salad, sweet French bread very closely resembles Greek bread, and the stuffed grape leaves may be omitted.

If you are able to find the rice-stuffed grape leaves, all you do is place them on a plate and serve at room temperature. You may garnish the dish with fresh mint (if available) and lemon wedges—a few drops of lemon juice on the leaf rolls is customary.

# Shellfish on Ice

## ASSORTED SHELLFISH ON ICE
Lobster, crab, shrimp, oysters, and clams

## VARIETY OF SEAFOOD SAUCES
Lemon Mayonnaise, Spicy Cocktail Sauce, Green Mayonnaise,
and Remoulade Sauce recipes on page 66

## ABALONE SEVICHE
Abalone marinated in lime juice with green chile salsa
Recipe on page 59

## CAESAR SALAD
Recipe on page 78

## ITALIAN BREAD STICKS AND SWEET BUTTER

## HOT AND COLD BEVERAGES
Champagne or Campari, white wine, espresso

Because you can buy the shellfish already cooked where necessary, this can be a practically effortless company dinner. Mix the sauces in advance, in a blender or by hand. The salad calls for quick last-minute showmanship. If you have time to spare, you can expend it on a festive table arrangement.

Consider first the setting—preferably out-of-doors, a cool protected spot with a lush green background. A small rustic plank or glass-topped table holds the buffet supper. Hurricane lamps, round glass Japanese floats, a fish net, seashells, ferns, and cut blossoms are among the many possibilities for decorating the buffet table. You might seat your guests at a large patio table, or supply trays for lap service.

When you seek icers for the shellfish, you might consider using colorful enamel-coated metal serving dishes. Or select trays with a raised edge, metal Chinese woks, or Indian brass serving trays with handles. Wooden soy tubs are also ideal for icing both the shellfish and the wine or other beverages. Just be sure the containers are deep enough to hold the water from the melting cracked or crushed ice.

For the entrées, choose the shellfish you think your guests would like best. For example, to serve eight persons, you might purchase the following: 4 Alaskan king crab legs (approximately 2 pounds); 2 or 3 Dungeness crabs, cooked and cracked; 1 or 2 spiny lobsters, cooked and split in half; 1½ to 2 dozen Eastern blue point oysters, rock cockle or cherrystone clams,

raw on the half shell; 3 pounds prawns, counting 8 to 10 to the pound, or the small local ocean shrimp, cooked; and 1 pound thinly sliced raw abalone for the Abalone Seviche.

The shellfish do not require any special preparation, but be sure to scrub them thoroughly while they are still encased in the shell. Break the king crab legs at the joints into serving-size pieces; with kitchen scissors, cut off half of the shell along the sides to reveal the crab meat, then serve the meat in the remaining half shell. Remove the lobster meat from the half shells and cut into inch-wide pieces; return to the shell. The oysters or clams on the half shell, the large whole prawns, and the cracked Dungeness crabs are ready for serving as is.

Embed the shells of crab, lobster, oysters, and clams in the ice. Small shrimp and the Abalone Seviche may be in bowls or shells embedded to the rim.

You might suggest to guests that the Lemon Mayonnaise suits the lobster, prawns, and crab. The Spicy Cocktail Sauce goes with oysters, clams, and shrimp. Green Mayonnaise is best suited to lobster and crab, Remoulade Sauce to all but oysters and clams.

# The Chinese "Hot Pot"

*FOR FOUR PEOPLE (QUANTITIES ADJUSTABLE TO SERVING MORE)*

**A SELECTION OF SLICED MEATS, SEAFOOD, AND VEGETABLES**

Cooked in simmering chicken broth by the guests

**CONDIMENTS FOR DIPPING COOKED FOODS**

Such as soy sauce, hot mustard, or other suggested sauces

**CHICKEN-NOODLE OR RICE SOUP**

Made from the broth in which foods have been cooked

**FORTUNE COOKIES OR ALMOND COOKIES**

**CHINESE TEA**

In China and neighboring countries rooms once were heated with charcoal in a small brazier. To conserve precious fuel, it was common to set a pot of broth over it and cook small pieces of food for a long, leisurely supper. Even today, too many cooks don't spoil the broth in the bubbling Chinese "hot pot." Everyone sitting around the table helps flavor the broth by cooking his own meal in it.

You may seat four to six "cooks" together around a small table or two groups at either end of a longer dining table. Each group shares a pot of bubbling chicken broth in which each person cooks his own meat, fish, chicken, and vegetables. (The pot may be an Oriental one especially made for this meal, but an electric frying pan works very well.)

Toward the end of the meal, the hostess adds cooked noodles or rice to the rich broth, which is by now well seasoned. Each person then has a cup of soup.

This supper is hard to beat for a company meal at which you'd like to have all guests feeling relaxed and congenial.

**The Cooking Pot.** The focus of interest on each table is the cooking pot. Most authentic is the charcoal-fired Oriental "hot pot"—available in Oriental hardware and import stores for $4 to $25. Some pots are sold only for ornamental use, so be sure the one you buy is lined with a metal safe for cooking.

But you don't need an Oriental "hot pot" to stage this supper. An electric frying pan is probably the easiest cooker to use because the heat is easily regulated. If you want to serve more than 4 or 6 people, you can easily borrow more pans.

You can also improvise a cooker, using a combination of charcoal or alcohol burner with a frying pan or flameproof casserole. The container should be at least 2-quart size and should sit firmly above a source of steady heat—hot enough to keep the broth just simmering.

For the traditional Oriental "hot pot," use good-quality, long-burning charcoal briquets. Light three or more coals; when they're glowing, arrange on the grill of the cooker with tongs. (For the small "hot pots," you may need to cut each briquet in half before starting.) Add additional ignited briquets as needed. Be sure that the room is well ventilated when you use charcoal indoors.

**The Table Setting and Utensils.** Each place setting should have a plate for eating (salad size is best if the table is small) and, if you choose, a plate of raw foods. For cooking, give each person a Chinese wire ladle (available at Chinese hardware stores), a flat Japanese tempura ladle (available at Oriental import and grocery stores), or a large slotted spoon. Those who know how to manipulate chopsticks well may use the metal or unfinished wooden ones for cooking.

Provide small dishes for condiments; inexpensive dishes are available at import stores.

**The Foods.** Whichever foods you choose to cook from those listed below, you will need the following basic ingredients:

**Chicken broth (canned or homemade)**
**Thin noodles or white rice**

To estimate the quantity of broth needed, first fill your cooking pot with water, about three-quarters full. Measure the water and also allow extra broth for adding as foods cook.

To estimate quantity of noodles, allow ¼ pound per each 4 persons; for rice, allow ½ cup (uncooked) for four.

Tender meats, fish, poultry, and vegetables are all suitable for this method of cooking. In the list below, some of the foods are traditional to the Chinese "hot pot," some are adaptations.

For four persons, serve six to eight foods (four or five meats and two or three vegetables). Choose from these:

    About ¾ pound flank steak; slice partially
        frozen meat very thin (cut steak in half
        lengthwise, then cut in ⅛-inch slices
        across the grain)
¾    pound boneless lean lamb, cut same as
        flank steak, above
1    whole boned chicken breast, cut in strips
        and marinated several hours in mixture
        of 2 tablespoons each soy sauce and
        salad oil, 1 teaspoon chopped fresh
        ginger, and 1 clove crushed garlic
1    pound medium-sized shrimp, shelled,
        sliced lengthwise, and deveined
¾    pound scallops, rinsed, dried, cut in half
1    jar (10 oz.) oysters, well drained
1    pound Japanese tofu or Chinese dow foo
        (soy bean curd), cut in 1-inch cubes
1    can (1 lb.) abalone, drained and sliced
        very thin
¼    medium-sized head Chinese cabbage,
        separated into leaves
½    bunch spinach, separated into leaves with
        stems cut off
¼    pound fresh mushrooms, sliced
¼    pound Chinese (edible pod) peas
1    small head cauliflower broken into
        bite-sized pieces
½    pound tender asparagus, cut in 1½-inch
        lengths
1    small bunch broccoli, cut in bite-sized
        pieces
2    medium-sized turnips, thinly sliced

For the condiments, select from the following list:

**Hot Chinese mustard**
**Soy sauce**
**Teriyaki sauce**
**Chinese oyster sauce**
**Chinese plum sauce**
**Hoy-sin sauce**

The traditional Cantonese dinner would include hot Chinese mustard and soy sauce. To make hot mustard, combine 4 tablespoons dry mustard with 2 tablespoons water and 1 tablespoon soy sauce; cover and let stand several hours to blend flavors.

If you like, garnish plates of food with following:

**Chopped green onion**
**Parsley or Chinese parsley (also called**
**    fresh coriander or cilantro)**

**The Serving.** The traditional Chinese way of presenting the foods to be cooked is to arrange each kind attractively on its own plate. This means the guests have to pass plates periodically if the plates aren't within reach. If table space permits, you might set up two plates of each food, with a complete selection available on either side of the hot pot.

Another way is to prepare a combination plate of uncooked meat, fish, poultry, and vegetables for each person. Have all foods cut in bite-sized pieces.

**The Cooking.** Shortly before dinner, cook noodles or rice, cover, keep warm. (They will be added to broth at end of meal to make soup.)

Just before the meal starts, fill the cooking container about three-quarters full of boiling chicken broth. A depth of 3 to 4 inches is best when using the wire ladles. Cover and return the broth to boiling; then seat the guests. Have more broth ready to add as needed.

To cook dinner, put about three items in your wire ladle and hold it in the broth until the foods are just cooked; most take 1 minute or less. Then empty the cooked foods onto your eating plate and place the refilled ladle back in the hot chicken broth. Eat the cooked foods with the sauces and condiments.

When your guests have finished meat and vegetables, add warm cooked noodles or rice to the rich broth, bring to boiling, then ladle soup into individual bowls.

# A Waffle Party

**ALTERNATE 1: GINGERBREAD WAFFLES**

With Ginger Cream (recipe follows)
and poached apple slices or apple sauce

**ALTERNATE 2: ORANGE SPONGE WAFFLES**

With berries, Honey Butter (recipe follows) or maple syrup, and
whipped cream or ice cream

Next time you invite friends in for an evening snack, treat them to an old-fashioned waffle party. Serve one or more kinds of waffles with a variety of toppings. Each guest can concoct his own waffle combination. Provide plenty of hot coffee or chocolate.

Along with these gingerbread and orange sponge waffles, you can serve plain waffles made from your favorite recipe or mix. For each type of waffle, specific toppings are suggested, but you might also serve some of these with any of the waffles: sweetened whipped cream, honey, ice cream in a variety of flavors, grated semisweet chocolate, and toasted sliced almonds.

For the waffles you can have the creamed mixture ready and the dry ingredients sifted together in advance. Save the remaining preparations to do while the waffle irons are heating: beat the egg whites, stir the dry ingredients into the creamed mixture, then fold in the egg whites. The batter should not be put together far in advance of baking.

## GINGERBREAD WAFFLES

¼ cup butter or margarine
½ cup **each** dark brown sugar (firmly packed)
    and light molasses
2 eggs, separated
1 cup milk
2 cups all-purpose flour
1½ teaspoons baking powder
1 teaspoon **each** cinnamon and ground
    ginger
¼ teaspoon **each** ground cloves and salt
1 cup heavy cream
2 teaspoons sugar
2 tablespoons finely chopped crystallized
    ginger

Cream together the butter or margarine and brown sugar; beat in the molasses, egg yolks, and milk. Sift flour (it isn't necessary to sift instant-type flour), measure, sift with the baking powder, cinnamon, ginger, cloves, and salt. Beat egg whites until soft peaks form. Stir dry ingredients into creamed mix-

ture, then fold in beaten egg whites. Pour batter into preheated waffle baker and bake until lightly browned. Makes about four 6 by 10½-inch waffles.

**Ginger Cream.** Whip cream and sweeten with sugar; fold in crystallized ginger.

## ORANGE SPONGE WAFFLES

4 eggs, separated
⅔ cup sugar
¼ cup milk
2 teaspoons grated orange peel
1 cup all-purpose flour
½ teaspoon salt
2 tablespoons sugar
½ cup softened butter or margarine
¼ cup honey

Beat egg yolks with the ⅔ cup sugar until thick and pale yellow; beat in the milk, and orange peel. Sift flour (don't sift instant-type flour), measure, sift with the salt. Beat egg whites until soft peaks form; gradually beat in the 2 tablespoons sugar until mixture is glossy. Fold egg yolk mixture and flour into beaten egg whites. Spoon batter into preheated waffle baker and bake until lightly browned. Makes four.

**Honey Butter.** Beat butter until creamy; gradually beat in honey.

# HOW TO SERVE UNEXPECTED GUESTS

The knowing cook is never without some kind of shock absorber to cushion the impact of unexpected guests. Somewhere in her cupboard, refrigerator, or freezer are the ingredients that allow her to insist with sincerity that guests stay for dinner.

Each cook has her own secret. Here are some of the ways the magic touch can be accomplished with ready-to-eat and frozen foods, plus staples nearly everyone is likely to have on hand.

## EASY SOUPS AS STARTERS

These quick versions of classic soups have the kind of rich flavor that usually comes only from long, slow cooking.

**French Cheese Soup.** Dissolve 4 beef bouillon cubes (or use beef stock concentrate) in 4 cups hot water. Add 2 teaspoons dehydrated onion soup mix, ½ teaspoon salt, and ½ teaspoon pepper; bring to a boil, cover, and simmer for 10 minutes. Meanwhile lay 6 thin slices toasted French bread in bottoms of oven-proof soup dishes. Cover each slice of toast with about ⅓ cup shredded Swiss cheese (2 cups total). Pour ¾ cup hot stock in each bowl. Heat in 350° oven for 10 minutes. Serve piping hot to 6.

**Egg Drop Soup.** In a pan, dissolve 4 chicken bouillon cubes in 4 cups hot water; add 1 cup diced raw tomato (optional) and simmer for 5 minutes. Beat 1 egg slightly; add to the soup; then stir constantly 1 or 2 minutes, or until the egg separates in shreds. Serve at once. Makes 4 to 6 servings.

## YOUR CHOICE OF ENTRÉES

Start with canned shellfish, canned ham, or frozen chicken (no need to thaw) to make these dishes.

**Twenty-Minute Paella.** In a medium-sized pan, stir together 1 package (7 oz.) precooked rice, 4 tablespoons instant minced onion, 1 can (1 lb.) stewed tomatoes, 1 can (7 oz.) minced clams and juices, 1 can (7 or 8 oz.) small oysters and juices, and 1 can (4½ oz.) wet pack shrimp and juices. Bring to a boil, cover, and simmer for 5 minutes. Turn off heat and let stand tightly covered (on gas or electric range) for 10 more minutes. Makes 4 or 5 servings.

**Fiesta Canned Ham.** Blend 1 package (8 oz.) soft Cheddar cheese spread or 1 package (8 oz.) softened cream cheese with 2 teaspoons prepared horseradish and 3 tablespoons white wine or whipping cream. Gently mix in 2 tablespoons finely chopped chives or green onions, ½ teaspoon seasoned salt, 2 tablespoons chopped canned pimiento, and ⅓ cup chopped ripe olives. Spread the cheese mixture

over the top and sides of a 3 to 5-pound canned ham or a piece of baked ham. Garnish with ripe olive rings and pimiento strips. Chill the ham until ready to slice and serve.

You can even use this mixture to dress up square loaves of canned luncheon meats.

**Chicken with Almond Sauce.** Into a pan put 1 broiler-fryer chicken (2 pounds, cut up), 3 cups water, and 1 teaspoon salt, and simmer until chicken is tender (about 35 minutes; 45 to 60 minutes if chicken is frozen). Remove chicken pieces and keep hot; reserve chicken stock. Melt 2 tablespoons butter in a small saucepan, add ½ cup slivered almonds, and cook over medium heat, stirring, for 3 to 5 minutes or until golden brown. Remove from heat; stir in 2 tablespoons flour. Gradually add 1 cup of the chicken stock, return pan to heat and cook, stirring, about 2 minutes or until thickened. Season with ¼ teaspoon salt, a dash pepper, and 1 tablespoon chopped parsley. Pour sauce over hot chicken. Serves 4.

## SALADS...OTHER THAN MIXED GREEN

A green salad is the handiest emergency salad. But occasionally you may be caught without enough on hand, or the greens may not be as fresh and crisp as you would prefer. You may have the ingredients for one of the following types.

**Antipasto Salad.** Arrange 4 lettuce cups on a platter. Open 1 jar (3 oz.) marinated mushrooms and 1 can (4¾ oz.) Portuguese sardines and spoon some on each cup. Place 2 pickled sweet red peppers on each salad. Cover and chill. Serves 4.

**Orange and Onion Salad.** Peel and slice oranges (one per person); remove seeds if any. Alternate with rings of sweet white or red onions on salad plates. Green pepper rings or pickled beet slices also make a colorful addition. The salads can be placed on a bed of lettuce, romaine, or watercress. Dress the salads with French dressing (add a little poppy or celery seed to the dressing if you wish, for flavor and appearance).

## SIMPLE, QUICK DESSERTS

One good choice to end almost any meal is ice cream or sherbet with a fruit, chocolate, coffee, or mint-flavored liqueur poured over it. Fresh fruit and cheese are also emergency standbys. See the sections on Elegant Ice Cream Finales (page 176) and Easy Fresh Fruit Desserts (page 191) for simple, quick dessert ideas.

# Japanese Sushi Picnic

*FOR FOUR PEOPLE*

**SUSHI RICE WITH VEGETABLE TIDBITS**

Including peas, carrots, mushrooms, shrimp, and egg strips

**SESAME-SOY CHICKEN**

Broiled and coated with toasted sesame seed
Recipe on page 112

**JAPANESE CUCUMBER SALAD**

Nippy with slivered fresh ginger
Recipe on page 80

**FRUIT**

**JAPANESE RICE COOKIES (OPTIONAL)**

**SAKE (OPTIONAL)**

Japanese rice wine, served warm if possible

**TEA**

Some weekend this summer when you decide to entertain guests by serving something special outdoors, consider this Japanese picnic menu. It's an elegant yet simple meal to share with one or two other couples on your patio. Or it packs neatly for transporting to a favorite picnic spot.

The only unusual item on the menu is the *sushi*, which is made from a slightly sweet-and-sour rice mixture and resembles a rice salad. It is easy to make ahead, contains familiar tastes or seasonings, and tastes best served at "room" temperature (never chilled).

Sushi shops are found everywhere in Japan, and also in Hawaii. No Japanese lunch box or picnic basket would be complete without it. A few West Coast Japanese restaurants prepare several different kinds, which you can order "to go." However, the type in this menu is easy and fun to make at home.

All sushi ingredients are readily available in any market, with the possible exception of the rice. You should use a short-grain rice. California-grown Pearl rice is fine for sushi, but oddly enough you will not find it in every store. Look for it in stores that cater to Oriental customers or in large supermarkets.

Marinate the chicken pieces in a soy mixture and either broil them in the oven before you leave or take them to the picnic in their marinade to cook there.

The chicken is good eaten hot or cold. Slice the cucumbers for the salad and chill them in their dressing. In many Western markets you can find Oriental cookies.

Sake or another Japanese rice wine is an elegant addition to the menu. Warm it in one of the miniature sake warmers you can get in Oriental import stores, or in a pan of water over a corner of the barbecue if you grill the chicken at the picnic. Carry the tea, hot or iced, in a vacuum bottle.

Prepare the components of the sushi first, then assemble and refrigerate them as much as 5 or 6 hours before packing the lunch.

**Patio Tempura Party Version.** If you serve this sushi menu for a patio party, you might like to substitute Curried Chicken Tempura (recipe on page 117) for the Sesame-Soy Chicken. Cook this crisp-crusted chicken in an electric frying pan right in front of your guests; serve piping hot.

## SUSHI RICE WITH VEGETABLE TIDBITS

2 packages (10 oz. <u>each</u>) frozen green peas
Sushi Rice (see following recipe)

Cook peas in salted water as directed on the package; drain. Put the Sushi Rice Mixture in a bowl with the drained peas; cut the Mushroom Strips and Carrot Strips (instructions follow) into short pieces and add to rice; mix all together carefully so you do not mash the rice grains. Turn into a serving dish, which might be a plastic container, square or rectangular pan, lacquered tray or bowl. Arrange the Egg Strips (instructions follow) and the Pink Shrimp attractively on top.

### MUSHROOM STRIPS:

2 ounce package of dried mushrooms
2 tablespoons <u>each</u> sugar, soy sauce, and
    water
1 teaspoon salt
¼ teaspoon monosodium glutamate (optional)

For Mushroom Strips, soak the mushrooms in water for 30 minutes to 1 hour. Drain and cut into long, thin strips. Put mushrooms into a small pan with 2 tablespoons *each* sugar, soy sauce, and water, 1 teaspoon salt, and ¼ teaspoon monosodium glutamate. Cover pan and simmer until the water is evaporated and mushrooms are tender, about 5 minutes.

### CARROT STRIPS:

2 large carrots
2 teaspoons white vinegar
2 tablespoons sugar
¾ teaspoon salt
¼ teaspoon monosodium glutamate (optional)
1½ tablespoons water

For Carrot Strips, cut carrots in long, thin strips. Put into a small pan with 2 teaspoons white vinegar, 2 tablespoons sugar, ¾ teaspoon salt, ¼ teaspoon monosodium glutamate, and 1½ tablespoons water. Cover pan and simmer until tender-crisp and the liquid is evaporated, about 5 minutes.

### PINK SHRIMP:

1 can (4½ oz.) broken shrimp
1 tablespoon sugar
    Red food coloring
1 teaspoon water

For Pink Shrimp, mix shrimp with 1 tablespoon sugar; add several drops of red food coloring, blended with 1 teaspoon water. Grind the shrimp mixture by pressing in a mortar with pestle, a Japanese *suribachi,* or a fine wire strainer until shrimp is flaky and color evenly distributed. Put into a small pan and stir over low heat until it is dry and fluffy.

### EGG STRIPS:

4 eggs
2 tablespoons sugar
½ teaspoon salt
4 teaspoons sake (Japanese rice wine),
    chicken stock, or water

For Egg Strips, mix eggs, 2 tablespoons sugar, ½ teaspoon salt, and sake, chicken stock, or water; beat with a wire whip or fork until well blended and the sugar is dissolved. Preheat an 8 or 10-inch frying pan on medium low heat (about 250° if you use an electric pan), oil it well, pour in ⅓ to ½ cup of egg mixture, and quickly tip and tilt pan to coat bottom evenly. When the egg is slightly browned, carefully turn to cook other side (if it should tear, patch it with a little of the egg mixture). When done, remove it to a piece of paper towel to absorb any excess grease. This will make about 2 "pancakes." Cut them into long, thin strips.

## SUSHI RICE MIXTURE

Use this quantity of sushi rice to prepare Sushi Rice with Vegetable Tidbits.

3 cups short-grain rice
3 cups cold water
4 teaspoons sugar
6 tablespoons white vinegar
4 tablespoons sugar
1 teaspoon monosodium glutamate (optional)
3 teaspoons salt

Put rice into a large, heavy cooking pan with tight-fitting lid. Add 3 cups cold water and 4 teaspoons sugar; soak about 2 hours. Cover and bring to a boil on high heat until the water begins to spew out from the lid. Without lifting the lid, turn heat immediately to low (on an electric range, have one of the units preheated to low and immediately transfer the pan of rice).

Cook for 12 minutes on low heat; remove from heat and let stand 10 minutes, all without lifting the lid. (If you should ever double the quantity of this recipe or use more than 5 cups of rice, cook it for 15 minutes on low heat instead of 12 minutes.)

Meanwhile, combine in a small pan the vinegar, 4 tablespoons sugar, monosodium glutamate, and 3 teaspoons salt; heat and stir just until the sugar is dissolved. Also have ready an electric hair dryer or have someone standing by who can fan the rice mixture to cool it quickly as you add the vinegar mixture (this prevents the rice from becoming soggy). Turn the cooked rice immediately into a large bowl and carefully fold in the vinegar mixture while fanning or cooling it with the hair dryer set on "cool," being careful to keep the rice grains whole.

# Portuguese Country Dinner

*FOR FOUR PEOPLE (RECIPES EASILY DOUBLED OR TREBLED)*

### CARNE DE PORCO CON VINHA D'ALHOS

Country-style spareribs in garlic wine
Recipe on page 108

### PURÊ DE BATATAS

Mashed potatoes (use your favorite method)

### COUVE CON CEBOLAS

Swiss chard, mustard, or kale with onions
Instructions follow

### COMPOTA DE MAÇÃ

Apple sauce (canned or freshly made)

### SALADA

Crisp lettuce with sweetened vinegar dressing
Instructions follow

### SUSPIROS

Traditional meringue cooky dessert
Recipe on page 193

This Portuguese dinner is simple and wholesome, and the foods are inexpensive; only the seasonings will strike you as being a little unusual. Since the complete meal can be on the table at one time, serving is simple. This is a good dinner to serve to guests you know are really "meat and potatoes" people.

Pork is the main dish in this meal based on authentic Portuguese recipes. Meaty country-style spareribs marinate for several days in a particularly mild and aromatic version of *vinha d'alhos,* freely translated "garlic wine." Then the ribs are roasted and the good brown drippings are ladled on mashed potatoes. Plain, unspiced apple sauce offsets the richness of the pork.

The greens you use for the cooked vegetable vary with the seasons. The typical (and low-calorie) slightly sweetened Portuguese vinegar dressing is mixed with crisp lettuce.

Pretty little meringue cookies are the dessert. They are traditionally served with tea, but have coffee if you prefer.

This is how you prepare the vegetable and salad:

**Swiss Chard, Mustard, or Kale With Onions.** Wash and coarsely chop enough greens (including stems if you use Swiss chard) to make 10 cups, lightly packed. Thinly slice 2 medium-sized onions and cook in a wide pan over moderate heat in 2 tablespoons salad oil or melted butter, stirring occasionally, until browned. Add the greens and ½ cup water. Cover and cook for about 10 minutes, stirring occasionally; or cook until greens are tender. Season with salt.

**Salad.** Mix 2 tablespoons vinegar with 2 teaspoons sugar. Sprinkle this over about 4 cups broken iceberg lettuce, then toss. If you like, add sliced tomatoes or green pepper rings for a little extra color and fresh flavor, plus salt and pepper to taste.

# Nouveau Riche Hamburgers

*FOR TWELVE TO TWENTY-FOUR PEOPLE*

**BURGUNDY BURGERS WITH ROQUEFORT**

**HAMBURGER BUNS WITH SESAME SEED**
From bakery or made from recipe on page 168

**ELEGANT ONIONS**

**BUTTER LETTUCE**

**BEEFSTEAK TOMATOES**

**FRENCH CHAMPAGNE MUSTARD**

When "just plain folks" suddenly come into a lot of money, they may begin to surround themselves with all sorts of elegant trappings. But their simple origins are difficult to disguise. That's why we call these "new rich" hamburgers. They are decked out fit to kill with some new and fancy trimmings, ready for a sophisticated party. But no one is fooled. They are still obviously plain old hamburgers at heart.

You dress the hamburgers up with wine and cheese, broil, and place on freshly home-baked buns, a real delicacy. Top them with dill-and-parsley-flecked onion slivers, leaves of tender butter lettuce, and thick slices of choice tomatoes. Then spread with imported mustard made with Champagne, bought at a gourmet food shop.

As special as these hamburgers sound, they are very practical to prepare. The meat patties can be shaped and marinated ahead. The buns may be frozen after baking, days in advance if you wish. The method of preparing the onions takes away some of the strong flavor and keeps them looking good long after they have been sliced. Butter lettuce leaves are just the right size to fit hamburger buns. Beefsteak tomatoes are solid, not juicy, so these elegant burgers can be tidily munched by the most refined.

**BURGUNDY BURGERS WITH ROQUEFORT**

- 8 pounds ground beef chuck
- 1 cup chopped parsley
- 1 cup chopped green onion
- 2½ tablespoons salt
- ½ teaspoon pepper
- 1 bottle (4/5 qt.) dry red wine
- 24 squares Roquefort or blue cheese (about 12 oz.)

Mix together the ground chuck, parsley, and the green onion; season with salt and pepper. Shape into 24 patties, making a depression in the center of each one. Place in a shallow pan and pour wine over patties, pouring into the depressions. Chill 2 hours or longer. Remove meat patties from marinade and broil over medium hot coals, for 8 to 10 minutes for medium rare. Place a small square of Roquefort or blue cheese on each meat patty just before serving so it will melt slightly.

**Elegant Onions.** Slice 4 large sweet onions in half lengthwise, then slice thinly, lengthwise. Sprinkle generously with salt, let stand 15 minutes. Squeeze in hands until limp, rinse well to remove salt, then mix with ½ cup chopped parsley and ½ teaspoon dill weed (optional).

# Wintertime Buffet

*FOR TEN PEOPLE*

**CREAM OF ASPARAGUS OR BROCCOLI SOUP**

Use canned asparagus soup or make from recipe on page 75
Recipe for Cream of Broccoli also is on page 75

**COLD SLICED TONGUE AND BEEF TENDERLOIN**

With fluffy horseradish sauce
Recipes on page 91

**PARSLEY-BUTTERED NEW POTATOES**

**SCALLOPED MUSHROOMS**

Buttered fresh mushrooms baked with crumb topping
Recipe on page 154

**GREEN SALAD**

**PUMPKIN ICE CREAM PIE**

Frozen pie of pumpkin mousse and vanilla ice cream
Recipe on page 186

This partly cold, partly hot buffet is a good choice for winter and especially holiday entertaining. Many of the foods can be prepared ahead, so you can easily organize your menu around the holiday rush.

## HAVE AN OLD-FASHIONED TAFFY PULL

A taffy pull can be fun for people of all ages. Since the taffy has to be prepared just before pulling, you may wish to plan some preliminary activity for your guests. It would be a good idea to ask each guest to bring his own apron, or you can provide them. Plan on offering liquid refreshments when the candy is being served.

Before pulling the taffy, be sure you either dampen your finger tips with water, dust them with cornstarch, or butter them.

Because this candy is made with brown sugar, it has a light coffee color. Each batch makes enough for three people to pull. If you want to make more, cook several batches in separate kettles rather than doubling the recipe.

**Brown Sugar Taffy.** Combine 2 cups brown sugar, firmly packed (slightly less than 1 lb.), ½ cup granulated white sugar, 2 tablespoons cider vinegar, 1 tablespoon butter or margarine, and ⅓ cup water in a deep saucepan. Cook over low heat and stir only until the sugar is dissolved. When the sugar is dissolved, wash off sugar crystals on the sides of the pan with a dampened pastry brush or fork wrapped with cheesecloth and moistened in warm water.

Without stirring, boil over medium high heat until a candy thermometer registers 272° (soft-crack stage). Pour the hot syrup on a buttered platter or large pan and let cool until it can be handled. (Dividing the mixture among several platters will speed up the cooling.) As it cools, fold the edges into the center and then pick up the whole batch of candy and pull and stretch for several minutes.

When the taffy is light colored and becomes rather hard to pull, stretch it in ribbons in a buttered pan; dent into bite-sized pieces with a knife. When cold, break apart. If there is any taffy remaining after the taffy pull, put in an airtight container.

# Supper Beside the Fire

*FOR FOUR PEOPLE*

**BARBECUED SIRLOIN WITH PARSLEY HERB BUTTER**

Prepared according to following instructions

**GRILLED FRENCH FRIES**

Cooked with the steak over the coals (see instructions)

**BUTTER LETTUCE SALAD**

**FRENCH ROLLS**

**ALTERNATE 1: FLAMING RUM BABAS**

Use canned babas, flame with rum

**ALTERNATE 2: COFFEE MOLD WITH FLAMING
NUT SAUCE**

Molded ice cream with brandy-flamed, Brazil-nut sauce
See recipe on page 176

When you gather a few friends around the fireplace at home to cook your supper and eat there, a successful evening with stimulating or merry conversation is almost guaranteed. The setting provides two elements seldom combined—glamor and informality. To further the warm glow if the weather is wet or icy, you can serve hot drinks or punch. The flaming dessert also contributes to the cozy yet elegant mood. Party clothes may be worn even by the person who cooks because the preparation is easily and neatly accomplished.

Prepare for the fire and cooking equipment ahead. For flamefree cooking that is easy to control, use charcoal briquets, instead of wood. If your grate has an open shape that will not hold charcoal, you can make an impromptu grate with a piece of fine-mesh hardware cloth. Cut the piece about 16 by 24 inches in size and bend up each side about 1½ inches to keep the charcoal from rolling out; place on top of grate or andirons.

An inexpensive, collapsible camp grill, available in hardware stores, makes a fine cooking surface for barbecuing steak and supporting other foods while cooking or heating.

Cook the steak and French fries simultaneously over the coals. To make potatoes for four people, place 2 packages (8 oz. *each*) frozen French-fried potatoes in a popcorn popper or other wire basket and place on the grill over the coals, shaking occasionally, for 10 to 15 minutes, or until browned and cooked.

Heat the rolls in a heavy foil pan, if you like.

Serve 1 can (12 oz.) rum babas, heated in their own syrup in a foil pan on the grill; if you wish, flame them with 2 tablespoons rum. If you choose the molded coffee ice cream, make the sauce and prepare the mold ahead using ready-made ice cream. At serving time, all you do is unmold it onto a chilled plate and top with flaming sauce.

**Barbecued Sirloin with Parsley Herb Butter.** Place a 1-inch-thick top sirloin steak (about 2 pounds) over coals on a grill and barbecue on both sides, allowing about 4 to 5 minutes on a side for rare meat. Cut in servings and serve with this parsley herb butter:

Finely chop together ½ cup chopped parsley, 2 cloves garlic, and the white part of 3 green onions. Heat ½ cup butter and stir in 2 teaspoons lemon juice and 1 teaspoon *each* anchovy paste and Dijon-style mustard. Remove from heat and stir in the minced greens. Makes 1 cup sauce. The steak will serve 4 people.

# The Fondue Party

*RECIPES MAKE FOUR MAIN-DISH SERVINGS, OR TWELVE TO SIXTEEN APPETIZER SERVINGS*

**ALTERNATE MENU 1: CHEESE FONDUE**
Guests dip bread cubes in melted cheeses

**KIRSCH**
Cherry brandy

**GREEN SALAD OR FRUIT SALAD**

———————————

**ALTERNATE MENU 2: BEEF FONDUE**
Guests cook meat chunks in hot butter

**SAUCES AND SEASONED BUTTERS**
Teriyaki Sauce, plus Onion, Blue Cheese, and Mustard butters

**BAKED POTATOES AND FRENCH BREAD**

**GREEN SALAD**

———————————

**ALTERNATE MENU 3: SEAFOOD FONDUE**
Guests cook fish, shrimp, and scallops in butter

**AVOCADO SAUCE, CHUTNEY SAUCE**

**BAKED OR PARSLEY BUTTERED POTATOES**

**COLE SLAW OR CAESAR SALAD**
Caesar Salad recipe on page 78

Guests enjoy the do-it-yourself aspect of preparing fondue or eating it from one of the special fondue pots with its own stand and heating unit. You can even use an electric frying pan for the meat or seafood types.

**The Cheese Fondue Party.** Once you've mastered making Cheese Fondue, you can serve this dish for many informal occasions, either as an appetizer or main course.

Each guest spears a piece of bread with a fork. He dips it in the pot, gives it a good stir (fondue needs to be stirred continuously), then twirls bread and cheese in the air until it stops dripping and cools.

By setting up several small tables, each with its own pot of fondue, you can provide for larger groups. The number of guests is limited only by the tables, fondue pots, and heating units you can collect, and by the pre-party helpers you can recruit. Making each pot of fondue requires the full attention of one cook for about 30 minutes while the cheese is gradually stirred into the hot wine.

A fondue party for two dozen guests can be staged by using six tables and inviting several friends to arrive a half hour or more early to help. Have the cheese shredded, wine measured into the pots, and everything ready for your helpers to stir the ingredients together.

To encourage guests to mingle and change tables, mark each person's fondue fork and glass or cup with his initial so he can move about, carrying those utensils with him. (Fondue forks have insulated handles and extra sharp prongs, but table forks can be used satisfactorily.) Have a small plate at each place for keeping bread cubes ready to dip. Dry white wine (usually the same wine used in the fondue) or hot tea is the only accompaniment needed.

Halfway through this feast, it is traditional to offer small glasses of kirsch (cherry brandy), which is said to promote digestion and stimulate the appetite.

As the quantity of fondue diminishes toward the end of the meal, the cheese tends to stick a little and form a crust on the bottom. In Switzerland, where this dish originated, the crust is considered a special delicacy. Once guests learn this, they may wage friendly battles for the last precious bits.

After the fondue, you could serve either a green salad with oil and vinegar dressing or light fruit salad —or just coffee and fruit for dessert.

**The Beef or Seafood Fondue Party.** Beef or seafood fondue differs from Cheese Fondue in that the pot contains bubbling butter and oil into which you dip cubes of steak, fish, or whole shrimp in order to cook them. After the cooking, which takes just a minute or two, you then swirl the chunks in little bowls of spicy sauce or flavored butter.

A meat or seafood fondue is quick to prepare with little potential for mistakes—you may not need to practice making the dish ahead of time. And, the sauces or butters, which can be made ahead, are very simple and foolproof. Just be sure you have a cooking utensil with which you can regulate the heat to keep the butter and oil at about 425°. An electric sauce or frying pan is ideal. If you use the traditional fondue pot with alcohol burner, check the temperature with deep-fat thermometer or practice regulating the heat ahead of time.

Like Cheese Fondue, the meat or seafood kind may be used either for an entrée or an appetizer. You may adapt the Cheese Fondue party plan to serve small or large groups. Just keep in mind that the pot of hot butter and oil could present some hazards. Be sure the cooking utensil is on a sturdy table, well centered, with handle, if any, placed where it is not likely to be jarred.

For individual servings of the sauces and butters, you might use some of the tiny Japanese dishes available in import shops. With seafood, abalone or scallop shells would be appropriate.

## CHEESE FONDUE

The recipe for Cheese Fondue is simple, but there are a few requirements. You must use the right cheese. Only *imported* Swiss and Gruyère reliably melt into the wine to make a smooth sauce.

Next in importance is the correct heat for melting the cheese—hot enough to keep it bubbling slowly, but not so hot that the cheese separates. You can melt the cheese in a heatproof earthenware dish directly over a denatured alcohol or canned heat flame. If you use a metal pan, place it over simmering water. (Use the water bath with a chafing dish, or a double boiler.) The heating unit you use at the table should be designed so you can regulate the heat.

| | |
|---|---|
| 1 | clove garlic, cut in half |
| 2 | cups light dry white wine (such as Riesling, Chablis, or Traminer) |
| ½ | pound imported Swiss cheese (Emmental), shredded |
| ½ | pound Swiss or Danish Gruyère (Samsoe), shredded |
| 1 | tablespoon cornstarch |
| 1 | teaspoon dry mustard (optional) |
| 3 | tablespoons kirsch (optional) |
| | Freshly ground nutmeg and pepper, to taste |
| 1 | small loaf French bread, cut in 1-inch cubes with some crust on each |

*Ingredients Tips.* Use a light, dry white wine of good quality for fondue. If a sweeter wine is used, you'll need to add 1 tablespoon vinegar.

To give an especially good flavor, the recipe calls for Swiss and Gruyère cheeses, but you can use Swiss entirely.

This recipe calls for the traditional kirsch, but brandy or light white rum can be substituted, or the liquors can be left out.

When you cut the bread into cubes, each piece should retain some crust; to get the crusty pieces, buy small loaves of French bread, either long and slim or shallow and round, or French rolls.

*Preparing Fondue.* Rub the fondue pot with the cut garlic. Add wine, and heat slowly until bubbles form and slowly rise to the surface. Combine the two cheeses, cornstarch, and mustard (if used). Add cheese mixture, a spoonful at a time; stir slowly and continuously until all the cheese is blended into a smooth sauce—it should bubble very slowly.

Stir in kirsch (if used) a tablespoon at a time, and again bring to a slow boil. (If the heat gets too high at any time, the fondue may separate.) Sprinkle with nutmeg and pepper, to taste. Take to the table with the bread cubes, and adjust heat so fondue keeps bubbling slowly.

If fondue gets too thick, thin with heated wine.
*(continued on next page)*

## BEEF FONDUE

**2 to 2½ pounds boneless beef sirloin or tenderloin**
**Melted butter and salad oil**

Cut the meat into bite-sized cubes and refrigerate until about 15 to 20 minutes before serving time.

Pour the melted butter and salad oil (equal amounts of each) into a Fondue Bourguignonne pot or an electric frying pan to a depth of 1½ to 2 inches. Heat just below the smoking point (about 425° in electric frying pan). When guests are seated and the butter-oil mixture reaches the correct temperature, start cooking. Each guest spears a cube of beef with a fork and holds it in the hot butter-oil until cooked, about 1 to 2 minutes. (Caution guests not to taste meat while on the hot cooking forks.)

Dip beef in one of the following sauces:

### TERIYAKI SAUCE:

**⅓ cup each canned consommé and Sherry**
**¼ cup chopped green onions**
**3 tablespoons each soy sauce, lime juice, and honey**
**1 clove garlic, mashed**
**2 teaspoons freshly grated ginger**

Blend together consommé and Sherry, green onions, soy sauce, lime juice, honey, garlic, and ginger. Heat to boiling; serve hot or cold.

### TOASTED ONION BUTTER:

**1 teaspoon toasted dried onions**
**¼ teaspoon each salt and Worcestershire**
**½ cup softened butter**

Combine the dried onions, ¼ teaspoon salt, Worcestershire, and ½ cup softened butter. Let stand several hours to blend flavors.

### BLUE CHEESE BUTTER:

**1 package (4 oz.) blue cheese**
**½ cup softened butter**

Mix blue cheese with the softened butter. Let stand several hours to blend.

### MUSTARD BUTTER:

**¼ cup prepared mustard**
**½ cup softened butter**

Mix together mustard and the softened butter. Let stand to blend flavors.

## SEAFOOD FONDUE

**½ pound each salmon steaks and swordfish steaks**
**¾ pound raw medium-sized shrimp**
**½ pound scallops**
**Dipping sauces (recipes follow)**
**3 lemons**
**2 bananas**
**¾ cup butter**
**1½ cups salad oil**

Cut salmon and swordfish into ¾-inch squares, discarding skin and bones. Peel and devein shrimp. Arrange fish and shellfish on a tray in separate sections, cover with plastic film, and chill until cooking time. Spoon the avocado and chutney dipping sauces into small bowls and chill. Cut lemons into wedges, place in a bowl, and chill. Just before cooking, peel bananas and slice in 1-inch rounds. Sprinkle with lemon juice.

To cook, heat butter and oil in a fondue pot placed over an alcohol burner until it starts to bubble. Arrange tray of fish and condiment sauces alongside. Let each person spear a piece of fish, shellfish, or banana with a fondue fork or a skewer and dip into the bubbling fat to cook. When fish takes on a tinge of brown on its edges, it is usually done.

### AVOCADO SAUCE:

**1 thawed can (8 oz.) frozen avocado dip (or 1 small avocado, peeled and puréed in a blender)**
**4 drops liquid hot-pepper seasoning**
**1 tablespoon lemon juice**

Mix avocado dip or puréed avocado with hot-pepper seasoning and lemon juice. Chill.

### CHUTNEY SAUCE:

**¾ cup sour cream**
**1 teaspoon curry powder**
**¼ cup chutney**

Mix together sour cream, curry powder, and chutney, chopped or puréed in a blender.

# Picnic for Patrons of the Arts

*FOR EIGHT PEOPLE*

**WIENER BACKHENDL**

Viennese fried chicken with crisp egg and crumb coating
Recipe on page 117

**VEGETABLE-FILLED AVOCADO HALVES**

With horseradish-flavored mayonnaise
Recipe on page 84

**RYE BREAD AND BUTTER SANDWICHES**

**DRY WHITE WINE OR FRUIT PUNCH**

**PUNSCHTORTE**

Lemon cake with whipped cream filling and rum butter icing
Recipe on page 187

**VIENNESE COFFEE**

Instructions follow

The pleasant tradition of picnicking is well adaptable to outdoor concerts and plays. There are many opportunities to attend outdoor performances where you may picnic either before or after.

An easy way to serve, particularly when you are dressed up, is to pack individual boxes for each member of the party. Folding cardboard bakery boxes are good choices. Carry along an extra basket for other picnic essentials.

If your portable cooler is large enough to hold them, pack in it the individually boxed meals, chilled wine, and a pressure can of whipped cream. In a basket carry two vacuum bottles of coffee, a corkscrew, paper plates, cups, and napkins. Wrap the wine glasses in extra napkins. Take along a supply of packaged chemically treated papers for wiping sticky fingers (or carry dampened paper towels in a plastic bag), and forks for the salad.

*Backhendl* is the Viennese variety of fried chicken, in some respects almost as typical of that city's cuisine as Wiener Schnitzel, which it resembles. Crisply crusted, it may be served hot or cold.

Cooked vegetable salads are popular in the German-speaking countries of Europe. This one has a Western touch—the vegetable mixture is heaped into avocado shells. Just before packing the lunches, fill the avocados, place in individual paper dishes, and cover with plastic film.

Make the cake (from lemon cake mix) as much as a day ahead. To prepare, cut in half lengthwise, then cut each half into 6 or 8 slices. Wrap them in plastic film and chill until boxes are packed.

California wine may not resemble the *Heuriger*, or new wine, of Vienna. But such white wines as chilled Riesling or Traminer will complement this menu nicely. (In areas where wine is inappropriate, substitute a tart fruit punch, kept cool in a vacuum bottle.)

To add a Viennese touch to your coffee, brew it strong and add whipped cream to each cup.

# Italian Fritter Meal

*FOR SIX PEOPLE*

### VEAL INDORATO
Batter-fried veal, artichokes, zucchini, and eggplant
Recipe on page 97

### TOSSED GREEN SALAD

### CRUSTY FRENCH OR ITALIAN BREAD

### SPUMONI OR NEAPOLITAN ICE CREAM

Italian fritters are seldom encountered in the numerous Italian restaurants—just in a few long-established places which continue to prepare old-style dishes. Fritters are usually an everyday meal in Italian homes. A full-scale production is called *Fritto Misto* and includes the four foods in Veal Indorato plus many others, such as chicken, brains, sweetbreads, chicken livers, crookneck squash, and mushrooms.

Naturally, the preparation of Veal Indorato (with just four kinds of food) is easier for a cook inexperienced in making such a meal. Also, the ingredients are more obtainable and more universally liked.

# Cold Salmon Buffet

*FOR TWELVE PEOPLE*

### WHOLE SALMON WITH TARRAGON DRESSING
Recipe on page 127

### GREEN BEAN AND ONION SALAD
Suggested recipe on page 81

### BREAD TRAY

### MIXED SUMMER FRUITS
See page 191 for interesting ways to serve fruits in season

This cold buffet is a do-ahead meal. The menu is appropriate for serving indoors or outdoors, depending on the weather and your serving facilities. You'll need to do most of your preparations a day ahead or early in the day you serve, as the fish and salad must chill.

# Tahitian Party

BUFFET FOR TWELVE TO SIXTEEN PEOPLE

### ICED WHITE WINE PUNCH

With pineapple chunks and fruit juices
Recipe on page 202

### CURRIED PRAWNS WITH STEAMED RICE

Simmered in white wine and butter
Recipe on page 130

### CONDIMENT CHICKEN SALAD WITH AVOCADO

With raisins, peanuts, chutney, coconut, and banana
Recipe on page 86

### HOT FRENCH BREAD SLICES

### FRUIT POË WITH COCONUT CREAM

Papaya and pineapple pudding
Recipe on page 183

### TAHITIAN COFFEE WITH COCONUT MILK

Recipe on page 201

You'll enjoy a Tahitian feast, scaled down to dinner-party size. It is a party that's easy to stage—no long-range planning or hours of food preparation. Yet the island dishes are sumptuous. French influence has given Tahiti perhaps the most highly refined cuisine of all the South Pacific islands. Although this is a Tahitian feast, it is not a typical *Tamaaraa*—a formidable affair with vast quantities of food, requiring days of preparation.

**Serving Dinner.** Fill the buffet with all the foods on the menu, even dessert and coffee. Tahitians don't have separate courses; all items for a meal are prepared and ready to eat at the same time.

Let each guest help himself to salad, bread, rice, and prawns, and perhaps coffee, then move on to card tables already set with silverware.

**Decorating.** Here are some ideas for decorating.

The *pareu* cloth ("par-a-oo") plays an important part in the Tahitian way of life. It is colored cotton with a bold contrasting flower or fern pattern in white. Tahitians use the cloth as a house decoration, for curtains, to cover pillows and cushions, as a tablecloth. Men and women use it as a garment (the men wind it around the waist; women wear it sarong-style).

*Ferns, broad green leaves, and flowers* are useful props for your Tahitian decor. Use sword ferns or broad-leafed cannas or buy ti leaves from your florist.

*Bamboo, reed, and straw,* in any form, lend a tropical touch. You can use baskets or trays as serving containers, filled with fruits and flowers, or as a lamp shield. Or pin a piece of straw matting on your wall.

*Tropical fruits* are useful—decorate with them wherever you wish.

*Ornaments from the sea*—you can use seashells, starfish, fish netting, imitation coral and seaweed, colored glass floater balls.

**Couronnes.** Tahitian men and women wear headbands of ferns and flowers, called *couronnes* ("cor-o-nas"). You can make them yourself for the guests, but it's more fun to have the makings on hand and let the guests create their own. Here are directions:

Select fairly sturdy leaves (sword fern or stephanotis would be fine). Using a heavy needle and thread, fasten the stem and tip of a leaf together to form a crown of the correct head size. (You may have to sew several leaves together to get enough length.) Then sew flowers, here and there, onto the fern band.

# Appealing Appetizers

In almost every country, appetizers typical of the native cuisine are used for snacks or a special beginning to meals. But in the United States, ideas have been adopted from all over the world with some typically American innovations added. It would be no surprise at all to attend a party where the hostess very tastefully combined a selection of snacks from Mexico, Japan, and Greece as well as an all-American dip with chips.

The recipes in this chapter reflect the international tastes of people in the United States, yet present choices for those who prefer less exotic combinations. Some require a bit of work and cooking skill, but most are easy to prepare completely or partially ahead.

A large part of the chapter consists of recipes for hot and cold treats that can be served with drinks to guests in the living room, on the patio, or wherever they might be sitting and milling about while talking before dinner. Most of these are easy to eat with fingers or with toothpicks, or to dip with a variety of suggested "dippers." Many are suitable snacks for entertaining when you don't serve a meal—at card parties, cocktail parties, or informal get-togethers.

The last group of recipes is for first-course or "sit-down" appetizers of the type usually presented on individual plates and eaten with a fork at the dinner table. These dishes are very pretty to see, so much so that they might be waiting as an appetizing greeting for guests when they come to the table. One of these recipes is for an Italian pasta customarily served as a first course. Usually at an American dinner, pastas are served with the entrée or after, but it may be a pleasant change to begin the meal this Italian way.

When you plan the menu for a company meal, it often is necessary to include "safe" dishes—those containing ingredients universally liked and prepared in a way acceptable to people who are not very adventuresome about food. But if you serve several appetizers, you have a chance to make at least one thing which is truly different to please those who appreciate a change. You can always include something conventional for the conventional, so that everyone will have something to his liking.

Appetizers can be the most enjoyable part of a dinner party for the guests, and the most fun for the hostess to prepare.

*Tiropetes (cheese pastries)—see page 56*

# DIPS, SPREADS, TIDBITS

The recipes in this section are for hot and cold appetizers which can be eaten with the fingers, nibbled from a toothpick or skewer, dipped, or spread on crackers. Here you may choose from vegetable, mushroom, cheese, bean, sea-food, and meat concoctions. These are cocktail-time treats to which guests may help themselves or which may be passed on trays. Many of these appetizers can be made ahead.

## Onion-Dill Dip

**MAKES ABOUT 3 CUPS**

**PREPARE 1 HOUR TO AS MUCH AS 1 DAY AHEAD**

2½ cups regular or low-fat plain yogurt
1 package (amount for 4 servings) dry onion soup mix
1 tablespoon minced parsley
¼ teaspoon garlic powder
1 teaspoon dill weed
Dash pepper

Raw vegetables are the most appreciated of appetizers, both by weight-watchers and by those who want to preserve appetite for the meal ahead. This dill dip complements all vegetables, including the more unfamiliar flavors of raw green bean, zucchini, turnip, or asparagus.

Combine all ingredients. Chill at least 1 hour to blend flavors. Serve with cherry tomatoes; pieces of crisp vegetables such as carrots, celery, radishes, or cauliflower; or some of the more unusual vegetables suggested above.

## Raw Radish Dip

**MAKES ABOUT 2 CUPS**

**PREPARE AS MUCH AS 2 TO 4 HOURS AHEAD**

1 large package (8 oz.) cream cheese, softened
1 tablespoon lemon juice
¼ teaspoon dill weed
1 teaspoon salt
1 clove garlic, mashed
1 cup chopped radishes

If you enjoy the convenience of dip and chips but have wearied of the usual kinds, this crunchy red radish dip will be refreshing. Serve with corn chips, other sturdy chips, or crackers.

In a small bowl, blend together cream cheese, lemon juice, dill weed, salt, and garlic. Add chopped radishes and stir until blended. Cover; refrigerate for at least 2 hours. You might garnish with a radish rose and parsley.

## Guacamole

**MAKES 6 TO 8 SERVINGS FOR INDIVIDUAL PORTIONS, MORE IF USED AS DIP**

**PREPARE NO MORE THAN A FEW HOURS AHEAD**

2 large ripe avocados
3 tablespoons lime juice
4 canned California green chiles, seeded, rinsed, and chopped
1 canned pimiento, chopped
¾ teaspoon ground coriander
About ½ teaspoon salt, or to taste
Tomato wedges
Parsley

This version of a Western favorite has two new flavor additions—chopped pimiento (which also adds color) and coriander, a frequently used spice in Mexico. Serve with corn chips or crisp fried tortillas.

Peel and pit avocados and mash coarsely with a fork. Blend in lime juice, chiles, pimiento, coriander, and salt to taste. Garnish with tomato wedges and parsley.

*Note: Instructions for making crisp fried tortillas are with Refried Bean Dip recipe on page 59.*

# Avocado Butter

Everyone enjoys an avocado spread, except perhaps the hostess. It is difficult to make sure the avocados reach ripeness on party day. Also, they are very perishable and should be prepared at the last minute. A solution is this spread molded with butter and gelatin, which can be made days ahead, even frozen.

Peel and mash the avocado, add soft butter or margarine, and beat until thoroughly blended. Soften gelatin in the cream, and stir in boiling water until gelatin is dissolved. Add gelatin to the avocado mixture, along with the lemon juice and garlic salt, if used. Turn into a small loaf pan or dish; spread smoothly. Cover and chill thoroughly. Cut into squares or individual pats to serve on crisp crackers.

**MAKES 32 APPETIZERS**

**CAN BE MADE A WEEK AHEAD, OR FROZEN**

1 medium-sized avocado
½ pound butter or margarine at room temperature (or use whipped butter or margarine)
½ envelope unflavored gelatin
2 tablespoons cream
2 tablespoons boiling water
2 tablespoons lemon juice
  Garlic salt (optional)

# Chilled Asparagus Spears

*WITH BROWNED BUTTER MAYONNAISE DIP*

Green spears of cold fresh asparagus, if cooked just until tender but still firm, make marvellous finger food to serve with dip. The spears look especially elegant standing upright in a crystal goblet or bowl.

Trim asparagus spears to the same length (save whatever tender ends you trim off to use raw and thinly sliced in green salads). In a wide shallow pan bring to a boil meat stock seasoned with carrot, lemon, parsley, onion, and salt. Add asparagus, keeping spears parallel, and cook covered just until tender. Chill in stock. Drain spears, and place upright in a bowl or flat on a tray; serve with Browned Butter Mayonnaise.

**Browned Butter Mayonnaise.** Heat butter until richly browned. Remove from heat and let cool slightly. Beat egg yolks until thick. Add warm butter 2 tablespoonsful at a time, beating constantly with a rotary beater (or whirl yolks in a blender for a few seconds, then add butter in a slow, steady stream). Serve immediately, or chill and whip to soften before serving. Makes about 1½ cups.

**ALLOW 3 TO 6 SPEARS PER SERVING**

**PREPARE AS MUCH AS A DAY AHEAD**

2 pounds fresh asparagus spears
3 cups rich meat stock
1 carrot, thinly sliced
1 lemon, thinly sliced (do not peel)
3 sprigs parsley
1 tablespoon diced onion
1 teaspoon salt

**BROWNED BUTTER MAYONNAISE:**

½ pound (1 cup) butter
4 egg yolks

# Crisp Artichoke Appetizers

Something really different in an appetizer *does* exist—these crisp cross sections of fresh artichoke, with intriguing shape and nutlike flavor. They are best served freshly fried.

Wash artichokes and drain. In a bowl, beat together the egg, water, salt, and pepper. Cut off top half of each artichoke; trim stem to 1 inch. Snap off tough outer leaves down to pale green leaves; trim base. Slice artichoke in half lengthwise; remove fuzzy choke. Cut "Y"-shaped cross sections ¼ inch wide. Cut remaining pieces at sides in half lengthwise.

In a 2-quart saucepan, heat shortening to 375°. Dip each artichoke slice into egg mixture, then coat in bread crumbs. Fry until golden brown, turning once; takes about 1 minute. Remove with slotted spoon, drain well, and serve hot. (These may be kept hot in a warm oven up to 1 hour on pans lined with paper towels.)

**MAKES 2½ TO 3 DOZEN SLICES**

**PREPARE NO MORE THAN 1 HOUR AHEAD; KEEP HOT**

5 medium-sized artichokes
1 egg
¼ cup water
½ teaspoon salt
¼ teaspoon pepper
2 cups shortening
  Fine dry bread crumbs

# Mushrooms à la Grecque

**PREPARE 1 DAY AHEAD**

- 1 **pound uniform mushrooms (preferably 1½ inches in diameter)**
- 1½ **cups water**
- ¾ **cup olive oil**
- 2 **tablespoons lemon juice**
- 1 **small clove garlic (put through the press)**
- 1 **stalk celery diced fine**
- 1 **tablespoon white wine vinegar**
- ¼ **teaspoon fennel seed**
- ¼ **teaspoon oregano**
- ¾ **teaspoon ground coriander**
- ½ **bay leaf**
- ¼ **teaspoon whole pepper**
- 1 **teaspoon salt**

The method of preparation is Greek, as well as the ingredients. Fennel, oregano, coriander, and bay leaf flavor these cooked mushrooms marinated in olive oil and lemon. Make in advance, serve at room temperature.

Clean mushrooms. Cut off gritty ends of stems and discard. In a pan combine all ingredients except mushrooms. (If you wish, tie spices in a cheesecloth bag so they may be removed before serving.) Simmer for 15 minutes, then add the whole mushrooms and cook another 5 minutes. Cool and chill for at least 24 hours.

## SIMPLE BUT SPECIAL APPETIZERS

The easiest appetizers are those from can or bottle. However, with little effort, you can prepare some of the following simple and beautiful tidbits, which reflect the attention to detail for which good hosts and hostesses are known.

**Edam Cheese Balls.** Slice 1½ inches off the top of an Edam cheese and use a melon ball cutter to scoop out balls. Refill the cheese shell with the balls.

**Fennel and Blue Cheese.** Arrange cheese on a bed of fennel leaves on tray. Add pieces of crisp raw fennel stalk. Provide knives for spreading cheese on fennel.

**Crudités (French-style raw vegetables) with Homemade Mayonnaise Dip.** Fill a small straw basket with a "nosegay" of fresh, raw relish vegetables such as cauliflower, Chinese (edible pod) peas, baby carrots, radishes, artichoke hearts, cherry tomatoes, cucumber, asparagus spears, green beans, and celery. Cut large vegetables into sticks, slivers, or other easy-to-dip shapes.

To make mayonnaise, place in a blender 1 egg, ½ teaspoon *each* sugar and paprika, 1 teaspoon Dijon-style mustard, and 3 tablespoons tarragon-flavored white wine vinegar. Blend a few seconds, and with motor running gradually pour in 1 cup salad oil, blending until smooth.

**Curried Almonds.** Use blanched or unblanched almonds. (To dry recently blanched almonds, spread them in a pan and bake in a 300° oven for 20 or 30 minutes.)

Heat ¼ cup salad oil in large frying pan. Add 2 pounds almonds; sprinkle with 2 tablespoons curry powder. Sauté, stirring, until nicely colored. Sprinkle with salt and drain on paper towels.

**Banana Chip Appetizers.** Thinly slice green-tipped, peeled bananas. Coat slices lightly with flour. Fry in deep fat heated to 375° for about 3 minutes or until golden brown. Drain on paper towels, sprinkle with salt or prepared cinnamon sugar, and serve hot.

**Melon with Meat.** Cut melon into bite-sized chunks and wrap with a paper-thin slice of one of the appropriate meats suggested. Fasten with toothpicks. Persian, Crenshaw, and Casaba melons and honeydew or cantaloupe are all complemented by prosciutto, Westphalian ham, and baked ham. Other meats which match well with most melons are pastrami, corned beef, tongue, smoked beef, Canadian bacon, Genoa or dry salami, smoked thuringer, Lebanon bologna, galantina, mortadella, and coppa.

**Cream Cheese Trio.** Arrange 3 packages (3 oz. *each*) cream cheese on narrow tray. Coat 1 block with toasted sesame seed, drizzle soy sauce over top. Press chopped chives into second cheese block to cover all of the surfaces generously. Spoon canned taco sauce over third cheese block; add additional sauce as required.

Serve with crisp crackers.

# Marinated Raw Mushrooms

Those who love raw mushrooms delight in their earthy flavor. Those who don't like them may change their minds when they taste fresh slices marinated with oil, vinegar, and tarragon.

Wash mushrooms and slice them lengthwise, right through stem and cap. Combine other ingredients and mix well with mushrooms. Let stand 5 or 6 hours before serving (don't chill).

**PREPARE ABOUT 6 HOURS AHEAD; DO NOT CHILL**

- 1 pound uniform mushrooms
- ¾ cup olive oil
- 3 tablespoons tarragon vinegar
- ½ teaspoon salt
  A little freshly ground black pepper
- 2 teaspoons minced parsley
- ½ teaspoon minced fresh or dried tarragon

# Ginger-Minted Carrots

Tangy with orange and ginger, these tiny cooked carrots brighten an assortment of less colorful appetizers, such as meatballs or pale cheeses. They also provide a low-calorie choice.

Combine carrots, orange juice, ginger, salt, and pepper in pan. Cover and bring to boil; simmer until carrots are just tender, about 3 minutes. Chill carrots, covered in liquid. Drain and spoon into serving bowl; garnish carrots with mint. Serve with picks.

**MAKES 6 CUPS**

**PREPARE 2 HOURS TO AS MUCH AS 1 DAY AHEAD**

- 3 packages (10 oz. each) frozen baby carrots
- 1 cup orange juice
- 1 teaspoon grated fresh ginger
  Dash each salt and pepper
- 1 tablespoon chopped fresh mint

# Skewered Swordfish and Cantaloupe

The combination of swordfish and melon may seem a weird one—until you taste it. Both have firm textures and mild, sweet flavors which the citrus and onion marinade enhances.

Cut swordfish into ¾-inch cubes. Place in a large bowl and cover with a marinade of lime or lemon juice, chopped green onion, and salt. Cover bowl and chill 1 hour. Remove rind and seeds from cantaloupe; cut in ½-inch cubes. Alternate cubes of swordfish and cantaloupe on long thin wooden skewers; allow three cubes per appetizer. Cook over hot coals or under preheated broiler. Serve with lime wedges.

**MAKES ABOUT 25**

**MARINATE FISH FOR 1 HOUR BEFORE BROILING**

**SKEWERS REQUIRED**

- 1 pound swordfish
- ¾ cup lime or lemon juice
- 2 tablespoons chopped green onion
- ¼ teaspoon salt
- 1 large cantaloupe
  Lime wedges

# Philippine Shrimp-Stuffed Tomatoes

Bite-sized stuffed tomatoes are so neat to eat that neither toothpick nor napkin accompaniment is needed. Therefore, they are ideal for large groups at stand-up parties.

Wash and drain tomatoes; cut a thin slice off the top of each and scoop out the pulp. Invert the tomatoes and set aside to drain. Chop the shrimp very fine and combine with the onion, olives, and soy sauce. Stuff this mixture into the tomato shells and refrigerate.

**MAKES 2½ DOZEN**

**PREPARE AS MUCH AS 6 HOURS AHEAD**

- 1 basket cherry tomatoes
- ½ pound cooked, shelled shrimp
- 1 green onion, chopped
- 3 or 4 pitted black olives, chopped
- 1 tablespoon soy sauce

# Cucumber-Cheese Slices

**MAKES ABOUT 40 SLICES**

**PREPARE 2 TO 8 HOURS AHEAD;
CHILL WELL**

2   packages (3 oz. <u>each</u>) soft
    chive cream cheese
¼   cup finely chopped pimiento-
    stuffed olives
3   cucumbers

These cheese and olive-filled cucumber slices have all the virtues of a good appetizer. They look beautiful, taste good, are easy to prepare, may be made ahead, and whet the appetite rather than satiate.

Blend cream cheese with olives. Halve each cucumber lengthwise and scoop out seeds with a teaspoon. Fill the hollow of each half with 2 to 3 tablespoons of the cream cheese mixture. Press halves together, wrap each cucumber individually in plastic film, and chill thoroughly. Cut crosswise in ½-inch slices.

# Tostadas de Harina

*TORTILLAS WITH BROILED CHEESE*

**MAKES 3 DOZEN**

**PREPARE FOR BAKING SEVERAL
HOURS AHEAD**

6   flour tortillas
2   cups shredded mild Cheddar
    cheese
2   tablespoons chopped, seeded,
    canned California green chiles

**VARIATION:**

2   chorizos
    (Omit green chiles above)

In Mexico the tortillas for Tostadas de Harina are made a giant size. You may find large ready-made ones in refrigerator cases at a few groceries now, but the regular-sized flour tortillas (7 inches in diameter) will certainly do as well.

Evenly sprinkle tortillas with cheese, leaving about a ½-inch margin around edges. Top with chiles. Bake on ungreased baking sheets in a 425° oven for 8 to 10 minutes or until edges are crisp and browned. Cut each tortilla into 6 wedges; serve hot.

**Variation: Chorizo Tostadas de Harina.** Omit green chiles. Remove casings from 2 chorizos; crumble meat and cook over medium heat until lightly browned. Drain meat, discarding fat. Evenly sprinkle cooked chorizo meat over cheese-topped tortillas as in Tostadas de Harina. Bake and cut as above.

# Tiropetes

*PASTRY TRIANGLES WITH CHEESE FILLING*

**MAKES 2½ DOZEN**

**MAY BE FROZEN, REHEATED**

1   large package (8 oz.) cream
    cheese, or 1 small (3 oz.)
    package cream cheese and
    ⅓ pound feta cheese
3   ounces Gruyère cheese, finely
    shredded
1   egg
2   tablespoons parsley
5   sheets fila dough (approximately
    14 by 20 inches). Buy prepared
    dough from Greek or gourmet
    shop.
½   cup (¼ lb.) butter, melted

Among the best Greek appetizers (*mezethakia*) are the *petes*, triangles of hot puffy pastry encasing cheese or meat filling. When you first read this recipe for the cheese version, you may think petes are tricky to make. But once you get the knack of how to fill them, you may decide they are one of the easiest specialties to prepare. (*Photograph on page 50.*)

Cream the cream cheese and feta cheese, if used, until light and mix in the Gruyère. Add the egg and beat until blended. Mix in parsley.

Lay out 1 sheet of fila and brush lightly with melted butter; then cut into 3-inch-wide strips about 14 inches long. Place 1 heaping teaspoon of cheese filling in one corner of a strip, fold over, making a triangle. Continue the folding, making sure the bottom edge is always parallel to the alternate side edge, until you fold over the last triangle at the end of the strip. Place on an ungreased baking sheet.

Repeat, until all the filling and fila are used. Bake in a 375° oven for 10 minutes, or until puffed and golden brown. After baking, they may be cooled and frozen. To reheat, place frozen pastries on baking sheet in 375° oven for 10 minutes again.

# A PRINCE OR PAUPER'S GUIDE TO CAVIAR

Glistening caviar is the most glamorous party appetizer. The choice and price range of fresh and preserved caviars from different fishes are great. You can choose the preserved dark caviars (prepared eggs or roe) of sturgeon, lumpfish, or whitefish; or fresh sturgeon caviar; or preserved red caviar of salmon. Lumpfish and whitefish caviars are dyed to simulate the natural gray, dark green, brown, or black hues of sturgeon caviar. Except for sturgeon caviar, which may be labeled just "caviar," the name of the fish is always on the label.

Some sturgeon caviar is labeled according to the variety. *Beluga caviar* is from the largest species of the sturgeon family; it is also the most expensive caviar available in this country. *Osetrova* (or *osetra* or *osetrina*) comes from a medium-sized sturgeon, and *sevruga caviar* from the smallest member of the sturgeon family.

*Malossal* is a term used to designate the finest grade of roe, not the type of sturgeon.

*Pressed caviar*, which has a consistency rather like jam, is made from broken sturgeon eggs and is less costly. Many connoisseurs prefer it.

Each caviar does have unique qualities, and you might keep in mind that fresh sturgeon caviar is usually salted more lightly than all others; preserved sturgeon caviar is more liquid in consistency; lumpfish caviar has an interesting crunchy texture; whitefish caviar is tiny and tender; salmon caviar is the most pungent.

Wide ranging as it is, price is no predictor of caviar's acceptance. Caviar costs range from about 15 cents to $5 an ounce (for the prized fresh Beluga Malossal), depending on the type of fish and quality or freshness. Caviar enthusiasts, not surprisingly, enjoy the expensive sturgeon roe, but also have an appreciative palate for caviars made from other fish roes. Those new to caviar usually enjoy each kind without decided preferences.

All caviar is prepared in essentially the same manner. Roe is taken from the fish before it spawns (this kills the fish); then the thin film, or sac, containing the eggs is carefully broken. The roe is gently rubbed through screens to separate the eggs. Salt is added, in varying amounts, to help preserve the eggs. Fresh caviar is lightly salted and kept under refrigeration; other caviar is sealed in jars or tins. (Freezing makes the eggs burst.)

Russia has long enjoyed a reputation as chief supplier of fine caviar, but since 1953 a revision of a trade agreement has made Iran our primary source. France, Denmark, Norway, Iceland, and even our own West Coast also prepare caviar from sturgeon caught in local waters. *Whitefish caviar* comes from a fresh-water fish taken presently in diminishing numbers from the Great Lakes. *Lumpfish caviar* is from an Atlantic Ocean fish, and *red caviar* from Alaska and Pacific Northwest salmon. (The word caviar, incidentally, is French, derived from Italian and, further back, from the Turkish word still used, *havyar*.)

**Caviar with Toast.** To the most appreciative palates, caviar is at its best when served very simply: icy cold with thin hot toast. A bowl of caviar can be embedded in a dish of crushed ice or solid block of ice. (See page 64 for how to use ice for elegant presentation.)

If the caviar is of the best quality, some consider it a sacrilege to offer chopped onion and chopped hard-cooked egg as accompaniments—lemon wedges are just barely permissible. On the other hand, lumpfish and whitefish caviar are delicious with these embellishments, and you won't feel you are violating any traditions. Leave the toast unbuttered; the caviar is rich. However, if you must use butter, buy it unsalted.

The traditional accompaniment is dry Champagne or vodka.

**Caviar with Deviled Eggs.** Shell 5 hard-cooked eggs, cut in half lengthwise. Mash yolks with 2 teaspoons lemon juice, 2½ tablespoons mayonnaise or sour cream; season with salt and pepper. Pipe or spoon the yolk mixture into the egg whites, leaving a small depression in the center of each; fill with about ¼ teaspoon black caviar.

**Artichoke with Red and Black Caviar.** Drain small marinated artichoke bottoms (about 1¼-inch diameter) and place, cap side up, in paper bonbon cups. Spoon about ½ teaspoon red or black caviar into each artichoke bottom.

**Avocado Dip with Red and Black Caviar.** Split 1 large, ripe avocado, discard pit, and carefully scoop out flesh, preserving shell. Mash pulp with ¼ cup sour cream, 2 tablespoons lime juice, and ⅛ teaspoon salt. Spoon into half shells.

With back of spoon, make a cavity in center of each mound of avocado; fill hollow of one with about 2 tablespoons black caviar; fill other hollow with about 2 tablespoons red caviar. Place avocado halves in a shallow basket and surround with tortilla chips or corn chips.

# Quiche Lorraine Appetizers

MAKES 40 PIECES ABOUT 2 INCHES
SQUARE

PASTRY SHELL MAY BE BAKED
AHEAD; BAKE QUICHE JUST
BEFORE SERVING

**Pastry (see recipe following)**
14 slices cooked bacon, finely
chopped
1¼ cups (about 6 oz.) diced or
thinly sliced Swiss cheese
4 eggs
1¼ cups heavy cream
½ cup milk
Freshly grated nutmeg (or
ground nutmeg)

**PASTRY:**
1½ cups unsifted all-purpose flour
⅛ teaspoon salt
9 tablespoons (½ cup plus 1
tablespoon) butter
1 egg

This variation of the classic *quiche* ("keesh") is baked in a shallow rectangular pan, rather than in the customary pie shape. This is so you can cut it into squares to serve as hot appetizers, either on napkins or little plates. You may also serve it as a first course at the table. The quiche has an egg pastry base with cheese and bacon custard topping.

Make the pastry (recipe below) and roll to fit a 10 by 15-inch rimmed shallow baking pan. Fit pastry flush with the top edge of pan and trim evenly if necessary. Prick bottom in about 20 places with fork. Bake in a 425° oven for 12 to 15 minutes, or until lightly browned. Cool. Wrap airtight if not used soon.

Evenly distribute bacon and cheese over the bottom of the pastry shell. Beat eggs until they are blended, then mix well with cream and milk. Pour liquid over the cheese and bacon. Grate a little nutmeg over the filling.

Bake in a 325° oven for 25 minutes or until filling appears set when gently shaken (if it puffs, prick with a fork to allow air to escape). Cut in small squares and serve while very hot. (This does not reheat well.)

**Pastry.** Measure flour into a bowl. Add salt and butter, cut in small pieces. With a pastry blender or your fingers break the butter into very small particles; the largest should be the size of small peas. Beat 1 egg and add to flour mixture, blending well with a fork. Shape mixture with your hands to form a compact ball.

Roll dough out on a well floured board; turn dough occasionally to prevent sticking. Gently fit pastry into pan (if it tears, just press edges together).

# Cheddar Cheese Spread

MAKES 1½ QUARTS

PREPARE 1 DAY OR MORE AHEAD

1 pound <u>each</u> aged sharp and mild
Cheddar cheese
2 cloves garlic, crushed
2 tablespoons Worcestershire
1 teaspoon <u>each</u> salt and dry
mustard
⅛ teaspoon liquid hot-pepper
seasoning
1 cup beer

A cheese spread made with beer is handy to have around for unexpected visitors. It keeps for several months and also can be used to top hot soup, vegetables, baked potatoes, and home-baked breads.

Cut cheese into ¼-inch slices and put into the large bowl of your electric mixer. Let stand at room temperature for 4 to 6 hours, or until very soft. Beat until light-colored and smooth. Add garlic, Worcestershire, salt, dry mustard, and liquid hot-pepper seasoning, and blend thoroughly. Add beer ¼ cup at a time, blending well after each addition, and continue beating until light and fluffy. Store in covered jars in the refrigerator.

# Fondue

*RECIPES WITH FONDUE PARTY MENUS—PAGES 44 TO 46*

Cheese, beef, or seafood fondue—often eaten as the main dish for dinner— also can be an appetizer, served wherever guests gather to converse before dinner or at the dining table. In the case of cheese fondue, cubes of bread are dipped in a hot cheese mixture; for beef or seafood fondue, pieces of the food are cooked in hot butter and oil, then dipped in sauce. In either case, the guests who must gather around the hot container to serve themselves mix and become acquainted easily. Instructions for the three kinds of fondue are included.

# Refried Bean Dip

Bland refried beans take on a new dimension when heated with cheese, onion, and taco sauce. They become a dip-type appetizer which nearly everyone instantly likes. Many won't recognize the main ingredient as just plain beans, and will ask what is in this new dish.

Mix beans, cheese, onion, salt, and taco sauce in a small pan or heatproof Mexican pottery bowl. Cook over coals, stirring, until heated. Keep warm on barbecue, or use chafing dish. Serve with crisp fried tortillas, or tortilla chips.

**Crisp Fried Tortillas.** Heat about 1 inch of salad oil in a frying pan over medium-high heat. Cut tortillas in pie-shaped pieces (cutting each into sixths). Fry about 8 at a time turning occasionally, until crisp and lightly browned, about 2 minutes. Drain on paper towels; sprinkle lightly with salt if desired.

**MAKES 3 CUPS**

**MIX INGREDIENTS SEVERAL HOURS AHEAD**

1   can (1 lb.) refried beans
1   cup (¼ lb.) shredded Cheddar
      cheese
½   cup chopped green onion
      (including part of the tops)
¼   teaspoon salt
2   to 3 tablespoons canned taco
      sauce
      About 1 dozen tortillas
      Salad oil
      Salt

# Iced Shrimp in Dill Marinade

*MENU FOR WINE-TASTING INCLUDES THIS DISH—PAGE 17*

A marinade seasoned with lemon juice, dill weed, minced onion, and allspice flavors the shrimp, which can be prepared well in advance.

Devein shrimp (see note below); drop in boiling salted water. Cook until shrimp turn bright pink. Drain; reserve ¾ cup of the stock. Shell shrimp and pour marinade over them. To make marinade, mix ¾ cup stock with lemon juice, dill weed, onion, sugar, 1 teaspoon salt, and allspice. Cover and chill for at least 4 hours (or overnight). Serve shrimp from a well-chilled or iced container. Garnish, if you like, with fresh dill or parsley sprigs. Serve with lemon wedges and rye wafer bread.

*Note: To devein shrimp without shelling, insert a slender wooden or metal skewer into the back of each shrimp just below the vein and gently pull to surface; repeat several times as required for each shrimp.*

**MAKES 6 SERVINGS**

**PREPARE 4 TO 24 HOURS AHEAD**

2   pounds large shrimp or prawns
      (about 40 to a pound)
      Boiling salted water
¾   cup stock from boiled shrimp
½   cup lemon juice
1   teaspoon dill weed
3   tablespoons minced onion
2   teaspoons sugar
1   teaspoon salt
¼   teaspoon ground allspice
      Fresh dill or parsley sprigs
      (optional)
      Lemon wedges
      Rye wafer bread

# Abalone Seviche

*MENU FOR SHELLFISH ON ICE INCLUDES THIS DISH—PAGE 33*

If abalone is among your seafood favorites, try this recipe for abalone marinated in lime juice, which "cooks" it without benefit of heat. An abalone shell makes a good serving dish.

Cut abalone into strips about 1 inch wide and 1½ inches long, and place in a small bowl. Mix together lime juice, salad oil, chile salsa, salt, pepper, garlic salt, sugar, and hot-pepper seasoning. Pour sauce over the abalone and mix well; then cover and refrigerate for about 4 hours or overnight.

At serving time, spoon into an abalone shell or other serving container, and garnish with lime, thinly sliced. Furnish toothpicks for serving.

**MAKES 8 SERVINGS**

**PREPARE 4 HOURS TO 1 DAY IN ADVANCE**

1   pound thinly sliced raw abalone
6   tablespoons lime juice
2   tablespoons salad oil
¼   cup canned green chile salsa
¼   teaspoon <u>each</u> salt, pepper, and
      garlic salt
½   teaspoon sugar
3   drops liquid hot-pepper
      seasoning
      Thinly sliced lime

# Shrimp Toast Canapés

MENU FOR CHAMPAGNE PARTY INCLUDES THIS DISH—PAGE 28

**MAKES 4 DOZEN**

**PREPARE FOR BROILING SEVERAL HOURS AHEAD**

1 **pound raw shrimp (12 oz. shelled and deveined frozen shrimp)**
1 **green onion, including part of green top**
4 **canned water chestnuts**
½ **teaspoon salt**
¼ **teaspoon garlic salt**
⅛ **teaspoon pepper**
1½ **teaspoons lemon juice**
1 **egg white**
12 **thin slices white sandwich bread, crusts removed**
**About 2 tablespoons melted butter**

For some strange reason, how to make this delicious hot canapé can be found in several Chinese recipe books. Perhaps the canapé is of Oriental origin, just as Italian spaghetti is said to be. Who knows?

Shell and devein the raw shrimp, or defrost frozen shrimp. Chop shrimp, onion, and water chestnuts into very fine pieces. Put into a bowl with the salt, garlic salt, pepper, and lemon juice. Mix until well blended. Add unbeaten egg white, mixing it in well. Put bread slices under the broiler until toasted on one side. Turn over and spread untoasted side with the shrimp mixture. This much can be done several hours ahead and the appetizers covered with clear plastic film or foil.

Just before serving, brush the top of each sandwich with melted butter and broil until the shrimp topping turns pink. Cut into quarters and serve hot.

# Indonesian Broiled Chicken

**MAKES 8 TO 10 SKEWERS**

**MARINATE MEAT, THREAD SKEWERS AHEAD**

2 **whole chicken breasts**
1 **package (8 oz.) broken walnuts (2 cups)**
⅔ **cup lime juice**
2 **tablespoons chicken stock or broth**
2 **green onions, cut up**
2 **small cloves garlic, mashed**
½ **teaspoon salt**
1 **cup yogurt or sour cream**

A classic Indonesian entrée has been adapted to a skewered appetizer which broils so quickly that even the most impatient or hungry guest may enjoy cooking his own. You can prepare the skewers with nut and lime coating ahead.

Cut the uncooked chicken from the bones in bite-sized pieces and set aside. Combine the nuts, lime juice, chicken stock, onions, garlic, and salt in an electric blender and whirl until the nuts are quite fine. Mix ½ cup of this nut mixture with the yogurt or sour cream to serve as a dip with the chicken; chill thoroughly.

Gently coat the pieces of chicken with the remaining nut mixture and refrigerate for 2 to 3 hours. Then string the coated chicken pieces on skewers and refrigerate until you are ready to cook the meat. Broil or grill the chicken about 5 inches from the source of heat for 5 to 7 minutes, turning once. Serve with the reserved sauce.

# Ham-Filled Mushroom Caps

MENU FOR CHAMPAGNE PARTY INCLUDES THIS DISH—PAGE 28

**MAKES 3 DOZEN**

**PREPARE FOR BAKING SEVERAL HOURS AHEAD**

1 **pound small whole mushrooms**
¼ **cup butter or margarine**
2 **cups ground cooked ham**
½ **cup sour cream**
2 **tablespoons minced chives**
6 **pitted ripe olives**

Small stuffed mushroom caps have a natural elegance that can be heightened by placing them in little fluted paper cups, convenient if the mushrooms are to be eaten with the fingers. Very large caps are equally elegant served on a plate for the first course at the table.

Remove stems from mushrooms and finely chop enough stems to make 1 cup. (Use remainder for another purpose.) Lightly sauté caps in melted butter and arrange in a buttered baking pan. Mix together ham, sour cream, chives, and the 1 cup chopped mushroom stems; pile inside mushroom caps. Bake in a 350° oven for 10 minutes. Garnish with sliced olive wedges.

*Ham Sauce in Artichokes—see page 63*

# Hawaiian Beef Sticks

**MAKES 4 DOZEN**

**MARINADE MAY BE MADE A DAY AHEAD**

**MARINATE MEAT 2 HOURS**

**SKEWERS REQUIRED**

    A 2-inch piece fresh ginger, sliced
2  cloves garlic, mashed
2  small onions, chopped
1  cup soy sauce
4  tablespoons sugar
8  small, dried, hot chile peppers
2  tablespoons red wine vinegar
4  teaspoons cornstarch
½  cup water
2  pounds beef sirloin

If you have spent any time in Hawaii, you probably have encountered these "meat sticks," Island classics ranking in popularity with *saimin, laulau,* and *sushi.* They are just a kebab variation of beef teriyaki with the sauce thickened so it won't drip off during broiling.

In a small pan, combine fresh ginger, garlic, onions, soy sauce, sugar, chile peppers, and vinegar. Cook over medium heat until slightly thick, about 20 minutes. Combine cornstarch with water. Gradually stir into sauce and cook, stirring until clear and thickened. Pour mixture through a wire strainer, pressing out all juices, and discard the pulp; cool. Cut beef into bite-sized pieces; add to marinade and allow to stand, covered, for 2 hours. Thread 2 or 3 pieces of meat on each skewer; barbecue over hot coals or broil.

# Sweet-Sour Sausage Balls

**MAKES 150 BALLS**

**PREPARE A DAY OR MORE AHEAD, OR FREEZE**

4  pounds bulk pork sausage
4  eggs, slightly beaten
1½  cups soft bread crumbs
3  cups catsup
¾  cup brown sugar, firmly packed
½  cup <u>each</u> white wine vinegar and soy sauce

This Hawaiian recipe uses a Chinese sweet and sour sauce spiked with a liberal amount of native American catsup. Especially suitable for serving a crowd, the meatballs are economical and easy to prepare, freeze, and reheat.

Mix together sausage, eggs, and bread crumbs. Using palms of hands, shape mixture into balls the size of small walnuts. Sauté in frying pan until browned on all sides; drain. Combine catsup, brown sugar, vinegar, and soy sauce; pour over sausage balls and simmer 30 minutes, stirring occasionally. Serve hot. (If made ahead, refrigerate or freeze sausage balls in their sauce. To serve, reheat in a 350° oven for 20 minutes.)

# Molded Chicken Liver Pâté

*MENU FOR CHAMPAGNE PARTY INCLUDES THIS DISH—PAGE 28*

**MAKES ABOUT 2 CUPS**

**PREPARE A DAY OR SO AHEAD**

¼  teaspoon unflavored gelatin
¼  cup <u>each</u> water and condensed consommé
¾  pound chicken livers
    Water
¾  cup soft butter or margarine
3  tablespoons finely chopped onion
1  teaspoon dry mustard
¼  teaspoon <u>each</u> salt, nutmeg, and anchovy paste
    Dash <u>each</u> cayenne and cloves
    Lemon slices and watercress for garnish

This is one of those elegant but easy dishes. A mound of shimmering amber gelatin tops this molded pâté, giving it a very special look. Yet the topping is very easily made from canned consommé. The entire dish may be made well ahead of party time.

Soften gelatin in the ¼ cup water. Add consommé and heat, stirring occasionally, until gelatin is completely dissolved. Pour into bottom of a 2½ to 3-cup mold; chill until firm.

Cover livers with water; bring to a boil and simmer for about 20 minutes, or until livers are very tender. Cool slightly in liquid. Drain livers and whirl in blender with butter until mixture is very smooth and fluffy (or press livers through a food mill or strainer; add butter and beat until smooth). Blend in onion and seasonings. Spread over gelatin in mold, pressing liver mixture in evenly; cover and chill until firm.

Unmold onto serving plate; garnish with lemon slices and watercress. Serve with crisp crackers or buttered rye toast.

# FIRST-COURSE DISHES

For beginning a very special meal, you may want to serve an appetizer course at the table rather than starting with soup or a salad. In addition to the following recipes, several in the preceding Dips, Spreads, and Tidbits section may also be suitable for a first course at the table.

## Antipasto Platter

Italian vegetable antipasto in decorative glass jars is sold by gourmet shops at prices in the truffle and *escargots* category. For a fraction of the cost, you can make the same thing. The homemade version will be just as good looking if you cut the vegetables in uniform, attractive shapes. Many vegetables in addition to those in the recipe can be used, such as artichoke hearts, tiny onions, and green beans.

Combine in a large pan the catsup, chile sauce, water, oil, vinegar, and lemon juice. Season with garlic, brown sugar, Worcestershire, horseradish, salt, and cayenne. Bring to a boil and simmer a few minutes.

Cut cauliflower into flowerets, peel and slice carrots, and slice celery diagonally into 1½-inch pieces. Add to the sauce the cauliflowerets, carrots, celery, mushrooms, and peppers; simmer slowly for 20 minutes, or until crisp-tender. Add drained tuna and simmer a few minutes longer.

Spoon into divided dishes, keeping each kind of vegetable and fish together. Cool and then chill. Garnish with anchovies, sliced olives, and parsley.

**MAKES 10 TO 12 SERVINGS**

**PREPARE AS MUCH AS 1 DAY AHEAD IF DESIRED**

- 1 cup each catsup, chile sauce, and water
- ½ cup each olive oil, tarragon vinegar, and lemon juice
- 1 clove garlic, minced or mashed
- 2 tablespoons brown sugar
- 1 tablespoon each Worcestershire and prepared horseradish
  Salt to taste
  Dash of cayenne
- ½ head cauliflower
- 3 medium-sized carrots
- 2 stalks celery
- ½ pound small whole mushrooms
- 1 jar (8 oz.) peperoncini (small peppers), drained
- 2 cans (7 oz. each) solid pack tuna
- 1 can (2 oz.) rolled anchovies with capers
  Pimiento-stuffed olives
  Parsley

## Ham Sauce in Artichokes

For a dramatic entrance to the dining table: whole artichokes with leaves spread out flower petal fashion, their centers filled with sauce, await each guest. *(Photograph on page 61.)*

In a bowl combine sour cream, mayonnaise, Worcestershire, garlic salt, pepper, and ham. Mix until well blended. Cover and let chill in refrigerator about 30 minutes if to be served cold (the sauce may also be used hot).

To prepare artichokes, cut off stem and top third of artichoke; discard. Trim coarse bottom leaves and cut off thorny points of remaining outer leaves with scissors. Cook artichokes in boiling water to cover with the juice of lemon and 1 teaspoon salt, for 30 to 40 minutes, or until a leaf can be pulled out easily.

Drain; place artichokes on individual serving plates. Spread leaves by taking a few outermost leaves at a time and pushing gently downward without breaking leaves away from heart; repeat until all leaves are fanned outward with only tender inner yellow leaves remaining. Remove remaining leaves and discard. Scrape out chokes, discard. Spoon ham sauce in center hollowed portion; serve immediately. If served cold, chill before spreading leaves.

**MAKES 4 TO 6 SERVINGS**

**PREPARE SAUCE AS MUCH AS 1 DAY AHEAD**

**ARTICHOKES TO BE SERVED COLD MAY BE COOKED SEVERAL HOURS AHEAD**

- 1 cup sour cream
- ½ cup mayonnaise
- ¼ teaspoon Worcestershire
- ½ teaspoon garlic salt
- ⅛ teaspoon pepper
- 1 cup finely chopped ham
- 4 to 6 large artichokes
  Boiling water
- ½ lemon
- 1 teaspoon salt

# Artichokes Vinaigrette

**MAKES 4 SERVINGS**

**PREPARE 4 HOURS TO 1 DAY AHEAD**

1 package (9 oz.) frozen artichoke
   hearts or 2 cups fresh trimmed
   and halved artichoke hearts
6 tablespoons olive oil
2 tablespoons red wine vinegar
3 tablespoons minced sweet pickle
1 tablespoon sweet pickle liquid
2 tablespoons <u>each</u> minced
   parsley and pimiento

Bits of pimiento, pickle, and parsley brighten this dish made from frozen artichoke hearts. They star as the first course at dinner.

Cook artichokes in boiling salted water as directed on package or until tender. Drain and place in a small deep bowl. Pour over them the olive oil and vinegar. Gently mix in the pickle, pickle liquid, parsley, and pimiento. Cover and chill at least 4 hours or overnight. Lift artichokes from marinade and arrange 6 to 8 halves on each individual plate. With a slotted spoon, remove some of the chopped ingredients from marinade and spoon over artichokes.

# Broiled Eggplant Salad-Appetizer

*RECIPE WITH TURKISH MEZE MENU—PAGE 20*

**EACH EGGPLANT MAKES ENOUGH
FOR 6 TO 8 PEOPLE**

**PREPARE SEVERAL HOURS AHEAD
OF SERVING**

Although called a salad in Turkey, its country of origin, this dish best fits American menus as an appetizer. Made from the mashed pulp of eggplants which have been broiled whole for smoky flavoring, it has a consistency much like that of guacamole, the avocado dip-spread. Serve with wheat crackers or toast triangles.

## ICY IDEAS FOR PRESENTING APPETIZERS

**Ice Bowl for Caviar or Dips.** Place an ice block in a shallow pan large enough to take care of melting; center the bowl you will use upside down on the block and trace around rim with an icepick. Hollow out ice within this tracing, testing with the bowl as you work, so that the bowl will fit inside the ice block, rim flush with top of ice. To speed work, put the bowl filled with hot water in the hollow to melt the ice, if you wish. Wipe up water underneath the bowl with sponge or cloth as ice melts. Slide a teakettle filled with hot water over ice to smooth out rough areas. Surround base of block with ice cubes or leaves to conceal pan.

**Ice Ring for Dips.** Fill a large ring mold with crushed ice; freeze. Unmold on large platter. Place a bowl of dip in the center. Stick crab legs, chunks of lobster, prawns, vegetable tidbits, olives, or pickles on toothpicks; stick into the cracks between the pieces of crushed ice.

For a solid, clear ice ring, fill a ring mold with boiled water and let stand until cool, stirring occasionally to remove air bubbles which would make the ice cloudy. Then freeze. After unmolding, arrange tidbits to be dipped around outside of ring.

**Fruit Appetizers on Ice.** Thread individual wooden skewers with an assortment of fruit (melon balls, pineapple cubes, orange and grapefruit sections, peach sections). Arrange on a deep tray filled with finely crushed ice. Let guests help themselves.

For individual servings of melon, layer long slices of honeydew and cantaloupe around a cone of crushed ice; accompany with lime wedges and chopped preserved ginger. Provide forks.

Melon or papaya halves may be nestled in individual bowls of crushed ice. Drained fruit cocktail or cubed fruits may be served on ice in a goblet.

**Seafood and Dip on Ice Platter.** Cover a large shallow platter, deep enough to collect melted water, with crushed ice; sink a bowl of cocktail sauce in the center. Arrange cooked and peeled prawns or crab legs over the ice.

For embellishment, you may spear a collection of relishes (lemon wedges, fancy pickles, small tomatoes, and green stuffed olives) on ornate silver skewers, and stick them into a crab shell or into the ice.

To clean a crab shell, scrub it well; boil in a baking soda solution 20 minutes; scrub again.

# Melon Appetizer

This simple melon cocktail should look as good as it tastes. Pile it in a crystal bowl, or even a vase, with a few lime slices. Or make individual servings in tall stemmed goblets, brandy snifters, or hollowed melon halves. Be imaginative with garnish.

Cut melons in halves, remove and discard seeds. Cut fruit into balls of different sizes, using melon (or French) ball cutter, or metal measuring spoons. Place fruit and all juices in a deep bowl. Mix together lime juice, honey, coriander, and nutmeg. Blend with the melon. Cover and chill. Spoon into serving bowls.

**MAKES 8 TO 10 SERVINGS**

**PREPARE SEVERAL HOURS IN ADVANCE**

- 1 <u>each</u> medium-sized Crenshaw melon and medium-sized Persian melon
- 2 tablespoons lime juice (or juice of 1 large lime)
- 2 tablespoons honey
- ¼ teaspoon <u>each</u> ground coriander and nutmeg

# Fettucine

## NOODLES IN CREAM AND CHEESE

Preparing *fettucine* is sheer show business. Razzle dazzle. Sleight of hand. Before the very eyes of your guests, you toss egg noodles with butter, cream, and Parmesan in a gleaming chafing dish. Serve and bow to applause. Those who shrink from exhibitionism may perform in the kitchen and still reap ovations. But be forewarned that a first course of fettucine is a hard act to follow.

Keep the noodles warm after cooking by floating in water that is hot to touch. In a wide frying pan or chafing dish over high heat on a range, melt butter until it is lightly browned. Add ½ cup of the cream and boil rapidly until large shiny bubbles form; stir occasionally. (Do this ahead, then reheat.)

Reduce heat to medium or place chafing dish over direct flame. Drain noodles well and add to the sauce. Toss vigorously with 2 forks, and pour in the cheese and the remaining cream, a little at a time—about three additions.

Season with salt and pepper and grate nutmeg generously over the noodles (or use about ⅛ teaspoon of the ground spice). Serve immediately.

**MAKES 4 TO 6 SERVINGS**

**PARTIALLY PREPARE SAUCE AHEAD, FINISH AT SERVING TIME**

- 3 cups hot boiled tagliarini or egg noodles (packaged or freshly made)
  Hot water
- 6 tablespoons butter
- 1¼ cups heavy cream
- 1 cup shredded Parmesan cheese
  Salt and pepper
  Fresh grated nutmeg (or ground nutmeg)

# Hot Stuffed Clam Appetizers

Here the French way of preparing *escargots* (snails) with garlic butter sauce has been adapted to small clams. Recently the wife of a French restaurateur convinced him that escargots should be removed from the menu of his world-renowned establishment. They are not chic, she says, and what's more, snails have no flavor—people only eat them because they like the sauce. Whether clams are chic or not, Americans will probably not care a fig. Littleneck or butter clams are bountiful, and the shells hold plenty of delicious sauce.

Put well-scrubbed clams in a large pan with the 2 tablespoons water; heat just until the shells open. When cool enough to handle, remove whole clams from shells; save half the shells.

Combine butter, garlic, parsley; and bread crumbs. Set each clam back on a half shell, spread with about 1 teaspoonful of the butter mixture, and arrange on a baking pan. (You can do this much ahead, then cover and refrigerate until time to serve them.) Set the clams about 4 inches from broiler unit and broil until lightly browned, 3 to 4 minutes.

**MAKES 2 DOZEN**

**PREPARE FOR BROILING UP TO 8 HOURS AHEAD**

- 2 dozen clams
- 2 tablespoons water
- ¼ cup (⅛ lb.) soft butter
- 1 large clove garlic, minced or mashed
- 2 tablespoons finely chopped parsley
- 3 tablespoons fresh bread crumbs (whirl about ½ slice bread in blender) or 1 tablespoon fine dry bread crumbs

# Shellfish Cocktails

*SAUCES USED WITH SHELLFISH ON ICE BUFFET—PAGE 33*

**LEMON BUTTER MAYONNAISE:**

- 3 egg yolks
- 1 teaspoon grated lemon peel
- 2 tablespoons lemon juice
- 1 tablespoon white wine vinegar
- ¾ teaspoon sugar
- 2 teaspoons Dijon-style mustard
- ½ teaspoon salt
- ½ cup each salad oil and melted butter (cooled to lukewarm)

**SPICY COCKTAIL SAUCE:**

- 1 cup chile sauce
- ½ teaspoon Worcestershire
- 4 drops liquid hot-pepper seasoning
- ⅓ cup lemon juice

**GREEN MAYONNAISE:**

- ¼ cup mayonnaise
- ½ cup sour cream
- 2 teaspoons lemon juice
- ⅛ teaspoon crumbled dried tarragon
- ¼ teaspoon salt
- 1 clove garlic, mashed
- ¼ cup each finely chopped watercress, spinach, and parsley

**REMOULADE SAUCE:**

- 2 tablespoons each finely chopped chives, capers, dill pickle, and parsley
- 1 cup mayonnaise

Here are four smoothly seasoned sauces to accompany the traditional seafood cocktail, always a delightful beginning to dinner. Lemon Butter Mayonnaise is excellent with lobster, prawns, Dungeness crab, and Alaskan king crab meat. The Spicy Cocktail Sauce goes with oysters, clams, and prawns. The Green Mayonnaise suits lobster and crab. Remoulade Sauce complements all but oysters and clams.

**Lemon Butter Mayonnaise.** In the container of your blender combine the egg yolks, lemon peel, 2 tablespoons lemon juice, vinegar, sugar, mustard, and ½ teaspoon salt; whirl at high speed for 30 seconds. With motor turned on at high speed, add the oil and butter in a slow steady stream. As mixture thickens, turn blender off frequently and blend oil in with a rubber spatula. Serve at room temperature.

*To make the mayonnaise with a mixer,* combine all ingredients but oil and butter; beat at high speed for 30 seconds. While beating at high speed, add oil and butter in a slow steady stream. This mayonnaise is thinner than that made in a blender, but you can chill it to thicken. Makes about 1¾ cups.

**Spicy Cocktail Sauce.** Mix together just until blended the chile sauce, Worcestershire, liquid hot-pepper seasoning, and ⅓ cup lemon juice. Cover and chill. Makes 1⅓ cups sauce.

**Green Mayonnaise.** Mix together the ¼ cup mayonnaise, sour cream, 2 teaspoons lemon juice, tarragon, ¼ teaspoon salt, and garlic. Mix in watercress, spinach, and ¼ cup parsley. Cover and chill. Makes about 1½ cups sauce.

**Remoulade Sauce.** Mix chives, capers, dill pickle, and 2 tablespoons parsley into the 1 cup mayonnaise. Makes about 1½ cups.

# Shrimp Saganaki

**MAKES 3 DOZEN APPETIZERS**

**KEEP HOT OVER WARMER**

**SERVE WITH COCKTAIL PICKS**

- 1 pound raw medium-sized shrimp
- 1 package (8 oz.) frozen artichoke hearts
  Boiling salted water
- 4 tablespoons olive oil
- ¼ pound small whole mushrooms (¾-inch diameter)
- 2 cloves garlic, finely minced
- ½ teaspoon salt
  Freshly ground pepper
- ½ teaspoon crumbled dried oregano
- 2 tablespoons lemon juice
- 2 tablespoons finely chopped parsley

*Saganaki* is a Greek word meaning "hot pan" and is the clue for presenting this dish. Serve in a heatproof pan or dish with candle warmer to make sure it remains a "saganaki" to the last bit of artichoke, mushroom, or shrimp. It may be appetizer, first course, or even entrée.

Peel and devein shrimp. Blanch artichoke hearts in boiling salted water for 2 minutes, then drain. Heat olive oil in a frying pan, add shrimp and mushrooms, and cook, stirring, until shrimp turn pink. Add artichoke hearts, garlic, salt, pepper, and oregano; heat until hot through. Sprinkle with lemon juice and stir lightly to blend flavors. Sprinkle with parsley.

# Coquilles St. Jacques

## SCALLOPS IN BUTTER

The most simple version of this classic is merely wine-poached scallops with parsley butter sauce. Its simplicity requires interesting serving dishes, either scallop shells or individual casseroles.

Wash and drain scallops. Put them in a pan with wine and water, if used. Bring liquid to a boil, cover, reduce heat, and simmer for 8 to 10 minutes. Remove scallops and cut them in large slices.

Arrange the sliced scallops in 4 shells or individual casseroles. Spoon 2 tablespoons melted butter over top of each filled shell. Sprinkle 1½ teaspoons parsley over each, then sprinkle them with paprika and heat in a 350° oven for 5 minutes.

**MAKES 4 SERVINGS**

**PREPARE FOR HEATING SEVERAL HOURS AHEAD**

**SHELLS OR INDIVIDUAL CASSEROLES REQUIRED**

- 1½   pounds scallops
- 1½   cups dry white wine (or ¾ cup wine and ¾ cup water)
- ½   cup (¼ lb.) melted butter
- 2   tablespoons chopped parsley Paprika

# Pâté en Croûte

## CRUST-ENCLOSED HAM AND VEAL PÂTÉ

This classic French dish takes time to make. But you will consider it time well spent as you watch your guests' delight when the flaky, golden pastry is cut to reveal ribbons of meat within. For an elaborate meal, thin slices may be the first course. Heartier portions can comprise an entrée if accompanied by good wine, salad, and dessert of fruit and cheese. However you serve Pâté en Croûte, let the setting be candlelit.

To make the filling, cut ham and veal into 1½-inch-wide strips, arrange in a shallow dish, and pour over the Cognac or brandy; let marinate 30 minutes. Mix together thoroughly the ground veal, sausage, eggs, salt, garlic salt, onion salt, and cream.

For the pastry, sift flour, measure, then sift again with salt into a bowl. Add butter, cut into small pieces, and add the mashed hard-cooked egg yolks; cut in until crumbly. Add the 2 unbeaten eggs, one at a time, mixing until blended.

Work dough with your hands until smooth. Roll out ¾ of the dough on a lightly floured board about ⅜ inch thick; make it about 1 inch larger all around than the bottom and sides of the pan you're using. (If you use a croûte mold, a special oval pan with removable bottom, butter mold lightly and dust with flour.) If you are using a 5 by 9-inch loaf pan, first grease pan, then line with foil, butter and flour the foil.

Fit pastry into the buttered, floured pan, letting it lap 1 inch over the sides of the pan. Take ¼ of the ground meat mixture and pat into the bottom of the pan, then arrange a layer of ham, and then veal. Repeat layers, ending with ground meat. Spoon in juices left from marinating.

Roll out the remaining pastry ⅜ inch thick; lay over the meat-filled pan, trim to fit, and pinch edges together. Decorate the top with pastry cutouts made from the pastry scraps, and make a slit in the top for steam to escape. Roll a small foil cone and poke it into this slit so juices won't spill over. Brush top lightly with milk.

Bake in a 450° oven for 10 minutes to set crust; reduce heat to 350° and bake 1 hour and 20 minutes longer. Let cool, and serve at room temperature.

*To serve a baked pâté that you have frozen, let it thaw completely, then reheat in a 375° oven for 15 minutes to freshen it; cool to room temperature before serving.*

**MAKES 8 TO 10 SERVINGS**

**BAKE SEVERAL HOURS AHEAD, OR FREEZE**

- ½   pound ham, sliced ⅛ inch thick
- ½   pound boneless veal steak, sliced ⅛ inch thick
- ¼   cup Cognac or brandy
- 1   pound ground veal
- ¼   pound bulk pork sausage
- 2   eggs
- ½   teaspoon salt
- ⅛   teaspoon <u>each</u> garlic salt and onion salt
- ¼   cup heavy cream

**PASTRY:**

- 2⅓   cups regular all-purpose flour
- ½   teaspoon salt
- ¾   cup butter or margarine
- 3   hard-cooked egg yolks, mashed
- 2   eggs
- 2   tablespoons milk

# *Soups and Salads*

AFTER THE APPETIZERS, and before the main dish of a meal, you may want to serve a soup or a salad or both, beginning with the soup. At some meals you may prefer to serve the salad with or after the entrée. This chapter gives you enough recipes for both soups and salads to enable you to make an appropriate choice.

The soups range from clear, light ones which will not be too filling if a heavy meal follows, to heartier versions. Some cold soups are included, which can be delicious in hot weather or a nice contrast after a hot appetizer.

Most soups are simple and easy to make, but tend to be rather plain in appearance. Fortunately, soups can be garnished just as easily as they are made. One or more of the suggestions for colorful toppings and garnishes will surely suit any recipe.

Although a tossed green salad is always appreciated, new and different salad recipes are included, plus interesting variations on old stand-bys. Some of these salads reflect the interest in foods of many nations; others just demonstrate the imaginative approach to salad-making that has earned a reputation for the western part of the country as being a sort of "salad center" of the world. Certainly nowhere else are the salads so varied, so beautifully presented, or so much appreciated.

Tips for making tossed salads and a long reminder list of all the greens and other colorful ingredients that may go into the salad bowl are a useful part of this chapter. These ingredients are well known to everyone, but sometimes it is difficult to think of just the right thing to add when you want to perk up or brighten a basic green salad.

A page of instructions on folding napkins in fancy shapes will aid in making your table appointments as interesting as the soup or salad you may choose to begin the meal.

# SOUPS

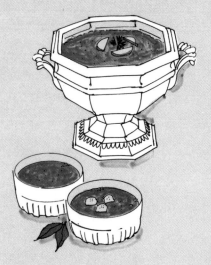

Soups appropriate for beginning a meal are included in this section. Most are clear or creamy, and light enough to whet the appetite. The hearty, filling soups which can be served as a main dish are included in the Entrées chapter, on pages 138 through 140; however, several of those main-dish soups could be used to begin a meal if served in small portions. Also, on page 140 are several recipes for crisp breads to accompany soups. Ordinarily you would only make these when soup is the main dish, but for a very special dinner party you might want such a bread to go with the soup course.

## Pacific Gazpacho

COLD SOUP-SALAD WITH AVOCADO AND BACON

**MAKES 6 SERVINGS**

**PREPARE AS MUCH AS 4 HOURS AHEAD**

6   medium-sized tomatoes
2   cups canned condensed beef broth
½   teaspoon basil
3   tablespoons lemon or lime juice
2   tablespoons olive oil
½   cup finely diced sweet onion
1   large avocado, peeled, pitted, and cubed
    Salt
    Avocado slices
    Thinly sliced onion rings
    Sour cream
6   slices cooked bacon
    Ice cubes

Icy cold *gazpacho* ("gaz-*pah*-cho") is a soupy salad or salad-like soup, whichever way you want to regard it. Originated by Spanish peasants, it is one of those dishes which tastes and looks much better than a description of it sounds. The classic (containing chopped cucumbers, onion, tomatoes, and garlic) is thinned with ice water, olive oil, and lemon juice or vinegar, then topped with bread cubes or crumbs. Ice may be dropped in for further chilling. This strange mixture is so appealing that the dish has been enthusiastically devoured for hundreds of years. Many variations have been devised, such as this brand-new Pacific Gazpacho with avocado, sour cream, and bacon.

Peel tomatoes and cut them in large pieces, saving the juice. Whirl smooth in a blender with beef broth. (Or chop the tomatoes very finely and blend with the broth.) Blend in basil, lemon or lime juice, olive oil, and onion. Gently stir in cubed avocado. Add salt if needed; the broth is usually salty enough. Chill well.

Ladle soup into shallow bowls. To each serving add several avocado slices, onion rings, about 1 tablespoon sour cream, 1 slice crumbled crisp bacon, and a few ice cubes.

## Iced Tomato Soup

**MAKES 5 TO 6 SERVINGS**

**PREPARE AS MUCH AS A DAY AHEAD**

1   can (1 lb. 12 oz.) pear-shaped tomatoes
1½  tablespoons lemon juice
1   bay leaf
1   chile pequin (or ½ small dried hot chile pepper)
1   teaspoon salt
    Dash ground cumin
1   strip orange peel
    Chopped green onions

You'll appreciate the magic an electric blender can work with simple ingredients when you make this quick cold soup out of nothing but canned tomatoes and a few subtle seasonings.

In a 5-cup electric blender container, combine tomatoes, lemon juice, bay leaf, chile pepper, salt, cumin, and orange peel (peel orange with vegetable peeler). Whirl smooth; garnish with chopped green onions, if you wish, and serve cold.

# Chilled Beet Soup

This borscht-type soup, to be sipped cold, is made in minutes in a blender. You can present it elegantly if you pour the soup into mugs or clear punch cups and nestle them in a bowl of crushed ice.

In a 5-cup electric blender container, combine beets and their liquid, broth, lemon juice, honey, caraway seed, salt, and clove. Whirl smooth and chill. Stir before serving. Garnish each serving with sour cream and a little chopped green onion.

**MAKES 6 SERVINGS**

**PREPARE AS MUCH AS A DAY AHEAD**

- 1 can (1 lb.) sliced beets
- 1 can (14 oz.) regular strength beef broth
- 3 tablespoons lemon juice
- 1½ tablespoons honey
- ⅛ teaspoon <u>each</u> caraway seed and salt
- 1 whole clove
  Sour cream
  Chopped green onion

# Wine Consommé

A dry red wine such as Cabernet or Zinfandel perfumes classic beef consommé. The soup can be served hot, cold, or jellied. Lemon serves both as a garnish and taste addition.

Heat beef stock to boiling point. To clarify it, stir in the egg white, and bring mixture to a boil; strain through a moistened muslin cloth, discard egg white, and return clarified stock to the pan. Bring again to a boil, and add wine, sugar, and lemon juice. Add salt and pepper to taste. Serve hot garnished with lemon slices.

**Variation: Jellied Consommé.** Soften gelatin in the water. Add gelatin mixture to boiling clarified stock (see preceding recipe) along with wine, sugar, and lemon juice; chill until set. Whip with a fork and serve with lemon wedges.

**MAKES 6 SERVINGS**

**PREPARE STOCK AS MUCH AS A DAY AHEAD**

- 4 cups regular strength beef stock
- 1 egg white, slightly beaten
- 1 cup dry red wine
- 1 teaspoon sugar
  Dash lemon juice
  Salt and pepper
  Thin lemon slices

**JELLIED CONSOMMÉ VARIATION:**

- 2 packages unflavored gelatin
- ½ cup water
  Lemon wedges (instead of lemon slices above)

# Avocado Bouillon

Hot chicken broth and clam juice, flavored with Sherry or lemon, contains cubes of avocado. A topping of whipped cream, parsley, and paprika is colorful and Christmas-like if you chose to serve it for the holidays.

Combine chicken broth, water, and clam juice. Heat piping hot. Meanwhile, peel and cube the avocados; spoon into each bouillon cup. Sprinkle with salt. Just before removing broth from heat, add Sherry. Pour over avocado cubes in cups. Top each with whipped cream and garnish with parsley and paprika. Serve immediately, with salted crackers, if you wish.

**MAKES 4 TO 6 SERVINGS**

**PREPARE JUST BEFORE SERVING TIME**

- 1 can (10½ oz.) condensed chicken broth
- 1 soup can water
- ½ cup canned or bottled clam juice
- 1 medium-sized or 2 small avocados
  Salt to taste
- 2 tablespoons Sherry or lemon juice
  About ½ cup cream, whipped
  Finely chopped parsley
  Paprika

# Palacsinta Soup

*HUNGARIAN PANCAKE STRIPS IN BROTH*

**USE ABOUT 1 PANCAKE AND ½ CUP BROTH PER SERVING**

**PANCAKES MAY BE FROZEN**

Hungarian Pancakes (see recipe on page 106)
Soup broth (chicken or beef)
Freshly chopped parsley

This attractive soup is nothing really but chicken noodle. However, the noodles are special and homemade. To prepare them, you cut easy-to-make Hungarian Pancakes (recipe on page 106) into long, thin strips. Make the pancakes far ahead and freeze them if you wish.

Cut Hungarian Pancakes into very thin strips, and place about ½ cup in the bottom of each large soup bowl. Just before serving pour hot soup broth over the pancake noodles. Garnish with freshly chopped parsley, if you wish.

# Les Halles Onion Soup Gratinée

**MAKES 6 SERVINGS**

**PREPARE SOUP AS MUCH AS A DAY AHEAD, BAKE JUST BEFORE SERVING**

6   large yellow onions, thinly sliced
2   tablespoons butter or margarine
1   tablespoon olive oil
6   cups Beef Stock (recipe follows) or canned beef broth
    Salt and pepper to taste
⅓   cup white or red Port
½   cup diced Gruyère or Danish Samsoe cheese
6   slices buttered, dry toasted French bread, sliced ½ inch thick
1   cup mixed shredded Gruyère and Parmesan cheeses
1   tablespoon melted butter

**BEEF STOCK:**

4   pounds cut-up beef and veal shanks (bones with some meat on them)
3   quarts cold water
2   scraped carrots
2   peeled onions
2   stalks celery
4   teaspoons salt
1   bay leaf
2   cloves garlic, peeled
2   whole cloves
4   whole black peppers
¼   teaspoon thyme

In the cafes of Les Halles district of Paris, countless bowls of this onion soup are served. Once chic Parisians stopped after parties for a nightcap of hot soup, and at dawn wholesalers and truckers working at the market there came in for a bowl of it. But now onion soup is not so chic and the market is being moved out of the city. These days, many of those who come for soup are tourists who gawk at each other and believe they are seeing the "real" Paris. *(Photograph of soup is on page 68.)*

Use a heavy-bottomed 3 or 4-quart covered pan. Sauté onions in butter and oil until limp. Cover and let simmer slowly for 15 minutes. Pour in Beef Stock (recipe follows) and simmer for 30 minutes. Taste, and add salt and pepper if needed. Pour soup and the Port into an ovenproof earthenware casserole, cover, and heat in a 350° oven for 30 minutes.

Remove from oven and sprinkle with the diced Gruyère cheese. Cover with an even layer of toasted French bread and sprinkle with the shredded cheeses. Dribble over the melted butter. Return to 425° oven for 10 minutes, then turn on the broiler and heat just until the cheese browns lightly on top. Serve at once.

**Beef Stock.** Place beef and veal shanks in an open roasting pan and put in a 450° oven for 20 to 25 minutes, or until nicely browned. Transfer to a 5 or 6-quart pan and add cold water, carrots, onions, celery, salt, bay leaf, garlic, cloves, black peppers, and thyme.

Bring slowly to a boil and simmer, covered, for 2 hours. Skim occasionally. Strain off stock (discard the meat and vegetables) and either skim off the fat or let stock chill, then lift off the cake of fat on top. Makes about 12 cups stock, or twice as much as needed for the preceding recipe. (You can freeze half the stock for later use.)

# Maritata

*CREAMY NOODLE SOUP WITH CHEESE*

*Maritata,* in Italian, means married; whether this soup is so named because of the fine blend or "marriage" of flavors or because it is sufficiently elegant for an occasion as special as a wedding is a subject for speculation. But Maritata is delightfully easy to prepare, and there is showmanship potential in its making. You cook a few strands of noodles in a rich broth—in a chafing dish right at the table—then add a velvety mixture of sweet butter, cheese, egg yolks, and cream.

Bring broth to boiling over direct heat (on a range top or over a denatured alcohol flame). Add vermicelli noodles (broken, if desired) and cook, uncovered, for 5 to 8 minutes or until noodles are tender to bite.

In a bowl blend the sweet butter with cheese and egg yolks, then gradually beat in the cream. (If you cook at the table, prepare this mixture in the kitchen.) Spoon a small amount of the hot broth into the cream mixture, stirring constantly, then pour this mixture back into the hot broth, stirring constantly. Extinguish heat, if using a chafing dish, or remove from heat. Ladle soup into bowls, including some of the vermicelli.

**MAKES 4 TO 6 MAIN-DISH SERVINGS, 8 TO 10 FIRST-COURSE PORTIONS**

**MAY BE PREPARED AT TABLE IN CHAFING DISH**

6   cups hot rich meat broth (all chicken, all beef, or combination of these, freshly made or canned)

2   ounces (⅛ of a 1-lb. package) vermicelli noodles

¼   pound (½ cup) soft sweet (unsalted) butter

¾   cup freshly grated Parmesan cheese

4   egg yolks

1   cup heavy cream

## GARNISH IDEAS FOR SOUPS

Often the difference between an everyday bowl of soup and one fit for company is the garnish. Even canned soups may not be recognized for what they are if imaginatively presented and decorated. Certainly you want to present the special soups you make at their best, too.

Most soup garnishes are simple. Familiar crunchy garnishes are floating croutons, pretzels, and small crackers. Toasted, slivered nuts or a sprinkling of buttered, toasted crumbs may suit certain soups.

Sour cream and yogurt also are familiar additions, but don't forget a dollop of whipped cream or a pat of melting butter for much the same effect.

In clear soups such as consommé, a small bay leaf or spices such as peppercorns, a clove, or a piece of stick cinnamon lend interest and flavor.

Egg and cheese can provide color. The cheese may be grated and sprinkled on, or cubed. Hard-cooked egg whites or yolks may be sieved for sprinkling on, or the whites may be cut in thin strips.

Parsley, herbs, watercress, and mint are the most frequently used green garnishes. Float a tiny sprig or two of any which has compatible flavor, or mince very, very fine to sprinkle on the soup or even on top of another floating garnish. Green onion tops also may be used; they are attractive cut in thin rings.

Paper-thin slices of lemon, lime, or orange to float or thin strips of peel not only give color but fragrance and flavor. If you have trees to provide them, floating citrus blossoms also are attractive.

Some bright-colored or crunchy vegetables may also be cut paper-thin—cucumber, carrots, radishes, beets, water chestnuts, and bamboo shoots.

Cold, jellied soups may be served in orange shells.

You may enjoy garnishing clear soups in the Japanese manner. Contrast should be considered and a delicate touch applied. Often three small garnishes of different shapes and colors are used. One might be round, oval, or flower-shaped—a leaf of watercress, slice of water chestnut, or carrot slice notched to resemble a flower. Another might be a strip or sliver—black mushroom, bamboo shoot, seaweed, celery, or green bean. The third might be something fragile of still different shape—parsley or dill weed sprig, green bean or celery slivered at one end to resemble a spray of pine needles, green onion ring, or piece of very thin noodle. Use your imagination and test the garnishes in the soup bowls you will use.

# Chicken-Cucumber Soup

Chopped cucumbers and fresh ginger root give this chicken soup a fresh-as-spring flavor. You can increase the amount of white wine in some servings to suit individual tastes.

Cut cucumbers into quarters, remove seeds, and chop finely. Sauté chopped cucumbers in butter for about 1 minute. Add chicken stock, ginger, and onion. Season to taste with salt and pepper. Simmer for about 15 minutes. Stir in wine and reheat quickly. Garnish with thin cucumber slices.

# Cream of Scallops

Bottled clam juice and scallops comprise this easy-to-make cream soup thickened with egg yolks, served hot. You can make the soup in just 5 to 10 minutes.

Heat clam juice, butter or margarine, Worcestershire, dry mustard, garlic salt, and celery salt in a pan. When just boiling, add cut-up scallops, and simmer gently about 3 minutes. Beat egg yolks with heavy cream or half-and-half; stir a little of the hot clam juice into the cream; then gradually stir the cream mixture into the remaining hot clam juice. Cook, stirring, about 1 minute, or just until liquid is slightly thickened. Garnish with chopped parsley or chives.

# Soupe au Pistou

*VEGETABLE SOUP WITH BASIL*

Pronounced "soup-oh-pea-stew," this soup is native to the French Riviera in and around Nice. It probably is related to Genoese minestrone, which contains a similar sweet basil sauce called *pesto.*

Place tomatoes and their juices and green beans in a large saucepan (at least 4-quart size). Peel potatoes and cut into ½-inch cubes (you should have about 3½ cups); add to tomato mixture along with water, salt, and pepper. Bring mixture to a boil, reduce heat, cover, and simmer for 1 hour. Add vermicelli and cook until tender, about 15 minutes longer; taste and add more salt, if needed.

  Stir about ½ cup of the simmering liquid into the pistou mixture in serving bowl. Then ladle in about two-thirds of the hot vegetables, vermicelli, and broth remaining in pan. Gradually add cheese, about 2 tablespoons at a time, stirring well after each addition. Blend in as much of the remaining soup as bowl will hold; serve immediately. (Any soup that doesn't fit into bowl can be added after you've removed several servings.)

**Pistou.** In a soup tureen or large deep bowl (at least 3-quart size) from which you can serve the soup, mix basil leaves, garlic, and olive oil. Stir mixture well so that oil coats the basil thoroughly. Then cover and let stand while you prepare the soup.

# Carrot Soup

Carrots make a smooth and colorful cream soup. The flavor is subtle, a little different. A dusting of nutmeg seems just the right finish.

Tie chicken and parsley in a bag formed from a single thickness of cheesecloth. Place in a deep pot. Add carrots, onions, 1½ teaspoons of the salt, and the water. Cover, bring to a boil, and simmer slowly for 2 hours. Let cool slightly, then lift bag from broth and drain well. Discard bones and parsley.

Remove carrots and onions from broth with a slotted spoon and whirl in a blender with some of the broth until smooth (or force through a wire strainer). Return vegetable purée to broth in pan, stir in cream, ¼ teaspoon of the nutmeg, and additional salt if needed. (You can do this much a day ahead and chill soup, covered, overnight.) Heat to simmering. Ladle hot soup into bowls or mugs, and dust each serving lightly with nutmeg.

**MAKES 10 TO 12 SERVINGS OF ABOUT 1 CUP EACH**

**PREPARE AS MUCH AS A DAY AHEAD**

- 4 pounds bony chicken pieces (backs, wings, necks)
- 6 or 8 sprigs parsley
- 10 or 12 carrots, peeled
- 2 large onions, sliced
- About 2 teaspoons salt
- 8 cups water
- 1 cup heavy cream
- About ¼ teaspoon nutmeg
- Salt (optional)
- Nutmeg

# Cream of Broccoli

*MENU FOR WINTERTIME BUFFET INCLUDES THIS DISH—PAGE 42*

Those who don't care for broccoli as a vegetable probably will welcome it in a cream soup similar to asparagus. For a change, serve the soup in pottery mugs, floating a pretzel in each. Pass them to guests in the living room before you leave to make last-minute dinner preparations.

In a medium-sized pan, combine broccoli, onion, and chicken stock; bring to a boil. Simmer for about 10 minutes, or until broccoli is tender. Whirl broccoli mixture in blender until very smooth, or press through a food mill or wire strainer. Melt the butter in a pan; add flour, salt, mace, and pepper, stirring until smooth. Slowly stir in half-and-half, then add broccoli purée. Cook over medium heat, stirring often, until soup bubbles. Serve hot.

**MAKES 10 TO 12 SERVINGS OF ½ CUP EACH**

**PREPARE AS MUCH AS A DAY AHEAD**

- 2 packages (10 oz. each) frozen chopped broccoli, thawed
- ¼ cup chopped onion
- 2 cups regular strength chicken broth
- 2 tablespoons butter
- 1 tablespoon flour
- 2 teaspoons salt
- ⅛ teaspoon mace
- Dash pepper
- 2 cups half-and-half (light cream)

# Cream of Asparagus

*MENU FOR WINTERTIME BUFFET INCLUDES THIS DISH—PAGE 42*

In Mexico a cup or small bowl of a light but distinctly flavored soup is one of the most typical beginnings to a special meal. This Mexican soup, which contains cream cheese rather than cream in the sense you might expect, may be made with frozen asparagus.

Combine the asparagus and broth in a saucepan and bring to boiling, uncovered. Stir to break apart asparagus and simmer gently, uncovered, for 10 minutes. Add salt to taste, if needed.

Cut the cream cheese into about ½-inch cubes and place in a soup tureen. Pour in the hot asparagus soup and serve at once. Or instead of using the cream cheese, you can pass sour cream to spoon into individual servings of the soup.

**MAKES 6 TO 8 SERVINGS**

**PREPARE JUST BEFORE SERVING TIME**

- 1 package (10 oz.) frozen cut asparagus
- 4 cups chicken broth, canned or freshly made
- Salt
- 2 small packages (3 oz. each) cream cheese or 1 cup sour cream

# Soupe de Légumes

*PURÉE OF VEGETABLES*

2   tablespoons butter or margarine
1   large onion, chopped
5   shallots or green onions, chopped
2   leeks, sliced (include a little green top)
2   cups cubed potatoes
2   cups diced turnips
1   medium-sized carrot, sliced
1   medium-sized tomato, peeled and diced
½   teaspoon salt
1   quart regular strength chicken broth or water
3   tablespoons heavy cream
    Parsley or crisp croutons for garnish

Gad-about travelers often bring back recipes for dishes they particularly liked while abroad, such as this French soup of six puréed vegetables.

Heat the butter in a large heavy pan, such as a Dutch oven. Add the onion, shallots or green onions, and leeks; sauté slowly, stirring, until the vegetables are golden, about 7 minutes. Add the potatoes, turnips, carrot, tomato, salt, and chicken broth or water; cover and simmer until all the vegetables are completely tender, about 20 minutes.

Whirl the soup, part at a time, in a blender until smooth. (Or put the soup through a food mill, or press through a wire strainer.) Add the cream to the puréed mixture, reheat, and serve each bowl garnished with a little fresh parsley or croutons.

## DRESSING UP GREEN SALADS

Although a salad may consist of a single salad green, a variety of greens in the bowl can be more interesting. Start with a large quantity of a mild-flavored green, such as romaine or one of the lettuces (iceberg, leaf, Australian, or butter). Add a smaller quantity of the nippier greens. Among these are chicory (curly endive), escarole (broad leaf endive), watercress, spinach, young beet tops, dandelion, young mustard greens, Bok Choy (Chinese chard), and Chinese cabbage. Snip in a little of the pungent herbs and leaves—regular or Chinese parsley, other fresh herbs, mint, green onions including tops, chives, celery tops, the feathery part of fennel, or even peppery nasturtium leaves. For crispness you may add slices of celery, fennel stalk, leek, bulb onion, or Belgian endive.

If you want to add other more hearty and colorful ingredients to a salad, this list may serve as a reminder or idea stimulator: croutons, raw vegetables (tomato, cucumber, carrot, cauliflower, avocado, zucchini, shredded cabbage, sliced asparagus, radishes), cooked vegetables (many of the preceding plus peas, Chinese peas, beans, artichokes, potatoes, garbanzos, beets, bean sprouts, bamboo shoots, water chestnuts), cheese, hard-cooked eggs, mushrooms (raw or cooked), olives, salami, cold meats and fowl, shrimp, lobster, crab, tuna, anchovies, pickled peppers, pimiento, capers, pickle relish, and nuts. If you exercise discretion, you may also combine fruits with greens.

Oranges, tangerines, grapefruit, apple, grapes, banana, papaya, and pineapple are often used this way.

Following are some party dressings for your salad bowl:

**French Dressing with Shallots.** Blend together ¼ cup finely slivered shallots, 1 tablespoon prepared Dijon-style mustard, 6 tablespoons wine vinegar, ½ teaspoon salt, and ¾ cup salad oil or olive oil. Cover and keep as long as 2 days. (If you put dressing in the refrigerator, use safflower oil, because it stays clear and liquid.) Shake to blend again before serving. Makes about 1 cup.

**Blue Cheese Dressing.** Mix together 1 cup salad oil; 3 tablespoons red wine vinegar; 1 teaspoon salt; ¼ teaspoon *each* pepper and paprika; 1 clove garlic, minced; ½ teaspoon celery salt; and 1 tablespoon *each* lemon juice and Worcestershire. Gradually mix this into ½ cup (4 oz.) crumbled blue cheese. Chill, covered, for at least 8 hours to mellow flavors. Makes 1¾ cups dressing; allow 1 tablespoon dressing for each cup of salad greens.

**Lime Salad Dressing.** (Use on salads containing fruit.) Combine ½ cup *each* fresh lime juice and salad oil. Add 2 to 3 tablespoons honey, 1 teaspoon salt, 6 drops liquid hot-pepper seasoning, and ½ teaspoon ground ginger; shake or beat well before using. Makes enough for 8 to 10 servings.

# SALADS

This section includes a wide choice of vegetable, fruit, and other salads suitable for accompanying a meal. Serve them before the entrée, with it (American-style), or afterward (European-style) where appropriate. With each salad you will find instructions for making any special dressing required. Some of the salads, such as those molded in gelatin or made of cooked vegetables, may be made as much as a day ahead. Recipes for salads which are filling and varied enough to be a main dish are found in the Entrées chapter on pages 141 through 143.

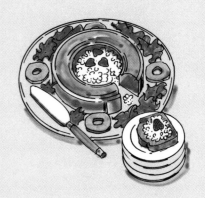

## Salad Tropical

This salad of whole fruits can be prepared so beautifully that it will double as centerpiece or buffet decoration. If you want to enjoy looking at it as long as possible, serve it for dessert—the sweet whipped cream dressing is just as suitable then. *(Photograph on page 79.)*

Slice top, with leaves intact, from pineapple and save. Peel the fruit, cut in thick crosswise slices (do not core), and restack slices, finishing with the decorative top and leaves. Set pineapple on a serving tray. Arrange the following fruit around the pineapple in such a way as to retain the identity of each fruit: the unpeeled pear, cored and cut in wedges; the peeled and seeded papaya, cut in wide crosswise slices; the peeled and pitted avocado, cut in lengthwise slices; and the litchis. Brush pear and avocado with lemon juice.

Peel and section the tangerines, removing all white material, and group the pieces on the fruit platter (or use mandarins). Also peel the oranges with a knife, cut in crosswise slices, and place on the tray. Garnish with lettuce. Place a portion of each fruit on individual serving plates and top with the Cardamom Dressing.

**Cardamom Dressing.** Thoroughly beat egg with lemon juice, cardamom, and honey. Whip cream until stiff; add egg mixture, and continue to beat until mixture is softly whipped. Serve at once. Makes about 2 cups.

**MAKES 8 TO 10 SERVINGS**

**PREPARE AS NEAR SERVING TIME AS POSSIBLE**

1 <u>each</u> large pineapple, large ripe pear, medium-sized or large papaya, and large ripe avocado
1 can (1 lb. 4 oz.) litchis, drained
Lemon juice
2 large tangarines or 1 can (11 oz.) mandarin oranges, drained
2 large oranges
Lettuce leaves

**CARDAMOM DRESSING:**

1 egg
1½ tablespoons lemon juice
⅛ teaspoon ground cardamom
1 tablespoon honey
½ cup heavy cream

## Pico de Gallo

*ORANGE AND VEGETABLE SALAD*

This salad combines elements of a fresh relish served in the state of Jalisco, Mexico, which typically includes *jicama,* a mildly sweet root vegetable. If you can find it, add ½ to 1 cup, raw, peeled, and chopped, to this salad. In Mexico the relish is eaten with the fingers. Some imaginative person, perhaps an expert in shadow plays, decided the human hand picking up the tidbits looks like a rooster pecking corn; so the name *pico de gallo,* meaning "rooster's bill," was applied.

Place romaine in a salad bowl. Arrange orange, cucumber, onion, and pepper on the greens. Garnish rim of the salad with tips of inner romaine leaves, if you wish.

Blend oil with vinegar and salt. Pour dressing over salad and mix lightly.

**MAKES 8 SERVINGS**

**PREPARE JUST BEFORE SERVING TIME**

2 quarts crisp, broken pieces of romaine
1 medium-sized orange, peeled and thinly sliced
½ cucumber, thinly sliced
½ sweet onion, slivered
½ green pepper, diced
⅓ cup salad oil or olive oil
⅓ cup wine vinegar
½ teaspoon salt

# Grapefruit-Avocado Salad

MENU FOR BARBECUED HAM BUFFET INCLUDES THIS DISH—PAGE 29

**MAKES 12 SERVINGS**

- 1 pink grapefruit
- 1½ large heads  romaine lettuce
- 1 avocado
  French dressing

The grapefruit for this salad can be prepared ahead; cover it with plastic film and refrigerate until you are ready to assemble the salad.

Cut away peel—including all the white membrane—from grapefruit; remove the sections. Shred lettuce and pile into salad bowl. Top with grapefruit. Peel and slice avocado and arrange on salad. Add your favorite French dressing.

# Green and Gold Salad

**MAKES 8 SERVINGS**

**PREPARE DRESSING 1 DAY OR MORE AHEAD**

- 1 cucumber, thinly sliced
- 1 can (11 oz.) mandarin orange segments, well drained
- 3 each bananas and avocados, peeled and sliced
  Leaf lettuce

**CHUTNEY DRESSING:**

- ½ cup each mayonnaise and sour cream
- ⅓ cup chutney
- ¼ teaspoon curry powder
- ½ teaspoon salt
- ⅛ teaspoon liquid hot-pepper seasoning
- 2 tablespoons salad oil
- 1 tablespoon white wine vinegar

The bland green flavors of avocado and cucumber combine well with oranges and bananas, especially when topped with a piquant chutney dressing. Contrasts of textures and colors make this salad pleasing.

Arrange cucumber and fruits on a large, lettuce-lined platter or eight individual salad plates. Brush bananas and avocados lightly with lemon juice if salad is to stand for a few minutes before serving. Drizzle about ½ cup of the dressing over all. Garnish with cucumber and banana; serve with remaining dressing.

**Chutney Dressing.** Place in blender container the mayonnaise, sour cream, chutney (including syrup), curry powder, salt, hot-pepper seasoning, oil, and vinegar. Whirl until smooth. Makes 1⅓ cups.

# Caesar Salad

MENUS FOR SHELLFISH (PAGE 33) AND FONDUE (PAGE 44) INCLUDE THIS DISH

**MAKES 8 SALADS OR 4 TO 6 MAIN-DISH SERVINGS**

**MIX AT LAST MINUTE**

- 1 clove garlic
- 2 large heads romaine
- ½ cup olive oil
- 2 eggs, simmered 1 minute
  Juice of 1 lemon (3 tablespoons juice)
- 8 anchovy fillets, chopped
- ⅓ cup grated Parmesan cheese
- 1 cup toasted garlic croutons
  Salt and pepper to taste

**MAIN-DISH VARIATION:**

- ⅓ cup more Parmesan cheese
- 1 cup more croutons
  Meat or seafood (see recipe for suggestions)

Caesar salad, the classic dinner salad, can become a hot weather entrée when you enrich it with meat, seafood, or poultry. The main-dish variation calls for mixing in salami, ham, corned beef, roast beef, chicken, or seafood.

Rub salad bowl with a crushed clove of garlic. Break romaine into bite-sized pieces and turn into the bowl. Pour over oil, and mix greens until well coated. Break the eggs into the salad and mix. Sprinkle with lemon juice and mix thoroughly. Add anchovies and cheese and mix again. Add the croutons and mix well. Taste; season with salt and pepper to taste. Serve at once.

**Variation: Main-Dish Caesar Salad.** Increase quantity of cheese above to a total of ⅔ cup, and use a total of 2 cups croutons.

You can add any one of the following meats or seafood: ⅔ pound assorted salami, thinly sliced and cut in strips; ⅔ pound sliced corned beef, cut in ½-inch strips; ⅔ pound sliced boiled ham, cut in ½-inch strips; ⅔ pound thinly sliced roast beef, cut in ½-inch strips; 2 cans (5 oz. *each*) small shrimp, rinsed and drained; or 2 cans (about 6 oz. *each*) lobster, rinsed and drained. Add meat or seafood when you toss in the croutons.

*Salad Tropical—see page 77*

# Japanese Cucumber Salad

*MENU FOR DINNER COOKED AT THE TABLE INCLUDES THIS DISH—PAGE 21*

**MAKES 4 TO 6 SERVINGS**

**PREPARE AS MUCH AS 4 HOURS IN ADVANCE**

2   large cucumbers
⅓   cup white vinegar
4   teaspoons sugar
1   teaspoon salt
½   teaspoon monosodium glutamate (optional)
2   slices fresh ginger, finely chopped or slivered

Japanese Cucumber Salad contains no salad oil—just white vinegar, a little sugar, salt, and slivered fresh ginger root. This salad can well accompany many types of roast meats, curries, or dishes with an Oriental or tropical flavor. To make it prettier and tastier, you can add bits of shrimp, lobster, or crab meat.

Cut cucumbers in half lengthwise and remove any large seeds. Slice crosswise into very thin slices. Marinate in a mixture of the vinegar, sugar, salt, monosodium glutamate, and ginger. Chill in the marinade an hour or longer. (If salad is to be carried to a picnic, take it in the marinade, perhaps in a vacuum bottle.)

# Greens with Dilled Shrimp

**MAKES 6 SERVINGS**

**MARINATE SHRIMP 1 HOUR**

¼   cup olive oil
1½   tablespoons white wine vinegar
1   tablespoon lemon juice
½   teaspoon dill weed
¼   teaspoon salt
⅛   teaspoon dry mustard
    Dash pepper
1   clove garlic, minced or mashed
½   pound cooked and shelled small shrimp
4   cups <u>each</u> chilled torn romaine and butter lettuce
¾   cup cubed Tilsit or jack cheese
½   cucumber, thinly sliced

Prepare everything for this salad, including the dill-marinated shrimp, ahead of time. All the ingredients can be cut or torn and refrigerated for tossing together when needed.

Combine oil, vinegar, lemon juice, dill weed, salt, mustard, pepper, and garlic; shake well to blend. Pour over shrimp; cover and let stand for about 1 hour in refrigerator. To serve, mix shrimp mixture lightly with romaine, butter lettuce, cheese, and cucumber.

# Marinated Mushroom Salad

**MAKES 6 SERVINGS**

**MARINATE MUSHROOMS 4 TO 8 HOURS**

**ASSEMBLE SALAD JUST BEFORE SERVING TIME**

¼   to ½ pound fresh raw mushrooms
1   medium-sized sweet onion, thinly sliced
⅓   cup salad oil (may be half olive oil)
¼   cup tarragon wine vinegar
1   or 2 drops liquid hot-pepper seasoning
½   teaspoon salt
2   teaspoons minced parsley (fresh or freeze-dried)
1   medium-sized head iceberg lettuce
1   large tomato, peeled (optional)

Plain tomato and lettuce salad gets dressed up for a party with a topping of marinated raw mushrooms and onions. Since you can prepare the mushroom mixture well ahead, assembling the salad is easy.

Rinse mushrooms, pat dry, and slice lengthwise through the stems. Combine the mushrooms and onions in the salad bowl. Over this pour salad oil, vinegar, hot-pepper seasoning, salt, and parsley; mix gently. Cover the bowl and let stand at room temperature for at least 4 hours.

Meanwhile wash the lettuce, drain well, wrap in a damp towel, and put into the refrigerator until well chilled and crisp.

Just before serving, break the lettuce into the bowl. If you use the tomato, cut it in wedges to add. Using a salad fork and spoon, mix all together lightly and well.

# Green Beans and Onions

MENU FOR COLD SALMON BUFFET INCLUDES THIS DISH—PAGE 48

Just because this familiar salad of green beans is not new does not mean it should be forgotten. It is colorful and tasty, especially suitable for buffet service. Make the day before, if desired.

Cook beans in water until tender; drain. Thinly slice onion and add to beans. Combine salad oil, salt, oregano, and pepper; pour over beans and onions. Refrigerate the salad overnight or until well chilled. Just before serving, stir in vinegar and lemon juice. Mix thoroughly. Spoon into serving dish, draining off most of the marinade.

**MAKES 12 SERVINGS**

**PREPARE 2 HOURS TO AS MUCH AS 1 DAY AHEAD**

4   packages (9 oz. <u>each</u>) frozen green beans
½   cup water
1   sweet onion
½   cup salad oil
½   teaspoon <u>each</u> salt and oregano
    Dash pepper
2   tablespoons <u>each</u> white wine vinegar and lemon juice

# Spinach with Pine Nut Dressing

All the recipes in this book have been selected because they are especially good. Yet this one is a star in an all-star cast. To make the salad very special, buy the freshest spinach in quantity and select only the smallest leaves. You might experiment with lemon juice in place of vinegar in the dressing.

To toast nuts, spread them in single layer on a pan; bake in a 350° oven for 5 minutes. Shake pan occasionally.

    Blend nuts with tarragon, lemon peel, nutmeg, salad oil, vinegar, and salt. Mix well before using. Allow 2 tablespoons dressing for each cup of greens. Sprinkle each salad lightly with nutmeg to serve. Makes about 1⅔ cups dressing, enough for about 3 quarts torn greens.

**MAKES 8 TO 12 SERVINGS**

**DRESSING MAY BE PREPARED A DAY AHEAD**

¾   cup toasted pine nuts, coarsely chopped
½   teaspoon tarragon
¼   teaspoon grated lemon peel
⅛   teaspoon nutmeg
½   cup salad oil or olive oil
⅓   cup vinegar
½   teaspoon salt
    Spinach leaves or half spinach and half butter lettuce
    Nutmeg

# Mixed Vegetables with Sweetbreads

The mild, smooth flavor of sweetbreads may have been appreciated in hot dishes; but it will be a taste experience for the adventuresome to have them cold, marinated in French dressing and tossed in a green salad. Anyone who does not care for sweetbreads may enjoy just the tossed greens.

Combine the oil, vinegar, herbs, salt, and dry mustard and pour over the sweetbreads, prepared according to the following instructions. Cover and refrigerate several hours or overnight. Just before serving, drain the sweetbreads, and combine with the salad greens, tomatoes, celery, and green pepper. Dress the salad with the remaining marinade.

**Preparing Sweetbreads.** Wash the sweetbreads well in cold water. Cover with cold water, and add 1 teaspoon salt and 1 tablespoon lemon juice per quart of water. Bring to a boil and simmer about 15 minutes. Drain and plunge the sweetbreads immediately into cold water for 5 minutes to cool them; drain.

    With the point of a sharp knife (and your fingers), remove as much of the white connecting membranes as possible, breaking the sweetbreads into small, bite-sized pieces. If you are not going to use the sweetbreads immediately, place them in a glass bowl, cover with cool water, and refrigerate. Use within 24 to 36 hours.

**MAKES 6 SERVINGS**

**PREPARE SWEETBREADS AS MUCH AS 2 DAYS AHEAD; MARINATE AS LONG AS OVERNIGHT**

½   cup salad oil
3   tablespoons white wine vinegar
2   teaspoons chopped parsley, chives, or basil
⅛   teaspoon <u>each</u> salt and dry mustard
1   pound sweetbreads, prepared as directed
3   cups mixed salad greens, washed, dried, and torn into pieces
2   tomatoes, peeled and cut in wedges
¼   cup <u>each</u> sliced celery and chopped green pepper

# Marinated Cauliflower

MAKES 6 SERVINGS

PREPARE 2 HOURS TO AS MUCH
AS 1 DAY AHEAD

1 medium-sized cauliflower
  Boiling salted water
½ cup olive oil or other salad oil
¼ cup white vinegar
¾ teaspoon salt
¼ teaspoon <u>each</u> pepper and basil
6 anchovy fillets, diced
2 tablespoons capers
¼ cup sliced ripe olives
  Salad greens

Cauliflower usually enters the salad picture raw. But in this case, flowerettes are very lightly cooked and marinated as long as overnight in a dressing redolent with essences of anchovies, capers, and olives.

Break cauliflower into flowerettes, wash, and drop into boiling, salted water. Cook for 7 minutes or so, until it is tender but still slightly crisp.

Drain, rinse in cold water, and drain again thoroughly. Put into a bowl. In another bowl or a glass jar, combine oil, vinegar, salt, pepper, and basil; shake or beat until well blended. Pour dressing over cauliflower. Add anchovy, capers, and olives; mix lightly. Cover and chill several hours or overnight, stirring several times.

To serve, lift the cauliflower with a slotted or runcible spoon, and arrange on the greens in the serving bowl. If you wish, serve the marinade as extra dressing to spoon over the salad.

# Greek Country Salad

*MENU FOR GREEK BUFFET INCLUDES THIS DISH—PAGE 32*

MAKES 8 TO 10 SERVINGS

PREPARE SALAD AT LEAST 2
HOURS AHEAD

4 large tomatoes
2 cucumbers
½ cup crumbled feta cheese or
  blue cheese
½ cup pitted ripe olives
3 tablespoons olive oil
½ teaspoon salt
  Freshly ground pepper
½ teaspoon whole oregano,
  crumbled

During the languid Aegean summer, everyone eats out-of-doors if possible, at little tables under an arbor or beside the sea. This salad may be one of the first dishes brought to the table. Everyone will nibble away at the tomatoes, cucumber, and cheese for appetizers. If you know where to buy white, salty *feta* cheese and black, salty dried olives, your salad can be authentic. But it will be just as good if you use easily available blue cheese and American ripe olives.

Peel and slice tomatoes and cucumbers. Arrange slices in a shallow salad bowl. Sprinkle with cheese and olives. Pour over a dressing made by blending olive oil, salt, pepper, and oregano.

# Green Peas in Sour Cream

MAKES 4 TO 6 SERVINGS

MAKE DRESSING AS MUCH AS 1
DAY AHEAD

ASSEMBLE SALAD NEAR SERVING

1 package (10 oz.) frozen small
  peas
1 tart, red-skinned apple
3 green onions, thinly sliced
  (include part of green tops)
½ cup sour cream
½ to 1 teaspoon prepared
  horseradish
¼ teaspoon salt
⅛ teaspoon pepper
2 teaspoons lemon juice
  Salad greens

At first reading this salad may sound like one of those concoctions invented by a committee of amateur gourmets who have been nipping on the cooking Sherry. Although the salad may be unusual, it is amazingly delicious if you use very tiny peas and prepare them just as the recipe says.

Turn the peas from the package into a colander or wire strainer and run hottest water from the tap over them just until thawed. Rinse in cold water, then drain thoroughly. (To hurry the draining, you might roll the peas on paper towels to absorb extra moisture.) Without peeling the apple, remove core and chop. Combine in a bowl the drained peas, chopped apple, and onion.

For the dressing, combine the sour cream, horseradish, salt, pepper, and lemon juice; add to the salad and mix together lightly. Serve in a bowl lined with crisp greens.

# FOLDED NAPKINS AND OTHER CUSTOM TOUCHES

At each guest's place in fine restaurants, often those with Continental influence, you may find a crisp starched napkin folded in an ornate shape. Such small details make dining more festive.

You can make a variety of fancy folded napkins at home with the instructions which follow. Other thoughtful touches might be: menu cards to let your guests know what courses to expect, especially appreciated when a sumptuous dessert is in the offing; individual salt dishes or salt and pepper shakers; a fresh flower tucked in napkin or laid beside silverware; several cigarettes, matches, and individual ash trays; fingerbowls with a floating lemon slice at the end of the meal; or steamy, damp finger towels in baskets Japanese-style.

**Napkin-folding.** With the following step-by-step directions and a little practice, you can be a master napkin-folder, turning out compliment-inspiring creations resembling fans, crowns, cones, and other interesting shapes.

White napkins are the most formal. You can also achieve lovely effects, especially for lunch or brunch, with colored, bordered, or print napkins.

Napkins today are usually smaller than in years gone by. If you have heirloom linens tucked away, this is the time to bring out grandmother's 22-inch-square napkins: the larger the napkin, the more dramatically it folds. Voluminous napkins aren't essential, however. You can do all these folds with more conventional 15 to 18-inch square napkins. But do use square napkins—most of the folds described cannot be accomplished otherwise.

To prepare napkins for folding, lightly starch them and press them flat (starch soft fabrics more stiffly). Store the napkins flat until you're ready to fold, then use a steam iron to press each fold (restaurant waiters don't do this, but ironing does help). You can prepare folded napkins hours or even days ahead.

For greatest success with the following instructions, read one step at a time and do that portion of the fold. Read the next bit and fold accordingly. If you continue this way throughout, you will produce a properly folded napkin with much more speed and less confusion.

**Triangle.** Fold in half away from you to make rectangle with fold toward you; fold left side over right one to make a square. Bring lower left corner to meet upper right corner, forming a triangle. Fold in half and stand napkin up with folded edge toward you.

**Pyramid.** Fold in half to make a rectangle with fold toward you. Bring upper right and left corners down to meet center of fold. Fold lower right and left corners up to meet at top edge. Turn over, end over end (by turning point facing you forward). Lift upper layer of bottom corner closest to you to meet top corner; lift center of this triangle into a peak, and cross bottom left corner over right corner.

**Cone.** Fold in half to make rectangle with fold at left; fold top edge down to bottom edge to make a square. To form a cone, start rolling tightly from lower left corner toward upper right one; keep point of cone at left and tightly rolled. Point will end at upper left corner, and wide open end at right. Turn up wide end forming cuff to hold napkin together.

**Bishop's Hat.** Fold in half to make a triangle with the point toward you. Bring upper left and right corners down to meet this point (the folded edges should come together). Fold the top corner down to within 1 inch of the point nearest you. Now turn this same corner back up to meet the last fold. Turn entire napkin over, and bring bottom corners together, tucking right corner inside left to hold in place. Stand.

**Crown.** Fold napkin in half to make a rectangle with fold toward you. Bring upper right corners down to meet center of fold, forming a triangle; bring lower left corner up to upper right corner to form a similar triangle. Turn over, with one of the new, long folded edges parallel to you. Fold edge closest to you to other edge, exposing a triangle at left, with point at bottom; turn over to expose two triangles whose points are at top. Tuck right end behind large left triangle; turn napkin over and repeat this to complete the crown. Stand upright.

**Fan.** Fold in half to make a rectangle with folded edge on left, open edges at right. Starting with short edge closest to you, crease in 1-inch accordion pleats. Pleat to within about 4 inches from top edge. Fold in half by turning the left half of rectangle underneath so that the pleats are outside and at the bottom. The folded edge will be at left. Turn down upper right corner, and tuck it behind pleat. Holding the tucked-in corner in one hand, place on table and spread the pleats into Japanese-fan shape. Use the portion with tucked-in corner as a stand at the back, which holds the open fan upright.

# Snow Peas with Sesame Dressing

**MAKES 4 TO 6 SERVINGS OF SALAD**

**PREPARE DRESSING A DAY AHEAD, VEGETABLES SEVERAL HOURS AHEAD**

1   package (7 oz.) frozen Chinese (edible pod) peas
    Boiling salted water
½   head cauliflower
1   can (5 oz.) water chestnuts, drained and sliced
1   tablespoon chopped pimiento

**SESAME SEED DRESSING:**

2   tablespoons sesame seed
⅓   cup salad oil
1   tablespoon <u>each</u> lemon juice, vinegar, and sugar
½   clove garlic, minced or mashed
½   teaspoon salt

Shouldn't those crisp green pea pods, so good in hot Chinese dishes, make a great salad, too? They do. This salad contains cauliflower and water chestnuts, often combined with the peas in stir-fry Chinese dishes. Toasted sesame seed contribute color and crunch. Now that Chinese peas are available frozen, the salad can be enjoyed anytime, everywhere.

Cook Chinese peas in a small amount of boiling salted water until barely tender, about 1 minute after water boils; drain. Separate cauliflower into bite-sized clusters (you should have about 2 cups); cook in boiling salted water until tender but still crisp, about 3 minutes after water boils; drain. Combine peas and cauliflower with water chestnuts and pimiento; cover and chill. Just before serving, mix with about 3 tablespoons Sesame Seed Dressing.

**Sesame Seed Dressing.** Place sesame seed in a shallow pan in a 350° oven for 5 to 8 minutes or until golden brown; cool. In jar with a lid combine salad oil, lemon juice, vinegar, sugar, garlic, salt, and toasted sesame seed. Cover and chill. Shake well before using.

# Vegetable-Filled Avocados

*PICNIC MENU INCLUDES THIS DISH—PAGE 47*

**MAKES 8 SERVINGS**

**MARINATE VEGETABLES AS MUCH AS A DAY AHEAD**

1   package (10 oz.) frozen mixed vegetables
¼   cup French dressing
¼   cup <u>each</u> finely chopped dill pickle and celery
2   teaspoons prepared horseradish
2   tablespoons mayonnaise
4   small avocados
    Lemon juice

A salad of cooked vegetables is just as good for stuffing avocados as a meat or seafood salad is. You may use frozen mixed vegetables or improvise other combinations from leftovers if you wish.

Cook vegetables until barely tender; drain well. Place in a bowl; pour French dressing over them. Cover, refrigerate, and let stand several hours or overnight; drain well.

    Fold in dill pickle, celery, horseradish, and mayonnaise until well combined; chill. Halve, pit, but do not peel, the avocados; brush cut surfaces with lemon juice to preserve color. Divide vegetable mixture evenly among avocado halves.

# Stuffed Avocado

**MAKES 4 SERVINGS**

**PREPARE 2 HOURS TO AS MUCH AS 1 DAY AHEAD**

2   avocados
    Lemon juice
2   tablespoons tarragon vinegar
1   teaspoon <u>each</u> salt and sugar
    Dash liquid hot-pepper seasoning
2   tablespoons <u>each</u> finely chopped chives, green pepper, and pimiento
1   teaspoon unflavored gelatin
½   cup cold water
    Crisp greens for garnish
¼   cup <u>each</u> mayonnaise and sour cream

Avocado halves are often filled with a salad. But in this case, all the green meat has been removed, puréed, and mixed with seasoned gelatin. The smooth mixture is molded and served in the glossy green shell.

Halve the avocados, discard seeds, and spoon out pulp, leaving about ¼ inch shell; brush inside each shell with lemon juice to prevent it from darkening. Combine avocado pulp in a blender with vinegar, salt, sugar, and hot-pepper seasoning; whirl until smooth (or mash together well). Stir in the chives, green pepper, and pimiento. Soften gelatin in water, then stir over hot water until dissolved. Stir gelatin into the avocado mixture. Chill until syrupy. Spoon into avocado shells and chill until set.

    Serve the salads on individual plates, with a garnish of crisp greens on each plate. Pass a dressing made by blending together the mayonnaise and sour cream.

# Beefsteak Tomatoes and Onions

Men love this salad. Choose the very best tomatoes—large, firm Beefsteaks *only*—and the sweetest red or Bermuda onions. Oregano in the dressing is the perfect simple seasoning.

Cut tomatoes in ½-inch-thick slices; slice onion. Place in alternate layers in a large bowl. Mix together olive oil, oregano, and salt. Pour over tomatoes, cover, and refrigerate for 1 hour or longer. Remove from the refrigerator about 10 minutes before serving.

**MAKES 6 SERVINGS**

**PREPARE SEVERAL HOURS AHEAD, CHILL**

2 large Beefsteak tomatoes
1 medium-sized Italian red or other mild sweet onion
¼ cup olive oil
2 teaspoons oregano
1 teaspoon salt

# Fresh Cucumber Mold

*MENU FOR PATIO BUFFET INCLUDES THIS DISH—PAGE 13*

This delicate mold of puréed cucumber is rich with sour cream, whipped cream, and mayonnaise. Horseradish and grated onion give it nip.

Soften gelatin in ½ cup water, and place over hot water to dissolve. Pare cucumbers, cut in half lengthwise, and remove seeds. Chop cucumbers and whirl in blender to make a smooth purée. Measure 3 cups purée and combine with sour cream, mayonnaise, horseradish, onion, salt, and white pepper. Stir in the dissolved gelatin. Chill until thickened (about 45 minutes). Fold in whipped cream. Turn into a lightly oiled 1½-quart salad mold. Chill at least 4 hours or until set. Unmold and garnish with thinly sliced cucumbers and watercress.

**MAKES 8 SERVINGS**

**PREPARE 5 HOURS TO 1 DAY IN ADVANCE**

**BLENDER REQUIRED**

2 envelopes unflavored gelatin
½ cup water
4 medium-sized cucumbers
¾ cup <u>each</u> sour cream and mayonnaise
2½ tablespoons prepared horseradish
2 tablespoons grated onion
1 teaspoon salt
¼ teaspoon white pepper
1 cup heavy cream, whipped
   Oil
   Thinly sliced cucumbers
   Watercress

# Tomato Aspic with Vegetables

This dark red aspic is very rich with tomato and vegetable bits, including avocado. To turn it into a luncheon entrée, add more cold shrimp. Use a mayonnaise or sour cream dressing flavored with lemon or horseradish.

Soften gelatin in the cold water. Bring 1 cup of the tomato juice to a boil; stir in the gelatin until dissolved. Add the remaining tomato juice, the tomato paste, vinegar, lemon juice, basil, salt, sugar, onion powder, black pepper, and Worcestershire. Refrigerate until partially thickened. Stir in the celery, green pepper, avocado, and olives. Pour into a 6-cup mold; refrigerate until set. Unmold and garnish with shrimp, if you wish.

**MAKES 6 TO 8 SERVINGS**

**PREPARE 4 HOURS TO AS MUCH AS 1 DAY AHEAD**

3 envelopes unflavored gelatin
¾ cup cold water
2½ cups tomato juice
1 can (6 oz.) tomato paste
¼ cup vinegar
3 tablespoons lemon juice
1½ teaspoons basil
1 teaspoon <u>each</u> salt and sugar
⅛ teaspoon <u>each</u> onion powder and black pepper
½ teaspoon Worcestershire
1 cup chopped celery
½ cup chopped green pepper
1 avocado, diced
1 can (2¼ oz.) sliced ripe olives
   Cooked, chilled shrimp for garnish, optional

# Macaroni Salad for a Crowd

RECIPE WITH SCANDINAVIAN BUFFET MENU—PAGE 27

**MAKES 50 SERVINGS**

**PREPARE AS MUCH AS 8 HOURS IN ADVANCE**

Sour cream and whipped cream, plus a tangy amount of horseradish, make this a different macaroni salad. It is easy to make in quantity and inexpensive. You may use an ice cream scoop to prepare individual servings in lettuce cups for a buffet.

# East Indies Cabbage Salad

**MAKES 6 SERVINGS**

**PREPARE DRESSING AS MUCH AS 1 DAY AHEAD**

**SHRED VEGETABLES SEVERAL HOURS AHEAD**

⅓ cup <u>each</u> creamy peanut butter and sour cream
1½ tablespoons brown sugar
1 teaspoon curry powder
2 tablespoons lime or lemon juice
1 tablespoon soy sauce
4 drops liquid hot-pepper seasoning
4 cups finely shredded crisp cabbage
½ cup <u>each</u> sliced celery and sliced green onion
Salted peanuts or pimiento

Raw cabbage, of all the salad ingredients, can profit most from a pungent and imaginative dressing. Here many ingredients of Southeast Asian cooking are combined in a sweet-and-citrus dressing with peanut, soy sauce, and hot-pepper seasoning.

For the dressing, combine the peanut butter, sour cream, brown sugar, curry powder, lime or lemon juice, soy sauce, and liquid hot-pepper seasoning in the container of your electric blender or in a bowl. Whirl or mix until the ingredients are well blended. This can be done ahead of time.

In a bowl combine the cabbage with the celery and green onions. Add dressing, and mix lightly. Garnish with a few salted peanuts or strips of pimiento, if you like. Serve immediately.

# Condiment Chicken Salad with Avocado

MENU FOR TAHITIAN PARTY INCLUDES THIS DISH—PAGE 49

**MAKES 12 SERVINGS**

**COMBINE INGREDIENTS WITH CHICKEN SEVERAL HOURS IN ADVANCE**

1½ cups mayonnaise
1 cup raisins
1 cup salted peanuts
1 cup mango chutney, cut into slivers
1 cup flaked coconut
2 pounds cooked chicken meat, diced coarsely
2 cups diagonally sliced ripe bananas
Salt and pepper to taste
Salad greens
Additional sliced bananas
Avocado slices
Lemon juice

This unusual chicken salad is rich with chicken meat and curry condiments. Mound the salad on a big bed of salad greens and garnish with thick slices of avocado. To plump the raisins, let them stand in white wine a few hours before making the salad.

Mix together the mayonnaise, raisins, peanuts, chutney, and coconut. Toss with chicken meat. Gently combine with sliced bananas. Season with salt and pepper. Mound into large salad bowl or on a platter lined with shredded lettuce and lettuce leaves. Garnish with slices of avocado and banana, which you have dipped into lemon juice.

# Turkish White Bean Salad

*RECIPE WITH COLD TURKISH MEZE BUFFET MENU—PAGE 20*

In Turkey white beans are cooked in olive oil with onions, potatoes, carrots, and garlic, then served at room temperature with lemon wedges which may be squeezed over the beans. These are good for a buffet, picnic, or wherever you want a hearty salad.

**MAKES 8 SERVINGS**

**PREPARE AS MUCH AS 1 DAY IN ADVANCE**

# Swiss Cheese Salad

In Switzerland, diced cheese with vegetables and sharp dressing is often served as a first course. You will find other ways to use such a salad in American meals if you compare it with potato or macaroni salad, which it most resembles. Whenever those two familiar salads are appropriate, cheese salad will be an easily accepted, easily prepared change.

Mix together the cheese, eggs, celery, and green pepper. In another bowl, blend together the mayonnaise, chives, vinegar, mustard, and salt. Stir the dressing into the cheese mixture and refrigerate the salad until serving time.

To serve, mound the salad on individual lettuce leaves or in a bowl lined with the lettuce. Press reserved egg yolk through a fine wire strainer and sprinkle over salad. Use cherry tomatoes to garnish. (They add color, and the tomato-cheese flavor combination is delicious.)

**MAKES 6 SERVINGS**

**PREPARE CHEESE MIXTURE AS MUCH AS 1 DAY AHEAD**

**ASSEMBLE SALAD JUST BEFORE SERVING TIME**

1   pound natural Swiss cheese, cut in ¼-inch cubes
3   hard-cooked eggs, diced (reserve 1 yolk for garnish)
½   cup <u>each</u> chopped celery and chopped green pepper
½   cup mayonnaise
1   tablespoon chopped chives
2   teaspoons white wine vinegar
1½   teaspoons prepared mustard
¼   teaspoon salt
    Lettuce leaves
    Cherry tomatoes for garnish

# Antipasto Potato Salad

This salad is so named because some of the ingredients are customarily part of Italian antipasto—salami, anchovies, and peppers. The potatoes are dressed with oil and vinegar rather than mayonnaise, as are most European potato salads; anise lightly flavors the dressing.

Scrub potatoes, and cook in their skins in boiling salted water until tender, about 40 minutes. Drain, peel as soon as possible, and cut into bite-sized ⅛-inch slices (you should have about 5½ cups). Place in bowl, and pour on Fennel Dressing. Cover and chill for at least 2 hours, or as long as overnight.

Add green pepper, onion, celery, and salami; mix lightly. Cover and chill for about 1 hour longer. Serve in a lettuce-lined bowl, garnished with hard-cooked eggs and chiles.

**Fennel Dressing.** Combine salad oil, vinegar, garlic, sugar, fennel or anise seed, salt, basil, pepper, and cayenne. Beat until well combined. Drain anchovy fillets, discarding oil from can; chop anchovies and add to dressing.

**MAKES 6 SERVINGS**

**PARTIALLY PREPARE 2 HOURS TO 1 DAY AHEAD; FINISH 1 HOUR OR MORE AHEAD**

5   medium-sized potatoes (about 2 lbs.)
    Boiling salted water
1   green pepper, seeded and finely chopped
¼   cup <u>each</u> sliced green onion and finely chopped celery
6   thin slices Italian salami, cut in ½-inch strips (about ⅓ cup)
    Lettuce
2   hard-cooked eggs, cut in wedges
    Pickled red and green mild chiles (for garnish)

**FENNEL DRESSING:**

⅓   cup salad oil
¼   cup red wine vinegar
1   clove garlic, minced or mashed
¾   teaspoon <u>each</u> sugar and fennel seed or anise seed, crushed
½   teaspoon <u>each</u> salt and basil
    Dash <u>each</u> pepper and cayenne
1   can (2 oz.) flat anchovy fillets

# Distinctive Entrées

THE ENTRÉE IS THE MOST IMPORTANT PART of a meal and the deciding factor in all the other things you serve before, with, or after. That is why so many recipes of such varied types are included here. There should be something which will be just right for any occasion you plan, informal or elegant, in any season and at any time of day. All the most popular meats and seafoods are represented, plus a few of the less available things such as game.

The recipes range from very, very simple to complex production numbers that even experienced cooks would attempt only for a particularly outstanding event. However, most of the recipes are a moderate challenge and use ingredients found at every market. They are distinguished by being particularly delicious or interesting in some way.

The foremost consideration in the selection of entrées has been whether they are practical for entertaining. Nearly all of these dishes may be made partially or entirely ahead; many may be frozen. Even those dishes which may seem complicated are really not, because most of the steps to their preparation may be done ahead. Some of the recipes with exotic titles and glamorous appearance have been chosen because their preparation belies the impression they give. They are, in reality, easy to make with convenience foods or using simple tricks and shortcuts.

In addition to the usual kinds of prepared dishes considered to be entrées, salads and soups substantial enough for a main dish are included. These have always been popular lunch dishes, but are increasingly served for evening meals, particularly informal or late suppers.

The finishing touch to either main-dish soup or salad may be a special crisp hot bread or crunchy bread sticks. Recipes for such savory accompaniments are included for those occasions when you go out of your way to make a meal as nearly perfect as possible.

*Coq au Vin—see page 118*

# BEEF AND VEAL

Beef is a most popular meat for company meals because it is the most universally liked. Delicate veal also is always welcome. Many of the following recipes include some new or interesting ways to prepare these meats for special party dinners.

## Pozharsky

*MEAT AND VEGETABLE CASSEROLE*

**MAKES 4 SERVINGS**

**PREPARE FOR BAKING UP TO 4 HOURS AHEAD**

|  | |
|---|---|
| About ¾ cup butter or margarine | |
| 1 | large potato, peeled and thinly sliced |
| 1 | pound boneless tender lean beef or veal, cut about ½ inch thick |
| 1 | large onion, sliced |
| ¼ | pound mushrooms, sliced (about 1½ cups) |
| 4 | whole slices eggplant, ⅜ inch thick |
| 1 | large tomato, peeled |
| 1 | package (9 oz.) frozen asparagus spears |
| | Boiling salted water |
| 1½ | tablespoons flour |
| 1 | cup beef broth |
| ½ | cup dry white wine |
| 1 | tablespoon <u>each</u> tomato paste and lemon juice |
| ¼ | teaspoon <u>each</u> salt, basil, and dry mustard |
| | Dash pepper |
| 3 | tablespoons brandy |

You'll find *pozharsky* (sometimes anglicized as *podjarka*) on the menus of some Russian restaurants. The word comes from the Russian *pozhar*, meaning "fire" —referring to the final flaming of the dish with brandy.

Heat 2 tablespoons of the butter in a large frying pan over medium heat. Cook potatoes, lifting and turning them often, just until tender and slightly browned. Arrange potatoes over bottom of a shallow 1½-quart casserole or 4 individual baking dishes (about 1 cup size). Add 2 tablespoons more of the butter to the frying pan; brown meat quickly on all sides over high heat. Cook meat to degree of doneness you prefer and arrange over potatoes.

Add 1 tablespoon of the butter to the same pan and sauté onions; spoon over meat. Then sauté mushrooms in about 2 more tablespoons of the butter or margarine, cooking until liquid from the mushrooms has evaporated; spoon over onion. Add 3 tablespoons of the butter to the pan and cook eggplant slices until tender and lightly browned on both sides. Arrange slices over vegetables in casserole.

Slice tomato in four thick slices and place on top of eggplant slices. Cook asparagus in boiling salted water just until tender; drain and arrange over tomato slices like spokes of a wheel, or around the side of the dish.

To make sauce, heat the remaining 1½ tablespoons butter or margarine in a pan and stir in flour; cook about 1 minute, browning lightly. Gradually add beef broth and wine, and cook, stirring, until sauce is smooth and slightly thickened. Stir in tomato paste, lemon juice, salt, basil, dry mustard, and pepper. Spoon sauce evenly over vegetables. (At this point, you can cover and refrigerate the dish, to be baked later.)

Bake, covered, in a 350° oven about 40 minutes for a large casserole or 25 minutes for individual dishes; sauce should be bubbly and vegetables and meat well heated. (If you refrigerate this dish before baking, increase baking time about 20 minutes.) Just before serving, warm the brandy, ignite, and pour flaming over the casserole (or casseroles).

## Danish Meatballs for a Crowd

*RECIPE WITH SCANDINAVIAN BUFFET MENU—PAGE 27*

**MAKES 50 SERVINGS**

**PREPARE MEAT MIXTURE AS MUCH AS 6 HOURS AHEAD**

Meatballs kept hot in a chafing dish are an excellent choice when you must serve many people. These tender Danish ones are made from both pork and beef, delicately seasoned with allspice. Add canned consommé to the chafing dish to keep the meatballs hot and moist.

# Cold Sliced Tongue and Beef Tenderloin

MENU FOR WINTERTIME BUFFET INCLUDES THIS DISH—PAGE 42

A horseradish sauce complements two kinds of chilled meat in this recipe. The sliced tongue and beef tenderloin are served together on a tray, with cherry tomatoes, stuffed green olives, and marinated artichoke hearts to add touches of color.

Place beef tongue in a deep pan with salt, allspice, onion, and water to cover. Bring water to a boil, then reduce heat and simmer until the tongue is fork-tender. (Allow about 1 hour per pound.) Cool tongue in liquid, remove, and cut off the bones and gristle at the thick end. Slit the skin on the underside, starting at the thick end; loosen the skin with a sharp paring knife, then peel and pull it off, working from the thick end to the tip. Chill and slice thinly.

Remove surface fat and connective tissue from the beef tenderloin; place the meat on a rack in a roasting pan. Tuck the narrow end of the tenderloin under to make a uniform thickness. Melt butter and blend with garlic; brush meat with the butter mixture. Roast the tenderloin in a 450° oven for 30 minutes for rare meat or 40 minutes for medium; baste occasionally with the garlic butter. Chill and slice the meat thinly to serve.

Arrange cold sliced meats on a large wooden tray. Alternate cherry tomatoes, stuffed green olives, and marinated artichoke hearts on wooden picks for garnish. Serve with Fluffy Horseradish Sauce.

**Fluffy Horseradish Sauce.** Whip cream until stiff; fold in horseradish, sugar, and lemon juice. Chill in the serving bowl for several hours, and sprinkle with chives just before serving. Makes about 2 cups.

**MAKES 10 TO 12 SERVINGS**

**PREPARE MEAT AHEAD TO CHILL FOR SERVING**

**MAKE SAUCE SEVERAL HOURS AHEAD**

2½ to 3-pound fresh beef tongue
1   tablespoon salt
8   to 10 whole allspice
1   small onion, sliced
    Cold water
4   to 6-pound beef tenderloin
¼   cup butter
1   clove garlic, minced
    Cherry tomatoes
    Stuffed green olives
    Marinated artichoke hearts

**FLUFFY HORSERADISH SAUCE:**

1   cup heavy cream
3   tablespoons prepared
      horseradish
2   teaspoons sugar
1   teaspoon lemon juice
    Chopped chives

# Javanese Satés

MENU FOR DINNER COOKED AT THE TABLE INCLUDES THIS DISH—PAGE 21

A table hibachi handles the barbecuing of interlaced steak strips and tropical fruits for this succulent Indonesian kebab. Guests spoon the assorted condiments into mounds on their dinner plates and intermingle them with both beef and fruits.

Toast sesame seeds in a 350° oven 10 minutes; pulverize in a blender until very fine or crush in a mortar and pestle; place in a small bowl. Slice round steak into four long strips, each about ¾ inch thick. Mix together the soy, Sherry, oil, onion, ginger, and garlic, and let meat marinate for 30 minutes. Thread on skewers in serpentine fashion (weave in and out on strip of meat lengthwise).

Peel papaya, halve, and remove seeds; cut in sixths. Peel back a 1-inch strip on each banana. Peel pineapple, halve, and cut in long slices. Purée chutney in a blender or chop finely; brush on fruit. Arrange fruit and meat on tray at table.

To cook, barbecue meat over hot coals, turning once (allow about 5 minutes to a side, or until meat is browned). Sprinkle lightly with toasted sesame seed. Meanwhile, skewer fruit lengthwise with bamboo sticks; place on barbecue along with meat (banana should have peeled side down) to heat through and brown slightly. Pass bowls of condiments.

**MAKES 4 SERVINGS**

**MARINATE MEAT AHEAD, COOK AT SERVING TIME**

**MAY BE COOKED AT TABLE**

½   cup sesame seed
1½  pounds top round steak,
      sliced ¾ inch thick
⅓   cup soy sauce
3   tablespoons Sherry
2   tablespoons salad oil
½   cup finely chopped onion
½   teaspoon ground ginger
3   cloves garlic, minced
1   papaya or small cantaloupe
4   small bananas
1   small pineapple
½   cup Major Grey chutney
    Condiments: chutney, toasted
      coconut, lime wedges, yogurt

# Steak, Mushrooms, and Asparagus

**MAKES 4 SERVINGS**

**PREPARE INGREDIENTS AHEAD,
   COOK AT LAST MINUTE**

1¼   pounds flank steak
½    pound mushrooms, sliced (about
      3 cups)
2    cups asparagus (about 1 pound
      fresh) cut in ½-inch diagonal
      slices
1    cup water
½    cup water
1    tablespoon cornstarch
¼    cup dry red wine
1    teaspoon salt
½    teaspoon thyme
¼    teaspoon <u>each</u> tarragon and
      garlic powder
3    tablespoons olive oil

Serve this quickly prepared beef, mushroom, and asparagus dish with an oil and vinegar-dressed salad, buttered brown rice, hard French rolls, and red wine. The information about wine on page 121 will aid your selection.

Cut flank steak in half lengthwise; slice each half, on the diagonal, into ¼-inch-thick strips. Place vegetables in a large, heavy frying pan that has a cover. Add 1 cup water. Cover, bring to a boil, and cook over medium-high heat for about 5 minutes or until asparagus is barely tender. Drain, reserving liquid, and place in an uncovered bowl.

Add ½ cup water to cornstarch gradually, blending until smooth; mix in wine, salt, thyme, tarragon, and garlic powder. Brown meat quickly in very hot olive oil; reduce heat, return vegetables to pan with cornstarch mixture, and cook for about 1 minute longer, stirring constantly, until sauce is thickened. Blend in about ⅓ cup of the reserved vegetable liquid if you prefer a thinner sauce.

## GARNISHING THE ENTRÉE

Have you ever noticed how glamorous even an ordinary dish seems in fine restaurants? Often it's the garnish that does it.

Elegant garnishes may take time, but they are a nice touch when you're entertaining.

**Easy Garnish Ideas.** A sautéed fish or broiled steak takes especially well to decorating; lay 3 or 4 ribbons of smoked salmon or anchovy fillets over the top, pour on melted butter, and add a wedge of lemon or sprig of fresh dill or watercress.

To garnish meat platters, fill artichoke bottoms (canned, if you wish) with tiny shrimp or sliced mushrooms cooked in butter. Large cooked mushroom caps may be filled with such tidbits as chicken livers, chopped ham, or sautéed onions. Cooked whole turnips, onions, or tomatoes can also be formed into cups to stuff with a rice or vegetable mixture or with butter-browned mushrooms.

Any meat platter or roast can be beautified with small fresh, cooked, or preserved fruits such as crab apples, kumquats, cranberries, cherries, grape bunches, or pineapple spears.

Cherry tomatoes, radish roses, scored mushroom caps (either raw or sautéed in butter), and toast points are other simple garnishes in addition to the frequently used sprigs or beds of watercress and parsley.

Citrus slices or wedges can be beautified with a sprinkling of finely minced parsley or paprika. A clove or parsley sprig stuck in the center of a slice is another variation.

Sliced rounds may be twisted into an interesting "S" shape (cut the round half way through to the center, then twist one of the cut sides to the left and the other to the right; stand up with the twisted points as bases).

**Fruit Brochettes.** To garnish a meat platter, thread small fruits or pieces of fruit on slender bamboo skewers. Use any fruit combination you like—pineapple chunks, banana slices, spiced figs or peaches, grapes, maraschino cherries. Coat fruits with lime juice and maple syrup, or with melted butter and a light sprinkling of curry powder. Just before serving, heat through under broiler or bake in a 450° oven just until hot.

**Cranberry Jelly Slices.** To ring a meat platter or top a casserole, slice cranberry jelly about ¼ inch thick and cut into interesting shapes with cooky cutters. Center on large orange slices or pineapple rings.

**Brandied Peaches.** Garnish platter with brandied peaches decorated with cinnamon stick stems and leaves cut from citron.

**Citrus Cups.** A serving platter of fish can be enhanced by individual lime or lemon cups brimming with tartar sauce. Slice off pointed ends of fruit halves to make a flat bottom. Ream, and score or scallop the cut rim of the cups, if you wish. Fill with sauce. (Seeded pepper halves could also be used.)

# Giant Beef-Lobster Kebabs

Meat for six people cooks on just two long skewers for these kebabs. If you use round steak, it might be wise to prepare it with instant meat tenderizer, following the directions on the container.

Thread skewers alternating lobster with beef cubes. An attractive way to do this is to wrap the lobster tail around a piece of beef and thread the skewer through the thick end of lobster tail, the beef cube, then the other end of the lobster tail. You can put three of these combinations onto each long skewer. Grill over hot coals for 8 to 12 minutes, or until lobster flakes and beef is done to your liking. Baste while cooking with a mixture of the wine, salad oil, and lemon juice. Serve hot with lemon wedges and Tomato Béarnaise sauce.

**Tomato Béarnaise.** Combine in blender the egg yolks and vinegar. Melt butter, turn blender on high speed and immediately pour in the hot butter in a steady stream. Add salt, tarragon, and parsley; whirl until blended, about 30 seconds. Mix in tomato purée. Makes about 2 cups sauce.

**MAKES 6 SERVINGS**

**PREPARE SAUCE AHEAD**

1½  to 2 pounds top sirloin or top round steak, cut in 2-inch cubes
3  frozen lobster tails (about 1½ pounds), split lengthwise and thawed
⅓  cup <u>each</u> dry white wine and salad oil
1  tablespoon lemon juice
   Lemon wedges

**TOMATO BÉARNAISE:**

3  egg yolks
1½  tablespoons tarragon vinegar
¾  cup butter
½  teaspoon salt
½  teaspoon tarragon
3  tablespoons finely chopped parsley
2  tablespoons tomato purée

# Beefsteak Pie

Beefsteak Pie, often with kidneys, is English in origin. This version is rich with fresh mushrooms and has a touch of red wine for flavor. A meat pie is ideal for entertaining because you can make it the day before and refrigerate unbaked until about 1½ hours before you plan to serve dinner.

Combine the 2½ teaspoons salt, pepper, herbs, and 6 tablespoons flour; dredge the meat cubes in the mixture. Brown the mushrooms in the 4 tablespoons butter over medium heat, stirring, until limp. Arrange half the meat cubes in a 2-quart casserole and half the mushrooms over the beef. Then add the remaining meat and finish with an even layer of the remaining mushrooms on top. Pour the red wine evenly over.

On a floured board, roll the pastry (recipe follows) to make a thick round about ½ inch thick and trim to fit the casserole top. Roll out the pastry trimmings and cut a long strip of dough about ¾ inch in diameter to fit the rim of the casserole. Moisten the edges of the casserole and press the pastry strip onto the rim. Arrange the pastry round over the filling and rim, moisten edges and press to flute, and fasten firmly onto the dough-topped casserole rim.

Roll out scraps of dough and cut leaf-shaped ovals to use for decoration. Prick pastry top, brush with the beaten egg, arrange leaf shapes on pastry, and brush again with egg.

Bake in a 350° oven for about 60 minutes or until meat is tender. You can test the meat with a long wooden skewer or knitting needle carefully probed through the pastry. If the top begins to brown too much, cover with brown paper or foil.

**Egg Pastry.** Measure 1½ cups unsifted flour into a bowl, stir in ½ teaspoon salt. Cut in ½ cup butter until mixture resembles fine crumbs. Add 1 egg, slightly beaten, and milk, mixing with a fork until dough holds together in a ball. Chill.

**MAKES 6 SERVINGS**

**PREPARE FOR BAKING AS MUCH AS A DAY AHEAD**

2½  teaspoons salt
¼  teaspoon pepper
1  teaspoon fines herbes (combination of thyme, oregano, sage, rosemary, marjoram, and basil)
6  tablespoons flour
2½  pounds top sirloin, cut in 1½-inch cubes (or 1½ lbs. sirloin and 1 lb. lamb kidneys, trimmed and cut in 1½-inch cubes)
1  pound mushrooms, sliced
4  tablespoons butter
¼  cup dry red wine
   Egg Pastry (recipe follows)
1  beaten egg

**EGG PASTRY:**

1½  cups unsifted flour
½  teaspoon salt
½  cup (¼ pound) butter
1  egg
4  to 5 tablespoons milk

# Beef Burgundy

MAKES 8 SERVINGS

COOK AHEAD, REHEAT

16  small white onions, peeled
      (about 1 pound)
 6  slices lean bacon, diced
 ¼  cup (⅛ lb.) butter or margarine
 4  pounds beef chuck, cut in
      1½-inch cubes, fat trimmed off
 ¼  cup brandy (optional)
1½  teaspoons salt
 ¼  teaspoon freshly ground pepper
 2  cups Burgundy or other dry red
      wine
 2  whole cloves garlic, peeled
 2  cups small whole, or sliced,
      fresh mushrooms
1½  cups water
     Bouquet garni: Tie in a piece of
      cheesecloth 1 or 2 sprigs
      parsley, 1 celery top, 1
      quartered carrot, a bay leaf,
      and a sprig of thyme (or 1
      teaspoon dried thyme).
 6  tablespoons flour
 ½  cup cold water

This entrée is a simple version of the traditional French Boeuf Bourguignonne. Lean chunks of beef are combined with pearl onions, fresh mushrooms, Burgundy, and seasonings. You can flame the meat with brandy if you wish. Beef Burgundy goes especially well with a wild rice casserole.

Brown onions with bacon and butter in a Dutch oven; remove onions and bacon with a slotted spoon, reserve. Add meat to the pan and brown well on all sides. If desired, pour brandy over the beef and set aflame, tilting pan to keep the flame going as long as possible. Sprinkle meat with the salt and pepper. Add the Burgundy, garlic, mushrooms, the 1½ cups water, bouquet garni, onions, and bacon. Cover and simmer about 1½ hours, or until the meat is tender.

Lift the beef, mushrooms, and onions out of the pan with a slotted spoon; arrange in a covered 3-quart casserole or baking dish, or in a serving dish if you plan to serve at once. Strain the liquid through a sieve, discarding bouquet garni, garlic, and bacon. Mix the flour to a smooth paste with the ½ cup cold water; stir into the meat stock and cook, stirring, until gravy is thick and smooth. Pour gravy over the meat and serve immediately, or refrigerate and reheat, covered, in a 350° oven for about 35 minutes, or until hot and bubbly.

# Stuffed Grape Leaves or Cabbage

MAKES ABOUT 40 ROLLS, OR 8 TO
10 SERVINGS

COOK ROLLS AS MUCH AS A DAY
AHEAD

 1  pound lean ground beef
 1  large onion, chopped
 ½  cup uncooked rice
 3  tablespoons butter or margarine
 ½  cup chopped parsley
 ¼  cup chopped mint
 2  teaspoons salt
 1  teaspoon each pepper and dill
      weed
 3  or 4 dozen canned grape leaves
      or 1 medium head cabbage
 1  cup water

AVGOLEMONO SAUCE:

 3  eggs
 3  tablespoons lemon juice
     Cooking liquid from leaf rolls

For centuries many Mediterranean countries have used grape leaves to enhance the flavor of different foods. Stuffed grape leaves, called *dolmathes* in Greek, are prepared with a variety of fillings and served as appetizer or main course. Grape leaves, packed in bottles, can be found in an increasing number of specialty food stores. Cabbage leaves are also used for dolmathes, sometimes called dolma, in various Near and Middle Eastern countries.

Combine ground beef, onion, rice, butter, parsley, mint, salt, pepper, and dill. Wash grape leaves in hot water; drain on paper toweling. (To use cabbage leaves instead, see instructions at end of recipe.)

Spread 1 grape leaf on a flat surface with the under side up and the stem end toward you; cut off the stem. Place about 2 teaspoons of filling near the stem end, then fold the sides of the leaf over the filling and roll away from you. Continue until all the filling is used. Do not roll tightly, as the rice will expand when it cooks.

Place close together in a large kettle (at least 6-quart size) on a layer of grape leaves. Add water and place a heatproof plate on top of rolls to prevent them from breaking apart. Cover pan and simmer for 40 minutes, or until rice is tender. Drain rolls, saving the cooking liquid. Serve with following sauce.

**Avgolemono Sauce.** Beat eggs until fluffy and add lemon juice, 1 tablespoon at a time. Gradually stir in the cooking liquid from the dolmathes. Pour sauce over the rolls.

*To use cabbage in place of grape leaves, separate the leaves from the head of cabbage and place in boiling water, letting them stand until they are quite pliable. Remove from water and trim away the thick stem. Place about 1 tablespoon of filling near the center of each leaf; fold sides of leaf over filling and roll.*

# STEAK—A FAVORITE PARTY ENTRÉE

The variety in names, sizes, and shapes of steaks understandably causes much confusion. To simplify this complex situation as much as possible, a division into three types helps—steaks from the loin, those from the rib, and those from other parts of the steer.

**Steaks from the Loin.** These are named according to the part of the loin from which they are cut. Club steaks are from the small end of the loin. Next cuts (and next in size) are the T-bones, then the porterhouse steaks (on one side of the bone is the fillet and the other the New York or strip, often cut and sold separately). Last and largest in size are the sirloins, which often are cut apart into three steaks—fillet, top sirloin, and culotte. The fillet muscle (also called filet mignon and tenderloin) runs from T-bone through sirloin sections and can, of course, be cut out in a whole long strip. When cut extra-thick for two persons, a fillet steak is called Châteaubriand.

**Steaks from the Rib.** Slices of the entire section containing rib bone, tender rib eye, and less tender top muscles are sold as rib steaks. When the choice central muscle or "eye" is cut out and sold alone, this is called a rib eye, market, or spencer steak. Some experts consider rib steaks the most flavorful of all, because of their generous streaking of fat.

**Steaks from Other Parts of the Steer.** These mostly are from the round and shoulder or chuck, and certain other muscles that are tender enough to broil or barbecue. The skirt steak, for instance, is from inside the rib cage and only two are on each animal.

All these steaks are less tender than loin, but they vary considerably in tenderness. Most of them need or at least profit by tenderizing with vinegar, wine, citrus juice, commercial powdered meat tenderizer, or some flavorful marinade. These steaks are most tender when done fairly rare; they become less tender when medium or well done.

A full round steak may be cut and sold in three different parts—top round (the most tender), bottom round (Swiss steak), and eye of round. Bottom and eye of round should be tenderized before broiling or barbecueing.

Center-cut cross rib steaks are the sliced center portions of a cross-rib chuck roast and are tender enough that marinating is optional.

Two other kinds of steaks come from the chuck—the blade-bone chuck and 7-bone chuck. These steaks should be cut about 1½ inches thick, cooked rare, and thinly sliced. Tenderize if you wish.

The skirt steak is a thin strip of meat, usually purchased rolled into a pinwheel and fastened with a wooden skewer. Tenderizing may improve these steaks, but is not necessary.

Lean flank steak, with coarse fibers, is at its best if scored before cooking, broiled rare, and sliced diagonally.

Another cut, the hanging tenderloin (there's only one to a steer), also benefits from the same treatment as flank steak; marinating enhances its flavor.

The sirloin tip, cut from between the sirloin and the round, is best cut an inch thick and tenderized.

## BAKE-BROIL METHOD FOR COOKING STEAKS

When you broil or barbecue a very thick steak, it's a bit tricky to make sure it's done to just the right degree—well browned on the outside, pink within.

This combination bake-broil method assures a medium-rare result. You begin by placing a 2-inch-thick steak in a very slow oven for 2 hours or more, then broil or barbecue it just long enough to brown the outside. Steaks prepared this way remain juicy and shrink little. There is also little spattering of fat.

This method is well suited to entertaining, for it enables you to time the serving of the steak precisely. Carve the steak as you would a roast, cutting in vertical ⅜ to ½-inch-thick slices.

**For Tender Steaks (Such as Porterhouse, Sirloin, Rib).** Stand a 2-inch-thick steak on edge in a V-shaped rack in a roasting pan. Place in a 200° oven for 2 hours. Then place flat on a rack and broil or grill on each side until well browned (3 to 5 minutes for each side). Season with salt and pepper.

**For Less-Tender Steaks (Such as Chuck, Sirloin Tip, Round).** Prepare meat by brushing lightly with water on each side; sprinkle each side with unseasoned meat tenderizer (allow a total of ½ teaspoon tenderizer per pound of meat), then pierce with a fork at ½-inch intervals. Stand steak on edge in a V-shaped rack in a roasting pan. Place in a 200° oven allowing 45 minutes per pound of meat. Then place flat on a rack and broil or grill on each side until well browned (3 to 5 minutes per side). Season with salt and pepper.

## AN ALL-PURPOSE STEAK SAUCE

The following classic steak sauce is delicious with any kind of steak.

**Blender Béarnaise.** Simmer 3 tablespoons white wine vinegar with 1 teaspoon *each* tarragon (crumbled) and chopped chives or green onions until reduced to about 2 teaspoons. Place in a blender container with 2 whole eggs and 2 tablespoons lemon juice. Blend a few seconds; then, with blender turned on, slowly pour in 1 cup hot melted butter. Turn into a sauce bowl. (If made ahead, reheat over a pan of hot tap water.) Makes 1½ cups.

# Veal Paupiettes à la Provençale

*BACON-STUFFED VEAL ROLLS*

**MAKES ABOUT 18 ROLLS, OR ABOUT 6 SERVINGS**

**MAY BE FROZEN**

2   pounds boneless veal cutlet, cut about ⅓ inch thick
1   pound sliced lean bacon
¼   cup minced fresh parsley
½   teaspoon <u>each</u> tarragon, basil, thyme, and rosemary
2   small cloves garlic, mashed
3   tablespoons butter, margarine, or salad oil
¾   cup <u>each</u> dry white wine and chicken stock
⅓   cup <u>each</u> chopped green pepper and chopped onion
1   sprig fresh parsley
1   bay leaf
¼   teaspoon thyme
    Dash pepper
1   tablespoon cornstarch blended with 2 tablespoons water

French *paupiettes* are paper-thin pieces of meat, poultry, or fish rolled around a ground-meat filling. The rolls are tied, browned, and then simmered in broth. They can be frozen at several stages—before browning and simmering, or after cooking (in this case, you just reheat the rolls in their sauce and thicken with cornstarch at the last minute).

To prepare the meat, cut away the fat from outside each slice. Place one slice at a time between pieces of waxed paper and pound lightly with the smooth side of a wooden mallet or empty wine bottle until the meat is about 1/16 inch thick. Pound the meat evenly; don't let it tear. Following the natural divisions, cut each pounded piece into rectangles about 3½ inches by 6 inches; cut away any fat.

For filling, cut bacon in short pieces and chop in electric blender, put through food mill, or chop very fine with sharp knife. Blend the minced parsley, tarragon, basil, thyme, rosemary, and garlic with the bacon. Spread about 1 tablespoon filling over the center of each piece of meat, but do not spread it to the edges. Leave a bare strip of meat about ¼ to ½ inch wide uncovered by filling all around the edges. To roll, fold up these uncovered edges on both long sides of the meat rectangle and begin rolling the meat over the filling from one of the short (3½ inch) sides. When the roll is completed, tie each end with string, or secure with small skewers or toothpicks.

Brown rolls in butter, margarine, or salad oil. Add wine, chicken stock, green pepper, onion, parsley sprig, bay leaf, thyme, and pepper. Cover, and simmer gently about 25 minutes, or just until meat is fork tender.

Remove skewers or string and place paupiettes on a warm platter. Strain cooking liquid (discarding the vegetables) and return liquid to pan. Blend in cornstarch and water, stirring, until gravy is slightly thickened; pour this sauce over meat.

# Veal Veronique

*WITH GRAPES IN WINE*

**MAKES 4 SERVINGS**

**SIMMER MEAT AHEAD AND KEEP WARM, ADD GRAPES JUST BEFORE SERVING**

1   pound boneless veal round, cut about ⅓ inch thick
2   tablespoons flour
½   teaspoon salt
⅛   teaspoon pepper
2   tablespoons salad oil
½   cup dry white wine
¼   teaspoon grated lemon peel
¼   teaspoon crumbled rosemary
½   pound seedless grapes, separated into small clusters

Green seedless grapes, often paired with delicate fish in French cuisine, are used here with mild veal simmered in white wine. The dish has a sumptuous look that belies the fact it is a dieter's delight.

Cut the veal into serving-sized pieces. Combine flour, salt, and pepper; gently pound into the veal. Heat the oil in a frying pan; brown meat on both sides. Add wine; sprinkle with lemon peel and rosemary. Cover and simmer slowly for about 15 minutes. Add the grapes, cover again, and continue cooking 5 minutes longer or until tender.

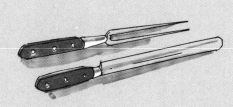

# Veal Indorato

*MENU FOR ITALIAN FRITTER MEAL INCLUDES THIS DISH—PAGE 48*

In Italian homes, a whole meal is made from a large assortment of meats and vegetables, batter-fried. This simpler version features only four ingredients— veal, zucchini, eggplant, and artichoke hearts.

Prepare for cooking as follows: Trim all membrane and tough connective tissue from veal. Place meat between sheets of waxed paper and pound with a flat-surfaced mallet until very thin (⅛ to ¼ inch).

Cut zucchini into diagonal slices, each about ⅜ inch thick. Slice eggplant crosswise into pieces about ¼ inch thick, or cut lengthwise into sticks about ⅜ inch thick. Break tough outer leaves from artichokes, cut off the top ⅓ (removing all thorns), and trim stem end. Cut in half or quarter each artichoke and place immediately in acid water (1 tablespoon vinegar to each quart water). Drain well to use. Season all foods with salt before cooking.

To cook, turn each piece in the flour and shake off excess, then dip into the beaten egg. Fry over medium-high heat in a wide frying pan containing about ½ inch of hot salad oil (or half butter) until each piece is richly browned. Add more fat as needed, and spoon out the small particles as they accumulate. Fry the vegetables first, then the veal; sauté veal just enough to brown lightly. Place browned pieces on baking sheets lined with paper towels; keep warm in a very slow oven or reheat later in a 350° oven.

Squeeze the juice of at least ½ lemon over each serving.

**MAKES 6 SERVINGS**

**PREPARE INGREDIENTS NO MORE THAN AN HOUR AHEAD**

**FRY AT LAST MINUTE IF POSSIBLE, OR KEEP WARM**

3  boneless veal round steaks (about 1¼ to 1½ lbs.)
2  or 3 medium-sized zucchini
1  small eggplant
6  small artichokes (sometimes called hearts) or about 12 thawed frozen artichoke pieces
   Vinegar and water
   Salt
   Flour
   Beaten eggs, about 4
   Salad oil or half butter, half salad oil
3  or 4 lemons, or more

# Veal Roast Orloff

This roast makes a dramatic appearance, yet is simple to do. You first roast a plain veal sirloin tip, then cut the meat into slices (handy for serving later). Between slices you insert Canadian bacon and Gruyère cheese. You also spread creamy onion sauce between the slices and over the top. The roast goes back in the oven long enough to heat meat, melt cheese, and brown the sauce. Everything except the final heating and browning can be done as much as a day ahead.

Sprinkle roast with salt and pepper. Place, fat-side up, on a rack in a shallow pan. Roast in a 325° oven for about 2¼ hours to a temperature of 160° on a meat thermometer. Remove from oven and let rest 15 minutes. Remove strings.

Cutting to within ½ inch of bottom, cut veal into ½-inch slices. Spread 1 cut side of each slice generously with Soubise Sauce (recipe follows), reserving half for topping. Insert a thin slice of Canadian bacon next to sauce on each slice, then insert 1 thin slice Gruyère cheese between bacon and each of the unspread surfaces of veal. Tie a string around roast to hold it together. Spread remaining sauce over the top; sprinkle with shredded Gruyère. If making ahead, cover loosely and chill.

Return to 325° oven; bake about 45 minutes, or until meat is heated through and sauce is lightly browned. Cut between slices to serve.

**Soubise Sauce.** Cook chopped onion in butter until soft. Use blender or food mill to purée; return to pan. Blend flour, salt, nutmeg, and pepper; stir into onion purée and cook about 2 minutes. Gradually add chicken broth and heavy cream. Cook, stirring constantly, until sauce is thick. Beat egg yolk; blend in a little of the hot sauce. Blend into remaining sauce and cook, stirring, until smooth and thick.

**MAKES 10 TO 12 SERVINGS**

**PREPARE AS MUCH AS A DAY AHEAD, REHEAT**

3  to 4-pound veal sirloin tip roast
   Salt
   Pepper
   Soubise Sauce (recipe follows)
½  pound sliced, fully cooked Canadian bacon
   About 6 ounces natural Gruyère cheese
2  tablespoons shredded Gruyère

**SOUBISE SAUCE:**

1  cup chopped onion
2  tablespoons butter
½  cup flour
½  teaspoon salt
¼  teaspoon nutmeg
   Dash pepper
½  cup <u>each</u> chicken broth and heavy cream
1  egg yolk

# LAMB

Lamb is much more popular in the West than in the rest of the country. Because it is so well liked and such a variety of ways to prepare it are possible, you may feature lamb at many kinds of guest meals. Most of the following recipes, some of foreign origin, have quite interesting seasonings.

## Lamb Chops in Pastry Crust

**MAKES 3 OR 4 SERVINGS**

**PREPARE MUSHROOMS SEVERAL HOURS AHEAD, WRAP CHOPS RIGHT BEFORE BAKING**

**FILA DOUGH MAY BE FROZEN**

- ⅓ pound mushrooms
- 4 tablespoons (¼ cup) butter or margarine
- 1 tablespoon instant minced onions
- ⅛ teaspoon <u>each</u> salt and thyme
- 1 tablespoon brandy or Cognac or dry red wine
- 2 tablespoons canned pâté de foie or liver paste
- 2 tablespoons fine dry bread crumbs
- 1 tablespoon chopped parsley
- 6 lean rib lamb chops, cut 1 inch thick
- ¼ teaspoon garlic salt

**FILA DOUGH:**

- ¾ cup unsifted regular all-purpose flour
- ¼ teaspoon salt
- 4 tablespoons water
- 1 tablespoon olive oil

A paper-thin crust encases lamb chops topped with mushroom-liver pâté. You can make the dough from the recipe included here or buy it frozen, usually called *fila* or strudel dough.

Wash mushrooms and chop finely. Sauté in 2 tablespoons of the butter with instant minced onions, salt, and thyme. Sprinkle with brandy and let cook a minute. Mix in pâté, bread crumbs, and parsley.

Trim lamb chops well, removing excess fat. Using a frying pan, brown chops quickly on both sides, about 2 minutes on each side. Sprinkle with garlic salt.

Melt remaining 2 tablespoons butter. Take 1 sheet of fila dough (recipe follows), or a double thickness of thin commercial dough—you may fold one large sheet in half for each chop—and brush it lightly with melted butter. Place 1 browned lamb chop in it, letting the end of the rib bone stick out of the pastry. Cover the top of the chop with a ⅓-inch-thick layer of mushroom stuffing. Wrap up meat in the pastry, encasing the meat completely and leaving the end of the rib bone free. Continue until all the chops are pastry-wrapped. Bake in 400° oven for 15 minutes, or until browned.

**Fila Dough.** Combine unsifted flour with ¼ teaspoon salt and mix in about 4 tablespoons water (you need enough water to make a firm ball); add olive oil, and knead until smooth. Cover with waxed paper and let sit 30 minutes. Divide the dough into 1-inch balls, and roll out each ball on a lightly floured board until it is as thin as paper and about 5 by 8 inches in size. Cover each sheet of dough with waxed paper to prevent it from drying out. You will need 6 sheets of dough.

## Mustard-Coated Lamb Roll

**MAKES 10 TO 12 SERVINGS**

**BEGIN ROASTING 1½ TO 2 HOURS AHEAD**

- 4½ to 5-pound boned, rolled leg of lamb
- ⅓ cup Dijon-style mustard
- 1 tablespoon soy sauce
- ¼ teaspoon <u>each</u> garlic salt and ground ginger
- 1 teaspoon dried rosemary (crumbled)
- 1 tablespoon salad oil

French mustard coats this boneless roast from a leg of lamb. If you have never tried lamb cooked medium rare rather than well done, try this roast that way— the meat is much more juicy and tender.

Place meat on a rack on a roasting pan. For coating, mix together mustard, soy sauce, garlic salt, ground ginger, rosemary, and salad oil.

Spread over roast, coating completely, and let stand at least 1 hour. Insert a meat thermometer and roast in a 300° oven until the thermometer registers 150° for pinkish rare meat (about 1½ hours) or 160° for medium well done. Remove to a platter and carve.

*Double Crown Roast of Lamb—see page 100*

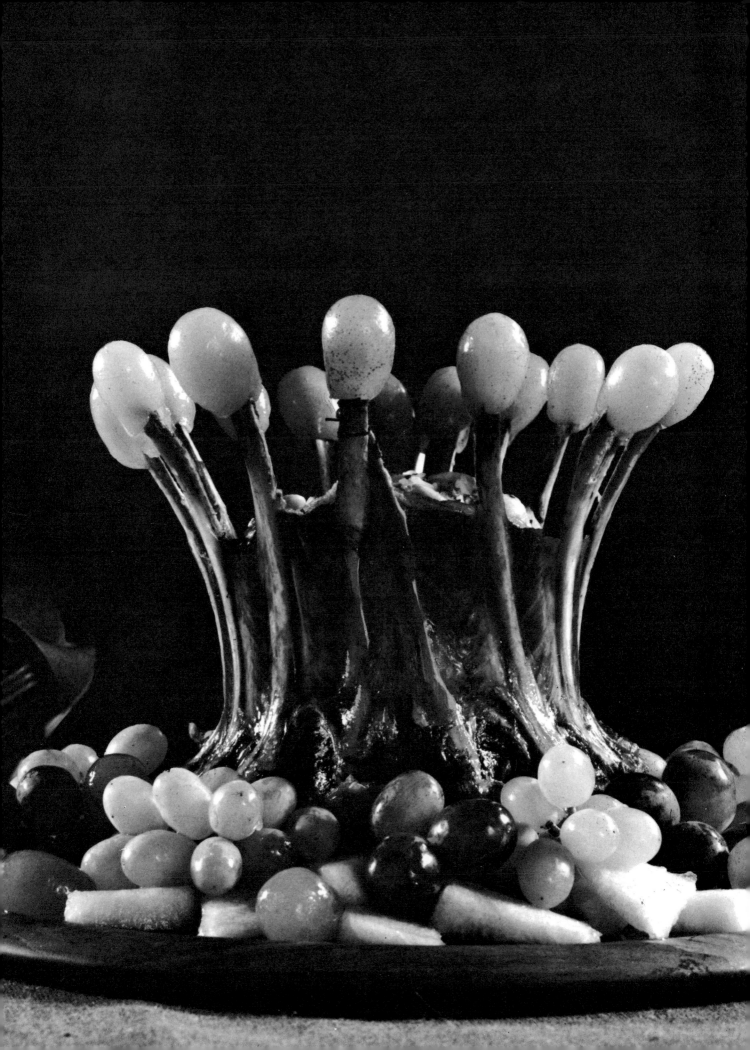

# Double Crown Roast of Lamb

*WITH RICE PILAF, INDIENNE*

**MAKES 7 SERVINGS**

**BEGIN ROASTING 3 HOURS AHEAD, PREPARE RICE PILAF IN MEANTIME**

- 14-rib double crown lamb roast, about 4 to 6 pounds (Have meat dealer cut meat back from ends of ribs and cut off backbone.)
- 1 cup orange juice
- ¼ cup finely chopped chutney (Major Grey type)
- ½ teaspoon curry powder
- 1 stick cinnamon

**RICE PILAF, INDIENNE:**

- ¼ cup (⅛ lb.) butter or margarine
- 1 large onion, finely chopped
- 2 cups long grain rice (uncooked)
- 6 cups boiling chicken stock
- 1 stick cinnamon
- 12 each whole peppers, whole cloves, and whole cardamom pods
- 2 cloves garlic, peeled
- 1 cup golden raisins
- ½ cup lightly toasted blanched almonds
- 2 green onions, chopped

**GARNISH:**

- 1 container (about 1 lb.) preserved kumquats
- 3 to 4 cups fresh fruit such as melon or pineapple spears and grapes

The most picturesque and festive meat dish of all is a crown roast of spring lamb. For this exceptional version, you have the butcher prepare a double crown of 14 ribs and then roast it with baste of orange juice, chutney, and spice. Fill crown with a savory pilaf resembling those of India, which contain curry spices, nuts, and raisins. Press glistening preserved kumquats onto the pointed bones which give the roast its "crown" name and heap cut-up fresh fruit around the base. This is indeed a dish fit for a king. *(Photograph on page 99.)*

To cook the roast, arrange crown on a rack in an open pan. Insert a meat thermometer into the thickest part of meat. Cover ends of ribs with foil to protect them from burning. To hold roast in shape, set a small heatproof bowl in its center.

Put into a 325° oven and roast until the meat thermometer registers the degree of doneness you like—about 160° for medium well done. During the last hour of roasting, baste several times with an orange sauce made by heating together the orange juice, chutney, curry powder, and 1 cinnamon stick (simmer 10 minutes).

**Rice Pilaf, Indienne.** Melt butter or margarine in a heavy 2-quart pan; sauté onion until golden. Add rice and continue cooking, stirring often, until lightly browned. Add boiling chicken stock and these spices tied in a cheesecloth bag: 1 stick of cinnamon (broken); whole peppers, whole cloves, and whole cardamom pods (crushed); and garlic. Cover and simmer 20 minutes. Add raisins and simmer 5 minutes longer, or until tender. Remove spice bag.

Spoon part of this pilaf in center of roast, serve the rest in a separate dish. Sprinkle top with almonds and chopped green onions.

**Garnishing the Roast.** Cut away excess fat from center and remove picks, if used. Have ready preserved kumquats and fresh fruit. Cut a cross in the ends of 14 kumquats and press one onto the end of each rib; mix remaining kumquats with fresh fruits to garnish the platter.

# Stuffed Provençal Lamb Shoulder

**MAKES 6 SERVINGS**

**BEGIN ROASTING ABOUT 2½ HOURS AHEAD**

- ½ pound ground pork
- 1 clove garlic, minced or mashed
- ¼ cup finely chopped onion
- ½ cup sliced pimiento-stuffed green olives
- ¼ teaspoon each salt and whole thyme
- Dash pepper
- 1 egg
- 3 slices whole wheat bread
- 2 tablespoons milk
- 3 pound boned lamb shoulder roast
- Olive oil

Stuffed with a mixture of pork and olives, this boneless lamb roast is easy to carve. Because of the pork inside, it should be cooked to a temperature of 170° on the meat thermometer.

Lightly mix pork, garlic, chopped onion, olives, salt, thyme, pepper, egg (slightly beaten), bread (crusts trimmed and cut in ½-inch cubes), and milk.

Fill cavity in roast with this mixture; sew edges closed with string or heavy thread. Rub olive oil lightly over surface of meat. Place stuffed roast on rack in an uncovered roasting pan in a 325° oven for about 2¼ hours or until meat thermometer inserted in thickest part registers 170°. Remove strings; place meat on a warm platter. If you like, you may skim and thicken pan drippings to make a sauce.

# PRESENTING THE PLEASURES OF WINE

The purpose of wine is pleasure, in the drinking and in the enhancement of good food. Wine, like music, can be as much a pleasure to the blissfully ignorant as to the expert. The only danger in a little knowledge of wines is that someone may worry about knowing too little and therefore spoil his pleasure.

**Wine Rules.** Rules for serving are not laws—you are not "wrong" if you break them. They are merely guides for getting the most pleasure out of the wine. They are based on reason and should be broken, too, when there is reason.

A good example is the rule which says wine bottles should be stored lying on their sides. This rule is reasonable—cork shrinks when it dries and lets in air which ruins the wine. However, if a bottle has a plastic stopper or screw cap, there is no reason to follow the rule.

The rules say white wines should be served chilled and red ones at room temperature. The reason is that flavor and aroma are at their best this way. However, some people like to keep their homes heated to 80 degrees, and "room temperature" usually means the European room of about 65 degrees. Light chilling of a red wine would be in order for these warmth-loving people; better yet, they would keep the wine in a cooler place such as the basement until serving. If the day is hot, light chilling may be desirable for more pleasant effect (some people prefer red wines slightly cooled at any time).

Generally, white wines should be served with seafood and chicken, red ones with meat and game. One reason is obvious—the milder, lighter foods are complemented by the lighter white wines. Another reason for the use of red wines with red meat is that these wines contain a greater amount of tannin, which enhances the hearty meat flavor but which may be unpleasant or overpowering with more delicate foods.

**When to Break the Rules.** Often there are reasons for breaking wine rules. One is personal preference, another is availability. If guests drop in and nothing but white wine is on hand to go with the roast, don't omit wine just because it isn't the "proper" one. Sometimes the seasonings of a dish may be the basis for disregarding the rule. A rich, highly spiced dish may do well with red wine and a creamy, light one with white, no matter what the main ingredient is. The experts and the people who live in wine-producing areas do not adhere religiously to the basic guidelines. They drink what they like, when they like.

In the West, you are often confronted with some menu situations which *must* break the wine harmony rules designed to enhance a Continental meal served in courses. What about the popular Chinese and Japanese meals, Scandinavian smörgåsbords, Hawaiian luaus, spicy Mexican and Indian dinners, as well as our own American buffet meals? How can white wine be served with the fish and a red with the meat when both meat and fish may appear simultaneously on the table, even in the same dish? Do we bypass wine just because some of these dishes may contain vinegar or spice which the experts say ruins wine?

Of course not. We probably decide that rosé wine would be fine with the subtle Chinese dishes, or a choice of red and white if the meal is served family-style to many people. A chilled Claret might be just the thing with Hawaiian roast pig and lomi salmon. A hearty Burgundy might be the most effective quencher of curry or taco sauce fires.

In addition to red and white wines, there are still other table wines which have their own sensible rules for serving. Dry Champagne and rosé wines should both be chilled and may be served with any kind of food.

**Appetizer and Dessert Wines.** These categories of wines too often are neglected. Dry Sherry, nutty in flavor, and sweet or dry Vermouth, herb-flavored, are delicious with the kinds of tidbits served before a meal. The Sherry may be chilled or not, depending on taste. Vermouth may be at room temperature, chilled, or over the rocks—with or without a twist of lemon zest.

The sweeter, rich-flavored wines which go with dessert or after are best at room temperature, with the exception of sweet Champagne, which should be chilled. Among the dessert wines (particularly outstanding with cheese, fruit, and nuts) are sweet and cream Sherry, Port, Muscatel, Tokay, Angelica, Malaga, Madeira, and sweet Marsala.

**Wine Glasses.** Common sense dictates choice of glasses for wine service. Wine usually should be served in clear glasses because they show off the beautiful color. However, it is perfectly reasonable to serve wine in tinted glass or a Japanese teacup if the container is also beautiful.

Even the shapes of glasses used for certain types of wines have logical reasons. Sherry or Port glasses are small and open because these wines are more potent in alcoholic content, flavor, and aroma. Red wine glasses have shorter stems and a more bulbous look because red wine is robust in color and flavor. Rhine wine glasses have slender, long stems so that the heat of the hand does not warm the wine, and a more fragile look to complement the delicate flavor and light, clear color. Champagne glasses are designed to display the bubbles and cause them to tickle the nose pleasantly.

If you don't have, or don't want, an array of the various types of wine glasses, the rules say a simple, stemmed, tulip-shaped glass may serve all purposes. This is reasonable—the glass has both delicate and sturdy qualities and catches aromas well. But, if you don't have enough wine glasses for a large crowd, use any kind of glass. After all, the purpose of wine is pleasure. In order to be drunk with enjoyment, the wine must first be poured into *something*—paper cups and thermos caps if need be.

# Molded Eggplant Moussaka

*MENU FOR GREEK BUFFET INCLUDES THIS DISH—PAGE 32*

**MAKES 6 TO 8 SERVINGS**

**MAKE SAUCE A DAY AHEAD**

**BEGIN BAKING MOLD 1 TO 3 HOURS AHEAD**

| | |
|---|---|
| 2½ | large eggplants (about 1½ lbs. each whole; choose long, slender ones) |
| | Salt |
| | About 1 cup salad oil or olive oil |
| 2½ | pounds ground lamb |
| 1 | large onion, chopped |
| 1 | clove garlic, minced |
| ½ | pound mushrooms, chopped |
| ½ | teaspoon crumbled rosemary |
| 2 | teaspoons paprika |
| 1 | cup packed, soft bread cubes |
| 1½ | teaspoons salt |
| 3 | eggs |
| | Tomato Sauce (recipe follows) |
| | Parsley |

**TOMATO SAUCE:**

| | |
|---|---|
| 1 | large onion, chopped |
| 2 | tablespoons butter |
| 3 | large tomatoes, peeled and chopped |
| 1½ | cups regular strength beef broth |
| ½ | teaspoon salt |
| ¼ | teaspoon pepper |

Moussaka is a dish so old that it has been integrated into the cuisine of almost every country of Asia Minor and the Balkans, plus several in North Africa. You'll find its name spelled many ways, but usually the pronunciation is something like "moo-*sah*-kah." It is a casserole of vegetables and minced meat. The vegetable most used is eggplant, with zucchini and potatoes running second and third. Tomatoes and cheese generally are incorporated in one way or another.

The most beautiful, elegant moussaka of them all is the one for which recipe is given here. The glossy purple skins of eggplant are used to line a mold into which a meat filling is poured and then baked. Turn the mold out on a very special serving dish, preferably one with a pedestal, and beautify further by drizzling with tomato sauce and topping with a nosegay of parsley.

*(See photograph on page 107.)*

Cut stems from eggplants, and quarter lengthwise. Sprinkle cut surfaces lightly with salt and let stand 20 minutes. Dry with paper towel. Heat enough oil to cover bottom of a wide frying pan, and cook cut sides of eggplant over medium heat until richly browned. Do not crowd eggplant, and keep a generous layer of oil in pan. Drain pieces on paper towels.

Let eggplant cool, then cut away the meaty centers of each section, leaving a shell about ⅜ inch thick. Chop eggplant meat and save. Arrange shells, skin side down, on a baking sheet, and broil about 6 inches below heat for 5 to 10 minutes or until browned (brush with a little oil if they look dry).

Crumble lamb in a large frying pan, and add 1 chopped onion, garlic, and chopped eggplant; cook, stirring, until lamb loses its pink color. Then add mushrooms, rosemary, paprika, bread, and 1½ teaspoons salt (or to taste); cook rapidly, stirring, until meat begins to brown slightly and vegetables are tender. Let cool slightly; spoon out excess fat. Mix in the eggs.

Arrange the shells vertically (skin side against dish) around sides of a deep 2-quart dish or charlotte mold; it may be necessary to put one section of skin across bottom of mold to cover area completely. A few gaps in the lining are unimportant, however. Spoon meat filling into center.

Set mold in a deep pan of hot water (water should come about half way up sides of moussaka) and bake in a 375° oven for 45 minutes. (When finished cooking, you can turn the oven temperature to warm and hold moussaka in oven up to 2 hours before serving.)

Remove moussaka from oven and hot water bath and let stand at least 10 minutes, then invert on a serving dish with rim, and remove mold. Drizzle some Tomato Sauce around moussaka and decorate with parsley. Cut in wedges to serve. Top each portion with more of the Tomato Sauce.

**Tomato Sauce.** Cook 1 chopped onion in butter until soft. Add chopped tomatoes, beef broth, ½ teaspoon salt, and pepper. Boil rapidly until reduced to 3 cups. For a smooth sauce, whirl in a blender. Serve hot.

# Herbed Leg of Lamb

*MENU FOR PATIO BUFFET INCLUDES THIS DISH—PAGE 13*

There is a growing trend to cook lamb the classic French way—medium rare or medium well done—instead of well done. The instructions following tell how to judge whatever degree of doneness you prefer.

A leg of lamb brought to the table on a carving board can be made quite beautiful with imaginative garnish. See page 92 for ideas on garnishing entrées. Bunches of grapes always make an appropriate decoration.

Rub all surfaces of lamb with 1 clove garlic, peeled and halved. Cut this clove and 1 more into slivers. Slit skin of lamb at intervals over the top surface; insert slivered garlic into slits. Blend dry mustard, salt, pepper, thyme, rosemary, and lemon juice. Spread over surface of the roast. Coat potatoes well with butter; place in pan with roast.

Place lamb on rack in an uncovered roasting pan in a 325° oven and roast for 2 to 2½ hours or longer, until thermometer in thickest part registers 150° (for medium rare); 160° (medium well done); or 175° (well done). Baste potatoes occasionally with pan drippings.

Remove meat and potatoes to platter; keep warm. For sauce, skim fat from pan drippings; reserve 1 tablespoon. Stir flour into fat in pan; heat until bubbly. Add water to skimmed drippings to make 1½ cups; blend into flour mixture, stirring constantly until thickened. Simmer for 3 to 5 minutes; pour through strainer to remove crusty particles.

**MAKES 6 TO 8 SERVINGS**

**BEGIN ROASTING ABOUT 3 HOURS AHEAD**

5½ to 6-pound leg of lamb
2 cloves garlic
1 tablespoon dry mustard
2 teaspoons salt
⅛ teaspoon pepper
½ teaspoon whole thyme
¼ teaspoon crushed rosemary
1 tablespoon lemon juice
10 to 12 medium-sized potatoes, peeled
Butter
2 tablespoons flour
Water

# Keema Curry

*RECIPE WITH AUTHENTIC INDIAN CURRY DINNER MENU—PAGE 11*

This curry contains ground lamb, a number of separate spices rather than curry powder, and peas. The other dishes suggested for serving with it are okra stuffed with spices, curried garbanzo beans, mint chutney, and a typical Indian pastry in syrup. However, Keema Curry, with just plain rice and a salad, makes a good, simple dinner for guests who love spicy food.

**MAKES 6 TO 8 SERVINGS**

**PREPARE AS MUCH AS A FEW HOURS IN ADVANCE**

# Arni Souvlakia

*GREEK-STYLE SHISH KEBAB*

You might alternate these lamb cubes on the skewers with small tomatoes and green pepper chunks, or cook vegetables on separate skewers.

Cut lamb into 1½-inch cubes. Dip each cube in lemon juice. Combine salt with pepper and oregano; sprinkle over the meat cubes. Thread meat on skewers. Broil over charcoal until the meat is brown but still juicy, brushing with olive oil two or three times during the cooking.

**MAKES 6 SERVINGS**

**MARINATE MEAT IN LEMON JUICE AHEAD**

**SKEWERS REQUIRED**

3 pounds boneless leg or shoulder of lamb
Lemon juice
1 tablespoon salt
1 teaspoon <u>each</u> pepper and oregano
Olive oil
Tomatoes (optional)
Green peppers (optional)

# Kebab Barg

*PERSIAN LAMB KEBAB*

**MAKES 10 SERVINGS**

**MARINATE MEAT 12 HOURS TO 2 DAYS AHEAD**

5 pound leg of lamb, boned and sliced ½ inch thick
1 cup grated onion
3 cups yogurt
About 1/16 teaspoon powdered saffron (optional)
Salt and pepper
Chelo Rice (optional), page 161
Butter (optional)
10 raw egg yolks in half egg shells (optional)
Raw green onions
Radishes
Pickles
Flour tortillas (optional)

The yogurt marinade gives this lamb an interesting tart flavor. It is traditionally served with Crusty Golden Rice, also called *Chelo* (recipe on page 161).

Trim fat off meat and cut meat in strips 2 inches wide by about 5 inches long. Mix onion with yogurt and saffron. Put lamb in yogurt marinade; refrigerate, covered, for 12 to 48 hours. Thread each piece of meat on two thin skewers, running them lengthwise through long edges of the meat. Sprinkle with salt and pepper, and broil over hot coals for 3 to 4 minutes on each side.

To serve with Chelo Rice, put about 1 tablespoon butter on each hot serving plate and cover with a mound of Chelo. Place a half egg shell containing a raw egg yolk on top of each mound and slip meat off skewers; arrange one piece of meat on each side of rice. Each guest will mix the egg yolk with the rice and butter on his plate. Serve with raw green onions, radishes, pickles, and flour tortillas, heated and cut into wedges.

# COOKING WITH WINE

Cooking with wine is easy if you use this cook book. The recipes tell just what quantities and types to use; you merely measure as you would any other ingredient. Wines for cooking purposes should be of fairly good quality—wines you'd enjoy drinking for their own sake.

In the case of an appetizer or dessert wine, the recipe specifies the exact kind of Vermouth, Sherry, or Port. Often a "dry white" or "dry red" wine is called for. In the case of white wines, you may use any non-sweet table wine such as Chablis, dry Sauterne, or Rhine types. Even dry Vermouth, which is an herb-flavored white wine, may be substituted in some recipes, particularly in dishes with herb seasoning or where a small quantity of wine is specified. A dry red wine may be either the Burgundy or Claret types, or Italian reds.

You may prefer to buy half-bottles of the table wines which are perishable. Larger opened bottles may be preserved by refrigeration. Frequently it is convenient to use some of the same table wine that will be served with dinner in preparing the food; this helps avoid leftover wine. Appetizer and dessert wines have a higher alcohol content and therefore are more resistant to spoilage. They may be stored on a shelf for several months after opening.

Wine used in cooking may serve several purposes. A few spoonfuls will point up or blend flavors, yet may remain unnoticed, just as a little lemon juice or garlic often is. If you have no wine on hand, such a small quantity can probably be omitted without changing the dish to any important extent. Larger quantities, usually called for by the cupful, contribute a definite flavor, and wine must be used if the dish is to taste as it should. Because wine also is a good tenderizer, it is useful in meat cookery; marinating or long simmering is necessary to take advantage of this characteristic. The dessert wines act much the way an extract does—several spoonfuls will impart a definite and identifiable flavor.

In experimenting with wine cookery, use a cautious approach as you would if trying new herbs or spices. Add a small amount and taste. However, wine added to cooking food does behave differently from herbs and spices, which may increase in pungency as the heat brings out their flavor. The alcohol in wine evaporates even below the boiling point, and heat seems to mellow the remaining flavor. Thus the taste will become subtler the longer cooking goes on, unless the liquid is reduced to such an extent that the wine in it is more concentrated.

When marinating foods in wine, be sure to use non-metallic containers. Utensils used for cooking foods with wine may be metal. In either case, cover the vessel to prevent evaporation of the essence.

Adding wine to foods is no more mysterious than adding salt. It is helpful to have a recipe which tells an exact amount of salt to use, but even a relatively inexperienced cook soon learns how to salt most foods without measuring. With a little practice the same kind of feel for adding wine can be acquired. Although over-salting can ruin a dish, "over-wining" is a seldom occurrence—wine does not need such precise measuring.

# PORK

A variety of ham recipes follows because this version of pork is so easily prepared in advance and makes such a handsome appearance at guest meals. However, some of the recipes in this section even glamorize the more humble chops, spareribs, or roasts.

## Stuffed Smoked Pork Chops

Smoked pork is quite similar to ham in flavor. The chops are particularly good stuffed; have your meatman cut a pocket in each for stuffing. This dish is appreciated by those who call themselves "meat and potatoes" people, yet it is special enough for a party.

Mix together the rice, raisins, green pepper, vinegar, pimiento, oregano, and bacon. Stuff each chop (do not pack); close with short skewers or wooden picks and lace with string. Brown chops on both sides in the butter or oil; add the water, cover, and simmer about 30 minutes, or until tender.

**MAKES 6 SERVINGS**

**STUFF PORK CHOPS SEVERAL HOURS AHEAD**

- 1 cup cooked rice
- ¼ cup each chopped raisins and chopped green pepper
- 1 tablespoon each vinegar and chopped pimiento
- ¼ teaspoon oregano
- 6 slices bacon, cooked, drained, crumbled
- 6 thick smoked pork chops, cut with pocket for stuffing
- 2 tablespoons butter or salad oil
- ½ cup water

## Braculine

*STUFFED PORK ROLLS*

These Italian rolls of pork are filled with a most unusual, flavorful stuffing of pine nuts, prosciutto (the salty Italian ham), and mashed hard-cooked eggs. The rolls are browned, then simmered in tomato sauce. Serve them with toasted pine nuts sprinkled on top and lemon wedges—a little lemon juice is just the right piquant finish.

To toast nuts, spread them in single layer in pan; bake in a 350° oven 5 minutes. Shake occasionally. Finely chop all but the 2 tablespoons nuts with a knife, or whirl a few at a time in a blender. Blend well with prosciutto, parsley, marjoram, and eggs, mashing together so mixture is slightly compacted. Set aside while you prepare meat.

Trim excess fat from tenderloin and discard; cut meat in 12 equal-size pieces. Place each portion of meat between sheets of waxed paper and pound very thin with a flat-surfaced mallet; the meat will tear apart easily but should have no holes. Divide filling evenly among pounded meat pieces and pat over surface. Roll to enclose filling and hold shut with small wooden skewers. (You can do this several hours ahead and keep cold, covered.)

Melt butter in a wide frying pan over moderate heat and lightly brown the filled rolls on all sides. Take care not to brown excessively as this hardens meat and makes it dry. Then add tomato sauce and water to pan, cover, and simmer over low heat for 12 to 15 minutes, turning rolls occasionally. Remove rolls to a serving dish and pour the pan juices over the meat. Sprinkle with the reserved 2 tablespoons pine nuts. Squeeze a little lemon on each serving.

**MAKES 6 SERVINGS**

**PREPARE STUFFING AND ROLLS SEVERAL HOURS AHEAD; COOK 20 MINUTES BEFORE SERVING**

- 1½ cups and 2 tablespoons pine nuts
- ⅛ pound (2 oz.) prosciutto, minced
- ¼ cup minced parsley
- ¼ teaspoon marjoram
- 2 hard-cooked eggs, mashed fine
- 2 pounds pork tenderloin
- 2 tablespoons butter
- ½ cup each canned tomato sauce and water
  Lemon wedges

# Layered Ham Pancakes

*RAKOTT SONKÁS PALACSINTA*

**MAKES 4 GENEROUS SERVINGS**

**FREEZE PANCAKES UNTIL NEEDED**

**PREPARE FILLING SEVERAL HOURS AHEAD**

**EIGHT-INCH CRÊPE OR FRYING PAN REQUIRED**

Hungarian Pancakes (recipe follows)
2    cups ground cooked smoked ham
1    cup sour cream
2    tablespoons finely minced green onions
¼    teaspoon salt
⅛    teaspoon Dijon-style mustard (or other prepared hot mustard)
     Dash of pepper
     About 1 tablespoon butter
     Sour cream

**HUNGARIAN PANCAKES:**

3    eggs
6    tablespoons flour
⅜    teaspoon salt
1    cup milk
     Butter (about 3 tablespoons)

Palacsinta (pal-a-*chin*-ta) is a thin Hungarian pancake that is not much different from the better-known French pancake, or crêpe, except that it is even more thin and eggy.

The French use crêpes in many ways, but Hungarian cooks have gone even further with palacsinta. They roll them, fold them, cut them, and stack them. They fill and embellish them with all sorts of savory and sweet mixtures. They use them as entrées, in soups, and for fancy desserts—but never for breakfast.

This "stack" of pancakes with minced ham filling is one of their most delicious entrée creations. It is a good idea to make Hungarian pancakes ahead of time and assemble them just in time to heat and serve. If you want to make the pancakes more than a day ahead, just freeze the cooled and stacked pancakes; allow to thaw completely before you work with them.

You'll need about 12 Hungarian Pancakes (one basic recipe below). For the filling, combine ham, sour cream, green onions, ¼ teaspoon salt, mustard, and a dash of pepper. Place one of the pancakes on a buttered baking dish or heatproof plate; spread with a thin layer of the ham filling. Repeat, using all the filling and pancakes, ending with a pancake on top. Dot the top with about 1 tablespoon butter.

Bake in a 350° oven for about 20 minutes or until heated through. Garnish with spoonfuls of sour cream. Cut in wedges to serve.

**Hungarian Pancakes (Palacsinta).** Beat eggs with a fork. Add unsifted flour and the ⅜ teaspoon salt; continue beating until batter is smooth. Gradually add the milk, beating again until smooth. Using an 8-inch crêpe pan or frying pan, heat butter (½ to 1 teaspoon for each pancake) over medium-high heat until bubbly. Pour in about 3 tablespoons batter (all at once) for each cake; quickly tilt and rotate pan so the batter completely covers the bottom of the pan. When lightly brown on bottom, turn with long, flexible spatula and lightly brown on other side.

# Ham and Bananas

**MAKES 4 SERVINGS**

**PREPARE RICE AHEAD, COOK MEAT AND FRUIT BEFORE SERVING**

2    tablespoons butter or margarine
2    tablespoons honey
2    tablespoons Sherry or apple juice
1    teaspoon lemon juice
⅛    teaspoon nutmeg
     Dash of ground cloves
1    center-cut ham slice, about 1 inch thick (1½ to 2 lbs.)
2    firm, ripe bananas
     Rice
     Raisins
     Dash of nutmeg

This dish is so quick to prepare that you might keep it in mind for those emergency times when guests drop in. You can also dress up the rice pilaf in a number of ways, depending on what ingredients you have on hand.

Combine in a small pan the butter or margarine, honey, Sherry or apple juice, lemon juice, nutmeg, and dash of ground cloves. Heat until butter is melted. Put ham slice in preheated broiler about 4 inches below the heat and broil 5 minutes, or until browned.

Meanwhile peel bananas and slice in half, lengthwise. Turn over ham slice, arrange half-slices of banana on top, then brush the butter-honey mixture all over top of ham and bananas. Put back under broiler and broil about 5 minutes more, or until browned, basting several times with the remaining butter-honey mixture. Serve the banana-topped ham on a bed of hot rice pilaf—add a handful of raisins and a dash of nutmeg to rice while it is cooking.

# Portuguese Spareribs in Garlic Wine

MENU FOR PORTUGUESE COUNTRY DINNER INCLUDES THIS DISH—PAGE 40

**MAKES 4 SERVINGS**

**MARINATE MEAT 4 DAYS**

**BEGIN BAKING 2 HOURS BEFORE SERVING**

4   pounds country-style spareribs
1   cup cider vinegar
3   cups water
½   cup dry white wine
2   teaspoons <u>each</u> crushed whole coriander and crushed whole cumin
5   to 6 cloves garlic
¼   teaspoon cayenne
2   teaspoons salt
½   cup water
4   to 6 tablespoons water

Like the German beef sauerbraten, which is marinated several days in vinegar and spices, these Portuguese ribs have a hearty, nose-tickling aroma.

Put spareribs in a deep glass or ceramic bowl. Blend together vinegar, 3 cups water, wine, coriander, cumin, garlic cloves (slightly broken), cayenne, and salt. Pour liquid over pork. Cover and refrigerate for 4 days; turn meat in marinade several times during this period.

On the fourth day, remove meat from marinade and let drain for about 30 minutes. Discard all liquid. Arrange meat in a single layer in a roasting pan and add ½ cup water. Bake uncovered in a 350° oven for 2 hours. Remove to a serving platter. Skim as much fat as possible from drippings, then add 4 to 6 tablespoons water to pan and bring to a boil, scraping free all the browned particles. Serve separately in a sauce dish. Cut between ribs to serve meat; it may require additional salt to taste.

# Ham in Pastry

**MAKES 12 TO 14 SERVINGS**

**PREPARE HAM FOR BAKING AS MUCH AS A DAY AHEAD**

4   cups beef stock (4 cups water plus 4 tablespoons beef stock base)
1   cup Madeira or Port wine
1   carrot, peeled and chopped
1   medium-sized onion, chopped
5   to 6-pound canned ham
1   pound mushrooms, chopped
3   tablespoons butter or margarine
    Juice of ½ lemon
3   tablespoons instant minced onions
2   green onions, chopped
¼   teaspoon <u>each</u> salt, thyme, and allspice
    Freshly ground pepper
1   can (2 or 3 oz.) pâté de foie or liver paste
½   cup fine dry bread crumbs
    Pastry (recipe follows)
1   egg yolk
1   tablespoon water

**PASTRY:**

2½   cups sifted regular all-purpose flour
½   teaspoon salt
¾   cup butter
3   egg yolks, slightly beaten
3   to 4 tablespoons cold water

Even a rather ordinary canned ham becomes a delicacy when you simmer it in a Madeira sauce and encase it in a mushroom stuffing and buttery pastry. This dish resembles the French masterpiece called *jambon en croûte*. You can assemble this entrée completely a day in advance, if you wish, then bake it just before you plan to serve it.

Using a large pan or Dutch oven, bring to a boil the stock, wine, and chopped carrot and onion. Add the ham, cover, and simmer for 1 hour; remove meat from stock and let drain; cool. Reserve stock.

Meanwhile, using a large frying pan, sauté mushrooms in the 3 tablespoons butter and sprinkle with lemon juice. Add the instant onion, green onions, salt, thyme, allspice, and pepper. Remove from heat and stir in pâté and bread crumbs. Cool.

Roll out rich pastry (recipe follows) about ⅜ inch thick to a rectangle large enough to enclose the meat—about 14 by 18 inches. Save pastry scraps for garnish.

Spread the mushroom filling over the pastry, pressing in firmly and leaving a 1½-inch margin on all sides. Place meat, top side down, with the long side of ham across the short side of pastry center. Wrap pastry around the meat and seal securely down the middle and at the ends, moistening pastry edges with water. Place, seam side down, on a greased baking sheet and garnish the pastry with designs cut from pastry scraps.

(You can wrap the pastry-covered ham in plastic film and refrigerate at this point. Before baking, let stand at room temperature for 1 hour.)

Brush pastry with a mixture of 1 egg yolk beaten with 1 tablespoon water. Bake in a 400° oven for about 30 minutes, or until well browned. Cut into ½-inch-thick slices, and serve hot with the strained, unthickened reserved stock. (You can leave vegetables in the stock, if you prefer.)

**Pastry.** Sift flour before measuring, then sift with salt into bowl. Cut in the ¾ cup butter until particles resemble fine crumbs. Mix in 3 egg yolks and 3 to 4 tablespoons cold water, mixing lightly. Press into a ball, cover, and chill.

# Charcoal-Barbecued Honeyed Ham

*MENU FOR BARBECUED HAM BUFFET INCLUDES THIS DISH—PAGE 29*

You needn't save barbecuing on the grill for entertaining out-of-doors. Often it is helpful to prepare the meat outside for a meal served indoors—this frees the oven for baking and prevents the house from being filled with cooking odors. If you set up the barbecue outside the kitchen, you'll have little extra walking to do to baste the meat while finishing other tasks in the kitchen.

Place a drip-catching pan in the fire bed beneath grill where the ham will be placed. If you don't have a suitable ready-made pan, you can make one of heavy-duty foil folded double. It should be about 3 inches longer and 2 inches wider than the ham, with sides about 2½ inches high.

Start two charcoal piles (one on each side of the drip-pan) of 20 briquets each, 30 to 45 minutes before you plan to start the ham (the briquets should burn down to an even gray). After each hour of cooking time, add about 6 briquets on each side.

Start the ham on the grill 3 to 5 hours before serving time, depending on the size and type of ham you buy. Plan on 15 to 20 minutes per pound if you buy a "tenderized" ham (or cook to 160° on meat thermometer); or 10 to 15 minutes per pound for a fully cooked ham (or 130° on meat thermometer).

As an added precaution to keep ham fat away from the barbecue fire, shape a "pan" of double heavy-duty foil loosely around lower half of ham. Sides should be about 4 inches high and should stand away from ham about 1 inch all around. Insert meat thermometer in thick portion of ham.

Set ham on the barbecue, centered over drip pan beneath. For slow heat, keep any draft opening small. Check the ham every half hour; if it begins to brown too quickly, lower heat by making draft openings smaller (but don't completely close them). If drippings accumulate excessively in the pan directly under the ham, remove them with a turkey baster. One hour before ham is done, remove from barbecue, drain off drippings, skin, score, and brush with honey glaze made by combining honey, Worcestershire, mustard, ginger, and pepper. Return to barbecue and brush with glaze about every 15 minutes. When ham is done, it will be easier to slice if you let it stand 15 to 20 minutes.

**MAKES 2 TO 3 SERVINGS PER POUND OF HAM (INCLUDING BONE)**

**SEE RECIPE TO ESTIMATE WHEN TO BEGIN COOKING**

Tenderized or fully cooked ham
3 tablespoons honey
1 tablespoon Worcestershire
1 tablespoon dry mustard
¾ teaspoon ground ginger
Dash of black pepper

# Pork Satés Bali

A Far Eastern spiciness permeates pork kebabs when you use puréed chutney in the marinade. Twirl the grilled kebabs in finely chopped peanuts to lend an authentic Indonesian flavor. Direct your meatman to bone a pork loin and slice it ¾ inch thick and then into 1-inch squares. This cut will grill quickly to a tender state.

Purée the chutney in a blender until smooth (or finely chop it). Turn into a bowl and add catsup, soy sauce, hot-pepper seasoning, and oil. Add meat squares and let marinate for several hours, turning occasionally. Impale meat on 6 skewers. Place under a preheated broiler (or barbecue over medium coals) and broil for about 15 minutes, turning to brown both sides. Immediately roll in finely chopped peanuts, spread out on a small tray or plate, to coat all sides.

**MAKES 6 SERVINGS**

**MARINATE MEAT SEVERAL HOURS**

**BROIL AT SERVING TIME**

**SKEWERS REQUIRED**

½ cup chutney
¼ cup catsup
1 tablespoon soy sauce
4 drops liquid hot-pepper seasoning
2 tablespoons salad oil
2 pounds boneless pork loin, cut ¾ inch thick in 1-inch squares
¾ cup salted peanuts, very finely chopped

# Baked Ham with Jewel Fruit Sauce

**ESTIMATE ABOUT ⅓ POUND MEAT
PER SERVING**

**PREPARE SAUCE AHEAD**

**CHECK HAM CAN FOR COOKING
INSTRUCTIONS**

7   to 12-pound canned ham

**JEWEL FRUIT SAUCE:**

1   can (1 lb. 14 oz.) fruits for salad
     (or 3½ cups canned fruits, a
     combination of your favorites)
1   tablespoon cornstarch
1   cup apple juice or cider
3   or 4 tablespoons brown sugar
1   tablespoon soy sauce
1   teaspoon dry mustard
2   tablespoons lemon juice
½   teaspoon grated lemon peel
2   or 3 tablespoons ham pan
     juices (optional)

This recipe is a jewel of a find for the hostess whose husband balks at the traditional male role of carving meat. The ham is presliced and tied by the meatman. The slices are skewered through the middle to hold them together after baking. At serving time, the skewer is gradually pulled out to release the slices one by one as needed.

Have your meatman slice and tie a flat-topped canned ham. Bake according to directions on can or in a 325° oven until meat is heated. Prepare sauce.

About 20 minutes before meat is done, drain off all pan juices. Pour the ½ cup fruit sauce you reserved for glazing over the ham; bake 20 minutes more. Pour rest of sauce, including fruit, over ham; bake until fruit is heated.

Place ham on a serving platter. Insert 1 or 2 skewers through slices and remove string. Arrange fruits over ham. Serve remaining sauce separately.

**Jewel Fruit Sauce.** Drain fruit, saving ½ cup syrup. (If you use several fruits, combine juices and then measure.) Blend cornstarch with a small amount of reserved syrup, combine with the remainder of the ½ cup syrup, apple juice, sugar, soy, mustard, lemon juice, lemon peel, and pan juices. Bring to a boil, stirring, and cook until clear and slightly thickened. Remove from heat; set aside ½ cup sauce for glazing ham. Add drained fruit to the rest of the sauce.

# Pork Loin with Sautéed Papaya

**MAKES 8 SERVINGS**

**BEGIN ROASTING ABOUT 3 HOURS
AHEAD**

4   pound pork loin roast
⅓   cup <u>each</u> catsup and orange
     juice
1   teaspoon grated orange peel
½   teaspoon ground ginger
1   papaya
2   tablespoons butter
     Juice of ½ lime
3   to 4 cups hot cooked rice
     Parsley

At the self-service meat counter, most pork loins have been partially cut into individual chops for easier carving at a guest meal. You can ask to have the roast cut this way if it's not already done.

Place roast on a rack in a shallow roasting pan; insert meat thermometer into thickest part. Combine catsup, orange juice, grated orange peel, and ginger; brush part of this sauce over meat. Roast, uncovered, in a 325° oven until meat thermometer registers 170°. Baste several times with remaining sauce.

Just before serving, peel papaya, halve, and scoop out seeds. Slice papaya and sauté slices in butter; turn to brown all sides lightly. Squeeze lime juice over papaya in pan. Spoon hot cooked rice onto a warm serving platter. Place roast or slices of roast on rice; arrange papaya slices around meat and pour any butter remaining in the pan over the fruit. Garnish with parsley, if you wish.

# Roast Pork, Hawaiian-Style

*RECIPE WITH PATIO LUAU MENU—PAGE 15*

**ALLOW ½ TO ¾ POUND MEAT
(WITH BONE) PER PERSON**

**MARINATE MEAT 2 HOURS OR
OVERNIGHT BEFORE COOKING**

Pit-roasted pork, main feature of the Hawaiian *luau*, can be successfully imitated by baking a pork roast in a packet of foil containing leaves, bananas, and sweet potatoes. This sweet, juicy meat may be prepared any time for many kinds of meals and need not be reserved for Hawaiian-style parties only. The sweet potatoes baked with the meat are especially tasty. Just add watercress salad and appropriate dessert such as Macadamia Nut Cream Pie (recipe on page 186) to complete a simple menu.

# POULTRY

Ways to prepare chicken, Cornish game hens, turkey, pheasant, and duck are featured in the following recipes. Although chicken is inexpensive, it always has an elegance appropriate for important entertaining. Most dishes of chicken and the other fowl are particularly suited to party meals because they need not be served at the precise moment they are done—they can be kept warm or reheated.

## Pilaf-Stuffed Chicken Legs

Inexpensive chicken legs become special enough for company dinner when they are stuffed with a spicy rice pilaf. The stuffing is very easily pushed under the loose skin; you'll be surprised to see that the skin will stretch so much that up to ⅔ cup of rice can be forced into each leg. This operation can be done ahead. Begin baking the chicken about an hour before serving time.

Sauté onion and rice in butter or margarine until onion is just tender. Blend in curry powder and add currants. Stir in chicken broth, cover, and cook about 20 minutes, or until rice is tender. Cool.

To stuff chicken legs, carefully lift up skin of thigh; spoon about ⅔ cup rice under skin of each leg, keeping skin and membrane intact as much as possible. Use your fingers to push rice down leg. Wipe away excess rice and pull skin over opening. Arrange in greased baking pan. (Cover and refrigerate until baking if you wish.) Bake, uncovered, in a 325° oven for about 50 minutes, or until chicken is just tender.

**MAKES 8 SERVINGS**

**STUFF CHICKEN UP TO 8 HOURS AHEAD**

- 1 medium-sized onion, chopped
- 1 cup long grain rice
- 2 tablespoons butter or margarine
- 1 teaspoon curry powder
- ¼ cup currants
- 2½ cups chicken broth
- 8 whole chicken legs (leg and thigh together)

## Freezer Chicken Kiev

Chicken Kiev—butter-filled boneless chicken breasts fried in a crusty coating—makes a dramatic company main dish. But usually it has one drawback: last-minute preparation is required. However, there is a new way to prepare this entrée so you can do it almost entirely ahead, freeze it, then complete the cooking in the oven in just a few minutes with no attention required.

Carefully remove skin from chicken so you do not tear flesh. Place chicken pieces, 1 at a time, between sheets of waxed paper. Pound gently with flat meat mallet until each piece is very thin and doubled in width. Sprinkle each piece evenly with tarragon, then lightly with salt and pepper. Cut butter into 8 sticks, each about 2 inches long; place a stick at small end of each chicken piece.

Roll tightly, folding in sides to enclose butter and make a compact roll. Fasten with small metal skewers or wooden picks. Coat each roll lightly with flour, then egg mixture, then bread crumbs. Fry, 2 at a time, in deep hot fat (350°) for 5 minutes, until golden brown. Drain on paper towels; when cool, remove skewers, wrap individually in foil, and freeze.

To serve, unwrap frozen rolls and let stand at room temperature for 1 hour. Bake on a rack in a shallow pan in a 450° oven for 20 to 25 minutes, until well browned.

**MAKES 8 SERVINGS**

**PARTIALLY COOK CHICKEN AND FREEZE; THAW, BAKE BEFORE SERVING**

- 4 whole chicken breasts (3 to 3½ lbs.), boned and halved
- 1½ teaspoons crushed tarragon
  Salt and pepper
- ½ cup (¼ lb.) cold butter
  Flour
- 1 egg, beaten with 1 tablespoon milk
- ½ cup fine dry bread crumbs
  Fat for deep frying

# Sesame-Soy Chicken

*MENU FOR JAPANESE SUSHI PICNIC INCLUDES THIS DISH—PAGE 38*

**MAKES 4 TO 6 SERVINGS**

**MARINATE SEVERAL HOURS
BEFORE BROILING**

2   pounds chicken legs and/or
    thighs
½   cup soy sauce
2   tablespoons sugar
1   teaspoon salt
    A 2-inch piece of fresh ginger,
    finely chopped
2   tablespoons sesame seed
    Melted butter or salad oil

This chicken is first marinated in a teriyaki-type mixture of soy sauce, sugar, and ginger, broiled, and then coated in toasted sesame seed. Sesame-Soy Chicken is good either hot or cold—it could be a tasty change from fried chicken for a picnic or other outdoor meal.

Wash chicken and pat dry. Marinate for 1 to 2 hours in a mixture of the soy sauce, sugar, salt, and ginger. If you plan to barbecue the chicken at a picnic, put it into the marinade just before you leave home. Also toast sesame seed either in a frying pan or in the oven until lightly browned.

Remove chicken from marinade and grill over medium-hot coals or in your broiler, brushing with some of the marinade and with melted butter or salad oil. Cook until nicely browned on both sides and the chicken is tender, about 30 to 40 minutes. Sprinkle with the toasted sesame seed when you remove it from the grill. Serve hot or cold.

# Shrin Polo

*PERSIAN CHICKEN AND RICE*

**MAKES 6 TO 8 SERVINGS**

**RICE SOAKS OVERNIGHT**

**CHICKEN CAN BE ASSEMBLED OR
COOKED A DAY AHEAD**

1½   cups long grain rice
     Water
2   broiler-fryer chickens, cut in
    pieces
10   tablespoons butter
1   teaspoon salt
1   large orange
3   cups shredded carrots
¼   cup slivered almonds
⅛   teaspoon saffron
1½   teaspoons sugar
1   teaspoon salt
2   tablespoons chopped pistachios
    or parsley

In old Persia, this festival dish might have been served at such a grand occasion as a wedding. Today this entrée in casserole form has special appeal to busy cooks because of its make-ahead possibilities. With salad, bread, and a dessert it is a complete meal—and a fine company choice. Typically the dish is quite sweet, but here the sugar has been adjusted to a level more acceptable to American tastes.

Cover rice with about 2 inches of cold water and let stand, covered, overnight in the refrigerator.

You can also cook the chicken one day ahead. Heat 2 tablespoons of the butter in a wide frying pan until melted. Sprinkle chicken pieces with 1 teaspoon salt and brown lightly in the butter over medium heat. Do not crowd pan; remove pieces as they are browned. When all are cooked, return the chicken pieces and accumulated juices to the frying pan, and add ½ cup water. Cover and simmer gently for about 45 minutes or until chicken is tender when pierced. (Refrigerate, covered, if cooked ahead.)

Thinly pare zest (the surface) from the orange with a vegetable peeler. Cut orange zest in slivers and cook in boiling water to cover for 3 minutes. Drain.

Melt the remaining ½ cup butter in a wide frying pan, add the carrots, and cook over medium heat, stirring, for 5 to 8 minutes; do not brown. Add the blanched orange zest, slivered almonds, ½ teaspoon salt, saffron, and sugar. Cook a minute or two longer, then add ¾ cup water and boil rapidly until liquid evaporates; stir frequently.

In the meantime, bring 3 quarts water with 1 teaspoon salt to a boil. Drain soaking rice and add to hot water. Boil for 8 minutes or just until rice is tender to bite. Drain thoroughly. Add rice to the carrot mixture and adjust salt.

Spoon the rice mixture into the center of a large casserole (about 3-quart size), arrange chicken pieces around the sides, and drizzle with the cooking juices or spoon them over. Bake immediately or cover and chill until ready to heat. Cover casserole and bake in a 375 oven for 15 to 20 minutes if ingredients are warm, or for 35 to 40 minutes if any of the ingredients are cold. Garnish with pistachios.

# Danish Chicken and Meatballs au Gratin

*THIS DISH IS FEATURED IN THE COVER PHOTOGRAPH*

Featured on the cover of this book, Danish Chicken and Meatballs epitomizes all that a good entrée for a special party should be. It is delicious, different (but not *too* different), and beautiful. Yet it is practical to make and serve. The ingredients may be found at any market, any time of year. Almost all the work is done ahead of time, far ahead if you wish. At serving time, you just assemble meats and sauce in an ovenproof dish, and broil a few minutes until glazed and bubbly. As an accompaniment serve Brandied Carrots, also in the cover photograph aflame in the chafing dish (recipe on page 154).

In a small saucepan, heat the 1 cup butter until bubbly, but not browned. Scoop slightly rounded teaspoonfuls of the meatball mixture and slide off spoon into hot butter. Cook several meatballs at once, turning as needed, just until browned, about 4 minutes. Drain meatballs on paper towels, then put into a 2-quart bowl; reserve the butter.

Slice chicken into ¼-inch-thick strips. Heat 4 tablespoons of the reserved butter in a frying pan and sauté chicken until white throughout; transfer to bowl with meatballs. Add butter to pan to make 2 tablespoons and sauté prepared sweetbreads until lightly browned; combine with meatballs.

For the sauce, heat the 2 tablespoons butter in a pan; add the flour and mustard and cook until bubbly. Gradually stir in broth, cream, and wine. Cook, stirring, until slightly thickened. Add cheese gradually, stirring, until melted. Remove from heat and stir in pimiento. (If you wish to serve later, cover and refrigerate sauce and meats separately.)

Just before serving, reheat cheese sauce. Add meat and cook slowly until heated through. Spoon into serving dish (one you can use in broiler), and broil about 5 inches from heat for 2 minutes, or until top is bubbly, but not brown. If you wish, garnish with mushroom caps, tomatoes, and parsley.

**Veal Meatball Mixture.** Combine in a bowl the veal, ¼ cup flour, egg, ⅛ teaspoon salt, pepper, onion, and milk. Beat with a spoon until very smooth, cover, let stand at least 5 minutes.

**Sweetbreads.** Wash sweetbreads. Simmer in 1 quart water with 1 teaspoon salt and lemon juice for 15 minutes. Drain, rinse in cold water, drain again. Peel and cut away membranes; break into bite-sized pieces.

**MAKES 6 SERVINGS**

**PREPARE SAUCE AND MEATS UP TO 1 DAY AHEAD**

**ASSEMBLE AND BROIL JUST BEFORE SERVING**

- 1 cup (½ lb.) butter or margarine
- Veal meatball mixture (directions follow)
- 2 large whole chicken breasts, boned and skinned
- Cooked sweetbreads (directions follow)
- 2 tablespoons <u>each</u> butter and flour
- ¼ teaspoon Dijon-style mustard
- ⅔ cup chicken broth (canned or freshly made)
- ½ cup whipping cream
- ⅓ cup dry white wine
- 1 cup shredded Danish Samsoe or Swiss Gruyère cheese
- 1 jar (4 oz.) sliced pimiento, drained
- 4 or 5 mushroom caps, lightly browned in butter (optional)
- Cherry tomatoes (optional)
- Parsley (optional)

**VEAL MEATBALL MIXTURE:**
- ¾ pound ground veal
- ¼ cup flour
- 1 egg
- ⅛ teaspoon salt
- Dash pepper
- 2 teaspoons grated fresh onion
- ½ cup milk

**SWEETBREADS:**
- 1 pound veal sweetbreads
- 1 quart cold water
- 1 teaspoon salt
- 1 tablespoon lemon juice

# Broiled Chicken Piquant

Broiled chicken is a calorie-saving dish even though it is brushed with seasoned oil as it cooks to enhance flavor and crisp the skin.

Sprinkle the chicken on all sides with salt and pepper. Shake together the oil, mustard, basil, and liquid hot-pepper seasoning; brush undersides of chicken with about half the oil mixture. Place skin-side down in a broiler pan without a rack. Broil for about 15 minutes, placing chicken about 8 inches from heat. Turn chicken and brush with remaining oil mixture. Broil 10 to 15 minutes longer, brushing occasionally with drippings, or until tender and well browned.

**MAKES 6 SERVINGS**

**BROIL JUST BEFORE SERVING OR SERVE COLD**

- 3 whole chicken breasts, split lengthwise
- Salt and pepper
- ¼ cup olive oil
- 2 teaspoons prepared hot mustard
- 1 teaspoon basil
- ¼ teaspoon liquid hot-pepper seasoning

# Cashew Chicken

*MENU FOR DINNER COOKED AT THE TABLE INCLUDES THIS DISH—PAGE 21*

This Chinese-style stir-fry dish takes only 5 minutes of cooking in an electric frying pan, making it an ideal cook-at-the-table entrée. Arrange the vegetables on a tray and put the sauce ingredients in pitchers to make sure the preparation moves speedily.

Bone chicken breasts and remove skin. Slice horizontally in ⅛-inch-thick slices, then cut in 1-inch squares. Arrange on a tray. Remove the ends and strings from the Chinese peas. Wash and slice mushrooms. Cut the green part of the onions into 1-inch lengths and then slash both ends several times making small fans; slice the white part ¼ inch thick. Drain bamboo shoots and slice.

Arrange all the vegetables on the tray in individual piles.

Pour chicken stock into a small pitcher. Mix together soy with cornstarch, sugar, and salt; pour into a small pitcher. Place oil and nuts in containers. Arrange at the table with electric frying pan.

To cook, heat 1 tablespoon oil over moderate heat (350°), add nuts all at once, and cook 1 minute, shaking pan, until lightly toasted; remove from pan and set aside. Add remaining oil to pan, add chicken, and cook quickly, turning, until it turns opaque. Add Chinese peas and mushrooms; pour in stock, cover, and simmer 2 minutes.

Add bamboo shoots. Stir the soy mixture into the pan juices, and cook until sauce is thickened, stirring constantly; then simmer 1 minute uncovered. Mix in the green onions. Sprinkle with nuts.

**MAKES 4 SERVINGS**

**PREPARE INGREDIENTS AHEAD, COOK AT SERVING TIME**

**MAY BE COOKED AT TABLE**

| | |
|---|---|
| 3 | whole chicken breasts, split |
| ½ | pound Chinese (edible pod) peas or 2 pkgs. frozen pods, partially thawed |
| ½ | pound mushrooms |
| 4 | green onions |
| 1 | can (15 oz.) bamboo shoots |
| 1 | tablespoon chicken stock base and 1 cup water |
| ¼ | cup soy sauce |
| 2 | tablespoons cornstarch |
| ½ | teaspoon <u>each</u> sugar and salt |
| 4 | tablespoons salad or peanut oil |
| 1 | package (4 oz.) cashew nuts |

# Chicken Momi

*HAWAIIAN—STYLE WITH SESAME SEED*

Hawaii, with its varied cultural heritage, contributes a host of good ways to cook and serve chicken. Chicken Momi, a meaty combination of boned chicken breasts enclosing a veal and pork stuffing, shows Philippine influence. *Momi* means "pearl" in Hawaiian, perhaps an allusion to the sesame-seeded surface of the chicken.

Pound inside of chicken breasts to flatten slightly; sprinkle with salt. Top each with a scant half cup of the stuffing and fasten with skewers or wooden picks. Place skin side up in a greased baking pan. Cream butter with honey; slowly beat in soy sauce. Spoon mixture over chicken. Bake in 325° oven about 45 minutes, basting occasionally with pan drippings, until chicken is tender. Sprinkle on sesame seed, increase temperature to 450°, and continue baking about 10 minutes longer or until well browned. Garnish with papaya and lime slices to serve.

**Veal and Pork Stuffing.** Pour half-and-half (light cream) over bread crumbs. Sauté chopped onion with water chestnuts in 2 tablespoons butter. Mix cooked onion mixture with softened bread, veal, pork, 1 egg, 1 tablespoon soy sauce, grated fresh ginger, monosodium glutamate, and cayenne.

**MAKES 6 SERVINGS**

**STUFF CHICKEN AHEAD, BAKE BEFORE SERVING**

| | |
|---|---|
| 6 | whole chicken breasts, boned |
| | Salt |
| | Veal and Pork Stuffing (recipe follows) |
| 2 | tablespoons <u>each</u> soft butter or margarine and honey |
| 1 | tablespoon <u>each</u> soy sauce and sesame seed |
| | Papaya and lime slices |

**VEAL AND PORK STUFFING:**

| | |
|---|---|
| ¼ | cup half and half (light cream) |
| 1 | cup soft bread crumbs |
| ⅓ | cup finely chopped onion |
| 1 | can (5 oz.) water chestnuts, drained and minced |
| 2 | tablespoons butter |
| ¼ | pound ground veal |
| ½ | pound ground pork |
| 1 | egg |
| 1 | tablespoon soy sauce |
| 1 | teaspoon grated fresh ginger |
| ⅛ | teaspoon each monosodium glutamate and cayenne |

*Buttery Barbecued Cornish Hens—see page 120*

ENTRÉES • CHICKEN 115

# HOW TO USE AND FUEL CHAFING DISHES

The term "chafing dish" comes from the French *chauffer,* meaning to make warm. By definition, a chafing dish is any pan or vessel placed over a source of heat to warm or cook food at the table.

You can buy a chafing dish as a complete unit, or you can improvise by setting a pan or a heatproof casserole over some type of burner unit (these can be purchased separately). When you shop for a chafing dish, you're sure to see many variations in vessels, burners, and fuels.

## CHAFING DISH COOKERY

You can prepare simple or elaborate dishes right before your guests with a chafing dish. Be selective in choosing a recipe for at-the-table preparation; if you are a novice, use a recipe designed for the chafing dish.

You should create the illusion that the recipe you prepare requires little effort. To do this, arrange a work tray with all the necessary ingredients ready to use, extra fuel, and a small towel. If the recipe is complicated or long-cooking, do the major preparation in the kitchen.

If you want to flambé (flame) food in the chafing dish, just be sure both the food and liquor to be burned are warm so they will ignite properly. To light, tilt the pan and touch match to edge. Use brandy, liqueurs, or any liquor of high alcohol content. Stir constantly to prolong the flames until all the alcohol has burned. Never pour more liquor into a flaming pan; the stream of liquid from the bottle can ignite with disastrous results.

## A VARIETY OF VESSELS

These are some of the most common chafing dish vessels.

**Omelet Pan.** A heavy, wide, shallow pan used over direct flame, it is ideal for quick heating and sautéing of meats, fish, eggs, and fruits. It is a good shape for flaming meats and fish which cook in it. Although "omelet pan" is its name, most experts agree that an omelet should be cooked on a range rather than in a chafing dish.

**Blazer Pan with Bain Marie.** The top pan, or *blazer pan,* is used for the cooking of the food. The bottom pan, or *bain Marie,* is a water bath.

For dishes requiring higher temperatures—browning, setting eggs, sautéing fruits—place the blazer pan over direct flame. If you cook something you would normally prepare in the top of a double boiler, cook it in the blazer pan over the water bath. Chafing dish recipes usually indicate whether or not to cook over the bain Marie.

**Earthenware Fondue Dish.** This flameproof dish is traditionally used for Swiss Cheese Fondue (see Fondue Party menu on page 44), but can also be used for heating and serving casseroles, stews, or soups.

**Fondue Bourguignonne Pan.** This small pan with an inward sloping side is designed for cooking cubes of meat on skewers or forks in hot fat (see Fondue Party menu on page 44). Place it over direct heat. Use it also to keep sauces or gravies warm.

**Heatproof Casseroles.** Use only those types suitable for use on top of a range unit. Casseroles of *pyroceram* (a glass-ceramic highly resistant to temperature change) are especially safe for dishes which involve cooking.

## FUELS FOR COOKING AND WARMING

**Alcohol Burners.** These come in a number of styles, but in two general categories: wick and compressed fiber. You regulate the flame by lengthening or shortening the wick on the first, and by opening or closing a damper (controlling the amount of air) on the second. The wick type has a disadvantage—after a few burnings, the wick must be replaced. The size of the alcohol container determines how long it will burn before refueling is necessary. Never add fuel until the flame is completely out.

Denatured alcohol is usually recommended for use in alcohol burners, but the less expensive isopropyl (rubbing) alcohol may be used. The two fuels have vastly different heating powers. Denatured alcohol heats much faster—use it for cooking. Isopropyl is better for rewarming or keeping a dish hot.

**Canned-Heat Burners.** These units consist of a stand with a holder for canned heat. The holder has a lid-like piece with a handle with which you can increase or decrease the size of the flame. Some units hold a large can (7 oz.), but most are designed for a small can (2⅝ oz.). A small can will last from 55 to 65 minutes and a large can for 4 to 5 hours. Fuel also comes in the form of cubes, which are placed in a container or empty can and used just as you use canned heat.

Canned heat has much the same heating properties as denatured alcohol. Use canned heat when high temperatures are necessary, for quick-cooking of meat and eggs, or for browning. You can also control it for low heat by partially covering the can opening.

**Candle Heating Units.** These units often come as a set—casserole with stand including a candle holder. Fireproof casseroles or pans can be placed on the stand.

The candle (buy one designated for warming) should be used only for keeping cooked foods warm. The flame is not hot enough to cook food, and its heat is too slow for heating cold things to a serving temperature.

# Wiener Backhendl

*PICNIC MENU INCLUDES THIS DISH—PAGE 47*

Viennese fried chicken is coated with egg and bread crumbs just as the famous veal cutlets, Wiener Schnitzel, are. The crispy chicken is good hot or cold.

Wash and drain broiler-fryers; sprinkle with salt. Coat on all sides with flour, then dip in eggs, and coat with bread crumbs. Place chicken quarters in a single layer in a preheated fry basket. Lower into deep fat preheated to 350°. Fry until well browned and tender, keeping temperature of fat at about 325°, for 8 to 10 minutes. Drain on paper towels. To serve cold, cool chicken, garnish with lemon slices topped with cherry tomato slices and parsley, and wrap in plastic film.

**MAKES 8 SERVINGS**

**PREPARE SEVERAL HOURS AHEAD IF SERVED COLD**

| | |
|---|---|
| 2 | small (under 2½ lbs.) broiler-fryer chickens, quartered |
| 2 | teaspoons salt |
| ½ | cup all-purpose flour |
| 4 | eggs, beaten |
| 2½ | cups very fine dry bread crumbs |
| | Oil for deep frying |
| | Thin lemon slices |
| | Cherry tomato slices |
| | Chopped parsley |

# Curried Chicken Tempura

Usually tempura consists of fish, shellfish, or vegetables, coated with an airy batter and fried crisp. Here tempura is an entrée of curried chicken wings that may be cooked at the table. To complete the meal, add rice or fried rice, green salad, and fruit dessert.

A patio setting is ideal for a tempura supper, and you avoid the possible problem of cooking odors in the house. An electric frying pan is the easiest way to cook tempura outdoors.

Cut the chicken wings off at the first joint (the wing tips and center sections can be simmered into a rich chicken stock for soup another day). Start at the small end of each large wing piece, and with a sharp knife cut the meat from the bone down to the end, leaving the meat attached to the bone at the large end. Pat excess moisture from wings with paper towels. (Wings may be prepared ahead.)

For the batter, break one egg into a measuring cup, beat with a fork, pour half into a small bowl (save other half for some other use); add water, cornstarch, flour, salt, sugar, curry powder, and monosodium glutamate; mix until well blended. Set the bowl inside a bowl of cracked ice to keep it cold while you use it.

To cook tempura at the table, use an electric frying pan or deep fat fryer with a good heat regulator. Set pan on a side table or tea cart (there may be some spattering of fat as you fry). Nearby arrange the prepared chicken wings, the batter in a bowl with ice, and a cake cooling rack over a shallow pan for draining the cooked food. For lifting the fried chicken out of the hot fat, you'll need a slotted spoon, tongs, or a Japanese flat wire strainer.

Heat the salad oil (about 1½ inches deep) in the pan to a temperature between 350° and 355°. If possible, use a deep-fat frying thermometer to check the temperature. Hold each chicken wing by the bone and dip into the batter, drain briefly, then put into the hot fat. Cook until golden brown, turning several times (takes about 2 to 3 minutes). Lift out with a slotted spoon and drain briefly.

Don't cook more than 4 or 5 pieces at one time or the fat will cool too much. Skim off any drops of batter that form in the fat so they won't burn and flavor the oil. Pass soy sauce at the table.

**MAKES ABOUT 4 SERVINGS**

**PREPARE CHICKEN AHEAD**

| | |
|---|---|
| 2 | dozen broiler-fryer chicken wings |
| ½ | egg |
| 10 | tablespoons water |
| 6 | tablespoons cornstarch |
| 6 | tablespoons all-purpose flour |
| 1 | teaspoon salt |
| 2 | teaspoons <u>each</u> sugar and curry powder |
| ½ | teaspoon monosodium glutamate |
| | About 2 quarts salad oil for deep frying |
| | Soy sauce |

# Stuffed Baked Papayas Congo

MAKES 4 TO 6 SERVINGS

PREPARE STUFFING UP TO
SEVERAL HOURS AHEAD

STUFF AND BAKE PAPAYAS JUST
BEFORE SERVING

2    half-ripe papayas
2    cups ground uncooked chicken
        (about 2 whole breasts and 2
        thighs)
½    cup soft bread crumbs
½    cup half and half (light cream)
1    egg, lightly beaten
1    teaspoon salt
       Pinch each freshly ground
         pepper, thyme, and marjoram
1    medium-sized onion, chopped
3    tablespoons butter
       Salt

In the Congo where this dish originated, they call papayas *pai pai* or *paw paw*. Whatever you call these fruits, this recipe calls for them to be filled with ground chicken and a most familiar, non-exotic stuffing. You'll recognize the other ingredients as those used for stuffing fowl American-style.

Cut off one end from each papaya. Scoop out the seeds and peel the papayas. Make a stuffing by mixing ground chicken with bread crumbs soaked in light cream, beaten egg, salt, pepper, thyme, and marjoram. Sauté onion in 2 tablespoons of the butter; add to chicken mixture. Mix well and stuff papayas. Melt remaining 1 tablespoon of butter in a baking dish, add the papayas, brush with melted butter, sprinkle with salt, cover, and cook in a 350° oven for 30 minutes. Remove cover, baste, cook 30 minutes longer, until tender and brown. Cut each papaya in half or into 3 pieces.

# Coq au Vin

*CHICKEN IN RED WINE WITH OLIVES*

MAKES 8 TO 10 SERVINGS

COOK AS MUCH AS A DAY AHEAD,
REHEAT

3    large broiler-fryers
        (approximately 3 pounds each),
        cut up
½    cup butter or margarine
¼    cup brandy
1    bottle (about 3¼ cups) dry red
        wine
1    tablespoon salt
¼    teaspoon nutmeg
½    teaspoon dried rosemary,
        crumbled
1    bay leaf
1    tablespoon chicken stock base
3    cloves garlic, minced or mashed
1½  pounds fresh mushrooms (caps
        about 1 inch in diameter)
1½  tablespoons lemon juice
4    slices extra-thick-sliced bacon
2    cans (about 1 lb. each) small
        whole onions
2    teaspoons sugar
⅓    cup each cornstarch and water
1    jar (7 oz.) pimiento-stuffed olives

Pimiento-stuffed olives accent this smoothly seasoned chicken. Its flavor actually mellows with reheating. If you prefer, do not serve the chicken backs, wings, and necks to guests, but cook them as directed, as they enrich the flavor of the red-wine sauce. *(Photograph on page 88.)*

Using 2 large frying pans, brown chicken pieces in ¼ cup of the butter, turning to brown all sides. Warm brandy slightly, ignite 1 spoonful, and spoon flaming over the chicken; pour on remaining brandy and let flame over chicken. Pour in wine to loosen the browned drippings, then transfer chicken and liquid to a large baking dish or Dutch oven (about 8-quart size) with a cover. Add salt, nutmeg, rosemary, bay leaf, chicken stock base, and garlic. Cover and simmer gently for 1 hour, or until chicken is barely tender. Remove from heat.

   Meanwhile, slice stems from mushrooms and leave caps whole; sauté stems and caps in the remaining ¼ cup butter along with lemon juice for a few minutes; transfer mushrooms and juices to the chicken.

   Finely dice the bacon and, using the same pan, sauté until crisp; remove from pan and drain on paper towels. Pour off all but 2 tablespoons bacon drippings and add well-drained onions to the pan. Sprinkle with sugar, and heat, shaking pan until onions are lightly browned. Add browned onions to the chicken.

   Blend cornstarch with water to make a paste. Drain the wine juices from the chicken into a saucepan and heat to boiling; stir in the cornstarch paste and cook until thickened, stirring constantly. Pour back over the chicken in the casserole. Add the drained olives and sprinkle with crisped bacon bits. (If made ahead, let cool and refrigerate at this point.)

   Cover and reheat in a 350° oven for 30 minutes if prepared continuously or for 1 hour and 15 minutes if refrigerated.

# Chicken with Lemon Sauce

*KOTA AVGOLEMONO*

The refreshing egg-thickened sauce with lemon, called Avgolemono, is much used in Greek cookery, particularly with chicken. Other than its marvelous flavor and ease of preparation, another virtue is its low calorie content. If you prepare this stew-type dish ahead, make the sauce at the last minute.

Using a frying pan with a cover, brown chicken on all sides in butter. Add garlic, salt, chicken stock base, and water; cover and simmer 25 minutes. Add vegetables to the chicken and simmer 10 minutes, or until tender. Transfer chicken and vegetables to a serving dish.

For sauce, beat eggs until light and blend in lemon juice. Slowly pour in the hot chicken juices, beating constantly with a wire whisk. Return juices to the pan and place over very low heat; cook, stirring, until sauce coats the spoon in an opaque layer (be careful not to overcook because sauce may curdle). Spoon over chicken and sprinkle with oregano.

**MAKES 4 TO 6 SERVINGS**

**PREPARE UP TO A DAY AHEAD, REHEAT AND FINISH SAUCE BEFORE SERVING**

1   large broiler-fryer chicken, cut up (3 lbs.)
1   tablespoon butter or margarine
3   cloves garlic, minced
1   teaspoon salt
1   tablespoon chicken stock base and 1 cup water
1   package (8 oz.) frozen Italian green beans
2   yellow crookneck squash, sliced
2   eggs
2   tablespoons lemon juice
½   teaspoon dried oregano, crumbled

## THE ART OF THE SMALL DINNER PARTY

Of all invitations, those that flatter us most are for small dinner parties. It's a very personal way to entertain, and satisfying to both hosts and guests. Following are some tips that can help you make an intimate dinner party especially successful.

**The Setting.** A decoration or two in the living room and on the buffet or dining table will make your home look festive. Simple arrangements of flowers, fruits, shells, or other ornaments are often sufficient.

The centerpiece itself is a challenge met in varied and imaginative ways. A large pink shell with a single full-blown garden rose is a striking example. Fruits or vegetables make beautiful and appetizing centerpieces. A golden Casaba melon and clusters of pale green Thompson seedless grapes are handsome in a low, black, free-form bowl. Flowers that float—begonia, camellia, azalea, or rhododendron blossoms—are good choices because you can keep the bouquet low. A few flowers arranged at the bases of candlesticks often suffice and are particularly suitable if your table is small and crowded.

**The Serving.** The clever hostess plans her menu to require only a few last-minute chores. Certain inevitable tasks like mixing the salad and getting dishes to buffet or table take one away from company long enough.

It's helpful to have chilled plates or bowls from the refrigerator for salad, and hot plates from the oven or warmer for the entrée.

If there is meat or poultry to be carved, let the host do it at the table (if he's willing). The hostess can then serve the vegetables, to speed up the process and keep food from getting cold.

**Combination Buffet—Sit-Down Dinner.** Many hostesses choose a combination plan where guests serve themselves at the buffet, then sit down at a set table. This procedure is easy to handle without outside help, and the guests are comfortably placed at an attractive table.

The partial buffet plan may also work another way. Serve your guests at the dinner table, perhaps having an attractive first course waiting at each place (a number of such suitable first-course recipes are on pages 63 through 67). Then let the dessert be buffet style in the living room. Set up coffee or tea service and a beautiful cake or pastry, with plates. Also place dessert wines or liqueurs and glasses there to pass around later. This helps get guests away from the table and lets those who would like a brief wait after the full meal serve themselves when they are ready.

# Cornish Hens under Glass

Wild Rice Stuffing (recipe
    follows)
¼ pound small whole fresh
    mushrooms
2 tablespoons butter
2 Rock Cornish game hens,
    thawed, washed, and dried
½ teaspoon salt
3 tablespoons melted butter
1 cup cooked fresh peas (optional)

**WILD RICE STUFFING:**
1 tablespoon butter
1 tablespoon minced onion
1 cup cooked wild rice (or
    combination wild rice and
    brown rice)
2 tablespoons crumbled blue
    cheese

*De rigueur* for a *tête-à-tête* dinner: something *sous cloche* (the French term for food served under glass). If it's elegance and romance you're after, the practical may not be worth mentioning. Nevertheless, the glass cover does make good sense—it keeps food hot and moist, holds all the aroma inside to release under the nose of the diner. (This marvellous scent has often proven more effective than French perfume with certain gentlemen.) If you don't have a glass bell made especially for dinner service, use an ovenproof glass bowl that fits serving plate or platter. A glass frying pan cover, if attractive, may work well, too. The ready-to-serve Cornish hens may remain covered in the oven with heat at lowest setting while you enjoy aperitif or first course.

Prepare the Wild Rice Stuffing, using the stems from the mushrooms. Sauté the mushroom caps in the 2 tablespoons butter until lightly browned and tender; reserve. Rub cavities of the game hens with salt, and fill with the Wild Rice Stuffing. To close the cavity, sew or skewer and lace with string. Tie the legs together. Brush with the 3 tablespoons melted butter, and roast, uncovered, in a 350° oven for 1 hour, or until tender. Baste occasionally with pan drippings.

Garnish with mushroom caps and arrange on heated serving plates. Spoon the peas on either side of the game hens, and spoon hot pan juices over the hens. Cover with hot glass (heat it in the oven for the last 5 minutes the chicken cooks). Keep hot in oven until ready to serve; do not remove glass until ready to eat.

**Wild Rice Stuffing.** Chop the mushroom stems and sauté in 1 tablespoon butter until tender; add minced onion and cook until lightly browned, about 3 minutes. Mix with rice cooked according to directions on the package. Add blue cheese, and mix until combined. Makes enough stuffing for 2 hens.

# Buttery Barbecued Cornish Hens

4 frozen Rock Cornish game hens
    (12 oz. to 1 lb. each), thawed
    Salt and pepper
    Herb Butter (recipe follows)
2 tablespoons lemon juice
¼ cup warm, strained apricot jam
    Watercress sprigs and fresh
    apricot halves, for garnish

**HERB BUTTER:**
½ cup (¼ lb.) soft butter or
    margarine
2 tablespoons chopped chives
    (fresh or freeze-dried)
¼ teaspoon rosemary, crushed

Herb butter blends with a glistening apricot glaze to flavor these juicy Cornish hens. They should be cooked on a barbecue that can be covered; the surface of the grill should be large enough for heat to circulate around the pan holding the hens. They also may be oven-roasted. *(Photograph on page 114.)*

Wash Cornish hens; pat dry, inside and out, with paper towels. Sprinkle skin and cavities lightly with salt and pepper. Place about 1 tablespoon of the herb butter in large cavity of each; fasten cavities closed with wooden picks or small metal skewers. Tie legs together.

Melt remaining herb butter with lemon juice. Place hens, breasts up, on a double thickness of heavy foil; turn up a 1-inch rim on all 4 sides to form a shallow pan. Place on grill over glowing coals. Cover barbecue, adjust drafts to keep fire burning slowly, and cook, basting occasionally with herb butter, for 45 minutes to 1 hour or until tender and golden brown.

If you wish to cook the birds in the oven, roast in 350° oven for about 1 hour.

When almost done, brush hens evenly with warm apricot jam; cover again and continue cooking until nicely glazed. Serve on wooden board or platter, garnished with watercress and apricots.

**Herb Butter.** Blend butter or margarine with chives and rosemary.

# A SHOPPER'S GUIDE TO WINE LABELING

The person shopping around for wines has every right to be confused by the great variety of labels he sees. Part of the confusion exists because no one system is used for naming wines.

As a starting point, it is useful to remember that there are five basic classes, and that all of the wines in each class bear some resemblance to one another. The classes are: white table wines, red table wines, sparkling wines, appetizer wines, and dessert wines. However, these class names do not appear on the bottle label—the wine buyer must learn which wines are of which class.

**How Wines Are Named.** Three systems are used. They are: for a geographic place (where the wine was actually made, or which inspired an imitator in some other region); for the name of the grape variety used; or for a name coined by the winemaker.

In France and Germany, most wines bear the name of the vineyard, commune, or region in which they were produced. Specific vineyards are exemplified by LaRomanée in Burgundy or Château Latour in Bordeaux. Communes are typified by Chablis (in the Burgundy region) or Sauternes (Bordeaux region). More general regions would be Burgundy, Bordeaux, Champagne, Rhône, etc. One French region, Alsace, practices varietal naming. The major wines of the region are called Gewürztraminer, Riesling, and Sylvaner, after the variety of grape used.

In the United States, and especially in California, wines are named after European place names, for the grape variety used, and, increasingly, the winemaker's coined name.

Most of California's early winemakers came from the wine districts of Europe. They brought grapes from Europe, attempted to make wines of the kind they had known there, and named them accordingly. That practice—called generic labeling—persists, but since the 1940's there has been increasing emphasis on varietal naming. Still more recently, many wineries have begun using coined names as alternatives to the generic ones.

**Making Comparisons.** In spite of the myriad names, there *are* ways to compare European and California wines, because many are made from corresponding grape varieties.

White Riesling and Sylvaner are the major grape varieties in the finest wines of the Rhine and Mosel in Germany. Varietals from each are made in California. These grapes, plus Traminer or Gewürztraminer, go into the best of Alsatian wines, which also find counterparts here.

Sauvignon Blanc goes into the white wines of Pouilly Fumé and the dry white Bordeaux called Graves. It and Semillon are used to make Sauternes and Barsacs, both very sweet. In California, those two grapes are used to make both dry and sweet wines.

Chenin Blanc, usually producing a slightly sweet white wine in California, predominates in the French wines of the Loire, especially Vouvrays.

Chardonnay (also called Pinot Chardonnay) is the grape used for white Burgundies of such different styles as Montrachets and Chablis, and for varietal wines of differing characters in California. Pinot Blanc, also grown in Burgundy, makes a varietal white in California.

Grenache, the grape of Tavel, produces a varietal rosé in California.

Cabernet Sauvignon grapes predominate in the château bottlings of Bordeaux reds, and are the grape in the varietal counterpart from California.

Pinot Noir grapes make the classic red Burgundies (Clos de Vougeot, Échézeaux), and produce a counterpart varietal in California.

Barbera is both a grape and an appellation in Italy and in California.

There are others—*Vitis vinifera*, the wine grape, has something like 8,000 varieties altogether—but these examples are enough to suggest how wines correspond. It should be noted that they only correspond; they are not identical. Tasting for comparisons is interesting, but not a final measure.

Beyond these most specific appellations (and most expensive wines) matches are harder to strike, but possible. A California wine called Rhine would resemble a German one called Liebfraumilch or Moselblümchen at similar price levels. A California wine called Claret would approximate a French one called Bordeaux or Médoc, again at a similar price level.

**Sherries.** Sherries originated in Spain. Similar wines are made in California, often by identical methods and using related or identical grapes. (There are several varieties.) The labeling adjectives differ. California calls its Sherries Dry, Pale Dry, or Cocktail Sherry when they are intended as appetizers, and Sweet or Cream Sherry when they are used as dessert wines.

Spain has many more distinctions. Manzanilla, Fino, and Amontillado are the cocktail types, ranging from dryest to less dry. The dessert types are called Amoroso, Oloroso, or Cream.

*Solera* means the wine is aged in banks of barrels. The oldest wine is at the lowest bank. The new wine goes into the top bank. Every year, each barrel is only partially emptied, and wine from the next higher bank is used to refill, assuring continuity of old wine in each bottling.

*Flor,* a yeast which imparts a specific taste to dry Sherries, is used in both Spain and the United States. California Sherry producers always state *flor* if the wine has been aged with the yeast present. Spanish Sherries are not always so labeled but almost all dry ones are *flor* Sherries.

# Rice Pilaf Stuffing for Turkey

**MAKES ABOUT 9 CUPS**

**PREPARE AS MUCH AS 1 DAY AHEAD; STUFF TURKEY JUST BEFORE ROASTING**

½ cup pine nuts or slivered almonds
½ cup (¼ lb.) butter or margarine
1 cup finely chopped onion
3 cups uncooked long grain rice
½ cup chopped parsley
¼ teaspoon <u>each</u> cinnamon and allspice
2 teaspoons salt
¼ teaspoon pepper
5 cups chicken broth or stock

When you roast turkey for the holidays, probably you want a traditional stuffing. However, a change takes the bird out of the Thanksgiving-Day category for entertaining at other times. In Turkey, where they *do* have turkeys, contrary to the impression left by some jokes, the birds are stuffed with a rice pilaf similar to this one. Cooks there sometimes add currants (as much as ½ cup may be added in this recipe).

For those who are curious about what they call the turkey in Turkey, the name is *hindi,* which means Indian (of the country India).

Lightly toast the nuts in a 350° oven for 5 to 10 minutes. In a wide frying pan, heat butter and sauté onion about 5 minutes. Add rice and cook, stirring, over medium-high heat for about 4 minutes. Blend in parsley, cinnamon, allspice, salt, pepper, and toasted nuts.

In another pan boil broth and pour over rice mixture; stir lightly. Reduce heat to low, cover, and simmer until moisture is absorbed (25 minutes).

# Turkey Tetrazzini

**MAKES 6 TO 8 SERVINGS**

**PREPARE FOR BAKING SEVERAL HOURS AHEAD**

6 tablespoons butter or margarine
5 tablespoons flour
2½ cups chicken broth (canned or freshly made)
1¼ cups half-and-half (light cream)
½ cup dry white wine
¾ cup shredded Parmesan cheese
¾ pound mushrooms, sliced
    Salted water
8 ounces noodles (spaghetti or tagliarini)
3 to 4 cups slivers of cooked turkey
    Salt

This classic dish of slivered cooked turkey is so delicious that you may reverse the usual procedure, serving the first turkey meal to family and Leftovers Tetrazzini to the most special of guests.

Melt 2 tablespoons of the butter, mix in flour and gradually blend in the chicken broth, cream, and wine. Cook, stirring, for about 3 minutes after mixture starts to simmer. Stir in ½ cup of the Parmesan cheese. Measure out 1 cup of the sauce and blend in remaining cheese.

Melt the remaining 4 tablespoons butter in a pan, add mushrooms, and cook quickly, stirring, until lightly browned. Bring a quantity of salted water to boiling, add noodles and cook until just tender to bite, but not soft; drain. Combine the large portion of sauce, mushrooms (save a few slices for garnish), hot noodles, and turkey; salt to taste. Turn into a large shallow casserole or individual casseroles. Spoon the 1 cup of sauce evenly over the surface and top with reserved mushroom slices.

Bake in a 375° oven until bubbling; allow 15 minutes for large casserole and about 8 minutes for individual ones. Broil tops until lightly browned.

# Turkey Schnitzel

**MAKES 6 TO 8 SERVINGS**

**MARINATE MEAT AN HOUR, COOK AT LAST MINUTE**

1 whole turkey breast (about 4 lbs.), split by meat dealer
¼ cup lemon juice
½ cup olive oil
¼ teaspoon <u>each</u> salt and pepper
½ cup flour
1¼ cups grated Parmesan cheese
    Butter

Treated in veal cutlet fashion, sliced boneless turkey breast is tender and flavorful. Marinate it first in an oil and lemon juice mixture.

Remove turkey from bone; skin, and cut meat crosswise into ½-inch slices. Pound slices slightly with a flat meat mallet to flatten to about ¼-inch thickness. Shake together lemon juice, olive oil, salt, and pepper. Pour over turkey slices in a shallow bowl; cover and refrigerate for about 1 hour. Drain turkey. Coat lightly with a mixture of flour and cheese. Quickly sauté turkey slices on each side in heated butter until lightly browned.

# Pheasant-in-a-Bag

When you roast pheasant inside a well-oiled paper bag, it stays juicy and acquires a beautiful reddish-brown color without basting. The classic Port wine sauce with orange peel makes a delectable accompaniment for any game bird.

Season pheasant with salt and pepper to taste. Sprinkle the inside of the cavity with Sherry. Quarter apple, remove core, and stick clove in an apple piece. Place apple pieces inside the cavity and truss bird. Pour salad oil over a clean heavy paper bag until it is all coated. Place bird inside the bag; fold over the top and secure with 2 paper clips. Place in a roasting pan and roast in a 375° oven for 1½ to 2 hours, or until tender.

**Cumberland Sauce.** Melt currant jelly in the top of a double boiler over hot water. Stir in orange juice and Port. Mix together lemon juice, mustard, and ginger and stir in. Cover orange peel with cold water, bring to a boil, and drain. Scrape off any white membrane and cut peel into matchlike pieces, about ⅛ inch wide and ½ inch long. Add peel to sauce. Serve in a sauce bowl accompanying the pheasant.

**MAKES 3 TO 4 SERVINGS**

**BEGIN ROASTING 1½ TO 2 HOURS AHEAD**

- 1 pheasant (2½ to 3 pounds)
  Salt and pepper to taste
- 1 tablespoon pale dry Sherry
- 1 small apple
- 1 clove
  About 3 tablespoons salad oil

**CUMBERLAND SAUCE:**

- ½ cup currant jelly
- ⅓ cup <u>each</u> orange juice and Port wine
- 2 tablespoons lemon juice
- 1 teaspoon dry mustard
- ½ teaspoon powdered ginger
  Whole peel of 1 orange

# Roast Duckling with Orange Sauce

MENU FOR DUCKLING DINNER INCLUDES THIS DISH—PAGE 16

The classic entrée, Canard à l'Orange, is based on the remarkable flavor compatibility of duckling with citrus fruit. Serve with white rice and hot fresh pineapple and papaya slices.

Peel oranges with a vegetable peeler and cut the thin skin into julienne strips about 1/16 inch wide and 1 inch long. Bring 3 cups water to a boil; add orange strips, cover, and simmer for 15 minutes; drain and reserve peel. Cut the oranges into neat, skinless segments; cover and chill until ready to use.

Rinse duckling inside and out and pat dry with paper towels; strip off all extra fat. Season inside and outside with 1½ teaspoons of the salt. Sprinkle ⅓ of the prepared orange peel inside the duckling. Tie legs and tail together; skewer neck skin to the back and tuck the wing tips underneath. Prick the skin every ½ inch around the thighs, back, and lower breast with a knife. Place duckling, breast down, on a rack in an open roasting pan.

Place in a 375° oven and roast for 30 minutes. Remove extra fat from the drippings with a bulb-type baster; pour ½ cup water into the pan along with the chopped onion and carrot. Turn duckling breast side up and continue roasting about 1½ hours longer, or until the legs move freely. Remove to a platter and keep warm; reserve pan drippings in roasting pan.

Meanwhile, simmer the giblets with the remaining ½ teaspoon salt and bay leaf in 3 cups water until tender, about 1½ hours. Remove giblets and bay leaf; cook down stock until reduced to 2 cups and add chicken stock base. Simmer wine vinegar and sugar until the liquid turns a caramel color; pour into the prepared duckling stock.

Skim fat from the roasting pan and discard. Add Port to the remaining drippings in the pan and heat, stirring to loosen bits stuck to pan. Pour through a wire strainer, discarding vegetables, and add drippings to the prepared duckling stock mixture; bring to a boil. Blend together the cornstarch and cold water and stir in. Cook, stirring constantly, until thick and smooth. Add the reserved orange peel and the curaçao. Taste for seasoning. Swirl butter into the sauce.

Garnish duckling with orange segments and pass sauce in a gravy dish.

**MAKES 4 SERVINGS**

**BEGIN ROASTING AT LEAST 2½ HOURS BEFORE SERVING**

- 3 oranges
  Water
- 4½ to 5-pound ready-to-cook duckling, thawed
- 2 teaspoons salt
- 1 onion, chopped
- 1 carrot, chopped
- 1 bay leaf
- 2 teaspoons chicken stock base
- ¼ cup red wine vinegar
- 3 tablespoons sugar
- ½ cup Port or Madeira
- 2 tablespoons cornstarch blended with ¼ cup cold water
- 1 tablespoon curaçao or other orange-flavored liqueur
- 1 tablespoon butter

# SEAFOOD

The variety of seafoods available in the West is such that it is impossible to include recipes for every kind. Nevertheless, one or more recipes for each of the most popular and easily available types follow. A page of instructions for cooking fish (page 128) presents basic techniques and sauces appropriate for any kind of fish you may want to serve. On the whole, these seafood recipes are both simple and imaginative. Many may be made ahead or very quickly prepared at the last minute.

## Individual Seafood Soufflés

**MAKES 6 SERVINGS**

**PREPARE 3 HOURS TO 1 DAY AHEAD**

**INDIVIDUAL 3-INCH SOUFFLÉ DISHES OR OTHER STRAIGHT-SIDED DISHES REQUIRED**

2  envelopes unflavored gelatin
½  cup dry white wine
1  bottle (8 oz.) clam juice
1  can (10 oz.) frozen shrimp soup, thawed
4  eggs, separated
3  packages (6 oz. <u>each</u>) frozen king crab meat, thawed
⅓  pound cooked small shrimp
¾  cup whipping cream
   Chopped chives
   Suggested garnishes: cherry tomatoes, sliced cucumbers, hard-cooked egg halves, diagonally sliced celery sticks, carrot sticks

Cold soufflés, unlike the hot kind, are not destined to fall sooner or later, because they are stabilized with gelatin. They are no more difficult to make than many gelatin salads, yet the cooked sauce and whipped cream within give a distinctive flavor and texture. Make the soufflés ahead and garnish the sides with chopped chives right before serving.

Sprinkle gelatin into a medium-sized pan, pour in wine and let stand until gelatin softens. Add clam juice and shrimp soup and heat until hot through. Beat egg yolks until light and gradually stir in part of the hot soup mixture. Return to the pan, and cook a few minutes, stirring constantly. Cool, then chill until mixture starts to set.

   Flake crab meat and reserve ½ cup for garnish. Mix in remaining crab meat and shrimp (save a few for garnish). Beat egg whites until stiff and fold in. Whip cream until stiff and fold in. Fold 8-inch strips of waxed paper into thirds lengthwise and place around six 3-inch individual soufflé dishes making 1½-inch collars; secure with paper clips. Spoon in soufflé mixture, letting it rise above the edge of the dishes 1 inch. Chill until firm.

   To serve, run a knife between the edge of the waxed paper and soufflé mixture and remove paper collars. Press finely chopped chives onto the sides of the rims of each soufflé. Arrange reserved crab and shrimp on top. Place soufflés on salad-sized plates and surround each with several cherry tomatoes, cucumber slices, 1 or 2 hard-cooked egg halves, celery or carrot sticks.

## Smoked Fish in Caper Cream Sauce

**MAKES 4 SERVINGS**

**PREPARE SEVERAL HOURS AHEAD, REHEAT**

1  to 1½ pounds kippered salmon or kippered cod
2  tablespoons butter or margarine
2  tablespoons flour
1  cup half-and-half (light cream)
1  tablespoon chopped capers
4  prepared patty shells or 4 slices toast

The description of this simple lunch or brunch main dish is a real tongue-twister, especially if you make it with cod rather than with salmon. Serve kippered, creamed, and capered cod on something crisp and crunchy—such as toast points or patty shells.

Steam the kippered salmon or kippered cod in any kind of steamer, improvised if necessary. (Set fish on rack above boiling water, cover, and steam just until heated through. A 1-pound piece of fish takes 10 to 15 minutes.) Using two forks, flake into bite-sized pieces while hot, removing the bones. Meanwhile, melt the butter or margarine in a pan; stir in the flour and cook until bubbly. Remove from heat while you slowly stir in the light cream. Add the chopped capers and cook, stirring, until thickened. Stir in the hot fish. Serve in the patty shells or on crisp toast points.

*Clams Bordelaise—see page 132*

# Freezer Seafood Newburg

MAKES ABOUT 4 SERVINGS

FREEZABLE

2   cups (about ¾ lb.) coarsely
        chopped cooked lobster,
        crab, or shrimp
2   tablespoons butter or margarine,
        melted
1   tablespoon each flour and rice
        flour
¼   teaspoon each salt and paprika
        Dash each cayenne and nutmeg
2   cups half-and-half (light cream)
¼   cup dry Sherry (optional)
        Toasted English muffins or hot,
        cooked rice
        Chopped parsley

This popular dish with Sherry-flavored cream sauce can be made from one or several kinds of shellfish. You freeze it in either large or individual casseroles, reheat without waiting for it to thaw. Rice flour is used in part to thicken the sauce because it withstands freezing better than flour or cornstarch. It is sold in health food stores and Oriental markets.

Arrange seafood evenly in four 4½-inch individual foil pans, one 8-inch foil cake pan, or a temperature-resistant 1-quart casserole. Drizzle evenly with melted butter. Mix flour, rice flour, salt, paprika, cayenne, and nutmeg in a small pan. Gradually stir in half-and-half to make a smooth mixture. Heat to simmering, stirring until thickened. Blend in Sherry. Pour sauce over seafood. Freeze quickly, then wrap well and store in the freezer.

To serve, bake uncovered in a 350° oven until sauce is hot and bubbly, about 30 minutes for individual casseroles or about 1 hour for a large one. Stir gently to blend sauce and seafood. Serve over toasted English muffins or cooked rice, sprinkled with chopped parsley.

# Lobster Imperial

MAKES 6 SERVINGS

COOK LOBSTER IN TOMATO SAUCE
    AS MUCH AS 1 DAY AHEAD;
    MAKE HOLLANDAISE A DAY
    AHEAD ALSO

4   tablespoons butter
1   tablespoon salad oil
6   frozen rock lobster tails
        (about 8 oz. each), thawed
        and split in half lengthwise
1   medium-sized carrot, finely
        chopped
1   medium-sized onion, finely
        chopped
2   cloves garlic, minced
½   teaspoon salt
⅓   cup brandy (optional)
4   tablespoons tomato paste
⅓   cup bottled clam juice
1½  cups dry white wine
½   teaspoon tarragon (crumbled)
½   pound medium-sized mushrooms
1   tablespoon lemon juice
        Hot steamed white rice

HOLLANDAISE SAUCE:

¾   cup butter
3   egg yolks
2   tablespoons lemon juice

This is a very special dish as the name implies. Not only are lobster tails on the expensive side, but you take the trouble to simmer them in one sauce and to glaze and broil them with another. Nevertheless, preparation is much simplified by doing part of the work beforehand, and the result is worth the effort.

Heat 2 tablespoons butter and 1 tablespoon salad oil in a large frying pan. Put in lobster tails, meat side down, and the carrot and onion; sauté on high heat for 2 minutes. Add garlic and salt. Warm brandy, ignite, and spoon flaming over the tails. Add tomato paste, clam juice, wine, and tarragon. Cover and simmer 5 to 6 minutes. Remove lobster tails from pan and let cool; loosen meat from shells. Chill until serving time.

Simmer sauce 10 minutes longer to blend flavors; then purée in a blender or push through a wire strainer. Slice mushrooms and sauté in the remaining 2 tablespoons butter with lemon juice; stir into the puréed tomato sauce. Chill.

To serve, place chilled lobster tails on a baking pan and heat in a 350° oven for 10 minutes. With a small spatula, spread a thick layer of Hollandaise over the lobster meat. Slip under the broiler and broil 1 minute, or until sauce browns. Serve on steamed rice; accompany with sauce bowl of reheated mushroom sauce.

**Hollandaise Sauce.** Heat ¾ cup butter until melted and bubbly. In a blender place egg yolks and 2 tablespoons lemon juice; blend a few seconds, then, with motor running, gradually pour in the hot butter in a slow steady stream. Blend just until the melted butter is incorporated into the sauce. Makes 1 cup. (Make this ahead and chill, but let warm to room temperature before using.)

# Swordfish Piraeus

A fish kebab, usually of swordfish, is much loved in Greece and neighboring countries. Whole bay leaves are threaded on the skewers for the smoky flavor they give the fish. Lemon juice and dried oregano are sprinkled over the fish after cooking. Sometimes in those countries, chunks of unpeeled lemon are also skewered between other ingredients—many people there consider the charred peel delicious.

For marinade, mix together in a bowl the oil, wine, lemon juice, salt, oregano, garlic salt, and onion. Cut fish steaks into 1¼-inch squares, place in the marinade, cover and chill overnight, turning several times. Cut pepper in half, remove seeds, and cut in 1¼-inch squares.

Compose 6 skewers in the following pattern: Alternate 1 piece swordfish, 1 square pepper, swordfish, bay leaf, tomato, swordfish, bay leaf, tomato, swordfish, pepper, swordfish, and end with a mushroom cap, stem removed.

Broil skewers in a preheated broiler (or barbecue over medium coals) for 10 minutes, turning to brown both sides and basting several times with the marinade. Accompany with lemon wedges and a small dish of oregano.

**MAKES 6 SERVINGS**

**MARINATE FISH OVERNIGHT, BROIL JUST BEFORE SERVING**

- ¼ cup salad oil or olive oil
- ½ cup dry white wine
- 2 tablespoons lemon juice
- 1 teaspoon each salt and dried oregano (crumbled)
- ¼ teaspoon garlic salt
- 1 tablespoon instant minced onion
- 3 swordfish steaks (about 2 pounds), cut ¾ inch thick
- 1 large green pepper
- 12 bay leaves
- 12 cherry tomatoes
- 6 mushrooms (about 1½ inches in diameter)
- 1 lemon, cut in wedges
  Oregano

# Salmon with Tarragon Dressing

*MENU FOR COLD SALMON BUFFET INCLUDES THIS DISH—PAGE 48*

A cold baked salmon with head and tail left on is the most attractive buffet dish. However, for other types of meals, a 6 to 8-pound piece of halibut or giant sea bass may be used instead of the salmon. A tapered piece from the tail end of the fish will look best when served. There is no need to cut the piece in half, as directed for the salmon, because it will fit on the baking pan. If more than about 3½ inches thick, the piece may take 15 to 20 minutes longer to bake. Chill, mask, and serve as directed for salmon.

Have fish cleaned but don't remove the head and tail. Sprinkle the 1 teaspoon salt and dash pepper inside the fish and dot with the butter. Cut fish in half crosswise.

Cover an 11 by 15-inch shallow baking pan with lettuce leaves and place both halves of the fish on the lettuce. Bake uncovered in a 400° oven for 1 hour or until fish flakes easily. Cool, then chill several hours or overnight.

To make the mask, mix together the mayonnaise (or mayonnaise and sour cream), tarragon, lemon juice, onion, ¾ teaspoon salt, and ¼ teaspoon pepper; chill.

To serve the fish, put the two halves together again on a large serving platter. (You may need to cut a thin slice from each cut end to allow the two halves to fit together neatly.) Then spread half of the mayonnaise mixture over the surface of the fish, leaving the head and tail exposed. Spoon the remaining mayonnaise mixture into a bowl to serve with the fish.

For the first servings, cut down only to the backbone of the salmon; when the top half has been completely served, carefully remove the spine and adjoining bones. The bottom side of the fish is then ready for second servings with the extra dressing. Garnish the whole fish with lemon slices, cherry tomatoes, and parsley.

**MAKES 12 SERVINGS**

**BAKE FISH AS MUCH AS A DAY AHEAD**

**FINISH PREPARATION SEVERAL HOURS AHEAD**

- 1 whole salmon, 6 to 8 pounds
- 1 teaspoon salt
  Dash pepper
- 3 tablespoons butter or margarine
- ½ small head lettuce
- 2 cups mayonnaise (or use half sour cream)
- 1 tablespoon crushed tarragon
- 2 tablespoons lemon juice
- 1 tablespoon minced onion
- ¾ teaspoon salt
- ¼ teaspoon pepper
  Lemon slices, cherry tomatoes, parsley for garnish

# FISH—SIMPLY COOKED AND ELEGANTLY SAUCED

Fresh fish, simply cooked, then served with an appropriate sauce, is something you can offer with pride to your most discriminating guests.

## COOKING THE FISH

Butter-sautéed, broiled, or barbecued fish is usually served hot, but poached fish is good either hot or cold. Cold, it's delicious in warm weather and easy on the hostess.

**Butter-Sautéing.** The French term is *à la meunière*. This method is most suitable for fillets of sole, flounder, or rockfish; for thin steaks of salmon or halibut; or for small, whole fish such as trout, perch, or smelt.

In a frying pan, heat butter, margarine, or part salad oil (¼ inch deep) until bubbly. Dip fish pieces in flour and sprinkle with salt and pepper. Sauté over medium-high heat until browned, turn, and brown other side—about 1 minute on each side for sole fillet, about 3 minutes on a side for trout.

*Sauce Beurre à la Meunière.* Sprinkle fish with chopped parsley. Add a little extra butter to the pan and brown lightly; add a few drops lemon juice and pour over fish immediately.

**Poaching.** This simple method is suitable for all types of fish. Much depends on having a good flavorful poaching liquid.

To prepare rich fish stock, ask your fish dealer for 1 to 2 pounds fish trimmings. Put fish trimmings into a large pan with 4 cups water (or 3 cups water and 1 cup white wine), 1 tablespoon lemon juice or vinegar, 2 teaspoons salt, 1 bay leaf, 1 medium-sized onion (sliced), 1 *each* carrot and celery stalk (sliced), a handful of parsley, and 3 whole black peppers. Bring to a boil, then reduce heat and simmer 1 hour. Let stand about 1 hour, then strain.

To poach fish, bring fish stock to a boil and pour over fish in a greased baking pan (or wrap fish pieces in cheese-cloth and gently lower into the boiling stock). Cover pan and put into a 425° oven—or reduce heat and simmer on top of the range—until fish flakes when tested with a fork. Watch carefully. Small pieces take only a few minutes. Serve with a sauce.

**Oven-Broiling.** Any fish steak, fillet, or small, dressed, whole fish can be broiled. White, lean fish should be dusted lightly with seasoned flour, then sprinkled with melted butter; fat fish such as salmon, trout, albacore, or swordfish need only be basted well with butter.

Put either type of fish on a well-greased broiler rack or hinged broiler and place in a preheated broiler about 2 inches from source of heat for thin pieces, to about 6 inches for thick fish. Broil until browned and the fish flakes with a fork; fillets are broiled just on one side; steaks and whole fish should be basted, turned, and broiled until browned on other side; this takes 4 to 10 minutes, depending on thickness.

**Barbecuing over Coals.** Good choices are fairly thick fish steaks or fillets (salmon, albacore, sea bass, swordfish, sablefish) or small whole fish (trout or mackerel). Place on greased grill or hinged broiler over moderately hot coals. Grill, turning once and basting often, until fish is browned and flakes with a fork. Baste with melted butter; with equal parts butter and lemon juice; or with equal parts of butter, lemon juice, and Sherry or Vermouth.

## FISH SAUCES

**Hollandaise with Cucumber** (for salmon, halibut, trout, albacore). Combine in the blender 3 egg yolks (at room temperature) and 1½ tablespoons lemon juice. Melt ¾ cup butter or margarine and heat until it bubbles—don't brown. Add 1 tablespoon hot water to the egg, turn blender on high speed, and immediately pour in hot butter in a steady stream (takes about 5 seconds). Add 1 teaspoon prepared mustard and ½ teaspoon salt and whirl until blended, about 30 seconds. Turn into a bowl and stir in 1 tablespoon *each* chopped parsley and chives, plus 1 peeled and seeded cucumber, chopped.

**Hollandaise with Shrimp** (for salmon, sole, halibut, sea bass, rockfish). Prepare preceding hollandaise sauce, except omit salt and cucumber. Stir in 1 can (about 5 oz.) shrimp (rinsed and drained).

**Tomato Sauce** (for halibut, rockfish, sea bass, swordfish, albacore). Sauté 1 medium-sized onion (chopped) in ¼ cup butter or margarine until soft. Add 1 crushed clove garlic, ½ teaspoon thyme, ¼ teaspoon crushed rosemary, and 1 can (1 lb.) stewed tomatoes (break up tomatoes with spoon). Simmer, uncovered, stirring occasionally, until reduced to about half—takes about 15 minutes. Add salt and pepper to taste.

**Brown Butter Almond Sauce** (for any fish, but best with salmon, halibut, trout). Heat 1 cup (½ lb.) butter until it turns a golden brown; cool to lukewarm. Into a bowl put 2 egg yolks, ½ teaspoon dry mustard, dash cayenne, and 1 tablespoon lemon juice; beat until blended. Slowly add the lukewarm butter (about 1 tablespoon at a time), beating constantly. As mixture thickens, you can beat in butter in a slow stream. Beat in 1 tablespoon *each* hot water and dry Sherry. Stir in ½ cup toasted, slivered almonds. If too stiff, beat in a little more hot water.

# Kauai Fillet of Sole

Delicate sautéed sole entrées demand last-minute cooking to be at their best. When you prepare this sole and avocado dish (named for the Hawaiian isle of Kauai) have ready the floured fillets, sliced avocado, and chopped macadamias. Have guests start eating salad; then cook the fillets in an electric frying pan right at the table, or on a serving cart.

Sprinkle sole with salt and pepper and 1 tablespoon of the lime juice; let stand for 10 minutes. Dip fish in flour to coat all sides, shaking off the excess. At the table, heat about half the butter in an electric frying pan set at 350°; add fillets and brown about 3 minutes on one side. Turn fillets, add remaining butter, and cook until nicely browned. Remove fish to a warm serving platter and sprinkle with remaining lime juice. To the pan add the cream and bring to a rapid boil, scraping browned particles free; spoon over fish. Top with avocado slices and the macadamia nuts. Serve at once. Pass lime wedges.

**MAKES 4 SERVINGS**

**PREPARE AT TABLE IN ELECTRIC FRYING PAN**

- 4 large sole fillets (1 to 1½ pounds)
  Salt and pepper
- 2 tablespoons lime juice
  Flour
- 3 or 4 tablespoons butter or margarine
- ¼ cup heavy cream
- 1 large avocado, peeled, seeded, and sliced lengthwise
- ¼ cup coarsely chopped macadamia nuts
  Lime wedges

# Sole Oyster Roll

Sole fillets are just the right size to serve as wrapper for a spoonful of savory oyster and onion filling. They are easily rolled up and quickly fastened with a toothpick. Poach the stuffed fillets in the oven.

Sauté the celery, parsley, and onion in the butter for about 3 minutes. Drain oysters and coarsely chop them. Add the chopped oysters to the vegetables and stir to blend over moderate heat; mix in the bread crumbs and continue to cook, stirring, for about 5 minutes. Spoon mixture onto lightly salted sole fillets; roll, and secure ends with picks.

Place the rolls in a greased, shallow baking dish or pan in about ½ inch of the mixture of wine and water (or water with a little lemon juice added). Cover and poach in a 350° oven for 20 to 25 minutes, or until the meat will flake when probed with a fork. When cooked, sprinkle lightly with pepper; remove to a warm platter, reserve stock.

Meanwhile, start heating the can of soup in a small pan; thin it slightly with 1 to 2 tablespoons of the fish stock. Place sole rolls on a serving plate and spoon the sauce over the top. Garnish with parsley or onion.

**MAKES 6 TO 8 SERVINGS**

**PREPARE ROLLS TO POACH SEVERAL HOURS AHEAD**

- 3 tablespoons chopped celery
- 2 tablespoons chopped parsley
- 1 tablespoon minced onion
- 3 tablespoons butter
  About 1 pint fresh oysters
- ½ cup soft bread crumbs
  Salt
- 8 small sole fillets (about 1½ lbs.)
  About ½ cup each dry white wine and water
  White (or black) pepper
- 1 can (10½ oz.) cream of celery soup
  Chopped parsley or sliced green onion

# Brazilian Baked Trout

A good catch of fresh trout is often reason enough for a party. Victorious fishermen, who want to savor the freshness of the fish, demand it be cooked simply. This Brazilian treatment is subtle, uses many of the traditional seasonings which bring out natural fish flavor.

Wash and dry trout with paper towels; rub outside with lemon juice and sprinkle with salt. Arrange the minced garlic in the bottom of a buttered, shallow baking dish large enough to hold trout in a single layer. Place trout in dish; pour wine over top. Sprinkle the parsley, green onion, and dry bread crumbs over trout; then spoon on butter. Bake in a 400° oven for 20 minutes. Serve from baking dish.

**MAKES 4 TO 6 SERVINGS**

**PREPARE FOR BAKING AHEAD, COOK JUST BEFORE SERVING**

- 4 to 6 medium-sized trout (about ½ pound each)
  Juice of 1 lemon
- 1 teaspoon salt
- 1 clove garlic, minced or mashed
- 1 cup white wine
- 2 tablespoons each chopped parsley, green onion rings, and dry bread crumbs
- 4 tablespoons melted butter

# Tahitian Curried Prawns

MENU FOR TAHITIAN PARTY INCLUDES THIS DISH—PAGE 49

**MAKES 12 SERVINGS**

| | |
|---|---|
| 2 | large onions, chopped fine |
| 6 | tablespoons melted butter |
| 5 | to 6 pounds (about 7 dozen) large prawns, washed and drained |
| 6 | cloves garlic, minced or mashed |
| 4 | to 5 teaspoons curry powder |
| 1 | cup sweet Sauterne |
| ½ | cup freshly chopped parsley |
| | About 8 cups steamed, hot rice |

Large Baja California prawns make a very good substitute for the fresh-water prawns found in Tahitian waters. Serve them over fluffy steamed rice, so the seasoned butter and wine cooking juices aren't lost. To eat, pick up the prawns in your fingers, suck out the juices, then break off the shell and eat the meat with fingers or with a fork.

Sauté onions in melted butter until yellow. Add prawns, then garlic and curry. Stir well. Add wine. Cover and cook over very low heat 15 minutes. Just before serving, sprinkle with the freshly chopped parsley. Serve with fluffy rice.

# Onigari Yaki

*JAPANESE SKEWERED SHRIMP*

**MAKES 6 SERVINGS**

**PREPARE SAUCE AND THREAD SKEWERS AHEAD**

**6 LONG SKEWERS NEEDED**

| | |
|---|---|
| ½ | cup Mirin (Japanese wine) or Sherry |
| 1 | cup soy sauce |
| 1 | tablespoon sugar |
| 36 | large shrimp or prawns (about 3 lbs.) |

In Japan these shrimp are threaded on bamboo skewers in a fancy serpentine design. The design pattern is not necessary, but definitely is worth the little bit of extra trouble it takes. To make this design, thread skewer through: (1) head of one shrimp, its body curved down; (2) head of second shrimp, body curved up; (3) tail of first shrimp; (4) head of a third shrimp, body curved down; (5) tail of second upcurved shrimp; (6) head of a fourth shrimp, body curved up; etc. Are you confused? Imagine how the poor shrimp feel!

In a small saucepan, combine wine or Sherry, soy sauce, and sugar; bring to a boil. Thread 6 shrimp or prawns on each of 6 skewers. Cook over hot coals, brushing constantly with sauce until shrimp are shiny and glazed.

# Oyster Pan Roast

**MAKES 2 SERVINGS**

**PARTIALLY PREPARE A FEW HOURS AHEAD, FINISH AT SERVING TIME**

| | |
|---|---|
| 5 | tablespoons butter |
| 2 | teaspoons minced shallots or green onions |
| 1 | medium-sized green pepper, seeded and finely chopped |
| ¼ | pound mushrooms, each cut in quarters |
| 1 | canned whole pimiento (or 1 tablespoon), chopped |
| 2 | tablespoons **each** chicken broth and dry red wine |
| 18 | oysters, each about 2 inches long |
| | About 8 hot buttered toast triangles or 1 cup hot cooked rice |
| | Parsley sprigs |

Green peppers, pimientos, and mushrooms give exceptional character to this remarkably quick entrée. The recipe is for two persons only, but you can easily increase quantities to serve more. Use fresh or frozen oysters (extra-small ones if possible—about 20 to 30 per pint).

Melt about 1 tablespoon of the butter in a wide frying pan and add the shallots, then the green peppers. Cook, stirring, over moderately high heat just until pepper turns brighter green; set aside in a shallow pan or dish.

In the same frying pan melt about 1 more tablespoon butter and add the mushrooms. Cook, stirring, over moderately high heat, just until mushrooms look moistened evenly by butter and are very lightly browned. Put in the pan with the green peppers but keep separate. Put the pimiento in the pan, also.

When you are ready to serve, melt the remaining butter (or about 3 tablespoons of it) in the same wide frying pan and add the oysters. Heat gently over moderate heat for about 1½ minutes, then add the pepper, mushrooms, pimiento, broth, and wine. Bring to a boil and simmer for 2 minutes to heat through.

With a slotted spoon, transfer oysters and vegetables to a serving dish and boil pan juices until reduced about half. Garnish the oysters with parsley sprigs and add toast or rice. Pour the pan juices over oysters.

# THE VERSATILE OMELET

The omelet is probably the most versatile dish ever invented, and the handiest solution for impromptu entertaining. Though your cupboard may be bare, you probably have plenty of eggs and butter in the refrigerator. You can invite a small group over for breakfast, lunch, light supper, or midnight snack whenever the mood strikes—and serve everyone in minutes. If you have bread or toast, breakfast meats or green salad, and fresh fruit, you have a complete meal. Undoubtedly you have other simple ingredients to add (such as grated cheese, sliced mushrooms, green onions, and herbs) if you want to perk up a plain omelet.

A good omelet is tender and golden, never browned, firm but delicate outside, smooth and creamy inside. Admittedly, it takes practice to produce such perfection, but few dishes are practiced so easily and quickly. Just make omelets instead of scrambled eggs for breakfast a few days in a row. Each should take only a minute or two to make. Soon you will have the knack and necessary confidence for serving a small group of people quickly.

Six or 8 guests are about the maximum suggested for an omelet meal. If an omelet is to be the entrée, plan to make a 3-egg one for each person. Sweetened omelets filled with jam or fruit are also good side dishes or desserts; one or two eggs per person will suffice for these.

**The Pan-Egg Ratio.** The success of your omelet depends on the size and shape of the pan and the number of eggs in the omelet. You can use a classic omelet pan or any fairly heavy pan with similar up-curved edges.

Measure the diameter of the rim to determine the number of eggs properly used in that particular pan: 6 to 6½ inches, one egg; 7 to 7½ inches, two eggs, 8 to 8½ inches, three eggs; 9 to 9½ inches, four eggs; 10 to 10½ inches, five eggs; 11 to 11½ inches, six eggs. An omelet any larger than six-egg size is awkward to handle.

**Care of Your Omelet Pan.** A good cook never uses an omelet pan for any other purpose and never washes it. Its oily seasoning can be ruined if other foods are cooked in it. Some omelet pans you may buy are treated so eggs won't stick. If not, season a pan by pouring in about ½ inch of salad oil and heating it until the oil smokes slightly; let oil cool in the pan; drain and wipe pan clean.

After cooking with your omelet pan, simply wipe it clean with a dry cloth or paper towel. If egg should cling, sprinkle with salt and rub clean. *Never* scour the pan with cleanser or other abrasive.

**Breaking and Beating.** Basic proportions are 1 teaspoon of water for each egg used, a little salt (¼ teaspoon for every three eggs), and a dash of pepper.

Break the eggs into a bowl (enough for one omelet at a time—or all the omelets you plan to make, so that you can later dip out single-omelet portions). Add water, salt,

and pepper. Beat vigorously with a fork for about 30 seconds, or until yolks and whites are blended.

**Heating the Pan.** Heat 1 teaspoon whole butter or margarine on medium-high heat until it bubbles, browns ever so slightly, and gives off a rich, nutlike odor.

**Pouring in Eggs.** Pour beaten eggs for one omelet all at once into heated pan. They should begin to set almost immediately. Slide pan rapidly back and forth on the burner, keeping omelet in motion and free from the bottom of the pan to avoid browning and sticking.

**Cooking.** As soon as the bottom of the omelet begins to set, slip a thin spatula well under the edges and let the uncooked eggs flow underneath to the center of the pan. This lifting, along with frequent shaking, causes the rippled surface and irregular edges characteristic of a good omelet.

*Most important to remember is that the omelet should never brown; it should be the same color outside as inside.* Browned egg will be tough, not crisp.

Your omelet is done when the egg no longer runs freely but the top still looks liquid and creamy. If you're going to add a filling, do so now—quickly. Spoon about 2 teaspoons filling per egg in the center of the omelet directly in line with the handle.

**The Final Turnout.** Hold pan with your left hand and tilt pan sideways, lifting left side off the heat. With your right hand, use spatula to fold right side of omelet (about ⅓) over the center. (If left handed, reverse process.)

Now holding the omelet pan in your right hand over a hot serving dish, rotate pan to where, as you shake the pan and ease with the spatula, the omelet will slip out.

Don't hesitate now. With a quick downward flick of the wrist, let the folded section of the omelet neatly fall over its extended edge on the hot plate.

# Clams Bordelaise

MAKES 4 SERVINGS

PREPARE CLAMS AND RICE JUST
   BEFORE SERVING

4   tablespoons butter
4   tablespoons finely chopped
      parsley
1   or 2 cloves garlic, minced or
      mashed
2   cups regular strength chicken
      broth
1   cup dry white wine (or ¼ cup
      lemon juice with ¾ cup
      chicken broth)
3   dozen small hardshell clams,
      washed well
1   to 2 cups hot, steamed rice

If you first start cooking the rice and then begin the clams, both should be ready to serve about the same time. Those who like plain steamed clams will find this dish equally pleasing in its simplicity. *(Photograph on page 125.)*

Heat the butter in a large, heavy pan. Add the parsley and garlic and sauté 1 to 2 minutes. Pour in the chicken broth and wine and bring to a boil. Add the clams, cover, and steam until clams open, about 5 to 10 minutes.

To serve, spoon some of the hot rice into each large soup bowl or soup plate. Arrange opened clams in each bowl, then pour over the broth and serve immediately.

# Chafing Dish Scallops

MAKES 4 SERVINGS

COOK AT LAST MINUTE IN
   PRESENCE OF GUESTS

¼   cup (⅛ lb.) butter or margarine
¾   cup sliced unblanched almonds
1½  pounds scallops
½   cup half-and-half (light cream)
3   tablespoons finely chopped
      parsley
½   teaspoon salt
⅛   teaspoon oregano
      Dash pepper
2   tablespoons dry Sherry
1   tablespoon cornstarch
1½  teaspoons lemon juice
      Hot cooked rice

These scallops with fluffy rice, green beans, flaky dinner rolls, and dry white wine will serve as lunch, supper, or after-theater meal. Have ingredients ready, cook the dish before the eyes of your guests.

Melt butter in blazer (top) pan of chafing dish over direct heat; add almonds, and cook until lightly browned. Stir in scallops; cook, gently stirring occasionally, until scallops lose their translucent look. Blend in half-and-half, parsley, salt, oregano, and pepper. Blend Sherry smoothly with cornstarch; stir into scallops and cook, stirring occasionally, until thickened. Blend in lemon juice. Serve with rice.

# Abalone Parmigiana

MAKES 6 SERVINGS

BREAD, FRY, AND BROIL JUST
   BEFORE SERVING

2   eggs
½   teaspoon salt
¼   teaspoon pepper
¾   cup fine dry bread crumbs
⅓   cup grated Parmesan cheese
6   slices abalone, fresh or frozen
      and thawed
⅓   cup olive oil
1   can (8 oz.) tomato sauce
2   tablespoons dry red wine
1   can (4½ oz.) sliced ripe olives,
      drained
1   package (6 oz.) sliced
      Mozzarella cheese

Prepared similarly to veal cutlets, this abalone has an Italian touch—cheese in the crumb coating and a pizza-like topping. Use instructions below if the abalone you buy is not already tenderized.

Beat eggs with salt and pepper until light. Mix together the bread crumbs and grated cheese. Pound abalone if it has not already been tenderized. Use a wooden mallet, empty wine bottle, or side of a hammer. Hit meat lightly and rhythmically until it feels soft and velvety, like a limp pancake.

Dip abalone slices in the egg mixture and then in crumbs. Using a large frying pan, fry steaks in olive oil about 1 minute on each side. Arrange in a 9 by 13-inch greased baking pan. Mix together tomato sauce, wine, and olives and spoon over the abalone slices. Arrange ½ slice of cheese over each piece of abalone. Place under the broiler until cheese melts.

# VARIED ENTRÉES

These recipes are for main dishes featuring mixtures of meats and/or seafood, pastas, mushrooms, vegetables, cheese, and eggs. Most are light dishes, suitable for lunches, brunches, or late suppers (you may want to use some of these for impromptu entertaining). Several of these dishes are hearty enough and contain such varied ingredients that they may comprise a whole meal if accompanied by a salad, bread, and simple dessert.

## Paella

*MENU FOR SPANISH PAELLA MEAL INCLUDES THIS DISH—PAGE 13*

Paella ("pah-*ey*-yuh") is the classic Spanish potpourri of saffron-flavored rice cooked with meats and other things—a liberal definition, perhaps, but one that suggests the extraordinary variety of combinations typical of this meal-in-one-dish. *(Photograph on page 135.)*

The Spanish cook it in a special wide, shallow frying pan called a paella pan. Such pans are available in kitchenware specialty shops in the larger cities here. If you have a frying pan 14 inches or more in diameter, it will be large enough; otherwise do the browning of the meats in two medium-sized frying pans, then blend all together in a big, deeper pan. The least tidy (and most aromatic) part of the cooking can be done the day before.

Have your meatman cut up the chicken as usual, then chop each piece into smaller sections. The cooked lobster is easier to eat if you free the meat from the shell and then put it back in place to serve. The shrimp are cooked in their shells; guests peel them to eat (you can shell before cooking, but the shrimp aren't considered as flavorful). *See note below about deveining shrimp.*

Heat 2 tablespoons of the oil in a very wide frying pan (or 2 regular-sized pans) and add onions; cook over high heat, stirring, until soft and lightly browned. Push onions to one side of the pan. Sprinkle pork and chicken with about 1½ teaspoons of the salt. Brown pork cubes on all sides over high heat, then push pork to one side of the pan. You will have to scrape free the accumulating browned particles continuously. Add chicken to pan, a few pieces at a time to avoid crowding, and as pieces become well browned remove to a small bowl.

Pour remaining oil into pan if needed. Crumble chorizos in pan, add tomato and rice, and continue cooking over high heat, stirring, until rice is lightly toasted. Return chicken and pork to cooked mixture. (At this point you can cool the mixture and refrigerate, covered, overnight. Reheat to use.)

Mix 4 cups of the chicken broth and saffron into the hot rice mixture. Cook rapidly, stirring, for 10 minutes. Then add the shrimp and lobster (thawed if frozen) and an additional 1½ cups broth. Cook rapidly, uncovered and stirring frequently, for about 20 minutes more or until rice is tender (add more broth if needed to prevent sticking).

Carefully fold in pimiento, ½ cup parsley, and salt to taste. If desired, keep the paella warm as long as 45 minutes in a 300° oven before serving. Arrange lobster and shrimp over surface of the rice and sprinkle with more parsley.

*Note: To devein shrimp without shelling, insert a thin wooden or metal skewer into the back of each shrimp just below the vein and gently pull to surface; repeat several times as required for each shrimp.*

**MAKES 8 SERVINGS**

**PARTIALLY PREPARE AS MUCH AS A DAY AHEAD**

| | |
|---|---|
| 2 | to 4 tablespoons olive oil or salad oil |
| 4 | large onions, chopped |
| 1 | pound lean, boneless pork, cut in ¾-inch cubes |
| 3 | pound broiler-fryer chicken, cut in about 2-inch pieces |
| | About 2 teaspoons salt |
| 2 | medium-sized (about 6 oz. total) mildly seasoned chorizos, casings removed |
| 1 | large peeled, seeded, and diced tomato |
| 1½ | cups uncooked long grain rice |
| 5½ | to 6 cups chicken broth (canned or freshly made) |
| ⅟₁₆ | teaspoon saffron |
| 1½ | pounds large shrimp, deveined and unshelled (see directions) |
| 4 | small (about ½ lb. each) rock lobster tails, split lengthwise |
| 1 | can (4 oz.) whole pimientos, thickly sliced |
| | About ½ cup minced parsley |

# Pastitsio

*MENU FOR GREEK BUFFET INCLUDES THIS DISH—PAGE 32*

**MAKES 10 SERVINGS**

**PREPARE FOR BAKING UP TO 8 HOURS AHEAD**

2 medium-sized onions, chopped
¼ cup (⅛ lb.) butter or margarine
2 pounds lean ground beef
Dash each cinnamon, cloves, and allspice
2 teaspoons salt
½ teaspoon pepper
½ cup water
2 tablespoons tomato paste
Macaroni Filling (recipe follows)
¾ cup grated Parmesan cheese
Cream Sauce (recipe follows)

**MACARONI FILLING:**

1 package (1 lb.) elbow macaroni
3 eggs
1 teaspoon salt

**CREAM SAUCE:**

6 tablespoons butter
¾ cup flour
1 quart milk
3 eggs
1 teaspoon salt

For those simple dinners where you might customarily serve spaghetti or some baked Italian pasta, try this similar and equally good Greek macaroni dish. Its very smooth texture is due to liberal use of eggs and cream sauce, which blend the other ingredients as they bake.

Sauté the onion in the butter until golden. Add meat and cook, stirring, until well browned. Add cinnamon, cloves, allspice, salt, and pepper. Stir in water and tomato paste; simmer 5 minutes. Set aside.

Spoon half of the macaroni filling (recipe below) in a buttered 9 by 13-inch pan, and sprinkle with ¼ cup of the Parmesan cheese. Place all of the meat mixture on top. Pour remaining macaroni filling over meat, and sprinkle with another ¼ cup of the Parmesan cheese. Then pour all of the cream sauce (recipe below) over the macaroni; sprinkle top with remaining ¼ cup Parmesan cheese. Bake uncovered in a 350° oven for 45 minutes, or until thoroughly heated (if refrigerated, bake 1 hour).

**Macaroni Filling.** Cook macaroni according to the directions on the package; drain and rinse. Stir in 3 eggs (slightly beaten) and 1 teaspoon salt. Mix until well blended. Set aside.

**Cream Sauce.** Melt 6 tablespoons butter in a pan. Gradually stir in flour and cook, stirring, until blended and bubbly. Gradually stir in milk and cook, stirring until sauce is smooth and thickened. Stir in 3 eggs (slightly beaten) and 1 teaspoon salt until well blended.

# Northern Italy Spaghetti

**MAKES 8 TO 10 SERVINGS**

**PREPARE SAUCE AS MUCH AS SEVERAL DAYS AHEAD**

1 pound round steak, cut into chunks
1½ pounds ground beef
1 teaspoon salad oil
4 cloves garlic, minced
2 medium-sized onions, chopped
1 green pepper, chopped
4 stalks celery, sliced
5 cans (6 oz each) tomato paste
1 large can (1 lb. 12 oz.) whole tomatoes
1½ cups red wine
1 small bunch parsley, chopped
2 tablespoons dried basil
1 tablespoon each oregano and marjoram
1½ teaspoons thyme
½ teaspoon rosemary
3 whole black peppers
4 dried chile peppers, crushed
About ¼ cup dried mushrooms
1 package (1 lb.) spaghetti, cooked

You can make this long-simmered sauce in a quantity to serve a very large group. Although it requires more than 4 hours on the range, it takes little tending and frees the cook for preparing the rest of the meal.

Brown the steak chunks and ground beef in the salad oil in a large frying pan; remove from pan. In the same pan, sauté the garlic and onions until golden, remove from pan. Then cook the pepper and celery until tender. Return these cooked ingredients to the pan and add tomato paste, whole tomatoes with liquid, wine, parsley, basil, oregano, marjoram, thyme, rosemary, black peppers, and chile peppers. Cover pan and simmer for 3 hours, stirring occasionally to prevent sticking. Then add the mushrooms and simmer for 1 to 1½ hours more. Pour over the cooked spaghetti.

*Paella—see page 133*

# Jamaican Stuffed Pumpkin or Squash

**MAKES ABOUT 8 SERVINGS**

**PREPARE PUMPKIN AND STUFFING AS MUCH AS A DAY AHEAD**

**STUFF PUMPKIN AND BAKE JUST BEFORE SERVING**

- 1 small whole pumpkin or Hubbard squash, 8 to 10 inches in diameter
- Boiling salted water
- Salt
- 2 tablespoons salad oil
- 2 pounds ground beef chuck
- 6 ounces ground smoked ham
- 2½ cups finely chopped onions
- 1 green pepper, finely chopped
- 2½ teaspoons salt
- 2 teaspoons <u>each</u> olive oil and oregano
- 1 teaspoon <u>each</u> vinegar and ground black pepper
- Dash crushed dried red pepper
- 2 large cloves garlic, mashed
- ¾ cup raisins
- ⅓ cup pimiento-stuffed green olives, chopped
- 2 teaspoons capers, drained and minced
- 1 can (8 oz.) tomato sauce
- 3 eggs, beaten

The cuisine of Jamaica shows the influence of the various peoples who settled this Caribbean island—Indian, Spanish, French, British, Dutch, Danish, African. As you might expect, the typical foods and seasonings are diversified. Some of these seasonings go into the savory meat filling of a whole pumpkin or squash, usually offered on a well-laden buffet table at native feasts there. It would be handsome for an October or Halloween dinner here. A crisp green salad, crunchy French bread or hot rolls, and dessert—perhaps fruit or ice cream—are all you need to complete the menu.

With a sharp knife, cut a circular top (about 5 inches in diameter) out of the pumpkin. Save this top for the lid. Scoop seeds out and scrape the inside clean. Place the pumpkin in a large pan and cover with salted water; cover pan. Bring the water to a boil, then simmer until the pumpkin meat is almost tender when pierced with a fork, about 30 minutes (the pumpkin should still be firm enough to hold its shape well). Carefully remove the pumpkin from the hot water, drain well, and dry the outside. Sprinkle the inside with a little salt.

Heat the salad oil in a large frying pan. Add the beef, ham, onions, and green pepper. Cook over high heat, stirring, just until the meat is browned and crumbly. Remove the meat from the heat. Mix together the salt, olive oil, oregano, vinegar, black pepper, red pepper, and garlic. Add to the meat along with the raisins, olives, capers, and tomato sauce. Mix well. Cover the pan and cook over low heat for 15 minutes, stirring occasionally. Remove from heat and allow to cool slightly; then mix in the eggs thoroughly.

Fill the cooked pumpkin with the meat stuffing, pressing the stuffing slightly to pack it firmly. Cover loosely with the pumpkin lid. Place the pumpkin in a shallow greased baking pan and bake in a 350° oven for 1 hour. Allow the pumpkin and stuffing to cool for 10 to 15 minutes before serving.

At serving time, carefully lift the hot pumpkin (support the bottom with a wide spatula) to a serving plate or carving board; garnish with fall leaves or flowers. Slice the pumpkin from top to bottom in fat wedges.

# Chicken Livers and Mushrooms

**MAKES 6 SERVINGS**

**COOK JUST BEFORE SERVING**

- 1¾ pounds chicken livers
- ¾ teaspoon salt
- ¾ pound mushrooms, sliced
- 1½ cups sliced celery (cut on the diagonal, ⅜ inch wide)
- ½ cup chopped onion
- About ½ cup butter or margarine
- Flour
- ½ cup Sherry
- 2 cups (1 pt.) sour cream
- Hot cooked rice
- Minced parsley

Both chicken livers and fresh mushrooms are at their best sautéed. This quick dish is finished with a luscious sour cream and Sherry sauce made from the buttery pan juices.

Have ready in the refrigerator, covered, chicken livers (cut in halves and sprinkled with about ¾ teaspoon salt), sliced mushrooms, sliced celery, and chopped onion.

To cook, place 2 wide frying pans over high heat and put ¼ cup butter or margarine in each. Add to one pan the mushrooms, celery, and onions. Dust chicken livers lightly with flour and place in the other pan (do not crowd). Cook the vegetables, stirring occasionally, until they are lightly browned; remove from heat and keep in a warm place. Brown chicken livers on all sides (you may need more butter) and add to vegetables as they are cooked. Pour Sherry into the pan in which the livers cooked, and bring to a boil, stirring to free browned particles. Reduce heat to low, and stir in sour cream; heat but do not boil.

Turn liver mixture into a serving bowl and pour the sour cream sauce over the top (or you can serve livers on the rice). Sprinkle liberally with parsley.

# Basque Artichokes with Eggs

Artichokes, filled with creamy scrambled eggs and surrounded by a tangy tomato sauce, are ideal for brunch or lunch.

Slice off the top fourth of each artichoke. With scissors, cut thorns from tips of lower leaves. Peel stem and remove small leaves around base. With a small-bowled, long-handled spoon, carefully scoop out choke and a few of the center leaves to make a cup. Place artichokes in boiling salted water to cover; add the lemon juice and 1 tablespoon of the oil. Cover and cook until stems are just tender, about 30 minutes; drain. Cut off stems so artichokes will stand flat; chop and reserve stems for sauce. Stand artichokes in a baking dish.

Sauté onion and garlic in remaining oil until soft; stir in tomatoes, reserved chopped artichoke stems, olives, and seasonings. Bring to a boil, reduce heat, and simmer, uncovered, for about 20 minutes. Spoon sauce around artichokes in baking dish. Cover and bake in a 350° oven for 10 minutes or until artichokes are heated. Fill artichokes with scrambled eggs, serve with cheese.

**Parsley Scrambled Eggs.** Beat eggs with half-and-half, ½ teaspoon salt, pepper, and parsley. Melt butter or margarine in a frying pan; scramble eggs in butter over low heat until cooked to taste.

**MAKES 6 SERVINGS**

**PREPARE ARTICHOKES AND SAUCE UP TO SEVERAL HOURS AHEAD**

| | |
|---|---|
| 6 | medium-sized artichokes |
| | Boiling salted water |
| 2 | tablespoons lemon juice |
| 3 | tablespoons olive oil or salad oil |
| ¼ | cup chopped onion |
| 1 | clove garlic, minced or mashed |
| 1 | can (1 lb.) tomatoes |
| ½ | cup halved, pitted ripe olives |
| ½ | teaspoon <u>each</u> salt, thyme, and oregano |
| | Dash of pepper |
| | Grated Parmesan cheese |

**PARSLEY SCRAMBLED EGGS:**

| | |
|---|---|
| 6 | eggs |
| 3 | tablespoons half-and-half (light cream) |
| ½ | teaspoon salt |
| | Dash of pepper |
| 2 | teaspoons chopped parsley |
| 2 | tablespoons butter or margarine |

# Mushroom and Sausage Pie

For brunch, serve this pie with plain or cheese omelets; for lunch serve a tart green salad with it; for supper or dinner, let it accompany a roast of lamb or veal.

Crumble sausage in a wide frying pan and add mushrooms. Cook over high heat, stirring frequently, until mushrooms and meat are lightly browned and all liquid from mushrooms has evaporated, about 15 minutes. Remove about 3 tablespoons of the sausage drippings from pan and discard. Mix parsley with mushroom mixture, return to heat and cook for 2 or 3 minutes.

Beat eggs with half-and-half and cheese, blend in the mushroom mixture, and add salt to taste; pour into pastry shell. Arrange mushrooms so that any stems showing are turned down into the liquid, and push the mushrooms down so pie is evenly filled. Bake on lowest rack in a 400° oven for 20 to 25 minutes, or until crust is well browned. Let pie stand about 10 minutes before cutting.

**MAKES 6 TO 8 SERVINGS**

**TO SERVE HOT: MAKE FILLING AHEAD, FILL AND BAKE BEFORE SERVING**

**TO SERVE COLD: BAKE SEVERAL HOURS AHEAD**

| | |
|---|---|
| ½ | pound bulk pork sausage |
| 1½ | pounds small whole mushrooms |
| ½ | cup minced parsley |
| 2 | eggs |
| 1 | cup half-and-half (light cream) |
| ½ | cup shredded Parmesan cheese |
| ¼ | to ½ teaspoon salt |
| | Unbaked 9 or 10-inch pastry shell |

# Jack Cheese Oven Omelet

This oven omelet requires no separating of eggs and beating of whites, but bakes to puffy perfection nevertheless. It makes a light meal for any time of day from breakfast to way-past-midnight.

Fry bacon until browned. Drain, reserving 1 tablespoon drippings. Sauté onions in drippings until limp. Beat eggs with milk and seasoned salt. Stir in bacon, onions, and 2 cups of the cheese. Pour into a greased, shallow, 2-quart baking dish. Bake, uncovered, in a 350° oven for 35 to 40 minutes until mixture is set and top is lightly browned. When almost done, sprinkle with remaining ½ cup cheese, and return to oven until cheese melts. Serve immediately.

**MAKES 6 SERVINGS**

**PREPARE AND BAKE 40 MINUTES AHEAD**

| | |
|---|---|
| 8 | slices bacon, coarsely chopped |
| 4 | green onions, thinly sliced |
| 8 | eggs |
| 1 | cup milk |
| ½ | teaspoon seasoned salt |
| 2½ | cups shredded jack cheese (about 10 oz.) |

# SOUP OR SALAD MEALS

Hearty soups and complex salads to feature as a main dish for a supper or lunch are included here. Lighter soups and salads to accompany meals are found on pages 68 through 87.

## Chile Verde

**MAKES 6 TO 8 SERVINGS**

**PREPARE UP TO 1 DAY AHEAD**

1½ pounds <u>each</u> boneless beef chuck and boneless, lean pork shoulder, cut in 1-inch cubes
3 tablespoons olive oil or salad oil
1 green pepper, chopped
1 large clove garlic, minced
2 large cans (1 lb. 12 oz. <u>each</u>) tomatoes
1 large can (7 oz.) California green chiles, seeded and chopped
⅓ cup chopped parsley
½ teaspoon sugar
¼ teaspoon ground cloves
2 teaspoons ground cumin
1 cup dry red wine, or ¼ cup lemon juice and ¾ cup beef broth
    Salt

This is a chile without beans, but definitely "con carne"—with *plenty* of meat. The *verde* (green) refers to the green chiles and bell pepper essential to the flavor. You may serve this thick soup in bowls or spoon it over cooked rice.

Brown about a quarter of the meat at a time on all sides in heated oil; remove with a slotted spoon and reserve. In pan drippings sauté green pepper and garlic until soft; add a little more oil, if needed.

In a large pan (at least 5 quarts) combine tomatoes and their liquid, green chiles, parsley, seasonings, and wine. Bring tomato mixture to a boil, then reduce heat to a simmer. Add browned meats, their juices, and sautéed vegetables. Cover and simmer for 2 hours, stirring occasionally.

Remove cover; simmer for about 45 minutes more until sauce is reduced to thickness you wish and meat is very tender. Taste and add salt.

## Petite Marmite

*BEEF AND VEGETABLE SOUP*

**MAKES 8 SERVINGS**

**PREPARE SOUP AS MUCH AS 1 DAY AHEAD**

3½ pounds beef shanks, cut 1 inch thick
3 quarts water
1 tablespoon salt
¼ teaspoon pepper
1 bay leaf
2 whole allspice
1 medium-sized onion, peeled
2 whole cloves
1 bunch carrots
2 turnips
3 stalks celery
3 leeks
½ pound chicken livers
1 tablespoon beef stock base or 3 beef bouillon cubes
2 tablespoons butter
¼ teaspoon paprika
3 tablespoons chopped parsley
1 cup shredded Parmesan cheese

Petite Marmite, "little pot," is really a full-meal soup, laden with succulent beef shanks, chicken livers, and assorted root vegetables. This version includes a special cheese that you lavish over each bowlful.

Place beef shanks in a large soup kettle; add water, salt, pepper, bay leaf, allspice, and onion stuck with cloves. Bring to a boil, skim off frothy scum on top, cover and simmer 2 hours, or until meat is tender. Lift out meat and let cool.

Peel and slice carrots. Peel and dice turnips. Slice celery thinly on the diagonal. Slice leeks thinly. Add vegetables, chicken livers, and beef stock to broth and simmer 20 minutes. Remove bones and fat and dice meat into bite-sized pieces. Add meat to soup.

Meanwhile make parsleyed cheese by creaming butter and mixing in paprika, parsley, and cheese. Reheat soup, ladle into bowls, and serve with the parsleyed cheese.

# Minestrone, North Beach Style

*MENU FOR BUILD-YOUR-OWN-SALAD LUNCH INCLUDES THIS DISH—PAGE 24*

The North Beach area of San Francisco is a place of contrasts with ever-changing nightclubs and restaurants. Most of these places are brassy and geared to whatever entertainment is the fad. But the little Italian family-style restaurants are still doing business here and there. You might share a tureen of hearty soup such as this with whoever happens to be sitting at your table.

First, prepare the stock. Cover beans with water and bring to a boil. Boil 2 minutes, remove from heat and let stand, covered, 1 hour. Add beef bones and beef shank; bring to boiling and simmer 2 hours. Let cool.

Remove meat and bones from beans, return lean meat to soup if flavor is good. Scoop marrow from bones and add to soup; discard bones. Mash half the beans by rubbing through a wire strainer; or whirl in a blender with some of the liquid. Return to whole beans in pan.

Next, prepare cooked vegetables. Heat 4 tablespoons olive oil or salad oil in a wide frying pan. Add onions, and cook until soft. Then add carrots, celery, and leeks and cook 5 minutes. Mix in tomatoes, mashing slightly. Simmer rapidly for 10 minutes or until most of the liquid has evaporated. Add to the prepared bean stock, and simmer 30 minutes. Season with about 2 teaspoons salt or to taste.

Then add raw vegetables. To the boiling soup, stir in potatoes and green beans. Simmer rapidly, uncovered, for 10 minutes, then add zucchini, cabbage, and macaroni. Simmer 5 minutes more. In another pan sauté parsley, garlic, and basil in 2 tablespoons olive oil until parsley is bright green. Mix into soup and serve. Sprinkle grated Parmesan cheese into each bowl.

**MAKES 24 TO 28 SERVINGS OF 1 CUP EACH**

**PREPARE AS MUCH AS SEVERAL DAYS AHEAD**

- 1   pound cranberry (or pink) beans
- 4   quarts water
- 4   marrow beef bones (each 3 inches long)
- 4   slices meaty beef shank (each 1 inch thick)
- 4   tablespoons olive oil or salad oil
- 2   large onions, diced
- 2   cups _each_ diced carrots, celery, and leeks
- 1   can (1 lb.) solid pack tomatoes
    Salt
- 2   or 3 large potatoes, diced
- 2   cups (½ lb.) green beans, cut in 2-inch pieces
- 4   small zucchini, sliced
- 3   cups shredded white cabbage
- ½   cup salad macaroni (ditalini)
- ½   cup chopped parsley
- 1   clove garlic, minced
- 2   tablespoons dried basil
- 2   tablespoons olive oil
    Grated Parmesan cheese

# Carmel Bouillabaisse

This Western version of the great seafood soup of southern France was created by the chef of a small French restaurant in Carmel, California. To make the bouillabaisse ("boo-ya-bess") ahead, prepare and refrigerate the tomato base up to the point of adding the saffron. Before serving, reheat it, add saffron and fish, and simmer until fish are cooked. Serve the soup with steamed rice; each diner spoons some rice into his bowl as he makes room for it.

Sablefish is sometimes sold under the name of black cod or butterfish; salmon could be used in its place. Any rockfish may be used; other names for it are rock cod, red snapper, and Pacific ocean perch. If you're unable to obtain clams in shells, use canned ones, drained.

In a large pan (about 5-quart size) combine tomatoes, water, salt, thyme, bay leaves, and pepper. Bring to a boil, reduce heat, and simmer, covered, for 20 minutes. Discard bay leaves; press tomato mixture through a fine strainer, reserving broth.

To prepare fish, shell and devein shrimp; rinse clams and scallops with cold water; cut lobster tails in half lengthwise; cut the sablefish and rockfish into about 1½-inch chunks.

Bring broth to a boil in a large deep pan (at least 6-quart size). Stir in saffron. Add shellfish and fish. Simmer, covered, for 10 to 15 minutes, or until shrimp and lobster turn pink and fish flakes easily. Remove from heat and loosen lobster meat from shells; return to fish mixture. Serve soup immediately, distributing some of all the fish into each bowl.

**MAKES 8 SERVINGS**

**MAY BE PARTIALLY PREPARED AHEAD**

- 3   large cans (1 lb. 12 oz. _each_) tomatoes
- ½   cup water
- 1   teaspoon _each_ salt and whole thyme
- 2   small bay leaves
- ¼   teaspoon white pepper
- 1½  pounds large shrimp or prawns
- 2   dozen small hardshell clams
- ½   pound scallops
- 4   frozen lobster tails, thawed
- 3   sablefish or salmon steaks (about 1½ lbs.), skinned and boned
- 1   pound rockfish fillets
- ⅛   teaspoon powdered saffron or ¼ teaspoon turmeric

# Hungarian Speckled Bean Soup

*BAB LEVES*

**MAKES 8 TO 10 SERVINGS**

**PREPARE AS MUCH AS 1 DAY AHEAD**

1 pound dried pinto or cranberry
    beans
    Cold water
2 large smoked ham hocks
    (about 2 lbs.)
2 pounds veal or beef bones,
    cut in 3 to 4-inch pieces
2 medium-sized carrots, peeled
1 parsnip, peeled
5 sprigs parsley
1 onion, peeled and halved
1 whole clove garlic
    About 1 teaspoon salt
1 tablespoon <u>each</u> butter and flour
2 teaspoons sweet Hungarian
    paprika or regular paprika
½ cup water
    Sour cream (optional)

Steaming bean soup makes a satisfying main dish at noon or a first course at dinner. If you serve this Hungarian *Bab Leves* (pronounced "bob *lev*-ahsh") as a main dish, accompany it with rye bread and cold meat or cheese.

Place beans in a bowl and cover with cold water; let stand for 4 to 5 hours or overnight. Drain beans, reserving water. Place ham hocks, veal bones, carrots, parsnip, parsley, onion, and garlic in a large deep pan (at least 6-quart size). Measure water drained from beans; add more water to make 3 quarts. Add the 3 quarts water to pan, cover, and simmer 2 hours, until ham is tender.

Pour soup through a strainer, reserving ham, carrots, and parsnip. Return strained broth to pan; add drained beans and simmer, covered, until beans are tender, about 1 hour. Slice carrots and parsnip; cut ham from bones, discarding skin, fat, and bones. Dice the ham. Add vegetables and ham to soup; taste and add salt as needed. If possible at this point, chill soup, then skim off fat and discard it; heat soup again to simmering.

Melt butter in a small pan, stir in flour and paprika, and cook until bubbly. Gradually add the ½ cup water, stirring constantly; cook until thickened. Blend flour mixture into soup, and cook about 5 minutes longer. Spoon a dollop of sour cream into each serving of soup, if you wish.

## CRISP BREADS TO ACCOMPANY SOUPS OR SALADS

Although rolls and muffins are delicious with soup or salad, perhaps the finest accompaniment of all is something crisp and savory. Soups, which are often creamy or contain ingredients cooked soft, particularly profit by bread sticks or thin breads which are crunchy and full-flavored. Fruit and gelatin salads also need this kind of contrast.

**Cardamom Tortilla Crisps.** Blend 3 tablespoons soft butter or margarine with ¼ teaspoon ground cardamom until smooth. Spread 4 flour tortillas with butter mixture; cut into quarters. Bake on ungreased baking sheets in a 400° oven for about 8 minutes or until crisp and golden. Serve hot. Makes 16.

**Swedish Flatbread.** In a bowl, blend 2¾ cups unsifted all-purpose flour with ¼ cup sugar, and ½ teaspoon *each* soda and salt. Cut in ½ cup (¼ lb.) butter or margarine until mixture resembles fine crumbs. Stir in 1 cup cultured buttermilk, using a fork, until mixture holds together.

Shape into a ball with your hands and break off small pieces to make balls an inch in diameter; separate on a floured board. Roll out each ball on floured board to make a round 4 to 5 inches in diameter, turning it over occasionally to prevent sticking. Space rounds slightly apart on ungreased baking sheets. Bake in 400° oven for 5 minutes, or until lightly browned; check frequently. Cool on wire racks. Store these thin, fragile, crisp rounds—they look like oversized crackers—in airtight containers until ready to serve (up to two to three weeks).

Serve cold or warm. To reheat, place in a 350° oven for 2 to 3 minutes. Makes about 6 dozen.

**Pine Nut Sticks.** Dissolve 1 package yeast, active dry or compressed, in ⅔ cup warm water; add ½ teaspoon crushed anise seed, 2 tablespoons *each* salad oil and olive oil, ¼ teaspoon grated lemon peel, 1 teaspoon salt, 1 tablespoon sugar, and 1 cup unsifted all-purpose flour. Beat until smooth. Add ⅔ cup pine nuts and about 1¼ cups unsifted all-purpose flour, or enough to make a stiff dough.

Turn out on a floured board and knead until smooth and elastic (about 5 minutes), using additional flour as needed. Place dough in greased bowl, cover with damp cloth, and let rise in a warm place until doubled, about 1 hour.

Punch down, divide dough in half. Cut each half into 20 equal-sized pieces; roll each piece, using palms of hands, into a 7-inch length. Place parallel on greased baking sheets about ½ inch apart. Cover and let rise until almost doubled, about 30 minutes; brush with 1 slightly beaten egg, and sprinkle lightly with 2 tablespoons coarse salt. Bake in a 325° oven for 30 minutes, until lightly browned. Makes 40 bread sticks.

# Salade Niçoise

*SEAFOOD AND VEGETABLE SALAD PLATE*

At restaurants along the Côte d'Azur, the French Riviera, Salade Niçoise is as much in demand as the mixed green salad is in the western United States. The classic Niçoise ("nee-*swaz*") is a vinaigrette of cooked potatoes and green beans, appetizingly arranged with tomato, olives, and anchovy fillets. But sweet red onions, pepper rings, radishes, cauliflower, asparagus, artichoke hearts, and a variety of seafoods can be added or substituted. The flavor of cooked ingredients improves if they are marinated a day or two. The entire salad can be assembled several hours before serving, and chilled.

For dressing, shake together oil, vinegar, salt, pepper, chives, and parsley; chill.

Cook unpeeled potatoes in boiling salted water 20 minutes, or until tender; cool immediately under cold water; peel and slice. Pour over just enough dressing to coat slices, mix lightly. Cover; chill at least 2 hours.

Cut off ends of beans and cut into 1½-inch lengths; cook in boiling salted water about 15 minutes or until crisp-tender; drain and cool immediately with cold water. Drain well again, then turn into a bowl and coat lightly with dressing. Cover and chill at least 2 hours.

Select a rimmed platter or large, shallow bowl and mound potato salad down the center. Arrange marinated green beans on each side. Peel tomatoes and cut in wedges. Quarter the hard-cooked eggs and alternate the egg quarters and tomato wedges beside the green beans. Criss-cross the anchovy fillets across the top of the potatoes.

Garnish with olives and sprinkle with capers. Cover with foil or clear plastic film and chill until serving time. When ready to serve, add a border of the inside leaves of butter lettuce and pour remaining dressing over them. Arrange tuna (in a round chunk, just as it comes from the can) on a side plate with watercress sprigs.

**MAKES 4 SERVINGS**

**PREPARE SEVERAL HOURS AHEAD**

| | |
|---|---|
| ¾ | cup olive oil |
| ¼ | cup red wine vinegar |
| ¼ | teaspoon salt |
| | Freshly ground pepper |
| 2 | tablespoons <u>each</u> finely chopped chives and parsley |
| 4 | large boiling potatoes |
| | Boiling salted water |
| 1½ | pounds green beans |
| 2 | large tomatoes |
| 2 | or 3 hard-cooked eggs |
| 10 | to 12 anchovy fillets |
| ½ | cup pitted extra large ripe olives |
| 1 | tablespoon capers (optional) |
| | Butter lettuce |
| 1 | can (7 oz.) solid-pack white albacore tuna (optional) |
| | Watercress (optional) |

# San Diego Salad

A salad named for San Diego would naturally be composed of foods much used in Mexican cookery—chicken, cheese, orange, avocado, olives, and tortilla. The dressing also has a Mexican tang of cumin and chile.

For each serving, arrange outer romaine leaves on a dinner plate. Finely chop a few inner leaves and arrange on top. Bone chicken breast, cut in strips, and place on lettuce. Add jack cheese (cut in strips), several slices of salami, orange, avocado, olives, and triangular wedges of crisp tortilla. Cover and chill. At serving time add Cumin Dressing.

**Cumin Dressing.** Blend sour cream and mayonnaise, then lemon juice, dry mustard, garlic, salt, cumin, and chile sauce. Chill. Serves 2 or 3.

**SALAD INGREDIENTS LISTED FOR 1 SERVING; DRESSING RECIPE MAKES 2 TO 3 SERVINGS**

**FOR EACH SERVING:**

| | |
|---|---|
| | Romaine leaves |
| 1 | cooked split chicken breast |
| | Jack cheese (cut in strips) |
| | Several slices of salami |
| 3 | or 4 slices orange |
| 3 | slices avocado |
| | Several ripe pitted olives |
| | Wedges of crisp tortilla |

**CUMIN DRESSING:**

| | |
|---|---|
| ¼ | cup <u>each</u> sour cream and mayonnaise |
| 1 | tablespoon lemon juice |
| ⅛ | teaspoon <u>each</u> dry mustard and garlic salt |
| ¼ | teaspoon ground cumin |
| 2 | tablespoons canned green chile salsa or chile sauce |

# Salmon Cornucopia Platter

MAKES 6 SERVINGS

PREPARE 2 TO 4 HOURS
IN ADVANCE

1  small package (3 oz.) cream
   cheese
1  teaspoon lemon juice
½  teaspoon grated lemon peel
½  cup heavy cream
12  slices smoked salmon (lox)
   Parsley sprigs for garnish
1  jar (8 oz.) cream-style preserved
   herring

**CAPER STUFFED EGGS:**

4  hard-cooked eggs
3  tablespoons mayonnaise
¼  teaspoon salt
⅛  teaspoon dry mustard
   Capers for garnish

**CUCUMBER-FILLED TOMATOES:**

1  unpeeled cucumber
¼  cup white wine vinegar
4  teaspoons sugar
1  tablespoon water
¼  teaspoon salt
⅛  teaspoon <u>each</u> freshly ground
   pepper and dill
3  tomatoes

Choose this decorative platter salad for a summer buffet luncheon or light supper. Cool cucumber-stuffed tomatoes and eggs balance the flavors of rich cheese-filled salmon cones and creamed herring.

For salmon filling, cream the cheese until light and blend in lemon juice and peel. Whip cream until stiff and fold in. Spoon mixture into a pastry bag with a star tip. Fold each salmon slice into a cornucopia shape and fill with the whipped cream and cheese mixture. Garnish the tip of each with a parsley sprig. Arrange on a platter.

Spoon herring into a large clam shell or scallop shell (or other serving dish) and arrange on the platter. Then place the Caper Stuffed Eggs and Cucumber-Filled Tomatoes (recipes follow) on the platter. Cover with clear plastic film and refrigerate until serving time.

**Caper Stuffed Eggs.** Halve eggs and remove yolks to a bowl. Blend in mayonnaise, ¼ teaspoon salt, and mustard. Pile yolks into the egg-white halves and garnish each with several capers.

**Cucumber-Filled Tomatoes.** Slice cucumber very thinly and place in a bowl. Mix together vinegar, sugar, water, ¼ teaspoon salt, pepper, and dill; pour over cucumber slices and let marinate at least 2 hours. Halve tomatoes crosswise and scoop out most of the pulp, making half shells. Drain cucumbers and pile into the tomato halves.

# Hawaiian Salad

SALAD INGREDIENTS LISTED FOR 1
SERVING; DRESSING RECIPE
MAKES 2 TO 3 SERVINGS

**FOR EACH SERVING:**

   Spinach leaves
¼  pound cooked, shelled large
   shrimp or roast pork strips
   (or some of each)
3  slices fresh pineapple
3  slices papaya
1  tablespoon chopped macadamia
   nuts

**CURRY DRESSING:**

¼  cup <u>each</u> sour cream and
   mayonnaise
1  tablespoon lemon juice
⅛  teaspoon <u>each</u> dry mustard and
   garlic salt
¼  teaspoon curry powder

Pineapple, papaya, and macadamia nuts are expected ingredients of this salad in the spirit of Hawaii. The shrimp is a reminder of the sea and the pork of a *luau*, or perhaps the open-air Chinese shops in Honolulu where the roast meat hangs from hooks, a delicious sight.

For each serving, line a dinner plate with spinach leaves and finely chop several more leaves to make a nest in the center. Arrange on the plate shrimp or roast pork strips (or some of each), pineapple, and papaya. Chill. Garnish with nuts, add dressing.

**Curry Dressing.** Blend sour cream and mayonnaise. Mix in lemon juice, dry mustard, garlic salt, and curry powder. Chill at least 1 hour. Serves 2 or 3.

# Hot Chicken Salad

Sesame seed, mustard, coriander, and lemon juice flavor this adaptation of a classic Chinese hot salad. You can have everything measured and ready to assemble, then heat the mixture right before serving.

In a pan, blend together the sesame seed, mustard, lemon juice, chicken stock or water, salt, sugar, coriander, and onions. Add the chicken and heat. Arrange the shredded lettuce on a warm platter and pour the hot chicken mixture over it. Serve immediately.

**MAKES 6 SERVINGS**

**PREPARE RIGHT BEFORE SERVING (INGREDIENTS MAY BE PREPARED AHEAD)**

- 2 tablespoons <u>each</u> toasted sesame seed, prepared mustard, and lemon juice
- ¼ cup chicken stock or water
- ½ teaspoon <u>each</u> salt, sugar, and ground coriander
- ½ cup chopped green onions
- 4 cups diced cooked chicken
  About 2 cups shredded iceberg lettuce

# Aïoli Meal

*RECIPE WITH FRENCH PEASANT AÏOLI MENU—PAGE 25*

Aïoli is the name of both a garlic mayonnaise sauce and a meal made from dipping hot or cold seafood and vegetables in this sauce. With the menu you will find a long list of suggested foods, as well as the sauce recipe. And, there's no reason why you can't simplify the dish for a light luncheon by serving just two or three foods, such as shrimp, whole artichokes, and hard-cooked eggs.

**MAKES 1¾ CUPS SAUCE**

**PREPARE SAUCE AS MUCH AS 4 DAYS AHEAD**

# Sole in Wine Aspic

This is an elegant dish, but it is easy to make and may be prepared ahead. A ring of wine and lemon gelatin encloses a surprise—rolls of poached fish and tiny shrimp. Crunchy bits of celery and green pepper provide color; a horseradish sauce gives zip.

Soften gelatin in ½ cup of the water. Roll each fillet; tie with string. Combine remaining 1 cup water, wine, lemon juice, salt, and liquid hot-pepper seasoning in a frying pan; bring mixture to simmering point. Place fish rolls in liquid and simmer, covered, for about 5 minutes or until fish is just tender. Remove fish rolls; set aside.

To clarify cooking liquid, stir in egg whites; bring to a boil and cook about 1 minute without stirring. Strain through damp cloth. Stir in gelatin until dissolved; add water to make 2¾ cups. Chill until syrupy.

Blend in celery, green peppers, chives, and shrimp. Pour gelatin mixture into a 4½-cup (8-inch) ring mold. Remove strings from fish rolls; arrange in gelatin. Chill until set, at least 3 hours. Unmold; garnish with greens; serve with sauce.

**Horseradish Sauce.** Blend sour cream, mayonnaise, horseradish, capers, sugar, and liquid from capers. Chill.

**MAKES 4 TO 6 SERVINGS**

**PREPARE 4 HOURS TO AS MUCH AS 1 DAY AHEAD**

**RING MOLD DESIRABLE**

- 2 envelopes unflavored gelatin
- 1½ cups cold water
- 6 small sole fillets (about 1 lb.), halved lengthwise
- 1 cup dry white wine
- ¼ cup lemon juice
- ¾ teaspoon salt
- ¼ teaspoon liquid hot-pepper seasoning
- 2 egg whites, beaten until frothy
- ⅓ cup <u>each</u> finely chopped celery and green pepper
- 2 tablespoons chopped chives
- ¼ pound cooked, peeled small shrimp
  Watercress or chicory

**HORSERADISH SAUCE:**

- ½ cup <u>each</u> sour cream and mayonnaise
- 2 tablespoons <u>each</u> prepared horseradish and drained capers
- 1 teaspoon <u>each</u> sugar and liquid from capers

# Accompaniments and Side Dishes

THE PERFECT DINNER is perfect because of the attention given to every detail. Even the vegetables, bread, or other starchy accompaniments such as rice or pasta reflect planning and originality. This chapter is devoted to these perfecting touches.

Vegetables prepared with originality are always a delightful surprise. It is little more trouble to make them out of the ordinary if you use the recipes in this chapter. Some are classics and others have been originated by creative cooks who believe vegetables deserve more attention than they often get.

Quite a few potato recipes are included. They are not intended to banish that all-time favorite—the baked potato with sour cream—from party menus, but to offer equally delicious alternatives.

The rice and pasta recipes are largely foreign in origin—and for good reason. Especially fine ways of preparing these foods have been perfected, sometimes over the centuries, in countries where they are staples in the diet. Some you may want to serve as a separate course, the way they are presented in their native lands.

Breads, of course, are tremendously varied. The recipes here are for those which might have the greatest adaptability to all sorts of entertaining and menus. Some are particularly delicious for buffet or smörgåsbord use. A few are sweet, to go with ham, turkey, pork, and other meats which take well to such accompaniments.

You will also find tips in this chapter for making basic yeast rolls in attractive party shapes and ways to mold butter for breads or to flavor it as a vegetable topping.

A page of information about cheeses will aid you in cooking with them or serving them at any time in the meal, from appetizers to dessert.

*Ratatouille (vegetable casserole)—see page 155*

# VEGETABLES

The following collection of recipes contains so many simple yet unique ways to glamorize vegetables that you may find yourself using this section of the book even for everyday cooking. When you entertain, attractive and imaginatively seasoned vegetables are essential to complement other carefully prepared dishes. Most of the vegetables included here are the colorful ones, which make a decorative as well as taste contribution to the meal.

## Baked Green Tomatoes

**MAKES 6 TO 8 SERVINGS**

**BEGIN BAKING 1 HOUR BEFORE SERVING**

8  medium-sized green tomatoes
   About 1½ teaspoons salt
½  teaspoon pepper
2  tablespoons chives or 1 teaspoon mixed herbs
¾  cup fresh bread crumbs, toasted
   Butter
¼  cup grated Parmesan cheese

Back in the days when tomatoes were seasonal, the last ones on the vine were picked green, before frost came, and cooked. Now tomatoes are enjoyed everywhere the year around, but many of these are picked green for shipping. Often you'll find a few which have not turned red yet on display, or you may ask the grocer to bring some out from the storeroom. The tart, rich flavor of green tomatoes is easy to like, particularly when enhanced with cheese and toasted crumbs.

Slice tomatoes and arrange in layers, sprinkling each layer with salt and pepper, a few chives or some mixed herbs, bread crumbs, and a liberal dotting of butter. Top with cheese, and bake in a 350° oven for 1 hour.

## Fresh Tomato Soufflé

**MAKES ABOUT 6 SERVINGS**

**SOUFFLÉ DISH OR OTHER STRAIGHT-SIDED BAKING DISH REQUIRED**

4  cups diced, peeled fresh tomatoes (about 6 medium-sized tomatoes)
½  cup chopped onion
1  large clove garlic, mashed
½  teaspoon sugar
¼  teaspoon basil
1  teaspoon salt
¼  teaspoon freshly ground black pepper
3  tablespoons butter
4  tablespoons flour
7  eggs, separated
2  tablespoons shredded Parmesan cheese (optional)

A fresh tomato sauce gives this soufflé a rich hue. Cheese sprinkled over the top when it has partially baked makes a particularly savory crust. Cold sliced ham and turkey, a marinated vegetable salad, and buttered rye bread will complement the soufflé.

In a pan combine tomatoes, onion, garlic, sugar, basil, salt, and pepper. Simmer rapidly, stirring, until the sauce is reduced to 1¾ cups. Whirl smooth in your blender or rub mixture through a wire strainer. Melt butter in a pan, stir in flour, and cook until bubbly. Remove from heat and stir in tomato mixture.
   Cook, stirring, until thickened. Remove from heat and beat in egg yolks. If necessary, return to heat and stir a few seconds to thicken again; set off heat. Whip egg whites until they hold short, distinct, moist peaks. Fold half the whites thoroughly into sauce; fold in remaining whites as thoroughly as you like. Pour into a buttered 1½-quart soufflé dish or other straight-sided dish.
   Bake in a 375° oven for about 35 minutes. Ten minutes before removing the soufflé from the oven, sprinkle cheese over the top. Serve immediately.

*Note: Instead of the fresh tomatoes, you can use 1 large can (1 lb., 12 oz.) whole tomatoes. Cook with the onion and seasonings until reduced to 1¾ cups, then continue recipe exactly as above.*

# Tomatoes Stuffed with Spinach

Spinach, bacon, and bread crumbs comprise this hearty and colorful stuffing. Be sure to select ripe but very firm tomatoes about 2½ inches in diameter.

Cut a thin slice off tops of tomatoes and use a grapefruit knife to cut and scoop out centers (use the tomato pulp in other cooking). Turn tomatoes upside-down to drain. Meanwhile cook bacon until crisp; drain, crumble, and set aside. Also cook the spinach in the water that clings to the leaves when you wash it, drain well, and chop. (Or cook the frozen spinach as directed, then drain well.)

Combine spinach, bread crumbs, bacon, and pepper. Sprinkle inside the tomatoes lightly with salt. Stuff the tomatoes with the spinach mixture and arrange them in a greased baking pan.

Bake, uncovered, in a 350° oven for 20 minutes, or until tomatoes are just tender but still hold their shape. Top each with a dollop of sour cream when you serve.

**MAKES 6 SERVINGS**

**STUFF AS MUCH AS AN HOUR BEFORE BAKING**

- 6 medium-sized tomatoes
- 6 slices bacon
- 1 pound fresh spinach (or a 10-oz. package frozen chopped spinach)
- ¾ cup soft bread crumbs (whirl fresh bread in blender)
- ¼ teaspoon pepper
  Salt
  Sour cream

# Celery Parmigiano

Celery, accented with Parmesan cheese, is baked just until golden to retain its characteristic fresh crispness.

Wash celery and cut off top branches and leaves. Cut each heart in half lengthwise. Add celery to boiling salted water to cover. Reduce heat to low and cook for 20 minutes or until almost tender. Drain and place in well-buttered, 9-inch square baking dish. Sprinkle with the cheese. Combine butter and cream, and pour it over the celery. Bake, uncovered, in a 325° oven for 20 minutes, or until tender and golden.

**MAKES 4 TO 6 SERVINGS**

**PARBOIL CELERY AND ASSEMBLE AHEAD, BAKE JUST BEFORE SERVING**

- 3 medium-sized hearts of celery
  Water
- 1 teaspoon salt
- ½ cup grated Parmesan cheese
- ¼ cup butter or margarine, melted
- ¼ cup heavy cream

# Baked Fennel

It's difficult to say why fennel hasn't become a more popular vegetable in this country. Italian cooks know it well, both as a salad ingredient and as a cooked vegetable—they call it *finocchio*. The French call it *fenouil*. Fennel has a delicate, licorice-like flavor. In fact, it is often called anise, and its flavor resembles that of the anise seed used in making licorice candy.

Cut the fennel heads lengthwise into quarters and drop into the boiling water; cook until just tender, about 8 to 10 minutes. Drain and arrange in a well-greased shallow baking dish. Spoon 2 tablespoons of the melted butter over the fennel. Combine the bread crumbs, cheese, egg, fennel leaves, and remaining 2 tablespoons melted butter; sprinkle over top. Add a sprinkling of paprika. Place in a 450° oven just until the crumbs have browned, about 10 minutes.

**MAKES 4 SERVINGS**

**PARBOIL FENNEL, PREPARE FOR BAKING AHEAD**

- 2 heads fennel, trimmed
  Boiling salted water
- 4 tablespoons melted butter or margarine
- 2 tablespoons fine dry bread crumbs
- 1 tablespoon grated Parmesan cheese
- 1 hard-cooked egg, chopped
- 1 tablespoon finely chopped fennel leaves
  Dash of paprika

# Spinach Pie

MAKES 6 TO 8 SERVINGS

**TO SERVE HOT: MAKE FILLING AHEAD, FILL AND BAKE BEFORE SERVING**

**TO SERVE COLD: BAKE SEVERAL HOURS AHEAD**

1 small package (3 oz.) cream cheese, softened
1 cup half-and-half (light cream)
½ cup soft bread cubes, lightly packed
¼ cup shredded Parmesan cheese
2 eggs, slightly beaten
1 cup cooked (about 1¼ lbs. fresh) spinach, very well drained and finely chopped
4 tablespoons butter or margarine
1 large onion, finely chopped
½ pound mushrooms, finely chopped
1 teaspoon tarragon
  About ¾ teaspoon salt
  Unbaked 9 or 10-inch pastry shell

Vegetable pie, a refreshing variation on the casserole, has the same merit of being preparable in advance. This spinach pie also is adaptable: It is good hot or cold, either as a light entrée or side dish for roast meats such as chicken or turkey. Consider spinach pie the next time you must take a dish somewhere, such as to a potluck dinner.

Mash cream cheese with a fork and gradually blend in half-and-half. Add bread cubes, Parmesan cheese, and eggs to cream cheese mixture and beat with a rotary mixer or wire whip to break up bread pieces. Stir in the spinach.

Melt butter in a wide frying pan and cook onion and mushrooms until lightly browned, stirring frequently; add tarragon when vegetables are soft. Blend hot vegetables with spinach mixture. Salt to taste.

Pour vegetable filling into pastry shell. Bake on lowest rack in a 400° oven for 25 minutes or until crust is well browned. Let stand 10 minutes and cut to serve hot, or let cool and cut to serve.

# Green Beans, Mediterranean Style

**MAKES 6 SERVINGS**

**PREPARE A DAY OR MORE IN ADVANCE**

1 pound fresh green beans
1 large onion, chopped
4 tablespoons olive oil or salad oil
½ green pepper, seeded and chopped
1 stalk celery, chopped
½ cup water

It's debatable whether these beans are better eaten hot or at room temperature. There's no debate about one point—they are just as good the day after they're made as when freshly cooked. If you refrigerate them, either heat or let thoroughly warm before serving.

Remove ends and strings from green beans. Cut beans in 2-inch lengths. In a wide frying pan, cook onion in oil over high heat, stirring, until onion is soft but not brown. Add green pepper and celery; cook over moderate heat, covered, for 5 minutes; stir occasionally. Add the beans to the cooking vegetables along with the water and continue to cook, covered, over moderate heat for 20 minutes, stirring occasionally.

# Green Beans with Water Chestnuts

*MENU FOR DUCKLING DINNER INCLUDES THIS DISH—PAGE 16*

**MAKES 8 TO 10 SERVINGS**

**PREPARE AT LAST MINUTE**

¼ cup (⅛ lb.) butter
2 cans (5 oz. each) water chestnuts, drained and sliced (reserve liquid)
1 teaspoon salt
4 packages (9 oz. each) frozen cut green beans
  Butter or margarine

Crunchy, sweet water chestnuts adapt to so many Chinese vegetables it would be only reasonable to try them with the green bean.

Melt butter in pan; stir in water chestnuts. Cook about 5 minutes. Blend in salt and beans. Using the liquid drained from chestnuts for liquid, cook beans until just tender, about 10 minutes. Season to taste with butter and additional salt if needed.

# Green Bean Casserole

Green beans have a mustard and ripe olive seasoning and a crunchy topping of fried onion rings in this casserole which, like many, is quickly assembled from packaged, canned, or frozen groceries.

Turn the cooked, drained green beans into a greased 1½-quart casserole. Melt the butter in a pan, then blend in the milk, dry soup mix, Worcestershire, mustard, and olives. Pour over the beans in the casserole. Then sprinkle the fried onion rings or crushed potato chips over the top.

Bake in a 350° oven for about 15 to 20 minutes, or until hot and bubbly.

**MAKES 6 SERVINGS**

**ASSEMBLE CASSEROLE AHEAD, ADD TOPPING AND BAKE AT LAST MINUTE**

3 to 4 cups cooked cut green beans (fresh, frozen, or canned), drained
2 tablespoons butter
1½ cups milk
1 package cream of leek dry soup mix (amount for 3 or 4 servings)
1 tablespoon Worcestershire
½ teaspoon prepared mustard
½ cup sliced ripe olives (2¼ oz. can), drained
1 can (3½ oz.) fried onion rings or 1 cup coarsely crushed potato chips

## FLAVORED BUTTERS FOR VEGETABLES AND FRENCH BREAD

Butter, flavored with herbs or other pungent seasonings, is an easy way to make vegetables outstanding. The butter may be prepared ahead and even molded into fancy shapes or balls (see page 165 for molding ideas). Just as you bring the serving dish to the table, put the butter on top. It will be pretty to see and good to smell.

Flavored butter has long been a favorite spread on slices of French bread before warming or toasting. At the end of each of the butter recipes to follow, it will be indicated when this particular kind is suitable for bread as well as vegetables. Each recipe also tells the kinds of vegetables most enhanced by this seasoning.

Flavored butters are not intended for long-time storage; for best flavor, plan to use them within a week or two.

For *each* of the following recipes, use ½ cup (¼ lb.) butter or margarine.

**Fines Herbes Butter.** Combine the butter and 1 tablespoon *each* minced parsley and chopped chives (fresh or freeze dried), ½ teaspoon *each* tarragon and chervil, ¼ teaspoon salt, and a dash of pepper; beat until fluffy.
*Suggested use:* Green vegetables; French bread.

**Basil Butter.** Combine in blender butter and ½ cup lightly packed, chopped fresh basil leaves (or 2 tablespoons dried basil), 2 tablespoons minced parsley, 1 tablespoon lemon juice, and ¼ cup grated Parmesan cheese; whirl until smooth (or crush basil and parsley with mortar and pestle, and beat together with other ingredients).

*Suggested use:* Spread on tomato slices before broiling; season baked potato, zucchini, eggplant, green beans, or green peas.

**Red Onion Butter.** Sauté 1 medium-sized red onion, finely chopped, in 2 tablespoons butter until soft, about 5 minutes; add 2 tablespoons dry red wine and cook until all liquid is evaporated. Cool thoroughly. Then combine onion mixture, the ½ cup butter, and ¼ teaspoon salt; whirl in the blender or beat until fluffy.
*Suggested use:* Fresh corn or almost any vegetable; French bread.

**Maître d'Hôtel Butter.** Combine the butter and 2 teaspoons *each* lemon juice and minced parsley, ¼ teaspoon *each* salt and thyme, and ⅛ teaspoon pepper. Beat until fluffy.
*Suggested use:* Many vegetables, especially carrots, onions, green peas.

**Mustard Butter.** Prepare Maître d'Hôtel Butter omitting thyme. Beat in 2 tablespoons Dijon-style mustard.
*Suggested use:* Asparagus, zucchini, or carrots.

**Dill Butter.** Press 2 hard-cooked egg yolks through a wire strainer; combine with butter and 4½ teaspoons dill weed, ½ teaspoon salt, and ⅛ teaspoon white or black pepper. Beat until fluffy.
*Suggested use:* New potatoes, carrots, green beans, or peas.

# Cold Broccoli with Cashews

MENU FOR PATIO BUFFET INCLUDES THIS DISH—PAGE 13

**MAKES 8 SERVINGS**

**PREPARE UP TO 8 HOURS AHEAD**

- 3 pounds broccoli
- ½ cup olive oil
- ¼ cup lemon juice
- ½ teaspoon salt
  Dash pepper
- 2 teaspoons chervil
- ½ cup salted cashews, coarsely broken

Cold vegetables are always good on a summer menu. They can serve as both salad and vegetable.

Cook broccoli until it is just tender; place in serving dish. Combine olive oil, lemon juice, salt, pepper, and chervil. Pour over the broccoli; chill. Just before serving, sprinkle with salted cashews.

# Skillet Zucchini

**MAKES 4 TO 6 SERVINGS**

**COOK JUST BEFORE SERVING**

- 6 medium-sized zucchini
- 1 clove garlic, minced or mashed
- 3 tablespoons olive oil
- 1 tablespoon finely chopped parsley
- 1 teaspoon whole oregano, crushed
- ¾ teaspoon salt
- ¼ teaspoon sugar
- ⅛ teaspoon seasoned pepper

Zucchini retain much of their color and firmness when sautéed with olive oil in a frying pan. Their high water content keeps them from browning too soon or toughening.

Slice zucchini about ¼ inch thick (do not peel).
   In a large frying pan sauté garlic in the oil for about 3 minutes. Add zucchini and cook, uncovered, over medium heat, stirring occasionally, for 8 to 10 minutes. Stir in a mixture of the parsley, oregano, salt, sugar, and pepper; cook for 3 to 5 minutes longer or until just tender.

# Squash à la Grecque

**MAKES 6 TO 8 SERVINGS**

**COOK JUST BEFORE SERVING**

- 6 each crookneck and zucchini squash
- ½ cup boiling salted water
- 4 tablespoons olive oil
- 2 tablespoons lemon juice
- ½ teaspoon crushed dried oregano
  Dash each salt and pepper

Two kinds of squash are colorful and tasty when cooked together, then seasoned the classic Greek way with olive oil and lemon juice.

Cut off the ends of squash and slice in half lengthwise. Place in a saucepan with boiling salted water and simmer for 8 minutes, or until tender. Drain. Blend together olive oil, lemon juice, oregano, salt, and pepper. Pour dressing over hot squash.

# Zucchini Fans

**MAKES 8 SERVINGS**

**STUFF ZUCCHINI UP TO AN HOUR AHEAD, COOK JUST BEFORE SERVING**

- 8 medium-sized zucchini
- 2 small tomatoes
- ¼ cup water
- 2 tablespoons olive oil
- ¼ teaspoon each salt and garlic salt

Select this vegetable dish when you need to add both color and interest to the dinner plate. The fan-cut slices of green zucchini interspersed with tomato are festive, pretty.

Cut the ends off the zucchini, and make 3 lengthwise cuts in each to within an inch of one end, forming a fan. Core tomatoes, cut in ⅓-inch-thick wedges, and insert a wedge between each zucchini slice. Place in a single layer in a large frying pan and add water, olive oil, salt, and garlic salt. Simmer for 15 minutes, or until tender. Lift out carefully.

# Asparagus with Cashew Butter

Nuts always dress up a vegetable. Cashews here take the place of the almonds so often used with asparagus.

Cook asparagus in salted water until tender, about 12 minutes, or, if using the frozen asparagus, cook as directed on the package. Drain cooked spears and arrange on the serving dish. Meanwhile, melt the butter in a small pan; add lemon juice, marjoram, and cashews. Simmer over low heat for 2 minutes. Pour over the cooked asparagus and serve.

**MAKES 2 OR 3 SERVINGS**

**PREPARE JUST BEFORE SERVING**

- 1 pound fresh asparagus or 1 package (10 oz.) frozen asparagus spears
- ¼ cup butter
- 2 teaspoons lemon juice
- ¼ teaspoon marjoram
- ¼ cup salted cashews, in lengthwise halves

# Asparagus Tips in Aspic

Fresh asparagus at its peak is so luscious it just demands special preparation for special springtime occasions. Here choice tips are molded in clear aspic with slices of lemon. This cold vegetable-salad is tantalizingly beautiful, refreshing with sour cream topping. *(Photograph on page 153.)*

In a large pan, combine the 2 cans of chicken broth, chicken pieces, carrots, onions, lemon, and tarragon. Bring to a boil and simmer gently, covered, for 50 minutes, strain mixture; discard bones and vegetables. Chill broth. Skim off solidified fat; discard.

Bring stock to a boil, whisk in the egg whites, and cook until stock resumes boiling. Remove from heat and let stand 1 or 2 minutes. Moisten a muslin cloth in cold water and wring dry. Line a large wire strainer with the cloth. Pour liquid through it; drain well (don't squeeze cloth). Discard egg white.

Measure stock; reserve 3 cups (save any extra for other uses such as cooking the asparagus). Soften gelatin in cold water, then dissolve over hot water and blend with stock. Cover and keep at room temperature.

Cut asparagus tips to fit individual molds—5-oz. custard cups or the classic egg-in-aspic mold—measuring to arrange tips horizontally. Cook asparagus in a wide pan in boiling salted water or chicken broth to cover, until just tender enough to pierce easily with tip of a sharp knife. Drain and chill.

Pour about ½ inch of the stock into each of 6 small molds and chill until set. Place a slice of lemon wedge on each aspic layer and top each with 1 or 2 asparagus tips. Pour in additional stock almost to cover spears. (If stock gels, warm over hot water to soften, but do not add to molds if it is warm.)

Chill again until aspic is set. Add 3 or 4 more tips to each mold, and again add stock barely to cover. Chill until set. Fill molds equally with the remaining stock. Chill again until set (covered if to be kept overnight). Dip molds in hot water briefly to loosen aspic. Unmold on individual plates or a tray. Garnish with parsley. Offer sour cream as a dressing.

**MAKES 6 SERVINGS**

**PREPARE AS MUCH AS A DAY IN ADVANCE**

**SMALL MOLDS OR CUSTARD CUPS REQUIRED**

- 2 cans (14 oz. <u>each</u>) chicken broth
- 1 pound bony chicken pieces
- 3 medium-sized carrots, chopped
- 2 medium-sized onions, sliced
- 1 lemon, sliced
- 1 teaspoon tarragon
- 4 egg whites, beaten slightly
- 1 envelope unflavored gelatin
- ¼ cup cold water
- 24 to 30 asparagus tips
  Boiling salted water or chicken broth
- 6 wedges of thin lemon slices
  Parsley
  Sour cream

# Brussels Sprouts with Pecan Butter

**MAKES 6 SERVINGS**

**PREPARE JUST BEFORE SERVING**

1½  pounds Brussels sprouts (about
    2 pints)
    Salted water
⅓  cup chicken stock
2  tablespoons chopped onion
½  teaspoon salt
½  cup sliced or chopped pecans
¼  cup butter or margarine
    Pimiento strips (optional)
    Parsley (optional)

Toasted pecans and strips of pimiento make this dish so festive you may want to serve it for one of the major holiday meals. Yet the dish is quick enough for enjoying any time.

Trim the Brussels sprouts and soak in salted water to cover for about 20 minutes. Drain and rinse with cold water. In a saucepan bring the chicken stock to a boil; add the sprouts, onions, and salt. Cook uncovered for 5 minutes; cover and continue cooking about 10 minutes, or until the vegetables are tender, but still slightly crisp. Drain, if necessary, and keep hot. Meanwhile in a small frying pan, sauté the pecans in butter for 2 or 3 minutes, until golden brown. Pour the butter mixture over the Brussels sprouts and mix lightly.
    Turn into a serving dish and garnish with pimiento strips and sprigs of parsley.

# Peas Cooked in Lettuce

**MAKES 3 SERVINGS**

**PREPARE AT LAST MINUTE**

    Outside leaves from iceberg
    lettuce
1  package (10 oz.) small frozen
    peas, partially thawed
½  teaspoon salt
⅛  teaspoon pepper
¼  teaspoon whole fresh thyme
    leaves or pinch of dried thyme
1  teaspoon scraped or grated
    onion, or ½ teaspoon instant
    minced onion
2  tablespoons butter or margarine

Use a heavy frying pan or electric frying pan to cook peas this French way. You'll need a few large lettuce leaves. You can easily double this recipe, using 2 packages of peas, the same lining of lettuce leaves, and about the same cooking time.

Wash the lettuce leaves, shake off excess water, and use them to line the bottom of a heavy frying pan (one with a tight cover) or electric frying pan.
    Empty a package of frozen peas; break any large pieces that are frozen together, and spread the peas on the lettuce. Sprinkle peas with the salt, pepper, thyme, and onion; dot the top with butter. Cover the pan, turn the heat to medium, and boil just until the peas are tender, about 3 minutes. Turn peas into a serving dish, discard the lettuce, and serve immediately.

# Limas and Peas Baked with Herbs

**MAKES 4 TO 6 SERVINGS**

**THAW VEGETABLES AHEAD, BEGIN
    BAKING 45 MINUTES BEFORE
    SERVING TIME**

1  package (10 oz.) frozen baby
    lima beans
1  package (10 oz.) frozen peas
¾  teaspoon <u>each</u> basil and salt
2  green onions, thinly sliced
    (including part of tops)
2  tablespoons butter or margarine
2  tablespoons water

Basil is the herb used with these green vegetables. Delicate green onion also brings out their flavors.

Thaw lima beans and peas for several hours at room temperature or in refrigerator overnight. Place in a greased 1½-quart casserole with basil, salt, and green onions; stir to blend. Dot with butter or margarine and sprinkle with water. Cover and bake in a 325° oven for about 45 minutes or until vegetables are just tender; stir occasionally.

*Asparagus Tips in Aspic—see page 151*

# Brandied Carrots

MAKES 4 SERVINGS

PREPARE AT LAST MINUTE

10 or 12 slender carrots
   Boiling salted water
3 tablespoons butter
¼ cup warm brandy

Turn pot roasts and stews into something special by ringing them with these brandy-flamed carrots. A fine roast of beef would also benefit from such garnish.

Scrape carrots. Cook in a small amount of boiling salted water in a wide, shallow pan until tender (about 10 minutes); drain off liquid. In the same pan or a chafing dish, melt butter; add brandy and set aflame. Sauté carrots until lightly browned, shaking back and forth to turn.

# Beets with Mustard Butter

MAKES 6 SERVINGS

COOK BEETS, PREPARE MUSTARD
   BUTTER AHEAD

¼ cup soft butter
1 tablespoon prepared mustard
1 tablespoon tarragon vinegar
3 cups diced cooked beets

Beets are such a robust peasant-type vegetable that it is surprising they aren't more often sauced with something hearty. This recipe uses healthy quantities of mustard and vinegar.

Beat together the butter, mustard, and vinegar. Heat beets, put in a hot vegetable dish, and add the mustard butter in small pieces. Mix lightly at table.

# Honey Parsnips

MAKES 6 SERVINGS

COOK AHEAD, REHEAT

6 medium-sized parsnips, peeled
   (about 1½ pounds)
   Boiling water
1 teaspoon salt
4 tablespoons butter or margarine
4 tablespoons honey
   Cinnamon

Honey-sweetened parsnips are especially good with ham or pork. Take care not to overcook them, or they will lose flavor and texture.

Cut parsnips lengthwise in thin slices, then cut slices into pieces about 1½ inches long. Place in medium-sized pan and cover with boiling water. Add salt and cook for 20 minutes, or just until tender. Drain. Melt butter in a large frying pan; add honey, and cook, stirring, until bubbly. Add parsnips, cover, and cook over low heat for 5 minutes. Just before serving, sprinkle with cinnamon.

# Scalloped Mushrooms

*MENU FOR WINTERTIME BUFFET INCLUDES THIS DISH—PAGE 42*

MAKES ABOUT 12 SERVINGS

MAY BE ASSEMBLED AHEAD,
   BAKED AT LAST MINUTE

1½ pounds fresh mushrooms,
   washed, drained, and sliced
3 cups soft French bread crumbs
   (fresh bread whirled in
   blender)
¾ cup butter, melted
   Salt and pepper
½ cup dry white wine

Toasty buttered bread crumbs top this mushroom casserole, which can be assembled ahead of time to be baked just before dinner if you want to free yourself for other tasks at the last minute.

Place about a third of the mushrooms in a buttered 2-quart baking dish; cover with about a third of the bread crumbs, and drizzle about a third of the butter over the crumbs. Sprinkle with salt and pepper. Repeat, using another third of the mushrooms, crumbs, and butter; add salt and pepper. For the top layer, cover with remaining mushrooms; sprinkle them with salt and pepper, and pour wine over all. Cover and bake in a 325° oven for about 35 minutes. Mix remaining butter and crumbs, and spoon over mushrooms. Bake uncovered 10 more minutes, or until crumbs are toasted.

# Carrot-Asparagus Platter

*MENU FOR BARBECUED HAM BUFFET INCLUDES THIS DISH—PAGE 29*

This colorful vegetable platter can be partially prepared ahead. You can cook the carrots a day ahead and refrigerate them; the potato border can be prepared early in the day it is to be served and then refrigerated until the final browning. *(Photograph on page 8.)*

Prepare instant mashed potatoes, adding salt, water, and milk according to directions on package. Add 4 tablespoons butter, 1 tablespoon minced onion, and eggs, beating until thoroughly blended. Spoon this mixture with teaspoon or press through cake decorator onto a large ovenproof platter or plank (about 18 by 24 inches) to make the decorative border for the carrots and asparagus; refrigerate until ready to cook vegetables.

While you glaze carrots and cook asparagus, brown potato border in a 375° oven for about 10 minutes. Arrange hot vegetables within the borders.

**Glazed Gingered Carrots.** In a small amount of water cook carrots, cut in chunks, until almost tender, 12 to 15 minutes. In a saucepan melt 3 tablespoons butter and stir in brown sugar, 1 tablespoon minced onion, ginger, ¼ teaspoon salt, ⅛ teaspoon pepper. Add carrots and stir carefully to coat them completely with the mixture. Turn carrots in pan over medium heat, until glazed and thoroughly heated, about 5 minutes. Arrange in center of platter.

**Buttered Parmesan Asparagus.** Cook asparagus in a small amount of water until tender, about 10 minutes. Drain and season with 1 tablespoon butter, ½ teaspoon salt, and ⅛ teaspoon pepper. Arrange on both sides of carrots on platter and sprinkle with Parmesan cheese.

**MAKES 12 SERVINGS**

**POTATO BORDER CAN BE MADE SEVERAL HOURS AHEAD, REFRIGERATED UNTIL FINAL BROWNING**

- Instant mashed potatoes (amount for 8 servings)
- Salt
- Water
- Milk
- 4 tablespoons butter
- 1 tablespoon instant minced onion
- 2 eggs

**GLAZED GINGERED CARROTS:**

- 4 cups carrots (2 pounds)
- 3 tablespoons butter
- 2 tablespoons brown sugar
- 1 tablespoon instant minced onion
- ½ teaspoon ground ginger
- ¼ teaspoon salt
- ⅛ teaspoon pepper

**BUTTERED PARMESAN ASPARAGUS:**

- 4 pounds fresh asparagus
- 1 tablespoon butter
- ½ teaspoon salt
- ⅛ teaspoon pepper
- 2 tablespoons grated Parmesan cheese

# Ratatouille

*MIXED VEGETABLE CASSEROLE*

Ratatouille ("rah-tah-*too*-yeh") is a summer vegetable stew that originated in the Midi, along France's sunny southern coast.

The appeal of making ratatouille ahead is the fact that it really tastes better after standing awhile. Serve it cold as a main-dish salad for hot weather, hot or cold as a meat accompaniment. *(Photograph on page 144.)*

Heat ¼ cup of the oil in a large frying pan over high heat. Add onions and garlic and cook, stirring, until onions are soft but not browned. Stir in the eggplant, zucchini, peppers, 2 teaspoons salt, basil, and minced parsley; add a little of the oil as needed to keep the vegetables from sticking. Cover pan and cook over moderate heat for about 30 minutes; stir occasionally, using a large spatula and turning the vegetables to help preserve their shape. If mixture becomes quite soupy, remove cover to allow moisture to escape.

Add the tomatoes to the vegetables in the pan and stir to blend. Also add more oil if vegetables are sticking. Cover and cook over moderate heat for 15 minutes; stir occasionally. Again, if mixture becomes quite soupy during this period, remove cover to allow moisture to evaporate. Ratatouille should have a little free liquid, but still be of a good spoon-and-serve consistency. Add more salt if required. Serve hot or cold. Garnish with parsley and tomato.

**MAKES 8 TO 10 SERVINGS**

**PREPARE AS MUCH AS 2 DAYS AHEAD**

- About ½ cup olive oil
- 2 large onions, sliced
- 2 large cloves garlic, minced or mashed
- 1 medium-sized eggplant, cut in ½-inch cubes
- 6 medium-sized zucchini, thickly sliced
- 2 green or red bell peppers, seeded and cut in chunks
- About 2 teaspoons salt
- 1 teaspoon basil
- ½ cup minced parsley
- 4 large tomatoes, cut in chunks
- Parsley
- Sliced tomato (optional)

# A GUIDE TO SERVING CHEESES

Probably as many as 100 cheeses are now sold in America. Following is a guide to about 65 of the most widely available kinds.

**Hard Grating Cheeses.** A few very hard cheeses are almost always grated for cooked dishes or for sprinkling on pastas and salads. Most familiar are sharp, piquant Romano, Parmesan, and dry Monterey Jack. Sapsago, a small cone-shaped cheese flavored and colored sage green with powdered clover leaves, is specified in a few recipes.

**Cheddar and Cheddar Types.** These range in flavor from mild to very sharp and in color from cream to deep yellow-orange. Cheddar originated in England, but most sold in this country is American-made, sometimes called American cheese or by a trade name. Several English Cheddar types — cream-colored, mild Caerphilly and crumbly, medium-sharp Cheshire — are now imported.

**Full-Flavored, Firm Cheeses.** Some of these compact cheeses have a very distinctive tang which leaves a bit of an aftertaste. Most pronounced is Port Salut or the Danish version of this cheese, Esrom. Tilsit (Danish Havarti), Beer Kaese, Münster, and mellow Brick are somewhat less assertive in flavor in varying degrees.

Of entirely different character, Greek Kasera (Kasseri) and American Fontinella resemble Parmesan but are soft enough to be sliced. If aged, they become hard enough for grating.

**Swiss and Gruyère Types.** Several cheeses have holes or "eyes" caused by certain bacteria, which also contribute a characteristic nutty flavor. Swiss with large holes and Gruyère with smaller ones are the best-known. Others similar are French Emmental, Danish Emmenthaler, and Danish Samsoe.

**Mild Cheeses (Firm to Semi-Soft).** Smooth Gouda and Edam are much alike in their nutlike flavor, yellow coloring, spherical shape, and red wax coating.

American Chantelle, Italian Fontina, and several Danish cheeses (Tybo, Elbo, Danbo, and a Fontina type) all have similar oily-rich texture.

White Monterey Jack and Teleme are more bland, slightly salty, and characterized by a somewhat elastic texture. Teleme softens as it ripens.

An even more elastic, resilient texture is shared by three Italian cheeses generally used for cooking because of their melting qualities. Pale yellow Mozzarella is the pizza cheese (Caciocavallo is similarly used). Smoky Provolone, well-aged, is excellent for appetizers.

Several cheeses with creamy, smooth texture and pleasant, light flavor have been recently introduced in Western America. Danish St. Paulin resembles Italian Bel Paese, which has been widely distributed for some time. Other relative newcomers are Pont L'Eveque with ochre crust,

mildly pungent Reblochon, and smooth Bonbel, usually purchased in a sphere coated with yellow paraffin.

**Blue-Veined Cheeses.** Genuine Roquefort, made only in France, is sharp and very crumbly when cool. Italian Gorgonzola is richer, less sharp, and more pungent; the fine English Stilton tends to be more restrained. Others streaked with blue or greenish mold are called "blue" in America or "bleu" in France. Such Danish cheeses may be labeled Danablu, Danish blue, or Mycella (which resembles Gorgonzola).

**Pungent Ripened Cheeses with Edible Crusts.** Soft-crusted with very creamy interior when ripe, these range from very strong to subtle (all a variation on what might be described as an earthy or mushroom-like flavor).

Infamous Limburger can scent a whole room. Liederkranz is similar, but less powerful and odoriferous.

Next down the potency scale is Camembert, which turns to a velvety cream when perfectly ripe; Brie is similar, but slightly more delicate.

Most mild are Neufchâtel and California-made Breakfast Cheese. When unripe, they resemble cream cheese, but become more and more zesty as they mature.

All these cheeses are relatively mild when young and increase in potency with the ripening process.

**Buttery, Creamy Cheeses.** Several very light French cheeses, somewhat like American cream cheese but more buttery, are now available at a few cheese shops. Delectable Boursault, Gervais, and Boursin are especially fine for dessert, served with fruit.

Danish white cream cheese also is becoming more widely distributed, often labeled Ballet or Castello.

**Specialty and Flavored Cheeses.** Some are so unique they are best described individually rather than categorized.

Kuminost is much like Jack, but is seasoned with cumin and flecked with caraway seeds. Dutch Leyden, also spiced with these seeds plus cloves, has a Cheddar-like color and texture.

Rich, white French Le Grappe is encrusted with the seeds and skins remaining after grapes are pressed for wine — this imparts a certain savoriness and may be eaten by those who like the crunchiness.

Two soft French types — Gourmandise and Nec Plus Ultra — are spiked with kirsch (cherry brandy) or walnut flavoring. (La Beau Pasteur is similar but unflavored.)

Norwegian Gjetost (pronounced "yeet-ost") is a very solid, caramel-flavored, brown goat cheese.

Italian Ricotta, much like cottage cheese, is used primarily for pastas and desserts.

No other cheese available in America is quite like Greek Feta, which is snow-white, salty, and crumbly but sliceable. Good with olives, Feta may be eaten with either fingers or forks, or used in cooked dishes.

# Spiced Baked Onions

Onion fanciers will enjoy these tiny baked onions on a party dinner menu. They are lightly spiced and topped with toasted almonds.

Peel onions; cook in boiling salted water for 5 minutes. Drain. Melt butter or margarine in a shallow 1½-quart baking dish; stir in brown sugar, salt, nutmeg or mace, cloves, cayenne, and white pepper. Add onions, stirring to coat with butter mixture. Cover and bake in a 325° oven for about 45 minutes or until onions are tender, stirring occasionally. Before serving, remove cloves, spoon some of the sauce over onions, and sprinkle with almonds.

**MAKES 6 TO 8 SERVINGS**

**PREPARE DISH FOR BAKING SEVERAL HOURS AHEAD**

24  small white boiling onions
Boiling salted water
3  tablespoons butter or margarine
1  tablespoon brown sugar
1  teaspoon salt
¼  teaspoon nutmeg or mace
6  whole cloves
Dash <u>each</u> cayenne and white pepper
¼  cup toasted, slivered, blanched almonds

# Scalloped Onions or Leeks

Poppy seed and cream cheese make this dish distinctive. A variation using leeks instead of onions is equally delicious.

Place sliced onions in a greased 1-quart baking dish. Sprinkle with salt, pepper, and poppy seed. In a small pan, stir the cream cheese over low heat until melted. Add milk and mix until it makes a smooth sauce. Pour over onions. Cover and bake in a 350° oven for 1 hour.

**MAKES 6 SERVINGS**

**ASSEMBLE SEVERAL HOURS AHEAD, BEGIN BAKING 1 HOUR BEFORE SERVING**

1½  pounds small white onions, peeled and sliced (or 3 cups thinly sliced leeks, including some of the green portion)
½  teaspoon salt
¼  teaspoon pepper
2  tablespoons poppy seed
1  package (3 oz.) cream cheese
½  cup milk

# Onion Soufflé

Onions give a mildly robust flavor to a soufflé that is good with simply cooked meat or fish. Baked in individual soufflé dishes, it would be a good choice for a patio supper featuring barbecued steaks. Have raw vegetable relishes and a cheese-flavored dip for guests to nibble while the steaks grill and the soufflé bakes. Serve hot buttered French bread and tomato wedges with the meat and soufflé.

Melt butter in a pan; add onions and cook until soft and lightly browned. Stir in flour, salt, thyme, and pepper and cook until bubbly. Remove from heat and gradually stir in milk. Cook, stirring, until thick. Either force this mixture through a wire strainer or whirl it in a blender until smooth. Return to the pan and heat to simmering, stirring. Remove from heat and beat in egg yolks. Heat and stir a few seconds, or until thick again; set off heat. Whip egg whites until they hold short, distinct, moist peaks. Fold half the whites thoroughly into sauce; fold in remaining whites as thoroughly as you like.

Pour into a well-buttered 2-quart soufflé dish or about 6 to 8 individual dishes. Bake in a 375° oven for about 40 minutes (15 to 20 minutes for small soufflés). Serve immediately.

**MAKES 6 TO 8 SERVINGS**

**2-QUART SOUFFLÉ DISH OR INDIVIDUAL SOUFFLÉ DISHES REQUIRED**

5  tablespoons butter or margarine
1  cup chopped onion
4  tablespoons flour
1  teaspoon salt
¼  teaspoon thyme
Dash freshly ground black pepper
1  cup milk
9  eggs, separated

# Potato Parmesan Soufflé

MAKES 8 TO 10 SERVINGS

PARTIALLY PREPARE SEVERAL
  HOURS AHEAD

SOUFFLÉ DISH OR OTHER
  STRAIGHT-SIDED BAKING
  DISH REQUIRED

8  servings instant mashed
     potatoes, prepared as
     package directs
6  eggs, separated
¾  cup shredded Parmesan cheese
½  teaspoon each salt and cream of
     tartar

Instant mashed potatoes speed the making of this impressive soufflé. If you need to hold the soufflé a few minutes before serving, leave it in the oven with the heat turned off.

Prepare instant mashed potatoes according to package directions for 8 servings. While still hot, beat in egg yolks, one at a time, and mix in cheese. (At this point, you can cover and let stand at room temperature a few hours.) About 1 hour before serving time, beat egg whites until foamy, add salt and cream of tartar, and beat until soft peaks form. Fold beaten whites into potato mixture. Spoon into two buttered 2-quart soufflé dishes or a 4-quart soufflé dish (or use baking dishes with straight sides).

Bake in a 375° oven, allowing 45 minutes for small soufflés or 1 hour for a large soufflé.

# Fluffy Potato Casserole

MAKES 6 TO 8 SERVINGS

PREPARE FOR BAKING UP TO 4
  HOURS AHEAD

2  cups hot or cold mashed
     potatoes
1  large package (8 oz.) cream
     cheese, at room temperature
1  small onion, finely chopped
2  eggs
2  tablespoons all-purpose flour
     Salt and pepper to taste
1  can (3½ oz.) French-fried onions

There's an interesting texture contrast between the creamy potatoes, containing cream cheese, and the crisp onion topping on this vegetable casserole. Use leftover seasoned mashed potatoes or prepare instant mashed potatoes as the package directs.

Put the potatoes into the large bowl of your electric mixer. Add the cream cheese, chopped onion, eggs, and flour. Beat at medium speed until the ingredients are blended, then beat at high speed until light and fluffy. Taste, and add salt and pepper, if needed.

Spoon into a greased 9-inch-square baking dish. Distribute the canned onions evenly over the top. Bake, uncovered, in a 300° oven for about 35 minutes. (If you prepare this dish ahead, add the onions just before putting it in the oven.)

# Potatoes with Fresh Tomatoes

MAKES 6 TO 8 SERVINGS

COOK POTATOES AHEAD, REHEAT
  AND ADD OTHER VEGETABLES
  JUST BEFORE SERVING TIME

4  medium-sized potatoes
2  medium-sized firm ripe tomatoes
1  medium-sized onion
½  green pepper
2  tablespoons shortening or
     salad oil
4  tablespoons butter
½  teaspoon salt
⅛  teaspoon pepper
½  teaspoon sugar

If you cook the potatoes in an electric frying pan, reduce heat to warm, sprinkle with tomato topping, and serve from the pan.

Peel the potatoes and cut into ½-inch dice. Peel the tomatoes, cut in half and gently squeeze out the seed pockets; dice. Peel and thinly slice onion and seed the green pepper and thinly slice.

In a heavy frying pan or electric frying pan, heat the shortening and 2 tablespoons of the butter over medium heat (about 350° on electric pan). Sauté the potatoes slowly, turning over as needed until golden and tender, about 25 minutes; sprinkle with salt and pepper.

Meanwhile in a small pan sauté the onion, green pepper, and tomato in remaining 2 tablespoons butter until soft, but not brown; sprinkle with the sugar and keep warm. Turn the potatoes into a warm serving dish and spoon the tomato mixture over the top. Serve immediately.

# Brown-Sugar-Glazed Potatoes

Brown-sugar-glazed sweet potatoes are a familiar treat, but small white potatoes can also be delicious this way.

Cook potatoes in boiling salted water until tender; drain and peel. Heat brown sugar, butter, and milk in large frying pan, stirring to blend. Add potatoes; cook 4 to 5 minutes, turning to glaze.

**MAKES 12 SERVINGS**

**COOK POTATOES AS MUCH AS A DAY AHEAD, GLAZE JUST BEFORE SERVING TIME**

| | |
|---|---|
| 2 | dozen small boiling potatoes |
| | Boiling salted water |
| ¾ | cup brown sugar |
| ¼ | cup butter |
| 3 | tablespoons milk |

# Skillet Potatoes Anna

Sliced potatoes, baked in a skillet with butter until they are crusty on top, can be a welcome change from the usual baked potato or French fries with steaks and barbecued meats.

Brush a 10-inch heavy frying pan (one that can be put into the oven) or shallow baking dish with part of the melted butter and overlap the potato slices in the pan, sprinkling each layer with salt and pepper to taste. Pour over the remaining melted butter. Bake uncovered in a 450° oven for 45 minutes, or until the top is crusty and the potatoes are tender.

**MAKES 10 SERVINGS**

**PREPARE FOR BAKING SEVERAL HOURS AHEAD**

| | |
|---|---|
| ½ | cup melted butter |
| 6 | to 8 large baking potatoes, peeled and sliced |
| | Salt |
| | Pepper |

# Potato-Onion Pancakes

With a topping of sour cream and crisp bacon on the side, these pancakes may be the main dish at supper or brunch. They are good accompaniments to hearty main dishes, particularly those of German origin, such as sauerbraten. Sausages and sauerkraut or smoked pork and apple sauce also are compatible.

Combine flour, salt, eggs, milk, parsley, and chives; mix to blend. Let stand at least 30 minutes. Blend in potato and onion. Divide batter evenly into 4 floured, well-buttered, 9-inch foil pie pans. Bake in a 425° oven about 25 minutes or until browned. Fold in half and serve hot.

**MAKES 4 SERVINGS**

**PREPARE BATTER AND VEGETABLES AHEAD, COMBINE AT BAKING TIME**

**FOUR PIE PANS REQUIRED**

| | |
|---|---|
| ⅔ | cup unsifted regular all-purpose flour |
| ½ | teaspoon salt |
| 3 | eggs, slightly beaten |
| 1 | cup milk |
| 1 | tablespoon <u>each</u> chopped parsley and freeze-dried chopped chives |
| 1 | cup shredded raw potato |
| ¼ | cup finely chopped onion |

# Pecan-Topped Sweet Potatoes

MAKES 8 TO 10 SERVINGS

COOK POTATOES UP TO A DAY
  AHEAD

ASSEMBLE CASSEROLE FOR
  BAKING SEVERAL HOURS AHEAD

2½ to 3 pounds sweet potatoes or
      yams, cooked and peeled
  2 eggs
  ¾ cup brown sugar
  ½ cup butter, melted
  1 teaspoon each salt and
      cinnamon
      Orange juice (up to 1 cup)
  1 cup pecan halves

A casserole of fluffy, orange-scented sweet potatoes can be a show-stopper. Arrange pecan halves close together to encrust the top completely. Put them in rows if your dish is square, or in concentric circles if round. The crunchy, brown-sugar-glazed nuts are a delicious sight, appetizing to cut through and spoon on top of each serving.

Mash sweet potatoes (you should have about 6 cups). Beat in eggs, ¼ cup of the brown sugar, ¼ cup of the melted butter, salt, and cinnamon. (If potatoes seem dry, beat in orange juice until moist and fluffy.) Put in a 1½ or 2-quart casserole. (Refrigerate if you wish.) Before baking, arrange pecan halves on top; sprinkle with the remaining ½ cup brown sugar and drizzle with remaining ¼ cup melted butter. Bake, uncovered, in 375° oven for 20 minutes, or until heated through.

# Sweet Potatoes and Apples Caramel

MAKES 8 TO 10 SERVINGS

ASSEMBLE CASSEROLE UP TO A
  DAY AHEAD

BEGIN BAKING AN HOUR BEFORE
  SERVING TIME

  ¼ cup granulated sugar
  ½ teaspoon salt
  ¼ teaspoon nutmeg
  4 tablespoons butter or margarine
      About 4 medium-sized sweet
        potatoes, cooked and peeled
  3 tart, crisp apples, peeled
  ¼ cup hot water
  ⅔ cup brown sugar, firmly packed

Serve this vegetable-fruit casserole with ham or pork or as a glamorous change from some of the sweet potato dishes traditional with Thanksgiving turkey.

Combine the granulated sugar, salt, and nutmeg; blend in butter with a fork. Thinly slice potatoes to make 4 cups, and thinly slice the apples.

In a flameproof 2-quart casserole or 9-inch square baking pan, make a layer of potatoes, then apples, then sugar mixture, using about ⅓ of each. Repeat making two more layers. Pour over the hot water; cover and bake in a 350° oven for 1 hour, or until the apples are tender. Remove from oven, uncover, and press the brown sugar through a wire strainer onto the top of the casserole to make an even layer.

Set under the broiler for about 2 or 3 minutes, or until the topping melts and bubbles—watch closely to prevent its scorching. Serve hot.

# Nut-Crusted Squash Squares

MAKES 6 SERVINGS

PARTIALLY PREPARE AHEAD

2½ pound piece of Hubbard or
      banana squash
      Water
  ⅓ cup finely chopped peanuts
  ⅓ cup crushed oven-toasted rice
      cereal
  ¼ cup brown sugar, packed
  ½ cup butter or margarine, melted

A crunchy peanut and rice-cereal coating is a simple but surprisingly good addition to baked squash. Serve this hearty, rich vegetable with ham, pork, or poultry.

Remove seeds from squash and place, cut side down, in a shallow baking pan. Add hot water to a depth of ⅓ inch. Bake in a 375° oven for 45 minutes, or until almost tender. Cool and peel. Cut into 6 squares. In a bowl, mix together peanuts, rice cereal, and brown sugar; set aside.

About ½ hour before serving, dip squares in melted butter to coat all sides, then dip in peanut mixture, coating all over. Arrange in a shallow baking pan, cover, and bake in a 400° oven for 15 minutes. Uncover and bake 5 minutes more or until lightly browned.

# PASTAS AND CEREALS

Starchy accompaniments include rice, bulgur (wheat), pastas, and dumplings, (in addition to potatoes, included in preceding pages of the vegetables section). So many dishes can be made from these basic ingredients that selecting just a few was not an easy task. Included in this section are those which are plain and all-purpose enough for serving with many types of entrées, yet different enough from the usual fare to lend interest to your party menus.

## Wheat Pilaf with Peas and Lemon

*Bulgur* (cracked wheat) has been used for pilaf and salads in the Middle East for centuries. American-grown wheat, nearly identical to that used for bulgur, is available at most markets in the rice section, usually packaged in boxes.

Melt the butter in a large, heavy frying pan. Sauté wheat and onion in the butter about 5 minutes. Add salt (amount depends on saltiness of liquid used), liquid, and lemon peel; reduce heat, cover tightly, and simmer until the water is absorbed, about 15 to 20 minutes. Stir in peas 5 minutes before cooking is finished. (The wheat will still be quite crunchy; you may prefer to add as much as 1 additional cup liquid and cook it 5 to 10 minutes longer.)

*Note: Instead of cooking the pilaf on top of your range, you can transfer it to a greased casserole and bake in a 400° oven. If the liquid in the recipe is hot when you add it, the pilaf will take about as long to bake as it does to cook on top of the range.*

**MAKES 6 TO 8 SERVINGS**

**SAUTÉ WHEAT AND ONION UP TO 2 HOURS AHEAD**

3   tablespoons butter, margarine, chicken or bacon drippings
2   cups quick-cooking cracked wheat (bulgur)
½   cup sliced green onion
    About 1 teaspoon salt
3   cups chicken stock or other liquid
1   teaspoon grated lemon peel
1   to 2 cups frozen peas (thawed)

## Crusty Golden Rice

*PERSIAN CHELO*

This Persian classic has a lovely buttery color and an appetizing top crust, which is crisped rice turned out from the bottom of the cooking pan.

Rinse rice with lukewarm water; drain, place in bowl, and add 2 teaspoons salt and cold water to cover. Let stand for 3 to 4 hours or overnight; drain well. In a large deep pan bring to boiling 2 quarts water and 1 tablespoon salt; add soaked rice, and boil, uncovered, for 12 to 15 minutes, stirring occasionally. Drain rice; rinse with lukewarm water, and drain again.

Melt butter or margarine in a small pan. Pour about ⅓ of the melted butter into a heavy 10-inch frying pan that has a tightly fitting cover. Add 1 tablespoon water to frying pan and tip back and forth to mix with the butter. Add drained rice, a spoonful at a time, to cover bottom of pan; pile remaining rice over this layer in the shape of a shallow cone. Drizzle remaining butter over top. Fold 3 paper towels, place gently over rice, and cover pan.

Place pan over medium-high heat for 5 minutes. Reduce heat to low and continue cooking for 30 minutes longer (if steam escapes around cover during cooking, place a folded towel over lid to help keep moisture inside pan). Carefully loosen edge and bottom of rice with a flexible spatula; invert rice in one large cake onto a warm plate (if part of the crust sticks to pan bottom, slide spatula under it, loosen, and invert crust over rice on serving plate).

**MAKES 6 SERVINGS**

**SOAK RICE 3 HOURS TO OVERNIGHT; BOIL RICE UP TO 8 HOURS BEFORE FINAL FRYING**

1½   cups long grain white rice
2    teaspoons salt
     Cold water
2    quarts boiling water
1    tablespoon salt
⅓    cup butter or margarine
1    tablespoon water

# Risotto

*ITALIAN RICE*

**MAKES 4 TO 6 SERVINGS**

**MAY BE HELD HOT IN WARM OVEN AN HOUR**

2 tablespoons <u>each</u> butter or margarine and olive oil
1 small or medium-sized onion, chopped
1 small clove garlic, minced or mashed
1 cup long grain rice
About 3½ cups hot chicken or beef broth
Salt to taste
½ cup freshly shredded or grated Parmesan, Asiago, or domestic Romano cheese (or ¼ cup imported Romano)
About 1 tablespoon butter

Unlike most other rice classics, Italian *risotto* has a creamy, flowing consistency. In Italy, where even the most simple meal is served in courses, the rice comes as the second or pasta course after the antipasto and before the meat or fish. But in American meals, risotto may come before, with, or after the entrée. For the best risotto, buy the best cheese and shred it yourself.

Heat the 2 tablespoons butter and olive oil together in a Dutch oven, heavy 2-quart saucepan, frying pan with a tight-fitting lid, or flameproof casserole. Add the chopped onion and sauté over medium heat until golden. Add garlic and rice and stir until the rice is milky in appearance, about 3 minutes.

Next add 1 cup of the broth, reduce heat, cover, and simmer until most of the liquid has been absorbed, about 10 minutes. Add the remaining hot broth in 2 or 3 additions, removing cover each time and stirring lightly with a fork; cook until the rice is tender and most of the liquid has been absorbed, about 20 to 25 minutes longer. (Exact amount of liquid needed and cooking time varies with rice and cooking pan you use.) Taste, and add salt if needed.

Remove from heat and add half the cheese and remaining 1 tablespoon butter; mix lightly with 2 forks. Turn into a serving dish or serve from the casserole, after topping with remaining cheese. You may also pass extra cheese.

# Egg-Foam Dumplings

*NOCKERLN*

**MAKES 4 TO 6 SERVINGS**

**COOK AT LAST MINUTE**

4 eggs, separated
⅛ teaspoon cream of tartar
½ teaspoon salt
4 tablespoons flour
Chicken broth, canned or freshly made, or from a stew

A light chicken stew, plain, or flavored with lemon or tarragon, makes a good companion for *nockerln;* you see the dumplings served this way in Austria and Switzerland. Remove the meat from the pot and keep it warm, then pour dumplings onto the broth (they cook in just a few minutes).

Beat yolks until light and thick. Whip whites with cream of tartar until whites hold short distinct peaks; fold in salt, flour, and yolks. Have broth just below boiling point in wide pan (10 to 12-inch diameter); pour in foam. Cover, cook 3 to 4 minutes or until foam is set on top. Do not allow stock to boil actively.

Cut through foam with slotted spoon; lift sections from liquid, draining. Serve with prepared chicken dish, or gravy. Spoon sauce over dumplings.

# Green Noodles with Sour Cream

**MAKES 4 TO 6 SERVINGS**

**PREPARE JUST BEFORE SERVING**

6 ounces noodle-shaped spinach macaroni
¼ teaspoon onion powder
½ teaspoon salt
2 tablespoons milk
3 tablespoons freeze-dried chopped chives
1 cup sour cream

Green noodles, made with spinach, are cooked and put together quickly with the simple sour cream sauce. They make a colorful accompaniment for chicken or broiled fish steaks.

Cook noodles in boiling, salted water until tender, about 8 minutes. Drain. Add seasonings, milk, and chives to sour cream and heat just until warmed through. Fold sour cream mixture into noodles, and serve immediately.

# Pasta a Pesto

MENU FOR WINE-TASTING INCLUDES THIS DISH—PAGE 17

The sauce for the pasta can be made several weeks ahead. To serve, you may wish to toss noodles with sauce in a chafing dish.

With a blender, or a mortar and pestle, reduce the basil, parsley, and garlic to a pulp, slowly adding olive oil to make a smooth paste. Add nutmeg, cheese, and 1 teaspoon salt. Cook noodles in a large amount of boiling salted water until tender. Drain, add basil sauce, and toss until well coated.

If you want to use a chafing dish, toss noodles with sauce in the dish over direct flame. Serve immediately, or cover and keep in the hot water bath of the chafing dish.

**MAKES 6 TO 8 SERVINGS**

**PREPARE SAUCE AS MUCH AS 2 WEEKS AHEAD**

¼ cup dried basil (or 1 cup of fresh leaves)
¼ cup chopped fresh parsley
1 or 2 small cloves garlic
⅔ cup olive oil
¼ teaspoon nutmeg
1 cup lightly packed, freshly grated Parmesan or Romano cheese
1 teaspoon salt
1 pound tagliarini (or other flat ribbon noodle)

# Parsley Spaghetti

Butter, onion, cheese, and a liberal amount of fresh parsley make a colorful, quick sauce for spaghetti. This is a good emergency dish for those times you suddenly find yourself playing hostess without having planned for it.

Cook spaghetti in boiling salted water as directed on the package; drain. Place on a platter and put in a 175° oven while you make the sauce.

Melt butter, add olive oil, and sauté the onion until it becomes translucent. Add parsley, nutmeg, salt, and pepper. Pour over spaghetti immediately. Sprinkle with cheese and leave in the oven for 5 minutes before serving.

**MAKES 4 TO 6 SERVINGS**

**PREPARE JUST BEFORE SERVING**

1 package (8 oz.) spaghetti
Salted water
¼ cup butter
1 tablespoon olive oil
1 small onion, minced
⅔ cup chopped fresh parsley
½ teaspoon nutmeg
¼ teaspoon each salt and pepper
2 tablespoons grated Parmesan cheese

## THE MYSTERIES OF WINE AGE AND VINTAGE

Unfortunately, the matters of wine age (how old) and vintage (what year) have put some people off fom getting better acquainted with wine.

Probably the most important misconception about wine age is that a wine must be old to be good. The truth is that most wines need not be held for any special aging. They are ready for drinking when they are bought. This applies to both European and California wines and is true for all rosé wines, most whites, and a great many reds. The exceptions are wines of particularly promising quality, especially the more full-bodied reds. Even a very good wine which could improve in certain ways with aging will still probably be a good wine when younger, with certain "young" qualities to be appreciated. Producers of fine wines the world over know when they have made a wine that will benefit by aging and often withhold it from the market until it is ready.

Vintage, the year in which the grapes are grown, is of importance only with French, German, or other wines grown on lands subject to climatic extremes and chancy weather. Grapes grown in California or elsewhere where the climate varies little from year to year differ in character from year to year, but are not subject to crop failure. Hence, "good years" and "bad years" are virtually unknown.

Many wines are not identified by vintage at all. Table wines of moderate price often are blends of different years. Sherries, most Champagnes, and most Ports are blends of wine from different years, whether made in America or in their country of origin.

# BREADS

Once an everyday cooking chore, bread-making is now most likely to take place when guests are expected because the daily bread we buy is so standardized and familiar. No greater treat can be presented at a meal for company than bread freshly baked at home. A simple meal can be glorified. Many of the breads in this section may be baked ahead and frozen to be ready whenever needed.

## Buttery Pan Rolls

**MAKES ABOUT 15 ROLLS**

**BAKED ROLLS MAY BE FROZEN**

- 2 packages active dry or compressed yeast
- ½ cup warm water (lukewarm for compressed yeast)
- 4½ cups regular all-purpose flour
- ¼ cup sugar
- 1 teaspoon salt
- 6 tablespoons butter or margarine, melted and cooled
- 1 egg
- 1 cup milk, scalded and cooled
- ¼ cup butter or margarine, melted and cooled

Light and good tasting, these yeast batter rolls rise quickly. You can serve them right in the baking pan.

Dissolve yeast in warm water and set aside until bubbly. Sift flour, measure, and sift 2 cups of it with the sugar and salt.

Add 6 tablespoons butter or margarine, egg, yeast mixture, and cooled milk to the flour; beat at high speed with an electric mixer about 2 minutes. Then beat in the remaining flour by hand. Cover bowl and let batter rise in a warm place until doubled in bulk, about 45 minutes. Pour half of the ¼ cup melted butter or margarine into a 9 by 13-inch baking pan, tilting pan to coat the bottom. Beat down batter and drop by spoonfuls into the buttered pan making about 15 rolls.

Drizzle remaining melted butter or margarine over dough. Let rise in a warm place until almost doubled in bulk, about 30 minutes. Bake in a 425° oven for 12 to 17 minutes, or until the rolls are lightly browned. Serve hot.

(You can also bake these rolls in muffin cups. Spoon about 1 teaspoon melted butter into each muffin cup. Fill cups half full; let batter rise until almost doubled. Bake as above.)

## Cheese Puff Ring

*GOUGÈRE*

**MAKES 7 PUFFS**

**BAKED ROLLS MAY BE FROZEN (REHEAT IN FOIL)**

- 1 cup milk
- ¼ cup butter or margarine
- ½ teaspoon salt
  Dash pepper
- 1 cup unsifted all-purpose flour
- 4 eggs
- 1 cup shredded Swiss cheese

The French serve *gougère* ("goo-*zhair*") for lunch with a mixed green salad and red wine. However, you might serve this cheese-flavored, popover-type bread with barbecued meats for dinner. To double recipe, double ingredients in the dough; then bake two rings of seven puffs each.

Heat milk and butter in a 2-quart pan and add salt and pepper. Bring to a full boil and add the flour all at once, stirring over medium heat about 2 minutes or until mixture leaves sides of pan and forms a ball. Remove pan from heat and beat in (by hand) 4 eggs, one at a time, until mixture is smooth and well blended. Beat in ½ cup of the cheese.

Using an ice cream scoop or a large spoon, make 7 equal-sized mounds of dough in a circle on a greased baking sheet, using about three-quarters of the dough. (Each ball of dough should just touch the next one.) With the remaining dough, place a small mound of dough on top of each larger mound. Sprinkle the remaining ½ cup cheese over all. Bake on center shelf of a 375° oven about 55 minutes, or until puffs are lightly browned and crisp. Serve hot.

# Egg Bagels

Bagels from the bakery may be either the egg or water kind. The egg type which this recipe makes is somewhat richer, suitable for breakfast as well as for the Jewish lox (smoked salmon) and cream cheese sandwich. Bagels are made differently from most other breads and rolls—they are first boiled like dumplings, then baked.

Soften yeast in ½ cup of the potato water (water in which peeled potatoes have been cooked). Beat eggs in large bowl; blend in the softened yeast, remaining potato water, salt, sugar, oil, and 2 cups of the flour. Stir in remaining flour.

Turn out on a lightly floured board and knead for about 10 minutes, adding more flour as needed to make a firm dough. Place the dough in a greased bowl, cover lightly, and let rise in a warm place until doubled in bulk (or place covered dough in refrigerator where it will rise slowly overnight—in about 10 to 12 hours).

Punch the dough down, and knead it for a few minutes on a lightly floured board until it is smooth. Roll the dough out to a rectangle, and divide into 32 pieces of equal size. Roll each piece between the palms to form a strand about 6 inches long and ¾ inch in diameter. Moisten the ends, and seal them together firmly to make doughnut-shaped rolls of uniform thickness. Let them rise on board for about 15 minutes.

Dissolve 2 tablespoons of sugar in 2 quarts of boiling water in a deep pot. Drop bagels in, one at a time. Do not crowd. As the bagels rise to the surface, turn them over. Boil for 3 minutes on the second side. Remove with slotted spoon and place on greased baking sheets; brush with egg yolk glaze. Bake in a 425° oven for 20 to 25 minutes, or until golden.

**MAKES 32 BAGELS**

**MAY BE FROZEN**

2　packages yeast, active dry or
　　compressed
2　cups warm potato water
　　(lukewarm for compressed
　　yeast)
4　eggs
1　tablespoon <u>each</u> salt and sugar
¼　cup salad oil
　　About 8 cups unsifted flour
　　Sugar
　　Boiling water
2　egg yolks beaten with 2
　　tablespoons water

## EVEN BUTTER CAN BE BEAUTIFUL

One of those special little touches that contributes to making entertaining special may be the butter you serve with your freshly baked breads—in fancy individual shapes on a bed of crushed ice. For shaping the butter, you will need to buy special utensils such as a cutter, curler, wooden paddles for making balls or "log" shapes, a "rose dish," which makes petal-shaped curls in the form of a blossom.

**Butter Pat Cutter.** The cutter, which resembles a wire egg slicer, cuts a stick of butter into restaurant-sized squares. Butter should be firm, and fresh from the refrigerator. Carefully place cutter on whole stick; press straight down, firmly. Put divided pats into ice water until you are ready to serve them.

**Butter Curler.** Pull curler, which looks much like a vegetable peeler, firmly across slightly softened butter; drop finished curls into ice water. Dip curler into hot water between curls. You can make several curls from each side of a stick of butter.

**Wooden Paddles for Butter Balls or "Logs."** You use two paddles which are scored to give the butter a textured finish. Use equal-sized chunks of slightly softened butter, and roll each into a ball between the paddles. Move paddles in tight circles, in opposite directions for ball, or back and forth for a log. Drop butter into ice water.

**Silver Rose Dish for "Butter Blossom."** Fill underside of dish with slightly softened butter. Set dish on its stand, press evenly to force the butter through patterned holes in dish; chill. Serve molded butter directly from dish.

**To Make Sweet Butter.** If you like sweet butter, yet consider it an extravagance or cannot find it to buy, make your own from ordinary salted butter. Cut the butter into chunks and cover it generously with ice water, then mix with an electric mixer or in a blender. Pour off and add fresh water at least twice, or until the salt is washed out. Drain, and knead or work with a spoon to remove the surplus water; then pack in jar, freeze until needed.

# Rieska

*FINNISH RYE OR BARLEY BREAD*

The wheatless bread called *rieska*, traditional in northern Finland and Lapland, is made in various thicknesses—the farther north you go there, the thinner you find the rieska. You can make it quickly, and it's best served freshly made, still hot, spread with butter. Serve it as you would any quick hot bread like biscuits or muffins (Finns serve it with beef stew or hot bouillon). Barley flour usually is sold only in health food stores, and rye flour is available in most supermarkets.

In a bowl combine the flour with the salt, sugar, and baking powder. Stir in the milk or cream and the melted butter until a smooth dough forms. Turn the dough out onto a well-buttered cooky sheet, dust your hands lightly with flour, and pat the dough out to make a circle about 14 inches in diameter and ½ inch thick.

   Prick all over with a fork, and bake in a 450° oven for 10 minutes or until lightly browned. Serve immediately cut in pie-shaped wedges and spread with plenty of butter.

**MAKES 8 TO 10 PIECES**

**HAVE DRY INGREDIENTS PREMEASURED; ADD LIQUID, SHAPE, AND BAKE JUST BEFORE SERVING**

| | |
|---|---|
| 2 | cups barley flour or rye flour |
| ¾ | teaspoon salt |
| 2 | teaspoons <u>each</u> sugar and baking powder |
| 1 | cup undiluted evaporated milk or light cream |
| 2 | tablespoons butter, melted |

# Whipped Cream Biscuits

In these fluffy biscuits, whipped cream is both the shortening and moistening ingredient.

Measure flour, salt, and baking powder into a large bowl. Blend in the whipped cream with a fork until a stiff dough forms. Turn onto floured board and knead slightly. Roll dough out to about ½-inch thickness. Cut into rounds with a 2-inch cooky cutter. Place well apart on an ungreased baking sheet and bake in a 425° oven for 10 to 12 minutes, or until golden brown. Serve immediately.

**MAKES 16 TWO-INCH BISCUITS**

**HAVE DRY INGREDIENTS PREMEASURED; WHIP CREAM AND FINISH PREPARATION JUST BEFORE SERVING**

| | |
|---|---|
| 1½ | cups unsifted flour |
| ¾ | teaspoon salt |
| 4 | teaspoons baking powder |
| 1 | cup heavy cream, whipped |

# Cheesy Spoonbread

Spoonbread will not suit some entertaining because it must be served right from the oven like a soufflé. But in cases where the rest of the meal requires little last-minute attention, nothing is more delicious, especially when the main dish is cold meat or a salad. The sight and smell of spoonbread being brought to the table will encourage guests to rush to their places, so you needn't worry that the bread will fall or cool before you can round up everyone.

Stir cornmeal, sugar, salt, and chile powder into milk; set over simmering water and stir until smooth and thickened, about 15 minutes. Beat eggs with an electric mixer until thick and pale yellow. Stir in cornmeal mixture and 2½ cups of the cheese. Pour into buttered 1½-quart casserole with straight sides and sprinkle remaining ½ cup cheese over top. Bake in a 425° oven for 50 to 55 minutes or until top is lightly browned and wooden pick comes out clean. Serve at once for it will fall a little as it stands.

**MAKES 8 TO 10 SERVINGS**

**BEGIN BAKING 1 HOUR BEFORE SERVING TIME**

| | |
|---|---|
| 1½ | cups yellow cornmeal |
| 1½ | tablespoons sugar |
| ¾ | teaspoon salt |
| ½ | teaspoon chile powder |
| 2½ | cups milk |
| 5 | eggs |
| 3 | cups shredded cheese: Cheddar, Swiss, or jack |

*Rich White Batter Bread—see page 168*

# Hamburger Buns

*MENU FOR NOUVEAU RICHE HAMBURGERS INCLUDES THIS BREAD—PAGE 41*

**MAKES ABOUT 24 BUNS**

**BAKED BUNS MAY BE FROZEN**

**USE FOUR-INCH FOIL PANS FOR BAKING IF POSSIBLE**

 2  packages yeast, active dry or compressed
 ½  cup warm water (lukewarm for compressed yeast)
 2  cups milk, scalded and cooled
 1  cup (½ lb.) butter or margarine, melted and cooled
 ¼  cup sugar
 4  teaspoons salt
 4  eggs, slightly beaten
 9½ cups unsifted all-purpose flour
 1  egg
 1  teaspoon water
    Sesame, celery, caraway, or poppy seeds or dried onion flakes

Warm homemade buns, topped with seeds (poppy, celery, caraway, sesame), dried onion flakes, or just left plain, are a special treat for a hamburger supper.

Dissolve yeast in the ½ cup warm water. Combine milk, butter, sugar, salt, the 4 eggs, and 4 cups of the flour in a large bowl. Beat well with an electric mixer about 2 minutes.

Beat in remaining flour by hand to make a soft dough. Turn out on a lightly floured board and knead until smooth and elastic, about 10 minutes. Place dough in a greased bowl, cover, and let rise in a warm place until doubled in bulk, about 1½ hours. Then punch dough down and shape it.

Lightly grease 24 foil pans, each about 4 inches in diameter. Form smooth-topped balls of dough about 2 inches in diameter. Place dough in pans, pressing to flatten. Beat the 1 egg with the 1 teaspoon water; brush buns. Sprinkle each with 1 teaspoon seeds or onion flakes. Set pans on baking sheets; let dough rise in warm place until almost doubled in bulk, about 30 minutes. Bake in a 375° oven for 12 to 15 minutes, or until lightly browned. Cool 5 minutes, then turn out on racks. Wrap when cool; freeze if you wish.

# Rich White Batter Bread

**MAKES 1 LARGE OR 2 SMALL LOAVES**

**FREEZE UNBAKED BATTER AS LONG AS 2 WEEKS; BAKED BREAD ALSO MAY BE FROZEN**

**COFFEE CAN (OR CANS) REQUIRED**

 1  package active dry yeast
 ½  cup warm water
 ⅛  teaspoon ground ginger
 3  tablespoons sugar
 1  can (13 oz.) undiluted evaporated milk
 1  teaspoon salt
 2  tablespoons salad oil
 4  to 4½ cups unsifted regular all-purpose flour
    Butter or margarine

**WHEAT BREAD VARIATION:**
See quantity adjustments in above ingredients suggested in instructions.

These tall, round loaves are light, moist, and fine textured. They rise and bake in coffee cans, which also act as containers both for storing the dough if you freeze it before baking and for keeping baked bread fresh. The plastic can lids not only aid storage, but also indicate—by popping off—when the bread has risen properly. The batter requires no kneading and only has to rise once. This bread is so easy to make you can treat guests to hot yeast bread often.
*(Photograph on page 166.)*

Dissolve yeast in water in a large mixer bowl; blend in ginger and 1 tablespoon of the sugar. Let stand in a warm place until mixture is bubbly, about 15 minutes. Stir in the remaining 2 tablespoons sugar and the milk, salt, and salad oil. With mixer on low speed, beat in flour 1 cup at a time, beating very well after each addition. Beat in last cup of flour with a heavy spoon; add flour until dough is very heavy and stiff but too sticky to knead.

Place dough in a well-greased 2-pound coffee can, or divide into 2 well-greased 1-pound coffee cans. Cover with well-greased plastic can lids. Freeze if you wish.

To bake, let covered cans stand in warm place until dough rises and pops off the plastic lids, 45 to 60 minutes for 1-pound cans, 1 to 1½ hours for 2-pound cans. (If frozen, let dough stand in cans at room temperature until lids pop; this takes 4 to 5 hours for 1-pound cans, 6 to 8 for the 2-pound size.) Discard lids and bake in a 350° oven for 45 minutes for 1-pound cans, 60 minutes for 2-pound cans. Crust will be very brown; brush top lightly with butter.

Let cool for 5 to 10 minutes on a cooling rack, then loosen crust around edge of can with a thin knife, slide bread from can, and let cool in an upright position on rack.

**Variation: Light Wheat Bread.** Use 1½ cups whole wheat flour and 3 cups all-purpose flour. Replace sugar with honey.

# Vörtbröd

*SWEDISH ROUND RYE LOAF*

Swedish *vörtbröd* is a round rye loaf made with beer, which gives it a piquant flavor and light texture.

In a large bowl, soften yeast in water. Add molasses, salt, fennel seed, orange peel, beer, and rye flour; beat to make a smooth batter. Blend in butter. Stir in 3¾ cups of the all-purpose flour to make a soft dough. Sprinkle rest of the flour on board; turn dough out on floured board and knead until smooth, about 5 minutes. Place dough in greased bowl; turn over to grease top. Cover; let rise in warm place until doubled, about 1½ hours.

Punch down; divide dough in half. Shape each half into a rounded loaf; place each on a lightly greased baking sheet. Cover; let rise until almost doubled, about 45 minutes.

Brush with egg. Slash loaf with razor blade to make a cross on top. Bake in 350° oven for 50 minutes, until browned.

**MAKES 2 LOAVES**

**BAKED LOAF MAY BE FROZEN**

| | |
|---|---|
| 2 | packages yeast (active dry or compressed) |
| ½ | cup warm water (lukewarm for compressed yeast) |
| 2 | tablespoons molasses |
| 1½ | teaspoons salt |
| 1 | teaspoon crushed fennel seed |
| 1 | tablespoon grated orange peel |
| 2 | cups beer |
| 3 | cups rye flour |
| 2 | tablespoons butter or margarine, melted and cooled to lukewarm |
| 4½ | cups unsifted all-purpose flour |
| 1 | egg, slightly beaten |

## FANCY SHAPES FOR DINNER ROLLS

Hot yeast rolls for a dinner party may be made in one or more decorative shapes. They are easy to do using packaged hot roll mix.

Prepare the dough and let it rise the first time according to package directions. Shape rolls as described in the following instructions. (Each 13¾-oz. box of mix will make 12 large rolls or 16 smaller ones.) Let rise a second time, as long as the package recommends.

Bake large rolls for 12 minutes in a 400° oven, smaller ones 10 minutes. Baked rolls may be frozen.

**Butterhorns.** Roll dough to an 8-inch circle, ¼ inch thick. Brush with butter. Cut circle into 6 pie-like wedges, roll each toward point. Place on greased pan, point down. For Crescents, bend to shape like horseshoes.

**Bowknots.** Roll each piece of dough into a smooth, even rope, ½ inch in diameter and 10 to 11 inches long. Gently tie each length once, as you would to start to make a knot.

**Snails.** Roll each piece of dough into a rope about ½ inch in diameter and 10 inches long. Starting at one end, wind strip of dough around and around; tuck outside end firmly underneath roll of dough.

**Braids.** Form long ropes, each ½ inch in diameter. Braid 3 of the ropes into 1 long braid, cut it into 3½-inch lengths. Pinch the dough together at each end; pull the braid slightly to lengthen it.

**Figure Eights.** Roll each piece of dough into a rope about ½ inch in diameter and 10 inches long. Pinch the ends of the rope together, forming a loop; twist dough once to form figure eight.

**Fan Tans.** Roll dough to an 8 by 15-inch rectangle, ¼ inch thick. Spread with butter; cut into 5 lengthwise strips, 1½ inches wide. Stack the strips evenly; cut into squares. Put in greased muffin pans with cut sides up.

# Honey-Pecan Cornbread Sticks

**MAKES 12 CORN STICKS OR 16 MUFFINS**

**PREPARE PANS WITH SYRUP AHEAD, ADD BATTER JUST BEFORE BAKING**

⅓   cup plus 1 tablespoon firmly packed brown sugar
2   tablespoons <u>each</u> honey and butter or margarine
1   package (15 oz.) cornbread mix
¾   cup chopped pecans

**MUFFIN VARIATION:**
See quantity adjustments in above ingredients suggested in instructions.

A sweet honey-flavored syrup tops these pecan cornbread sticks when you turn them out of the pans right after baking.

In a small pan combine brown sugar, honey, and butter; stir occasionally over low heat until it boils and sugar is dissolved. Meanwhile prepare cornbread mix as directed on package. Sprinkle about 1 tablespoon chopped nuts into each of 12 average-sized cornstick forms; then spoon over about 2 teaspoons of the hot syrup. Divide cornbread batter into cornstick forms; bake 25 minutes or until lightly browned. Immediately invert onto serving platter; serve hot.

**Variation: Muffins.** Increase packed brown sugar to ¾ cup, honey and butter to 3 tablespoons *each*, and chopped pecans to 1 cup. Divide as directed above into 16 greased 2½-inch muffin cups.

# Pumpernickel Twist Bread

**MAKES 2 LOAVES OR 1 LARGE TWIST LOAF**

**BAKED LOAVES MAY BE FROZEN**

2   packages yeast, active dry or compressed
½   cup warm water (lukewarm for compressed yeast)
2   cups milk scalded and cooled to lukewarm
2   tablespoons <u>each</u> dark molasses and Postum
1   tablespoon caraway seed
2   teaspoons salt
3½  cups unsifted regular all-purpose flour
1   cup whole bran cereal
2½  cups rye flour
    Egg white

The most simple buffet of cold cuts and cheeses from the delicatessen will be out of the ordinary if you offer homemade bread. This pumpernickel can be made in twisted loaves or in regular bread pans.

Dissolve yeast in water in mixing bowl. Add milk, molasses, Postum, caraway seed, salt, and 2 cups of the all-purpose flour; beat with electric mixer on medium speed about 3 minutes. Then beat in remaining 1½ cups all-purpose flour and the bran cereal by hand. Turn out on board and gradually knead in the rye flour to make a stiff dough. Knead firmly about 10 minutes.

Put dough into greased bowl, turning to grease top of dough; cover and let rise in a warm place until almost doubled in volume, about 1 hour. Stir down dough and knead about 5 minutes on a lightly floured board.

*For one twist loaf,* divide dough in half. Roll each half to an even strand about 16 inches long. Place rolls parallel on a lightly greased baking sheet and twist them together; handle dough as little as possible, twisting without stretching it. Make twists even and parallel. Brush dough lightly with a slightly beaten egg white. Let rise in a warm place about 30 minutes. Bake loaf in a 350° oven for 30 minutes or until crust is lightly browned.

*For two thinner, buffet-sized loaves,* divide dough into four parts. Roll each part into a strand about 16 inches long. Twist each two pieces together as in making a single large twist loaf (see above). Brush with slightly beaten egg white and let rise about 20 minutes. Bake in a 375° oven about 25 minutes.

*To bake in regular loaf pans,* shape the dough into two loaves and let rise in two lightly greased 5 by 9-inch loaf pans until almost doubled in volume, about 25 minutes. Bake in a 375° oven about 45 minutes, or until lightly browned.

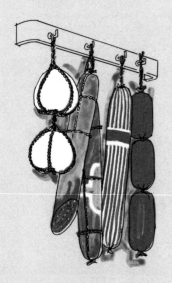

# Upside-Down Lemon Muffins

Each of these lemon muffins is coated with a brown sugar and coconut mixture. Turn them out of the pans as soon as they're baked; serve upside down. They would make an interesting accompaniment to a fruit salad plate, roast turkey, or pork.

Make coconut topping by blending coconut, brown sugar, the 2 tablespoons flour, 3 tablespoons melted butter, and ⅛ teaspoon nutmeg. Divide topping evenly into 12 well-greased 2½-inch muffin cups; press against bottoms and sides.

Sift and measure flour; sift into a bowl with baking powder, salt, ¼ teaspoon nutmeg, and sugar. Beat egg lightly with milk, the 3 tablespoons butter or oil, lemon peel, and lemon juice. Stir milk mixture into dry ingredients just until combined. Fill prepared muffin pans about ¾ full.

Bake in a 400° oven for about 20 minutes or until well browned. Turn muffins from pans immediately; serve upside down.

**MAKES 1 DOZEN**

**PREPARE TOPPING AND COMBINE DRY INGREDIENTS AHEAD**

- ½ cup <u>each</u> flaked coconut and firmly packed brown sugar
- 2 tablespoons flour
- 3 tablespoons melted butter
- ⅛ teaspoon nutmeg

**MUFFINS:**

- 2 cups regular all-purpose flour
- 3 teaspoons baking powder
- ½ teaspoon salt
- ¼ teaspoon nutmeg
- ¼ cup sugar
- 1 egg
- 1 cup milk
- 3 tablespoons melted butter or margarine, or salad oil
- 1 tablespoon <u>each</u> grated lemon peel and lemon juice

# Finnish Coffee Bread

*MENU FOR FINNISH COFFEE SMÖRGÅSBORD INCLUDES THIS BREAD—PAGE 12*

Wrap loaves of this bread tightly in foil or a plastic bag and they will stay fresh at least a week. Or put in your freezer to store longer. Be sure to follow this method of combining the ingredients. Adding the melted butter after the first addition of flour (rather than earlier, as in most yeast doughs) gives the bread its distinctive texture.

Scald milk; cool to lukewarm. In a large mixing bowl, sprinkle or crumble yeast in ¼ cup warm water; stir to dissolve. Stir in the lukewarm milk, sugar, 2 beaten eggs, cardamom, salt. Sift flour before measuring. Gradually stir 5 cups flour into the mixture in bowl; beat with a spoon until dough is smooth. Add melted butter; stir until blended. Add 3 to 4 cups more flour, mixing to make a stiff dough. Turn out on lightly floured board and knead until dough is smooth and satiny. Place in greased bowl; cover and allow to rise in warm place until doubled in bulk, about 1 hour. Punch down and allow to rise again until almost doubled in bulk, about 30 minutes.

Turn dough onto lightly floured board; divide into 3 portions (each to be formed into a braid loaf). For each loaf, divide dough portion into 3 parts; roll each between hands to form a strand about 14 inches long. Place 3 strands on board; braid. Repeat to make 2 more braided loaves. Lift braids onto greased baking sheets; allow to rise in a warm place for about 20 minutes (not until doubled). Gently brush tops of loaves with 1 beaten egg. If you wish, sprinkle the top of each loaf with about 1 tablespoon *each* chopped almonds and crushed sugar. Bake in a 425° oven for 25 to 30 minutes or until golden brown (do not overbake). Slip onto wire rack to cool.

**MAKES 3 LOAVES**

**MAY BE FROZEN**

- 2 cups milk
- 1 package yeast (active dry or compressed)
- ¼ cup water (warm for dry yeast, lukewarm for compressed)
- ¾ cup sugar
- 2 beaten eggs
- 2 teaspoons crushed cardamom
- 1 teaspoon salt
- 5 cups all-purpose flour
- ½ cup melted butter
- 3 to 4 cups all-purpose flour
  Beaten egg
- 3 tablespoons <u>each</u> chopped almonds and coarsely crushed lump sugar (optional)

# Distinguished Desserts

SOMETIMES YOU WANT TO SERVE a simple, light dessert and other times an awe-inspiring creation. In this chapter, you will find just the kind of sweet to suit the time you can spend and the occasion, whether it be the finale to dinner or party refreshment.

Great variety is included, but most recipes have one aspect in common—they may be partially or entirely made in advance, often a day or more ahead. It is preferable to have as little work as possible to do on party day; and at dessert time especially, no hostess wants to spend many minutes in the kitchen.

Few standard recipes, such as the more ordinary pies and cakes, will be found here. Even the old familiars have new or intriguing treatments which make them exceptionally good.

Some very helpful ideas for easy desserts using ice cream and fruits, as well as for ways of garnishing them beautifully, are included. Such lighter finishes to a meal are often most appreciated, especially when they look so good they completely satisfy the eye if not entirely the appetite.

You will also find instructions for making fancy ice cream or sherbet molds, called *bombes.* These can be made far ahead with great ease, but are highly impressive if garnished imaginatively.

Most of the dessert recipes may be prepared at any time of year, but some call for seasonal fruits. Usually, however, you will find optional suggestions making it possible to use what is available.

Few special baking pans or utensils are needed to make these desserts. If so, the particular requirement is mentioned in the tips accompanying each recipe. Unusual or hard-to-find ingredients have also been kept at a minimum. Only a half-dozen or so recipes call for anything which will require a trip to a gourmet shop.

*Sweet Country Cheese with Berries—see page 182*

# Pineapple Sherbet

MENU FOR HAM BUFFET INCLUDES THIS DISH—PAGE 29

**MAKES 6 TO 8 SERVINGS**

**LET SHERBET SOFTEN IN REFRIGERATOR 20 TO 30 MINUTES BEFORE SERVING**

2   eggs, separated
¾   cup sugar
1   can (9 oz.) crushed pineapple
2   tablespoons lemon juice
2   cups buttermilk
1   teaspoon (part of a package) unflavored gelatin
1   tablespoon water

**RASPBERRY VARIATION:**
    Omit crushed pineapple above
1   package (10 oz.) frozen raspberries

**LIME-PINEAPPLE VARIATION:**
    Omit lemon juice in basic recipe above
1   can (6 oz.) frozen daiquiri mix or frozen lime concentrate
2   teaspoons grated lemon peel

**ORANGE VARIATION:**
    Omit crushed pineapple in basic recipe above
1   can (6 oz.) frozen orange juice concentrate

This fruit-flavored sherbet is made with buttermilk, which contributes to its tangy flavor and smooth texture; it's actually less crystalline than most sherbets. To mellow the flavor, make the sherbet at least the day before you want to serve it.

Combine the egg yolks, ½ cup of the sugar, the pineapple (including the syrup), lemon juice, and buttermilk in the blender; whirl until blended (or beat together with rotary beater). Soften the gelatin in water; stir over hot water until dissolved; then blend into buttermilk mixture. Pour into a 2-quart container and freeze until firm around the outer edges of the container, about 1½ hours.

Beat the egg whites until soft, moist peaks form; gradually beat in the remaining ¼ cup sugar and continue beating until egg whites hold firm peaks. Break the partially frozen sherbet into chunks, pour it into a chilled bowl and beat until fluffy, then fold into egg white mixture. Return to freezer container and freeze until it is firm. Makes about 1½ quarts.

**Variation: Raspberry Sherbet.** Follow recipe for pineapple sherbet but substitute frozen raspberries, thawed, for the crushed pineapple. (If you do not have a blender, press the raspberries through a wire strainer, then beat together with the buttermilk, lemon juice, and ½ cup sugar.)

**Variation: Lime-Pineapple Sherbet.** Follow recipe for pineapple sherbet but omit the 2 tablespoons lemon juice. Instead, add daiquiri mix or lime concentrate, thawed, and lemon peel to the buttermilk mixture in blender.

**Variation: Orange Sherbet.** Follow recipe for pineapple sherbet but substitute orange juice concentrate, thawed, for the crushed pineapple.

# Maple Parfait

*CRYSTALLINE FROZEN CREAM*

**MAKES 6 TO 8 SERVINGS**

**LET FROZEN DESSERT SOFTEN A FEW MINUTES PRIOR TO SERVING**

4   eggs
⅛   teaspoon salt
1   cup sugar
½   cup water
½   teaspoon __each__ maple flavoring and lemon juice
2   cups heavy cream, whipped

When you dip a spoon into this frozen dessert, you'll observe its distinctive crystalline structure. But when you taste, you'll discover a creamy texture. The dessert is much like ice cream, but its elongated crystals are the result of fast freezing without stirring.

The name given to this type of dessert is French Parfait though it is not the parfait of popular terminology, built up of layers of ice creams, sherbets, and sauces. Parfait means "perfect"—a term quite appropriate.

Using the large bowl of your electric mixer, beat the eggs with the salt until light and fluffy. In the top of a 2-quart double boiler, combine the sugar, water, maple flavoring, and lemon juice. Bring to a boil, over direct heat, and boil 3 minutes without stirring. Pour the hot syrup in a fine stream into the beaten eggs, beating constantly at a high speed. Pour this beaten mixture back into the top of the double boiler and cook over hot water, stirring constantly with a wooden spoon, until the mixture is slightly thickened (about 10 minutes).

Remove from the heat and set the pan in a bowl of cold water; continue beating until the mixture is cooled. Fold in the whipped cream and pour into a pan or mold; freeze quickly until firm. Makes about 1¾ quarts.

# Meringue Shell Glacé

*WITH FLAMING STRAWBERRY SAUCE*

Expect this meringue shell to be soft and marshmallow-like; it simply melts when you bite into it. The suggested trio of ice creams makes a stunning combination with fresh strawberries and flaming berry sauce.

Place egg whites and cream of tartar in a mixing bowl and beat with an electric rotary mixer until foamy. Gradually add sugar, 1 tablespoon at a time, beating thoroughly after each addition; continue beating several minutes longer, until stiff and glossy. Beat in vanilla. Spoon into a well-buttered 10-inch pie pan, making a depression in the center.

Bake in a 300° oven for 1 hour, or until very lightly browned. Let cool. When made in advance, cool, then slip into a plastic bag and store in the freezer.

Scoop ice cream into small balls and refreeze. When ready to serve, let meringue shell thaw at room temperature and fill with alternating flavors of ice cream. Arrange 1 cup of whole strawberries between ice cream balls. Spoon flaming sauce over ice cream.

**Flaming Strawberry Sauce.** Purée berries with their syrup in a blender until smooth; then blend in orange juice concentrate and currant jelly. Turn into a small serving saucepan and add the 1 cup whole strawberries. Heat sauce just until bubbly. Warm brandy and orange liqueur, ignite a spoonful, and spoon flaming over the strawberry sauce; then spoon over the remaining warm liqueurs.

**MAKES 10 SERVINGS**

**MERINGUE MAY BE FROZEN; SAUCE AND BERRIES MAY BE PREPARED AHEAD**

- 5 egg whites
- ¼ teaspoon cream of tartar
- 1¼ cups sugar
- 1 teaspoon vanilla
- 1 pint each vanilla, chocolate, and pistachio ice cream
- 1 cup strawberries, washed and hulled

**FLAMING STRAWBERRY SAUCE:**

- 1 package (10 oz.) frozen sliced strawberries, thawed (or 1¼ cups sliced strawberries mixed with ¼ cup sugar)
- 3 tablespoons undiluted orange juice concentrate
- 1 tablespoon currant jelly
- 1 cup fresh whole strawberries, washed and hulled
- 1½ tablespoons each brandy and orange-flavored liqueur

# Pineapple Baked Alaska

This spectacular dessert is quite easy to assemble. You fill pineapple half shells (leaves still on) with ice cream, pineapple chunks, and meringue, and quickly brown the meringue just before serving. Accompany with homemade fruit sauces or bottled berry syrups.

Wash pineapple; but do not remove leaves. With a sharp knife, cut pineapple in half lengthwise, leaves and all. Using a grapefruit knife, cut out the pineapple and remove from shell. Dice the fruit, discarding the core. Spoon half the fruit back into the pineapple shells. Spoon toasted almond ice cream into one pineapple half shell, and spoon the pistachio ice cream into the other. (Or use vanilla ice cream for both.) Cover the ice cream with the remaining pineapple chunks. Place in the freezer until ice cream is firm again.

To prepare the sauces, place raspberries and their syrup in a blender and blend until smooth. Then press through a wire strainer to remove seeds. Stir in lemon juice. (Or you can substitute bottled raspberry syrup for the frozen raspberries and lemon juice.) Pour into a small pitcher for serving. Turn canned apricots into a blender and pureé until smooth; add enough of their syrup to make a sauce consistency. Pour into a small pitcher.

To prepare the meringue, beat egg whites until foamy; add salt and cream of tartar, and beat until soft peaks form. Gradually beat in ½ cup sugar, beating until stiff. Spread the meringue over the pineapple half shells, covering completely. Place in a 450° oven for 5 minutes, or until meringue is slightly browned. Serve at once with the raspberry and apricot sauces.

**MAKES 8 SERVINGS**

**PREPARE PINEAPPLE SHELLS AND SAUCES AS MUCH AS A DAY AHEAD**

- 1 large ripe pineapple
- 1 pint each toasted almond and pistachio ice cream or 1 quart vanilla ice cream
- 1 package (10 oz.) frozen raspberries, thawed
- 2 teaspoons lemon juice
- 1½ cups canned apricots and syrup
- 4 egg whites
- ⅛ teaspoon each salt and cream of tartar
- ½ cup sugar

# ELEGANT ICE CREAM FINALES

Ice cream is always a welcome end to a fine meal. The quality of ice creams you can buy is so great that dishes for the most discriminating can be created with little effort. Sometimes the secret of individuality is a sauce, other times molding with fresh or candied fruit. Following are ways to make ice cream desserts beautiful enough for the most special dinner party.

**Ginger Sundaes.** To make sauce, combine 2 cups sugar, ¼ teaspoon cream of tartar, and 1 cup water in a pan. Bring to a boil; simmer about 6 minutes or until temperature reaches 232° on a candy thermometer (syrup spins 2-inch thread when dropped from spoon). Cool about 10 minutes. Put 7 pieces preserved ginger and 1 tablespoon *each* lemon juice and syrup from ginger into blender; whirl smooth. Blend in ¼ cup whipping cream or ice cream, cooled syrup, and 1 drop yellow food coloring. Serve warm or chilled over vanilla ice cream. Top with fresh fruit, nuts, or chopped candied ginger, if you wish.

**Ice Cream with Chocolate-Chestnut Sauce.** Drain into a pan the syrup from 1 jar (7 oz.) chestnuts in vanilla-flavored syrup (marrons in syrup). Add 2 ounces semisweet baking chocolate and ¼ cup double-strength coffee. Stirring, heat until the chocolate is melted and sauce is smooth. Stir in 3 tablespoons rum, brandy, or Cognac. Slice the candied chestnuts and add to the sauce. Serve warm over coffee, toasted almond, vanilla, or chocolate ice cream.

**Ice Cream in Chocolate Cups.** Melt 1 package (6 oz.) semisweet chocolate pieces over hot but not boiling water. Using a pastry brush, spread chocolate evenly in 8 paper baking cups placed in 2½-inch muffin pans. Chill until hardened, about 2 hours. Carefully peel off paper; store chocolate cups in a cool place, or freeze until ready to use. Marinate ½ cup thinly sliced candied cherries in 2 tablespoons crème de cacao for 8 hours or more. Fill shells with 8 scoops vanilla ice cream to serve; top with cherries. Serves 8.

**Coffee Mold with Flaming Nut Sauce.** Let ½ gallon coffee ice cream soften slightly; then pack into a fancy 2-quart metal mold, cover with foil, and return to the freezer for at least 2 hours, or until solidly frozen. When ready to serve, dip mold in hottest tap water for about 10 seconds, then turn upside down on a large chilled plate. Return to the freezer while preparing sauce.

Coarsely chop ¾ cup Brazil nuts. Melt 2 tablespoons butter in a small serving pan, add nut meats, and brown them lightly. Warm ¼ cup brandy slightly.

Assemble the dessert at the table before guests. First spoon out a tablespoon of the warmed brandy, ignite, and pour it over the nut meats in the pan. Then pour the remaining brandy over the nuts and spoon the flaming sauce over the ice cream. Makes 10 servings.

**Cherries Jubilee.** Pack 1½ quarts slightly softened vanilla ice cream into a festive metal mold, or scoop ice cream into large balls; freeze. Drain the syrup from 2 cans (1 lb. *each*) dark Bing cherries into a saucepan. Add ⅓ cup currant jelly. Heat to boiling and stir in a blend of 2 tablespoons cornstarch and 2 tablespoons water; cook, stirring until thickened. Add cherries and heat through.

Dip mold into hottest tap water for about 10 seconds, then invert onto chilled serving plate. Return ice cream to freezer.

At serving time, reheat cherry sauce and take molded ice cream from freezer. Warm ⅓ cup kirsch (cherry brandy). At the table, ignite kirsch and spoon flaming over the hot cherry sauce; serve over the ice cream. Accompany with sweetened whipped cream and grated milk chocolate, if you wish. Serves 8.

**Cassata.** Line a 2-quart mold with 1½ quarts slightly softened vanilla ice cream; freeze until firm. Cover with a layer of 1 quart slightly softened chocolate ice cream; freeze until firm. Whip ½ cup heavy cream and fold in 1 teaspoon vanilla or 1 tablespoon maraschino liqueur. Beat 1 egg white until soft peaks form, and beat in 2 tablespoons powdered sugar; fold into cream. Then fold in 2 tablespoons *each* chopped candied red cherries, citron, and orange peel. Spoon into center of mold. Cover and freeze until firm.

To unmold the ice cream, dip the mold into hot water for about 10 seconds, then turn upside down over a cold serving plate. If it doesn't release immediately, repeat, dipping in water a shorter time. Refreeze 30 minutes before serving. Decorate with whipped cream, candied cherries, and citron. Serves 10 to 12.

**Cantaloupe Stuffed with Berries and Orange Ice.** Select a large ripe cantaloupe for every 4 servings, and cut a 2-inch plug from the stem end. Discard seeds and stringy portions, and spoon out meat, leaving a good thick shell. Cut meat into pieces, and combine with about 2 cups sugared, sliced strawberries, raspberries, or blueberries. Flavor with a liqueur, if you wish. Chill melon shell and berries. Have ready 1 pint of soft orange sherbet; combine with berries, and fill melon shell. Replace plug and serve at once by slicing into quarters. Or you can put the filled melon in your freezer. Before slicing and serving, allow about 10 minutes at room temperature for it to soften.

# Raspberry Torte

*MENU FOR DUCKLING DINNER INCLUDES THIS DISH—PAGE 16*

If make-ahead desserts appeal to you, this handsome freezer torte is ideal. You can make it days or even weeks ahead, store in the freezer (at 0° or colder).

Purée the berries in an electric blender. Press through a wire strainer to remove seeds, measure (you should have 2 cups purée), and add sugar to taste *only* if you have used fresh berries. Frozen berries need no extra sugar.

Combine the 1½ cups sugar, water, and corn syrup in a small pan; bring to a boil and cook over high heat until the temperature reaches 238° (soft ball stage) on a candy thermometer. Beat egg whites with an electric mixer until soft peaks form, then gradually beat in hot syrup. Continue beating at high speed for 8 minutes, or until meringue mixture cools to room temperature. Fold in raspberry purée and kirsch. Whip cream until stiff; fold into meringue.

Line the buttered sides of a 9-inch cheesecake pan (a pan with removable bottom or spring-release sides) with split ladyfingers. Pour in the raspberry mixture. Cover and freeze until firm (8 hours or longer). To serve, remove pan sides, garnish the top with berries, and cut into wedges.

**MAKES 12 SERVINGS**

**KEEP TORTES FROZEN UNTIL SERVING TIME**

**CHEESECAKE PAN REQUIRED**

2 packages (10 oz. <u>each</u>) frozen raspberries (or 2½ cups fresh raspberries and sugar to taste)
1¼ cups sugar
⅓ cup water
1 teaspoon light corn syrup
4 egg whites
2 tablespoons kirsch (cherry brandy), optional
2 cups (1 pt.) whipping cream
1 package (3 oz.) ladyfingers (about 2 dozen split ladyfingers)
Raspberries for garnish

# Orange Shells Glacé

Scooped-out navel oranges, filled with citrus mousse and then frozen, make a handsome winter dessert.

Slice the tops off 8 of the oranges. Using a grapefruit knife, remove sections, holding the fruit over a bowl to catch the juice. Scoop out any remaining pulp with a spoon, then turn shells upside down to drain. Reserve the fruit for another purpose.

Measure ¾ cup juice; combine with sugar in a pan and cook until the temperature reaches 220° (jelly stage) on a candy thermometer. Place egg yolks in the top of a double boiler and slowly beat in the hot orange syrup with a portable mixer or rotary beater. Place over hot water and beat constantly until stiff peaks form, about 7 minutes. Remove from heat, place over cold water, and continue beating until cold.

Whip cream until stiff and fold in vanilla and lemon juice or orange-flavored liqueur, and the grated citrus peels. Fold into yolk mixture. Spoon mousse mixture into hollow orange shells, mounding the top. Cover and freeze until firm. At serving time, slice remaining orange thinly into half slices and garnish.

**MAKES 8 SERVINGS**

**FREEZE UNTIL FIRM**

9 medium-sized navel oranges
1 cup sugar
6 egg yolks
1 pint (2 cups) whipping cream
2 teaspoons vanilla
2 tablespoons lemon juice or orange-flavored liqueur
1 teaspoon <u>each</u> grated orange and lemon peel

# Crème Royal Viking For Fifty People

*RECIPE WITH SCANDINAVIAN BUFFET MENU—PAGE 27*

Enriched with eggs and whipped cream and firmed with gelatin, this dessert is topped with apricots and chocolate curls. Chill the cream in small individual paper dishes so that it may be removed from the refrigerator and served when needed.

**MAKES 50 SERVINGS**

**PREPARE AS MUCH AS A DAY IN ADVANCE**

# Chilled Zabaglione Cream

MAKES 6 SERVINGS

CHILL CREAM AS MUCH AS 2
DAYS AHEAD

6   tablespoons sugar
1   teaspoon unflavored gelatin
½   cup Marsala or dry Sherry
6   egg yolks
1   tablespoon brandy or ¼
    teaspoon brandy flavoring
1   teaspoon vanilla
½   pint (1 cup) whipping cream
3   egg whites
⅛   teaspoon <u>each</u> salt and cream
    of tartar
½   square (½ oz.) semisweet
    chocolate

You can prepare this refreshing cream a day or two in advance and refrigerate it. This gives it an advantage over its namesake, frothy hot Italian Zabaglione, which must be made right before serving.

Using the top of a double boiler, mix together 4 tablespoons of the sugar and the gelatin. Stir in wine. Beat egg yolks until light and lemon colored and stir in. Cook over hot water, stirring constantly, until thickened. Remove from heat and stir in brandy and vanilla. Cool.

Whip cream until stiff and fold in. Beat egg whites until foamy, add salt and cream of tartar, and beat until stiff. Beat in the remaining 2 tablespoons sugar. Fold meringue into the custard and spoon into tall, slender parfait glasses or dessert dishes. Chill for 1 hour or longer. Garnish with chocolate curls (use a vegetable peeler to make the curls).

# Almendrado

*ALMOND PUDDING*

MAKES 6 SERVINGS

PREPARE CUSTARD UP TO 24
HOURS AHEAD

CHILL PUDDING AS LONG AS 6
HOURS

1   envelope unflavored gelatin
¼   cup cold water
5   egg whites (yolks used in sauce
    recipe)
¾   cup sugar
½   teaspoon almond extract
¼   teaspoon grated lemon peel
    Red and green food coloring
    (optional)

ALMOND CUSTARD SAUCE:

5   egg yolks
¼   cup sugar
2   cups milk
¼   teaspoon grated lemon peel
¼   teaspoon almond extract
¾   cup slivered almonds, toasted

Almendrado, in Spanish, means almond-like; it is also the very appropriate name of a Mexican almond-flavored pudding. In Mexico, part of the meringue pudding is white and the balance tinted pink and green. The mixture is layered into a mold. The dish is also pretty assembled in fluffy mounds.

Soften gelatin in cold water, then dissolve over hot water. Add to the egg whites in the large bowl of an electric mixer. Beat whites at highest speed until they form a thick, white foam. Continue beating and add the ¾ cup sugar 1 tablespoon at a time, gradually sprinkling in each spoonful over a period of 1 minute. When whites hold soft, curving peaks as the beaters are withdrawn, add the ½ teaspoon almond extract and ¼ teaspoon lemon peel and beat in.

If you want to make the typical Mexican-style Almendrado, tint ⅓ of the meringue a pale pink with a few drops of red food color, and tint another ⅓ of the meringue a pale green with a few drops of green food color. Pile the pink, white, and green meringue mixtures side by side in a shallow bowl (or just mound the all-white meringue) and chill at least 2 hours or as long as about 6 hours. With a cap of foil, cover the meringue without actually touching it, as it is easily marred.

Spoon the meringue into dessert bowls and pour sauce over each serving.

**Almond Custard Sauce.** In the top of a double boiler blend thoroughly the egg yolks, ¼ cup sugar, milk, and ¼ teaspoon grated lemon peel. Cook, stirring constantly, over gently simmering water until mixture thickens enough to coat the back of a metal spoon in a velvety layer. (If there is any sign of graininess at any time, remove custard from heat at once and set in cold water, stirring to cool quickly.) Add ¼ teaspoon almond extract and almonds to custard, then set pan in cold water and stir to cool. Cover and chill (as long as overnight).

*Chilled Orange Chiffon Soufflé—see page 181*

# Souffléed Omelet

**MAKES 4 SERVINGS**

**COOK JUST BEFORE SERVING**

**OMELET PAN DESIRABLE**

4 eggs, separated
2 tablespoons sugar
½ teaspoon vanilla
 Dash salt
2 tablespoons flour
¼ cup milk
 Butter
 Honey

This hot dessert is not much like what its name implies. Although called an omelet, it is more like a tender egg pancake folded over thick meringue. Although called soufflé, it is surprisingly durable and will not fall.

Beat the egg whites until frothy; add the sugar, vanilla, and salt; beat until the mixture is satiny and will form stiff peaks; reserve.

Use a fork to blend the flour and egg yolks together; stir in milk until it is smooth.

Melt about ½ teaspoon butter in a 7½ to 8½-inch omelet pan and place over medium heat until butter browns slightly. Pour in ¼ of the yolk mixture (about 3 tablespoons) and spread it evenly by rotating the pan. Immediately spoon ¼ of the beaten whites on one side of the yolk layer; cook about 1 minute. Use a spatula to lift up the side *with* the beaten white filling and fold it over the free yolk side—it will only partially enclose the filling. Cook about 1 minute longer so whites will be heated through. Remove from pan with a broad spatula.

Repeat process for each omelet, adding butter each time. Place cooked omelets in a 175° oven until all are cooked. Serve with honey.

## TWO BEAUTIFUL DESSERT GARNISHES

Chocolate leaves and praline crust—two handsome garnishes—can be used on a number of desserts, including ice cream, puddings, cakes, and fruit cups. They can be made much in advance to be ready for a planned party or impromptu entertaining.

**Chocolate Leaves.** Choose any thick, textured leaf with an attractive pattern on the underside, such as camellia, fatshedera, ivy, rhododendron, magnolia, or fig. Leave on a section of stem. Wash well and dry thoroughly. Prepare melted painting chocolate as directed in instructions below.

Then brush the chocolate on the underside of a leaf in a layer about ⅛ inch thick, using a small brush about ⅜ to ½ inch wide with a square-cut tip and fairly stiff bristles. Leave a tiny margin around edge of leaf. Coat well along heavy central vein. Place on a pan, chocolate side up, and chill.

Carefully peel real leaf from chocolate one; protect chocolate from heat of your fingers with folded paper. Remove one leaf at a time from refrigerator to peel.

Store chocolate shapes in the refrigerator until just before serving, wrapping airtight if you plan to store them for more than several hours.

*To prepare painting chocolate,* fill the base of a double boiler with water, set top in place, and heat water to simmering. Reduce heat to lowest setting, just to keep water hot. Put 1 bar (14 oz.) milk chocolate, coarsely chopped, and 1 package or 6 squares (6 oz.) semisweet chocolate in top part of pan. Stir occasionally until mixture is melted smooth and blended thoroughly. (Stir occasionally while using.)

**Praline Lace Crust.** Those who enjoy the flavor of caramel and the crunch of pralines will discover many uses for this lacy brown sugar crust in dressing up desserts. You may break it in pieces, crumble it, or finely crush it to top ice cream, fruit, or pudding. A triangle or square of it could be inserted at the side of such dishes to be eaten like a cooky. Or you could carefully cut the crust to fit the top of a baked custard to make a mock Crème Brûlée.

To make the crust, heavily butter a chilled cooky sheet (one without side rims). Sprinkle with an even layer—⅛ to ¼ inch deep—of brown sugar rubbed through a wire strainer. Leave a border of at least 1 inch on all sides.

Place 6 inches beneath heat in broiler. Watch very carefully, turning pan if necessary to cook evenly. When sugar is bubbling (this may take less than 1 minute so be careful not to scorch it), remove from heat and let cool until you can just touch pan comfortably. Then quickly and gently loosen crust with a long, flexible spatula. Store crust flat, wrapped airtight in foil or clear plastic wrap; or break in small pieces and store in a jar. Crust will stay crisp for about a week if in foil, or indefinitely if in a jar.

# Chilled Orange Chiffon Soufflé

Orange juice concentrate and citrus peel flavor this low-calorie dessert. Cold soufflés, firmed with gelatin, do not fall as hot ones do. In fact, they must be made ahead. *(Photograph on page 179.)*

Mix gelatin, ¾ cup of the sugar, and salt in the top of a double boiler; stir in water and heat over direct heat until gelatin dissolves. Beat yolks of the 6 eggs until light and stir in the gelatin mixture. Return to the double boiler, place over a pan of hot water, and cook, stirring, until mixture coats the spoon. Remove from heat and stir in the orange juice concentrate, lemon juice, and grated citrus peels. Chill until it starts to congeal.

Beat the 6 egg whites until soft peaks form and gradually beat in the remaining ¼ cup sugar. Fold meringue into the chilled orange mixture. Fold a 20-inch length of waxed paper into thirds lengthwise and place around a 2-quart soufflé dish to form a collar; secure with paper clips. Spoon in the orange soufflé mixture, letting it come up above the rim of the mold. Chill until set.

When ready to serve, slip a knife between the waxed paper and soufflé and remove paper strip. Then press the almonds around the rim of the soufflé. Garnish with strawberries or other fresh fruit, and serve with chilled custard sauce.

**Soft Custard Sauce.** Scald milk in the top of a double boiler. Beat 3 egg yolks until light and mix in ⅓ cup sugar and cornstarch blended together. Blend in the hot milk; return to the top of the double boiler, and, stirring constantly, cook until thickened. Stir in vanilla. Cool, then chill.

**MAKES 10 TO 12 SERVINGS**

**PREPARE CUSTARD AND CHILL SOUFFLÉ UP TO 24 HOURS AHEAD**

**SOUFFLÉ OR OTHER STRAIGHT-SIDED DISH REQUIRED**

- 2 envelopes unflavored gelatin
- 1 cup sugar
  - Dash salt
- 2 cups cold water
- 6 eggs, separated
- 2 cans (6 oz. <u>each</u>) frozen orange juice concentrate, thawed
- ¼ cup lemon juice
- ½ teaspoon <u>each</u> grated orange and lemon peel
- ⅓ cup toasted slivered almonds
  - Fresh strawberries (or other fresh fruit) for garnish

**SOFT CUSTARD SAUCE:**

- 2 cups milk
- 3 egg yolks
- ⅓ cup sugar
- 1 tablespoon cornstarch
- 1 teaspoon vanilla

# Hot Chocolate Soufflé

If you've shied away from a soufflé because you thought it difficult to make at the last minute, here's the way out: Make the cream sauce ahead of time—a soufflé is nothing but an egg-thickened cream sauce into which beaten egg whites have been folded. The sauce can stand as much as an hour, covered. About half an hour before serving, fold in beaten egg whites, and bake the soufflé.

Butter the bottom and halfway up the sides of a 1½-quart soufflé dish, or 5 individual baking dishes, with 1 tablespoon of the butter. Coat with 1 tablespoon of the sugar.

Melt remaining butter and blend in flour. Add milk gradually, and cook, stirring, until thick and smooth. Stir in cocoa and 2 tablespoons of the sugar. Separate eggs and beat yolks until thick. Add a little of the hot mixture to them, then combine the 2 mixtures. Cook a minute or so longer over low heat, stirring constantly, until mixture thickens again. Add vanilla. (This custard sauce may be made as much as an hour before the final preparation.)

Beat egg whites with salt until soft peaks form; then add remaining sugar gradually, and continue beating until stiff peaks form. Fold in chocolate sauce in 2 parts, and turn into the baking dish. Fit a "collar" (a 1½-inch-wide strip of paper 12 inches long) around the inside of the dish, if you wish, to make soufflé rise higher. Bake in a 400° oven 30 minutes for a large baking dish, 20 minutes for individual baking dishes, or until the soufflé feels set when touched lightly with your finger. Remove collar (if used) and serve at once.

**MAKES 5 SERVINGS**

**MAY BE PARTIALLY PREPARED AHEAD**

**SOUFFLÉ OR OTHER STRAIGHT-SIDED DISH REQUIRED**

- 3 tablespoons butter or margarine
- ½ cup sugar
- 2 tablespoons flour
- ¾ cup milk
- 2 tablespoons cocoa
- 3 eggs
- 1 teaspoon vanilla
- ¼ teaspoon salt

# Natillus with Crunchy Caramel

*MENU FOR PAELLA MEAL INCLUDES THIS DISH—PAGE 13*

MENU FOR PAELLA MEAL INCLUDES THIS DISH—PAGE 13

**MAKES 6 SERVINGS**

**PREPARE CUSTARD 2 HOURS TO A DAY AHEAD**

**BAKE MERINGUES 2 TO 8 HOURS AHEAD**

**ASSEMBLE NO MORE THAN 4 HOURS IN ADVANCE**

---

6   eggs
⅛   teaspoon <u>each</u> salt and cream of tartar
1   cup plus 2 tablespoons sugar
1½  cups half-and-half (light cream)
1½  cups milk
     Grated peel of 1 lemon
2   teaspoons vanilla

This variation of Spanish *Natillus* or French Floating Island *(Oeufs à la Neige)* has caramel syrup decoratively dribbled over the meringue floating in custard. The caramel hardens into crunchy candy, a marvelous contrast. If you make the dessert in advance, top with the syrup no more than 4 hours ahead so it will be crisp.

Separate 3 of the eggs. Beat the 3 egg whites until foamy, add salt and cream of tartar, and beat until stiff, then gradually beat in 6 tablespoons of the sugar. Pour 1 inch of hot water into a 9 by 13-inch baking pan, and spoon meringue in 6 balls onto the water. Place in a 425° oven and bake for 8 minutes, or until lightly browned. Remove from oven. Holding meringues with a spatula, drain off water. Let stand at room temperature.

Pour half-and-half and milk into the top of a double boiler, place over hot water, and heat until scalded. Beat remaining 3 whole eggs and the 3 egg yolks until light; gradually beat in ½ cup of remaining sugar. Pour hot milk into egg mixture, return to top of double boiler, and add grated lemon peel. Stirring constantly, cook until custard coats the spoon in a thick, velvety, opaque layer. Stir in vanilla. Immediately remove from heat and place in a pan of cold water to cool. When cool, pour into a serving bowl or individual dessert bowls, cover, and chill.

When ready to serve, gently spoon the meringues onto the custard. Pour remaining ¼ cup sugar into a heavy saucepan and place over moderate heat just until sugar turns amber and melts into a syrup (shake pan frequently to prevent scorching). Slowly pour hot sugar syrup over custard and meringues. Serve at once or hold up to 4 hours.

# Sweet Country Cheese with Berries

**MAKES 8 SERVINGS**

**PREPARE AT LEAST A DAY AHEAD; SERVE WITHIN 1 TO 2 DAYS**

---

4   cups (2 pints) sour cream
6   egg yolks
1   package (8 oz.) cream cheese
1   cup sugar
3   or 4 strips lemon peel
     Strawberries
     Plain unsalted crackers

This soft cheese is made from sour cream, eggs, sugar, and cream cheese, flavored with lemon peel. It is drained in cheesecloth, then molded into as simple or elaborate a shape as you feel artistically inclined to execute. Serve with strawberries and crackers. *(Photograph on page 172.)*

In the top of a double boiler heat sour cream, stirring, until scalding. Blend some of the hot cream with the egg yolks thoroughly beaten with cream cheese and sugar. Return all to double boiler. Add lemon peel. Cook over simmering water, stirring frequently, until thickened, about 15 minutes.

Remove from heat. Cover and let stand in the hot water for 15 minutes more; discard lemon peel. Line a large wire strainer or colander with 3 or 4 thicknesses of cheesecloth; arrange over another pan for draining. Pour in cheese mixture. Let stand about 2 hours at room temperature, then gently draw up loose edges of cheesecloth and fasten lightly over cheese. Continue draining while it chills overnight. Mold cheese or shape with a spatula. Makes about 3 cups.

# Tahitian Fresh Fruit Poë

*MENU FOR TAHITIAN PARTY INCLUDES THIS DISH—PAGE 49*

Tahitians make many varieties of poë desserts. (Tahitians would make it with arrowroot starch rather than cornstarch.) The chilled coconut cream poured over the top in this version is made of coconut milk and evaporated milk.

Peel papayas and remove seeds; peel and core pineapple. Purée in blender or force through food mill to make 4 cups puréed fruit. Stir in cornstarch and sugar. Turn into greased and floured baking pan (8 by 10 inches). Bake in a 350° oven for an hour or until set and caramelized at corners. Allow to cool in pan a few minutes. Cut into 1-inch squares. Lift onto shallow tray or into serving bowl. Sprinkle with grated coconut. For coconut cream topping, combine coconut milk and evaporated milk and pour over warm cubes of poë.

**MAKES 12 SERVINGS**

**PREPARE COCONUT MILK AS MUCH AS 1 DAY AHEAD, OR FREEZE**

About 2 papayas and 1 fresh pineapple (to make 4 cups puréed fresh fruit)
2 cups cornstarch
2 cups sugar
Grated fresh coconut (or packaged flaked coconut)
1 pint (2 cups) chilled coconut milk (purchased frozen or made from recipe on page 203—right column)
2 cups chilled evaporated milk

# Cranberry Fruit Soup

Fruit soups are well known in the Scandinavian countries, Germany, Poland, and even in Oriental cuisine. The consistency varies from almost as thin as punch to as thick as cornstarch pudding; some are served hot, others cold. The thinner, tarter soups may be used just as a soup would be—before dinner. Those which are thicker and sweeter are best as dessert, as is this ruby-red, cold cranberry soup with whipped cream and almond garnish.

Combine cranberry juice, water, sugar, cornstarch, cinnamon, and cloves in a pan. Bring to a boil; simmer, stirring, until juice is clear and slightly thickened. Chill. Serve in individual glasses, top with whipped cream and almonds.

**MAKES 12 SERVINGS**

**PREPARE AS MUCH AS SEVERAL DAYS AHEAD**

3 cups <u>each</u> cranberry juice and water
¾ cup sugar
6 tablespoons cornstarch
1 stick cinnamon
2 whole cloves
Whipped cream
Sliced almonds

# English Fruit Pudding

Mincemeat is usually associated with winter holidays, but its spicy fruit flavor is good in desserts at almost any time. This pudding resembles a pie (it's composed of a crust and filling), but is mound-shaped because you bake it in a bowl.

Sift flour with baking powder and the salt into a bowl. With a fork, cut in butter until mixture resembles coarse crumbs. Stir in ice water, a tablespoon at a time, to make a dough that holds together in a ball. Turn out onto a lightly floured board and roll out to make a circle 14 inches in diameter.

Cut out exactly ¼ of the dough, just as you would cut a wedge of pie (a fourth of the pie); save to cover top of pudding. Fit the larger piece of dough into a buttered 1½-quart ovenproof bowl; moisten cut edges and press together to seal.

Prepare the filling by combining mincemeat, apples, and nuts; pour into the dough-lined bowl. Roll out the reserved fourth of the dough to fit top; place over filling, moisten edges, and seal. Prick top with a fork and bake in a 375° oven for 1 hour, or until golden. Cool 20 minutes, then invert onto serving dish; dust with powdered sugar.

**MAKES 8 SERVINGS**

**MAY BE BAKED AHEAD AND REHEATED**

**OVENPROOF BOWL (1½ QUARTS) OR SIMILAR MOLD REQUIRED**

2 cups unsifted flour
2 teaspoons baking powder
¼ teaspoon salt
¾ cup butter
7 to 8 tablespoons ice water
1 can (1 lb. 12 oz.) prepared mincemeat
3 cups chopped fresh apple
1 cup chopped nuts
Powdered sugar

# Persian Baklava

4 cups very finely chopped, blanched almonds (about 1¼ lbs.)
2 cups sugar
2 teaspoons cardamom
1 pound unsalted butter, melted
1 package (1 lb.) fila
  Rose Water Syrup (recipe follows)
  Halved pistachios for garnish (optional)

ROSE WATER SYRUP:

2 cups sugar
1 cup water
2 tablespoons rose water

Persian baklava is a little different from that you may have tasted before, not only in ingredients but in texture. Rose water and cardamom are new flavor additions. The texture is more crystalline. Although exotic, baklava is extremely easy to make if you can just find the proper ingredients. It keeps a number of days without refrigeration. To serve this sweet at tea time the Middle Eastern way, put one or two pieces on each dessert plate and provide both knives and forks. Water is usually served to drink while eating. Then afterward you serve tea or coffee. (For Turkish coffee recipe, see page 201.)

Mix almonds, the 2 cups sugar, and cardamom. Brush bottom of a 9 by 13-inch baking pan generously with some of the butter. Carefully fold 3 sheets of fila to fit pan; place in pan 1 at a time, brushing each with butter. Sprinkle about ⅓ cup of the almond mixture over the top sheet of fila. Fold 1 more fila sheet to fit; brush on butter; sprinkle with ⅓ cup more almond mixture.

Add more layers, using 1 folded sheet of fila, a generous brushing of butter, and about ⅓ cup of the almond mixture for each, until nut mixture is used up (you should have about 12 nut-filled layers). Fold remaining 4 to 6 sheets of fila to fit pan, brush each with butter, and stack on top.

With a very sharp knife, carefully cut diagonally across the pan to make diamond shapes about 1¾ by 2½ inches, cutting all the way to the bottom of the pan. Pour any remaining butter evenly over the top. Bake in a 300° oven for 50 minutes to 1 hour, until lightly browned.

Then pour Rose Water Syrup evenly over the top of the hot pastry; decorate each piece with half a pistachio, if you wish. Cool before serving.

**Rose Water Syrup.** Bring the 2 cups sugar and 1 cup water to a gentle boil in a 1½-quart pan. Boil gently, uncovered, for 15 to 20 minutes until syrup reaches the thread stage (230° to 234°). Stir in rose water. Keep warm.

*Shopping Hints. Paper-thin sheets of dough (called fila in Greek) are used throughout the Near and Middle East. In this country you will usually find the dough, fresh or frozen, rolled into a long, thin package at Greek or gourmet food shops. Rose water may be bought at the same shops or at some pharmacies (be sure not to buy the cosmetic kind with glycerin). If you can't find rose water, omit it or substitute 2 teaspoons lemon juice. Salted butter can be used for baklava, but the unsalted is much to be preferred.*

# Mincemeat-Cheese Pie

4 packages (3 oz. <u>each</u>) cream cheese
2 eggs
½ cup sugar
  Grated peel of 1 lemon
1 tablespoon lemon juice
2 cups mincemeat
  Baked 9-inch pastry shell
1 cup sour cream
2 tablespoons sugar
½ teaspoon vanilla
  Lemon slices

This pie has three layers — one of mincemeat, another resembling smooth cheesecake, and a topping of sour cream. If you like to serve traditional dishes during the winter holidays, but still welcome them with a different twist, this recipe will provide just the right balance between the new and the old.

Beat together cream cheese, eggs, ½ cup sugar, lemon peel, and lemon juice with an electric mixer until very smooth. Spoon mincemeat into pastry shell. Pour cream cheese mixture evenly over mincemeat.

Bake in a 375° oven for 20 minutes. Mix together sour cream, the 2 tablespoons sugar, and vanilla. When pie has baked the 20 minutes, remove from oven and spread sour cream mixture evenly over top. Return to oven for 10 minutes. Then chill pie before cutting and serving. Garnish with twisted lemon slices and lemon leaves (if available).

# Pink Grapefruit Chiffon Pie

This pleasantly tart pie uses pink grapefruit juice; you can expect to squeeze ¾ to 1 cup of strained juice from a large grapefruit. The texture of the filling is refreshingly light.

Cut the peel and all the white membrane from grapefruit; lift out sections and drain well. Soften gelatin in 1 cup of the grapefruit juice. Beat egg yolks and combine in a pan with remaining ½ cup grapefruit juice, ½ cup of the sugar, salt, lemon peel, lemon juice, and grapefruit peel. Cook over low heat, stirring constantly, until mixture bubbles and lightly coats a metal spoon.

Remove from heat, add softened gelatin, and stir until gelatin is completely dissolved. Add a few drops food coloring to tint a medium pink. Chill gelatin mixture until it is thick enough to mound on a spoon. Beat the 3 egg whites with cream of tartar until frothy; add the remaining ¼ cup sugar and continue beating until stiff peaks form. Beat gelatin mixture until light and frothy. Fold in grapefruit sections, reserving several for garnish; then fold in the beaten egg whites. Spread in pastry shell; chill until firm, several hours or overnight.

To serve, garnish with reserved grapefruit sections and dollops of whipped cream, if you wish.

**MAKES A 9-INCH PIE**

**CHILL PIE AS MUCH AS A DAY AHEAD**

- 1 medium-sized pink grapefruit
- 1 envelope unflavored gelatin
- 1½ cups fresh pink grapefruit juice
- 3 eggs, separated
- ¾ cup sugar
- ¼ teaspoon <u>each</u> salt and grated lemon peel
- ¼ cup lemon juice
- ½ teaspoon grated pink grapefruit peel
  Few drops red food coloring
- ¼ teaspoon cream of tartar
  Baked 9-inch pastry shell
  Sweetened whipped cream (optional)

## BOMBES FOR A BURST OF COMPLIMENTS

The most elegant of molded frozen desserts, *bombes*, are easy to make with either homemade or commercial ice creams and sherbets. If you have a freezer that holds at 0° or colder, you can make them several days, or even weeks, before a party.

Originally spherical, bombes had an indentation at the top where a brandy-soaked wick was inserted. The bombe was served flaming, to resemble the large round bombs once used in warfare.

Later, other shapes were used, and they held an important place in *la haute cuisine*. Escoffier alone listed over 80 variations, from *Bombe Aboukir*, a shell of pistachio ice filled with a rich praline filling and garnished with pistachio nuts, to *Bombe Zamora*, coffee ice with a curaçao filling.

**Hints on Making Bombes.** Bombes can be simpler. They can be made with ice creams you buy and molded in anything from a melon-shaped mold to a glass bread pan. They may be frozen in the freezer, or packed in ice — three parts cracked ice to one part ice cream salt.

**Measure the Mold.** If homemade ice cream or a high-quality commercial ice cream is used, 2 quarts will fill a 2-quart mold. However, some commercial ice creams are

whipped so that they contain a large quantity of air. These lose volume when pressed into the molds, so extra ice cream is required.

**Chill the Mold.** Before filling the mold, chill it thoroughly in the freezer or in a pan filled with cracked ice. Have the ice cream soft enough so that it can be spread easily.

**Line Mold.** Use either ice cream or sherbet; press an even layer on sides and bottom with spoon while keeping the mold in pan of ice. Smooth with a spatula and cover with lid or foil; freeze until firm.

**Spoon in Filling.** Use ice cream or sherbet of a contrasting color and harmonious flavor, or vanilla mousse made by flavoring stiffly whipped cream with sugar and vanilla. After filling, smooth the top with spatula; then cover with wax paper or foil. Put on cover and press down firmly; or use heavy foil, pressing down around sides. Freeze at least 5 to 6 hours.

**Unmold.** Dip bottom of mold quickly in hot water (about 6 seconds) and turn out on a well-chilled plate. Bombes can be unmolded, garnished, refrozen, wrapped, and stored for several months.

# Pumpkin Ice Cream Pie

*MENU FOR WINTERTIME BUFFET INCLUDES THIS DISH—PAGE 42*

**MAKES A 9-INCH PIE**

**REMOVE PIE FROM FREEZER A FEW MINUTES BEFORE SERVING TIME**

| | |
|---|---|
| 1½ | pints vanilla ice cream |
| 1 | cup canned pumpkin |
| ¾ | cup brown sugar, firmly packed |
| ½ | teaspoon <u>each</u> ground ginger and cinnamon |
| ⅓ | cup candied orange peel or mixed candied fruit, finely chopped (optional) |
| 3 | tablespoons rum (or ¼ cup orange juice) |
| ¾ | cup whipping cream |
| | Pecan halves for garnish |

The filling for this pie is pumpkin mousse; you freeze it inside an ice cream "crust." Make it days ahead, if you wish, and remove it from the freezer a few minutes before serving.

Put a 9-inch pie pan into the freezer when you remove the ice cream; allow ice cream to stand at room temperature a few minutes, until slightly softened. Then spread ice cream evenly over the bottom and sides of pie pan; set back in freezer if it gets too soft. Keep in freezer while you prepare the filling.

For the filling, combine pumpkin, sugar, ginger, and cinnamon in a saucepan. Stir over medium heat until mixture is just below the simmering point. Stir in candied fruit and rum (or orange juice); refrigerate until well chilled. Whip cream and fold into chilled pumpkin mixture. Pour into ice-cream-lined pie pan and freeze. Garnish with pecan halves just before serving.

# Macadamia Cream Pie

**MAKES 6 TO 8 SERVINGS**

**CHILL PIE AS MUCH AS A DAY AHEAD**

| | |
|---|---|
| ½ | cup plus 1 tablespoon sugar |
| 1 | envelope unflavored gelatin |
| 3 | tablespoons cornstarch |
| ¼ | teaspoon salt |
| 1 | small package (3 oz.) cream cheese, softened |
| 6 | tablespoons sour cream |
| 1¾ | cups milk |
| 2 | eggs, separated |
| | About 1 cup (3½ oz. jar) unsalted, chopped macadamias (see recipe for how to use salted nuts if unsalted ones are unavailable) |
| 1 | cup heavy cream |
| 1 | teaspoon vanilla |
| | Baked 9-inch pie shell |

A pie similar to this is one of the delights remembered by vacationers at a luxury hotel on Maui in Hawaii. This recipe combines the best qualities of a chiffon and a cream pie.

In the top of a double boiler, mix the sugar with gelatin, cornstarch, and salt (omit salt if salted nuts are used). Blend cream cheese with the sour cream until smooth; gradually stir in the milk. Slowly blend the liquid mixture into the dry ingredients in the double boiler. (Or combine sugar, gelatin, cornstarch, salt, cream cheese, and sour cream in a blender and whirl, gradually adding milk, until mixture is smooth. Put in double boiler.)

Cook over gently boiling water, stirring frequently, until very thick and smooth and about the consistency of a thick cream sauce; takes 10 to 15 minutes. Blend some of the hot liquid with the egg yolks, then return to sauce. Cook, stirring, for about 2 minutes more. Remove pan from heat and take top of pan out of the hot water. Whip egg whites until they hold short, distinct stiff peaks, then fold the warm sauce into them. Chill until mixture is cool, but is not set.

Meanwhile, prepare macadamias. *(Note: If unsalted, chopped nuts are unavailable, buy whole salted ones. Roll in a towel and rub to remove as much salt as possible; then chop.)* To toast chopped nuts, spread them in an even, shallow layer in a pan. Bake in a 350° oven for about 5 minutes, shaking occasionally, until lightly toasted.

Whip heavy cream until stiff, and fold the cream, vanilla, and ½ cup of the macadamia nuts into the cooked mixture. Pour this filling into the baked pie shell; do not smooth top. Chill for 2 to 3 hours, then sprinkle remaining nuts over the surface of the pie and serve.

# Sultana Raisin Cake

*GATEAU SULTANA*

Expect this sultana cake to be compact, with a texture similar to that of pound cake. If tightly wrapped, it stays moist up to 4 days.

Cover raisins with water and let soak 30 minutes. In a large bowl, cream together butter and sugar. Add eggs, one at a time, beating well after each addition. Blend in rum, lemon juice, lemon peel, and milk. Sift flour; measure; sift again with baking powder, salt, and soda. Add gradually to creamed mixture until well blended.

   Drain raisins; use paper towel to remove excess water. Mix into batter. Pour batter into well-greased and floured 10-inch tube cake pan or 10-cup mold. Bake in 325° oven for 1 hour and 20 minutes or until inserted pick comes out clean.

   Cool in pan 10 minutes, then invert on rack; when completely cool, dust lightly with sifted powdered sugar.

**MAKES 12 SERVINGS**

**BAKE UP TO 4 DAYS AHEAD**

**TUBE PAN OR MOLD REQUIRED**

| | |
|---|---|
| 1½ | cups golden raisins |
| | Water |
| 1¼ | cups butter or margarine |
| 1½ | cups sugar |
| 5 | eggs |
| 1 | tablespoon light rum |
| 2 | tablespoons lemon juice |
| 2 | teaspoons grated lemon peel |
| ½ | cup milk |
| 3½ | cups regular all-purpose flour |
| 3 | teaspoons baking powder |
| ½ | teaspoon <u>each</u> salt and soda |
| | Sifted powdered sugar |

# Punschtorte

*PICNIC MENU INCLUDES THIS DISH—PAGE 47*

The tortes of Vienna are notable for variety, richness, and complexity. Using a lemon cake mix as the basis of a Punschtorte simplifies its preparation without sacrificing traditional elements. The lemon, raspberry, and rum flavors of the cake may remind you of a rum *Punsch* (the German spelling).

Butter and flour sides of a 9 by 13-inch baking pan; line the bottom with brown paper. Prepare lemon cake mix as package directs; bake as directed for a 9 by 13-inch pan. Cool in pan about 10 minutes; turn out onto a rack and cool completely. Cut in half to get 2 rectangles about 9 by 6½ inches each; split halves horizontally to get 4 layers. Sprinkle all surfaces with 2 tablespoons rum.

   To assemble the torte, place bottom cake layer on a cutting board; spread with ¼ of the raspberry preserves and then ⅓ of the Whipped Cream Filling (recipe follows). Spread ¼ of the preserves over the cut surface of the next cake layer and place it, preserves side down, over the whipped cream. Repeat with the remaining cake layers, preserves, and ⅓ of the filling. Then put the 2 sets of layers together with remaining filling between.

   Trim sides and ends evenly. Spread Rum Butter Icing (recipe follows) over sides and top; reserve part of icing and pipe on in a decorative border of rosettes. Chill for several hours or overnight.

**Whipped Cream Filling.** Soften gelatin in cold water; dissolve over hot water. In a chilled bowl, whip cream until it begins to thicken. Add ⅓ cup powdered sugar, and gradually beat in 3 tablespoons rum. Slowly pour in gelatin mixture, beating until just stiff enough to hold shape. Use immediately, or cover and chill 2 to 3 hours and beat again before using. Makes about 3 cups.

**Rum Butter Icing.** Cream soft butter with 1 cup powdered sugar until fluffy. Add ⅓ cup rum; gradually blend in 4 cups sifted powdered sugar, beating until creamy.

**MAKES 12 TO 16 SERVINGS**

**MAKE UP TO A DAY AHEAD**

| | |
|---|---|
| 1 | package (about 1 lb. 3 oz.) lemon cake mix |
| 2 | tablespoons light rum |
| ¾ | cup seedless raspberry preserves |

**WHIPPED CREAM FILLING:**

| | |
|---|---|
| 1½ | teaspoons unflavored gelatin |
| 2 | tablespoons cold water |
| 1½ | cups heavy cream |
| ⅓ | cup sifted powdered sugar |
| 3 | tablespoons light rum |

**RUM BUTTER ICING:**

| | |
|---|---|
| ½ | cup (¼ lb.) soft butter |
| 1 | cup sifted powdered sugar |
| ⅓ | cup light rum |
| 4 | cups sifted powdered sugar |

# Finnish Old Times Cake

*MENU FOR COFFEE SMÖRGÅSBORD INCLUDES THIS DISH—PAGE 12*

Bake pastry layers ahead of time (wrap cooled layers individually in waxed paper, then overwrap in foil), but assemble cake just before serving. The layers are quite fragile so handle with care.

Sift the flour before measuring, put into a bowl. With pastry blender or 2 knives, cut in butter until particles are fine. Sprinkle in 7 to 8 tablespoons cold water, mixing with fork to form a dough. Gather together into a ball. On a floured board, roll dough into a log. Divide into 8 portions, graduated in size from about a 2-inch ball to a 4-inch ball. Roll out each into a circle about ¼-inch thick, using additional flour as needed to prevent sticking; keep unrolled portions chilled as you work (rounds should range from about 3 inches to 10 inches in diameter). Trim rounds into even circles with notched pastry cutter, if you wish. Place on lightly greased baking sheets. Prick all over with a floured fork. Brush surface of each very lightly with cool water and sprinkle with sugar (about 4 tablespoons altogether). Bake in a 375° oven for about 10 minutes or until golden; cool on wire racks.

Drain strawberries well. Whip cream with sugar and vanilla to taste. To assemble cake, place largest round on flat plate; top with a layer of sliced strawberries, then spread with part of the whipped cream. Repeat layering to make a pyramid-shaped cake, ending with whipped cream. Decorate, if you wish, with whole strawberries and fresh flowers. With a very sharp, thin-bladed knife, cut through top four layers to make wedge-shaped servings. Cut narrower wedges from bottom 4 layers.

**MAKES 18 SERVINGS**

**BAKE PASTRY LAYERS AHEAD, ASSEMBLE JUST BEFORE SERVING TIME**

- 3 cups all-purpose flour
- 1½ cups (¾ lb.) butter
- 7 to 8 tablespoons cold water
  Sugar
- 2 packages (10 oz. <u>each</u>) sliced frozen strawberries, or 1½ cups fresh strawberries with ½ cup sugar
- 2 cups whipping cream
  Sugar
  Vanilla
  Whole strawberries

# Chocolate-Caramel Torte

Crackly caramel glazes this multi-layered chocolate-frosted cake. In flavor, it closely matches the authentic Hungarian Dobos with its dozen layers. Firm pound cake you buy is used; you freeze the cake to slice it thinly with ease. *(Photograph on facing page.)*

Melt chocolate in the top of a double boiler over hot water; let cool to room temperature. Cream butter until light and gradually beat in powdered sugar. Add egg yolks, one at a time, and beat until smooth. Beat in vanilla and the cool melted chocolate.

While cake is still slightly frozen, slice the top crust layer off the cake (you can eat it), then slice the cake horizontally into 6 or 7 very thin layers. Set aside the top layer for the caramel topping. Spread the chocolate frosting between remaining layers, reserving about ½ cup of the chocolate to coat the sides.

Heat the granulated sugar in a small pan (preferably with a nonstick fluorocarbon finish) until it melts and turns amber-colored. Place the reserved top cake layer on a sheet of foil or waxed paper and quickly pour over the hot caramel syrup, coating the top of the layer evenly. Arrange this layer on top of the last frosted layer of cake.

Heat the blade of a wooden-handled knife or spatula (not your best one) in the flame of a gas range or on an electric element and immediately mark the caramel topping into serving-sized slices.

Frost sides of cake with remaining frosting. If desired, pipe a small border of whipped cream around the top and bottom edge of the cake. Chill.

**MAKES 8 SERVINGS**

**CHILL CAKE AS MUCH AS A DAY OR TWO AHEAD**

- 4 ounces semisweet chocolate
- ½ cup (¼ lb.) butter or margarine
- ½ cup unsifted powdered sugar
- 2 egg yolks
- 1 teaspoon vanilla
- 1 frozen loaf-sized pound cake
- ⅓ cup granulated sugar
- ½ cup heavy cream, whipped (optional)

*Chocolate-Caramel Torte—see recipe above*

# Orange Cheddar Cheesecake

*MENU FOR PATIO BUFFET INCLUDES THIS DESSERT—PAGE 13*

**MAKES 10 SERVINGS**

**BAKE AS MUCH AS A DAY OR TWO AHEAD**

**USE CHEESECAKE PAN**

1 cup crushed orange-flavored
    cooky wafers
2 tablespoons melted butter
2 large packages (8 oz. <u>each</u>)
    cream cheese, softened
½ cup finely shredded Cheddar
    cheese
¾ cup sugar
2 tablespoons flour
3 eggs
¼ cup beer
¼ cup whipping cream
¼ teaspoon <u>each</u> grated orange
    peel and grated lemon peel
½ teaspoon vanilla

Grated citrus peels add zest to the unusual blend of Cheddar cheese and beer in this cheesecake. For a pretty display, garland the cake with clusters of frosted grapes nestled on leaves. To frost the grapes, dip in slightly beaten egg white, then granulated sugar.

Mix the cooky crumbs with the melted butter and pat into the bottom of a buttered 9-inch cheesecake pan (one with removable bottom or spring-release sides). Bake in a 350° oven for 8 minutes. Whip the cream cheese until light and fluffy and blend in the Cheddar cheese. Gradually beat in the ¾ cup sugar mixed with the flour. Add eggs, one at a time, beating until smooth. Mix in the beer and cream. Add the grated orange and lemon peels and vanilla, mixing well. Turn into crumb-lined pan and bake in a 350° oven for 30 minutes. Cool, then chill.

# Four Seasons Cake

**MAKES 12 TO 16 SERVINGS**

**CHILL CAKE AS LONG AS 24 HOURS**

**USE 10-INCH TUBE PAN**

1 package angel food cake mix
3 cups fresh, frozen, or canned
    fruit, well drained
1 envelope unflavored gelatin
¼ cup cold water
6 egg yolks, beaten
    Dash salt
½ cup sugar
½ teaspoon grated lemon, lime, or
    orange peel
½ cup lemon, lime, or orange juice
6 egg whites
½ cup sugar
1 cup heavy cream, whipped
    About ¾ cup fresh, frozen, or
    canned fruit, well drained, for
    garnish
    Fresh mint sprigs (optional)

This delicious-looking cake makes use of fruit that is in season. It's made with a packaged angel food cake mix, fruit, and either lemon, lime, or orange-flavored filling.

In fall and winter, use grapes, pears, melons, papaya, pineapple, or oranges. In spring, try strawberries, papaya, melons, or grapes. Summer combinations are seeded, halved grapes with lemon filling; strawberry halves with lemon or orange filling; papaya or cantaloupe slices with lime filling; pitted, halved cherries with lemon or orange; peach slices with lemon; apricot slices with orange.

Any time of year you can use well-drained canned or frozen fruits: pitted cherries, peaches, pears, apricots, or mandarin orange segments. (Dip fruit that darkens into an ascorbic acid mixture, following the label directions; drain.)

Bake angel food cake according to package directions, using a 10-inch tube pan. Invert cake to cool; then remove from pan and wash pan. Prepare fruit and drain on paper towels.

Soften gelatin in water. In top of a double boiler, beat together egg yolks, salt, ½ cup sugar, peel, and juice. Cook over hot water, stirring constantly, until mixture coats a spoon. Add gelatin and stir until dissolved. Set custard aside to cool, stirring occasionally. Beat egg whites until soft peaks form; gradually add remaining ½ cup sugar, beating until glossy. Fold slightly cooled custard mixture into egg whites.

Slice cake into 4 horizontal slices of equal width. Return bottom layer to tube pan, spoon ⅓ of the citrus filling over it, and arrange 1 cup of the fruit on filling. Repeat, using next two slices of cake and ⅓ of filling and 1 cup fruit for each layer. Add top cake slice, cover pan with foil, and refrigerate several hours or overnight.

Loosen cake from pan and invert on serving plate. Frost with whipped cream and garnish with fruit and mint, if used. Refrigerate. To serve, slice with a sharp knife.

# EASY FRESH FRUIT DESSERTS

Often fruit is the most welcome dessert after a meal of rich dishes.

A simple fruit dessert can be just as interesting as the rest of an elaborate meal. Following are some suggestions for attractive ways to present whole fruits, ways to use ice for chilling and eye-appeal, and delicious fruit combinations with wine, liqueurs, or sauces.

Many of these ideas will be lifesaving solutions for dessert when unexpected guests arrive.

**Fresh Fruit Trays.** Arrange identical individual servings of fruit on small trays, preparing the fruit in pretty and appetizing fashion.

To make an orange "flower," cut the peel six times around lengthwise—from stem nearly to the other end (make cuts equidistant). Pull loose peel halfway back, then tuck points down and in toward fruit to make petal effect.

Cut figs in half to show off their rosy interiors. Leave stems on choice strawberries and dip tips in sugar.

To make a banana boat, cut hard section off each end of a banana. Use a sharp knife to slit the peel from end to end along the center of the inside curve. Pull edges of the peel apart slightly, and tuck under the fruit on either side. Using the tip of the knife, cut the fruit into bite-sized pieces, leaving it in the skin. Sprinkle with lemon juice and powdered sugar. Serve with mint sprigs set into each end of the boat, if you wish.

**Strawberries, Oranges, and Champagne in Orange Shells.** Slice off a little more than the top ⅓ section of 6 large navel oranges (each about 3 inches in diameter). Squeeze juice from tops and save; discard tops. With a grapefruit knife, cut fruit from each orange, carefully removing as large and whole a portion as possible. Cover shells and chill.

Cut fruit from membrane and place in a deep bowl. Squeeze juice from membrane into bowl and add juice reserved from the orange tops. Gently mix in 4 cups whole hulled strawberries, 1 cup chilled Champagne, and 3 to 4 tablespoons sugar (depending on sweetness of berries). Cover and chill at least 3 hours; stir carefully several times.

Mound fruits into orange shells. Set shells in individual serving dishes that are partially filled with crushed ice. Pour as much of the marinade as possible into each shell. Garnish with mint leaves and serve immediately. Makes 6 servings.

**Iced Red Fruits in Wine.** Combine ½ cup sugar and ¼ cup water and bring to boil; chill. Wash and drain 2 cups *each* raspberries and strawberries. Wash, drain, stem, and pit 2 cups sweet red cherries. Chill fruit and serving dishes. If you use icers, fill bottoms with finely crushed ice.

Spoon fruit into top containers of icers or into chilled dishes. Pour syrup over fruit. Pour 1 small bottle (12 or 13 oz.) chilled pink Champagne, sparkling Burgundy, or crackling rosé over fruit and serve. Makes 6 to 8 servings.

**Fruit on Ice.** For each serving, slightly mound finely crushed ice in a handsome dish or goblet. Top with sliced sugared fruit (such as peaches or figs) or small whole berries. Drizzle with a flavorful liquid such as a liqueur like Cointreau, rum, or fruit juice concentrate. Eat the fruit, then sip the chilled liquid through a straw.

**Melon Mélange in Watermelon Shell.** Combine 1 cup sugar and ½ cup water and bring to a boil; remove from heat and add ⅓ cup kirsch or Cointreau; chill. With melon ball cutter, make 10 cups assorted melon balls, or dice melon. (Suggested melons: cantaloupe, Casaba, honeydew, Persian melon, watermelon.) Just before serving, pile melon balls in watermelon shell or in a large serving bowl. Pour liqueur-flavored syrup over fruit. Garnish with sprigs of mint. Makes 10 to 12 servings.

**Fruit with Sour Cream Sauce.** Gently stir into 1 cup sour cream, ½ cup powdered sugar, 1 teaspoon *each* grated lemon peel and lemon juice, and ¼ teaspoon vanilla. Cover and chill for several hours before serving. Spoon over fruit; sprinkle sauce lightly with nutmeg to serve.

**Pineapple or Pears with Brown Sugar Rum Sauce.** Beat yolks of 2 eggs until thick and light and gradually beat in ¼ cup brown sugar. Beat egg whites until soft peaks form and gradually beat in another ¼ cup brown sugar. Fold the yolk mixture into the meringue. Whip 1 cup heavy cream until stiff, stir in 2 tablespoons rum or ½ teaspoon rum flavoring, and fold into the egg mixture. Turn into a sauce bowl and dust the top with nutmeg. Chill. Serve over fresh sliced fruit.

**Baked Apples or Bananas with Orange Cream Sauce.** Place 1 cup heavy cream, 3 tablespoons frozen orange juice concentrate, and 3 tablespoons sugar in a bowl. Whip until stiff. Serve over hot baked fruit.

# Sweet Lemon-Yogurt Cake

*MENU FOR GREEK BUFFET INCLUDES THIS DISH—PAGE 32*

**MAKES 12 SERVINGS**

**BAKE UP TO 2 DAYS AHEAD**

**TUBE PAN REQUIRED**

- 1 cup (½ lb.) butter or margarine
- 2 cups sugar
- 6 eggs, separated
- 2 teaspoons grated lemon peel
- ½ teaspoon lemon extract
- 3 cups cake flour
- 1 teaspoon soda
- ¼ teaspoon salt
- 1 cup yogurt
- 2 tablespoons brandy (or substitute more yogurt)

In the eastern Mediterranean countries, yogurt is used for cooking and baking as often as we use milk or cream. Serve slices of this unfrosted Greek cake with ice cream or fruit. Cakes will keep several days if wrapped well.

Beat butter and 1½ cups of the sugar with an electric mixer until creamy. Add egg yolks, lemon peel, and lemon extract and beat until thick and pale yellow.

Sift the flour, measure, and sift again with the soda and salt. Into the creamed butter mixture alternately mix the flour and the yogurt (and brandy, if used). Beat the egg whites until soft peaks form; then gradually add the remaining ½ cup sugar, beating until glossy. Fold batter into beaten egg whites and pour into a greased 10-inch tube pan. Bake in a 350° oven for 45 minutes or until done. Cool 15 minutes in pan, then turn out on a rack.

# Finnish Orange Torte Cookies

*MENU FOR COFFEE SMÖRGÅSBORD INCLUDES THIS DISH—PAGE 12*

**MAKES 18 SLICES**

**BAKE AS MUCH AS A DAY IN ADVANCE**

- 1½ cups all-purpose flour
- ¼ cup sugar
- ½ cup (¼ lb.) butter or margarine
- 1 egg yolk
- 2 teaspoons slightly beaten egg white
- 1 cup ground almonds
- ¾ cup sugar
- ¼ cup sifted powdered sugar
- About 1 tablespoon orange juice
- Strips of candied orange peel
- Candied cherries

This long, slender, log-shaped torte is filled with ground almonds and sugar. You cut it into thin slices to make cookies.

Sift flour, measure 1½ cups, and sift again with ¼ cup sugar into large mixing bowl. With pastry blender or two knives, cut butter or margarine into flour and sugar until particles are fine. Stir in slightly beaten egg yolk. Gather the crumbly mixture together to form a ball; work between your palms for about 2 minutes or until the warmth of your hands makes a smooth dough. On a lightly floured board, roll dough out into a rectangle 5 by 10 inches.

Mix together slightly beaten egg white, almonds, and ¾ cup sugar. Turn mixture onto board; press together firmly to form a log about 8 inches long; place lengthwise down middle of dough rectangle. Bring up the two long sides of dough to encase the filling, overlapping edges slightly to seal; press to make a smooth seam. Pinch ends together to seal. Carefully lift filled roll onto a lightly greased baking sheet. Bake in a 400° oven for 15 minutes or until golden. Cool. Drizzle top with icing made by mixing powdered sugar and orange juice. Decorate with orange peel and cherries. To serve, cut into thin slices.

# Persian Cardamom Cookies

**MAKES ABOUT 4½ DOZEN**

**KEEP SEVERAL WEEKS IN AIRTIGHT CONTAINER**

- ¾ cup soft butter or margarine
- ½ teaspoon vanilla
- 1 cup powdered sugar
- 2 egg yolks
- 3½ cups cake flour
- ¾ teaspoon cardamom
- Pistachio nuts

These spice-scented treats from Iran have green pistachios pressed in their centers. The cookies are traditionally served with a refreshing cucumber punch (the recipe is on page 199).

Beat together butter or margarine, vanilla, and powdered sugar until fluffy. Beat in egg yolks, one at a time, beating until light colored. Sift and measure cake flour, sift with cardamom. Stir flour mixture into butter mixture until soft and well blended. Shape dough into ¾-inch balls. Press a small piece of pistachio in center of each. Bake on ungreased baking sheets in a 375° oven for 12 to 15 minutes, or until cookies are lightly browned.

# Suspiros

*MENU FOR PORTUGUESE DINNER INCLUDES THIS DISH—PAGE 40*

The name of these Portuguese dainties means "sighs." They are soft as a sigh and very sigh-inspiring.

Beat egg whites with cream of tartar until whites are thick and foamy. Gradually add sugar, beating constantly. Continue whipping until whites are stiff enough to hold high peaks that curl downward.

Force meringue through a pastry bag fitted with a fancy tip (or drop by generous teaspoonfuls) onto baking sheets lined with brown paper or other special baking-pan lining paper. Leave about an inch between each cooky. Bake in a 325° oven for 30 minutes or until an even gold in color. Carefully remove cookies from paper immediately, using a spatula, and cool on wire racks. They must be sealed airtight (such as in a heavy plastic bag) until serving time if prepared ahead.

**MAKES 1½ TO 2 DOZEN COOKIES**

**BAKE AS MUCH AS 1 WEEK IN ADVANCE**

3 egg whites
⅛ teaspoon cream of tartar
½ cup sugar

# Three Finnish Cookies

*MENU FOR COFFEE SMÖRGÅSBORD INCLUDES THESE—PAGE 12*

Here a basic dough makes three kinds of different-tasting, beautifully shaped cookies. They may be frozen if made ahead.

In a large mixing bowl, cream soft butter or margarine and sugar until light and fluffy. Sift flour before measuring, gradually beat flour into creamed mixture. Gather the crumbly mixture together; work between your hands until the warmth makes a smooth dough. Divide into three parts. Use one portion to make each of the following cookies:

**Raspberry Strip Cookies.** On a lightly floured board roll basic dough with palms of hands into logs about ½ inch in diameter and long enough to fit length of baking sheet. Place logs on lightly greased baking sheet. With side of your little finger, press a groove down the middle of each log, lengthwise. Bake in a 375° oven for 10 minutes. Remove from oven and fill groove with jam. Return to oven and bake 10 minutes more until dough is set and very light golden. While hot, brush with glaze made by mixing powdered sugar and about 2 tablespoons water. Cut warm logs diagonally into cookies about 1 inch wide. Allow to cool on baking sheet on a wire cooling rack. Makes about 2 dozen cookies.

**Horseshoes.** Thoroughly mix 1 egg yolk with ball of basic dough. Place dough into a cooky press fitted with a star tip. Force out long strips of dough onto board. Cut strips into 3-inch lengths; bend each to make a U-shape. Place on lightly greased baking sheet. Bake in a 375° oven for 12 minutes or until lightly browned. When cool, dip ends of horseshoes into chocolate melted over hot water. Makes about 18 cookies.

**Cinnamon Half-Moons.** Thoroughly mix 1 egg yolk with basic dough. On a lightly floured board, roll out dough about ⅛ inch thick. With a circle cutter, cut into rounds 2 to 2½ inches in diameter. Cut each round in half. Place on lightly greased baking sheet, brush lightly with a beaten egg white. Sprinkle cookies with a mixture of ¼ cup sugar and the cinnamon. Bake in a 375° oven for 12 minutes or until lightly browned at edges. Makes about 2 dozen cookies.

**MAKES 5½ DOZEN COOKIES**

**BAKE AS MUCH AS A DAY AHEAD, OR FREEZE**

1 cup (½ lb.) soft butter or margarine
½ cup sugar
3 cups all-purpose flour

**RASPBERRY STRIP COOKIES:**
About 6 tablespoons seedless raspberry jam or other jam
½ cup powdered sugar
2 tablespoons water

**HORSESHOES:**
1 egg yolk
2 ounces semisweet chocolate

**CINNAMON HALF-MOONS:**
1 egg yolk
Beaten egg white
¼ cup sugar
½ teaspoon cinnamon

# Hot and Cold Drinks

MANY HOT AND COLD DRINKS, some unusual and some familiar, are described in this chapter.

Recipes are included for cool fruit and milk drinks suitable for young people or breakfast-brunch service. Sophisticated concoctions containing liqueurs and wines, many of which are rich and sweet enough to make a delightful substitute for dessert, are appropriate for adult meals or refreshment. Some exotic drinks from other countries will interest the adventuresome. Both the cold and the hot, spicy wintertime punches will be convenient to serve at large parties.

Coffee has been given lengthy consideration. A variety of recipes will be found for coffee drinks from countries around the world, including the well-known Italian, French, and Turkish varieties. Some of these are rich enough to serve wherever you might want a dessert, while others are meant to be black and strong finales to a heavy meal or a contrast to a very sweet pastry.

You will find many tips on presenting beautiful drinks and ideas for using ice not only to keep drinks cold but to glamorize them as well. How to improvise punch bowls and ice them also is discussed.

Many of the drinks in this chapter are excellent to serve with sweets or snacks when you entertain informally without serving a complete meal.

Some of the drink and punch recipes contain wine. You will, however, find more information elsewhere to aid in selection and serving of wines—how to have a wine-tasting, page 16; how to serve wine, page 101; cooking with wine, page 104; selecting wines, page 121; wine age and vintage, page 163.

# Cranberry-Mint Cocktail

MENU FOR HAM BUFFET INCLUDES THIS DRINK—PAGE 29

**MAKES 12 SERVINGS**

**COCKTAIL BASE MAY BE MADE A DAY AHEAD**

- 2 cups cranberry juice
- ¼ cup crushed fresh mint leaves
- 2 cups (16-oz. can) jellied cranberry sauce
- 4 cups (1 quart bottle) ginger ale

Fresh mint adds a refreshing note to cranberry juice and jellied cranberry sauce in this cocktail; ginger ale is added just before serving.

In an electric blender, whirl together 1 cup of the cranberry juice and the mint leaves. Add 1 more cup cranberry juice and jellied cranberry sauce and whirl for 3 to 4 seconds or until smooth. Pour into a large pitcher and refrigerate. Before serving, add the ginger ale, mixing well. Serve with an ice cube in each glass.

# Lemon Frappé

**MAKES 6 TO 8 SERVINGS**

**IF MADE AHEAD, WHIP AGAIN BEFORE SERVING**

**CHILL GLASSES**

- 1 cup whipping cream
- 1 quart cultured buttermilk
- 1½ teaspoons grated lemon peel
- 4 tablespoons lemon juice
- ½ cup sugar
  Cinnamon or cinnamon sticks

Serve this sweet-tart and frosty beverage for dessert or for midday refreshment. One ingredient is buttermilk; but, since it loses its identity, you might keep it secret from anyone who is anti-buttermilk.

Using a rotary beater, whip cream into soft peaks; set aside. Using the same beater, without washing it, whip buttermilk with lemon peel, lemon juice, and sugar until frothy. Fold whipped cream into buttermilk mixture, then pour into a chilled pitcher and serve in tall glasses. Sprinkle a dash of cinnamon on top, or add a cinnamon stick stirrer to each glass.

If refrigerated, whip with a rotary beater just before serving.

# Chocolate-Mint Fizz

**MAKES 4 SERVINGS**

**WHIP CREAM AHEAD**

**CHILL GLASSES**

- ½ cup chocolate syrup
- ¼ cup heavy cream, whipped
- 2 bottles (7 oz. each) club soda
- 1½ pints peppermint ice cream

The tang of soda water enhances the combination of chocolate syrup and peppermint ice cream.

Place 2 tablespoons chocolate syrup into the bottom of each of 4 glasses (approximately 10-oz. size). Spoon 2 tablespoons whipped cream into each and stir well with a spoon. Pour in about 2 tablespoons soda and stir until foamy. Add 2 scoops of ice cream to each glass. Pour soda into each glass, filling to the top, and stir lightly. Serve with straws.

# Alexander Icicle

**MAKES 4 SERVINGS**

**BLEND AT SERVING TIME**

- 1 pint vanilla ice cream, softened
- 2 tablespoons each crème de cacao and brandy

Soft ice cream blended with liqueurs is fun to sip through straws. Be sure you chill the glasses well so the ice cream won't melt.

Put the ice cream and liqueurs into a chilled blender container. Blend just until smooth. Pour into chilled small glasses or sherbet glasses. Add short, fat straws.

# Mexican Almond Horchata

*HORCHATA DE ALMENDRAS*

Horchata ("ore-*shah*-tah") is made from nuts or seeds steeped in a light sugar syrup. One type found in Curaçao, Netherlands West Indies, is made of sweet and bitter almonds. In Mexico you may have tasted a version made of cantaloupe seeds, or this *Horchata de Almendras*, garnished with a floating fragrant blossom. *(Photograph on page 194.)*

Boil the water and sugar together until the sugar is dissolved. Pour over the ground almonds and allow to stand at room temperature for 1 hour. Strain through 4 thicknesses of cheesecloth, squeezing out all the liquid; discard nuts. Stir in the orange blossom water and kirsch, cover, and chill for 8 hours or more. Stir before serving. Pour over ice in wide, shallow stemmed glasses, and float a blossom on each.

**MAKES 6 SERVINGS**

**CHILL AT LEAST 8 HOURS**

4½  cups water
9   tablespoons sugar
1½  cups blanched almonds, finely ground
1   tablespoon <u>each</u> orange flower water and kirsch (cherry brandy)
6   washed fragrant blossoms, such as orange or lemon (optional)

# Double Fruit Soda

Bottled berry syrup provides an excellent flavoring base for this fruit soda made with sherbet and ice cream.

Place 2 tablespoons strawberry syrup in the bottom of 6 tall (12 to 14 oz.) glasses. Spoon 2 tablespoons whipped cream into each and stir well with a spoon. Pour in about 2 tablespoons soda and stir until foamy. To each glass add 1 scoop *each* orange sherbet, vanilla ice cream, and strawberry ice cream. Pour soda into each glass, filling to the top, stir lightly, and add a dollop of whipped cream. Garnish each drink with a strawberry. Cut a slit just to the center of each orange slice and insert a slice over the side of each glass.

**MAKES 6 SERVINGS**

**WHIP CREAM AHEAD**

¾  cup bottled strawberry syrup
½  cup heavy cream, whipped
1  quart club soda
1  pint <u>each</u> orange sherbet, vanilla ice cream, and strawberry ice cream
6  fresh strawberries for garnish
1  orange, sliced with peel on for garnish

# Fresh Fruit Yogurt Coolers

Now that fruit-flavored yogurt has become so popular everywhere, these drinks should be enjoyed by many people who would not even have been acquainted with yogurt a few years back when it was regarded as just a "health" food. Yogurt beverages are not a new idea. They have been popular in the Middle East for centuries.

Chill fruit. If you have no blender, force fruit through food mill or wire strainer; then blend with yogurt, milk, and sugar to taste. If you use blender, whirl fruit, yogurt, milk, and sugar together until smooth. Then pour through strainer to remove seeds if raspberries or blackberries are used. Serve cold at once, or chill as much as 3 hours. Makes 3 cups.

**MAKES 2 TO 3 SERVINGS**

**MAKE NO MORE THAN 3 HOURS AHEAD**

**CHILL GLASSES**

1  cup sliced strawberries, crushed blackberries, crushed raspberries, or sliced peaches
1  cup cold yogurt
1  cup skim or whole milk
   Sugar

# Kahlua Frost

**MAKES 4 SERVINGS**

**WHIP CREAM AHEAD**

**CHILL GLASSES**

4 tablespoons Kahlua or other
coffee-flavored liqueur
¼ cup heavy cream, whipped
2 bottles (7 oz. <u>each</u>) club soda
1 pint coffee ice cream
4 cinnamon sticks

Coffee liqueur and coffee ice cream give smooth flavoring to this summery beverage for grownups.

Place 1 tablespoon Kahlua in the bottom of 4 large (8-oz. size) wine glasses or sherbet glasses. Add 1 tablespoon whipped cream to each glass and stir until blended. Pour about 2 tablespoons soda into each glass and stir until foamy. Add 1 large scoop of ice cream to each glass and pour in sufficient soda water to fill to the top.

Add a dollop of whipped cream and insert a cinnamon stick into each glass to serve as a stirrer.

# Milk Punch

**MAKES 4 TO 6 SERVINGS**

**BLENDER DESIRABLE**

1 cup brandy
2 cups cold milk
6 tablespoons powdered sugar
½ teaspoon vanilla
6 to 8 ice cubes, coarsely crushed
Nutmeg

Usually such a punch is a cold-weather drink, but ice is added to this version to make it refreshing for hot weather—or any season.

Pour brandy into blender with milk, sugar, vanilla, and crushed ice cubes. Whirl the mixture until it is frothy and well blended. Pour into glasses or punch cups, and sprinkle with nutmeg.

# Mexican Chocolate

**MAKES 6 SERVINGS**

6 cups milk
¾ teaspoon cinnamon
6 ounces coarsely chopped sweet
cooking chocolate
½ cup heavy cream, whipped
2 tablespoons sugar
6 cinnamon sticks

Mexican hot chocolate is beaten until frothy, spiced with cinnamon, topped with whipped cream, and spiked with a cinnamon-stick stirrer.

Heat milk with the ¾ teaspoon cinnamon until steaming. Add chopped chocolate and stir until melted. Beat with a rotary mixer until mixture is frothy. Have ready heavy cream, whipped stiff with the sugar. Pour hot chocolate into cups and top each with a spoonful of the cream. Drop a cinnamon stick in each cup if you wish.

# Mocha Cooler

**MAKES 6 SERVINGS**

**CHILL GLASSES**

1½ quarts chocolate ice cream
2 cups chilled milk
2 tablespoons instant coffee or
malted milk powder
1 teaspoon vanilla
Chocolate curls for garnish

For this chocolate milk shake, you have a choice of instant coffee or malted milk powder for a subtle second flavoring. Serve this drink with spoons for eating the ice cream floating in it.

Place in a blender 1 pint ice cream, milk, instant coffee, and vanilla; blend just until smooth (or beat with a rotary beater until smooth). Scoop 1 pint ice cream into 6 tall glasses. Pour over the mocha milk shake and top with scoops of the remaining ice cream and shaved chocolate.

# Persian Cucumber Punch

Iced cucumber punch—from Iran, where cucumbers are regarded as fruits—is refreshingly tart on a warm afternoon, served with Persian Cardamom Cookies (recipe on page 192). To garnish the punch bowl for a party, make an ice ring with unpeeled cucumber and lemon slices frozen in it (see "Icy and Imaginative Ways to Serve Drinks" below for how to freeze the ring).

Peel, quarter, remove seeds, and coarsely chop cucumbers. Whirl about ⅓ at a time, in blender until puréed; strain out and discard pulp (you should have about 2½ cups juice). Just before serving, mix 2 cups Punch Base (recipe follows), 8 cups cold water, cucumber juice, and ¼ cup lemon juice. Pour over ice to serve.

**Punch Base.** Combine 1 cup water, sugar, vinegar, and ½ cup lemon juice; bring to a boil and cook until syrup reaches 230° on candy thermometer (spins a 2-inch thread). Remove from heat and add chopped mint; cool. Strain; store in a covered jar. Makes about 2 cups.

**MAKES 3 QUARTS PUNCH**

**PUNCH BASE MAY BE MADE
1 DAY AHEAD**

6   medium-sized cucumbers
2   cups Punch Base (recipe follows)
8   cups cold water
¼   cup lemon juice

**PUNCH BASE:**

1   cup water
3   cups sugar
¾   cup cider vinegar
½   cup lemon juice
1   tablespoon chopped fresh mint
    or ½ tablespoon dried mint

## ICY AND IMAGINATIVE WAYS TO SERVE DRINKS

The simple purity and gleam of ice is often all the garnish a cold drink needs. Following are a number of ways to use ice for individual drinks and in punch bowls. Other ways to make drinks appealing are also suggested.

**Watermelon-Shell Glass Chiller.** Cut a large watermelon in half the long way and scoop out meat; fill shell with crushed ice. Turn punch glasses upside down and push into ice.

**Fiesta Ice Cubes.** Put mint leaves, maraschino cherries, lemon and orange wedges in compartments of an ice tray; pour half full of water, fruit juice, or ginger ale; freeze. Fill to top and freeze again.

**Iced Bottle.** Put empty bottle from which drink will be poured in center of half-gallon wax milk carton. Pour water up to the bottom of the neck of the bottle and freeze. Peel off carton and fill bottle with ice-cold high-proof liquor such as aquavit or vodka. Return to freezer if you wish (the liquor will not freeze). To serve, place bottle in shallow bowl and wrap small towel around neck of bottle.

**Ice Cones.** Pack two V-shaped glasses with crushed ice. Unmold one onto the other. Pour on liqueur or fruit juice concentrate. Insert straw.

**Orange-Shell Cups.** Stand short straws in plain or fancy cut orange shells. Pack with crushed ice; pour in liqueur or fruit juice concentrate.

**Flower-Lei Straws.** Thread one end of a soda straw or thin bamboo skewer through the centers of several fragrant flowers. Insert other end in drink.

**Improvised Punch Bowls.** If you don't have a punch bowl, use an ice bucket, fish bowl, kitchen kettle, soy tub planter lined with plastic bucket, insulated picnic cooler, or colorful enamel mixing bowl.

**Ice Ring for Punch Bowl.** Fill a ring mold with boiled water and let water sit for awhile, stirring occasionally to remove air bubbles which will make ice cloudy. Freeze and unmold into punch bowl. To center edible decorations (such as mint leaves, berries, cucumber slices, or maraschino cherries) in the ice, first freeze the ring a third full of water, add garnish, then add water to fill two-thirds full. Freeze again. Then fill to top and freeze again.

# Spicy Citrus Punch

**MAKES ABOUT 40 SERVINGS**

**PREPARE PUNCH BASE UP TO 8 HOURS AHEAD**

| | |
|---|---|
| 4 | quarts water |
| 1 | tablespoon whole cloves |
| 1 | teaspoon whole allspice |
| 2 | sticks whole cinnamon |
| 6 | lemons |
| 6 | large oranges |
| ⅓ | cup tea leaves |
| 3 | cups sugar |
| | Orange for garnish (optional) |
| 6 | whole cloves (optional) |

You can make this tea-based punch ahead; serve it cold or reheated.

Put 2 quarts of the water in a pan and add the 1 tablespoon cloves, allspice, and cinnamon. Using a vegetable peeler, remove the thin outer zest from peel of the lemons and oranges; reserve the fruit. Add fruit peel to spices; cover, bring to simmering. Reduce heat and steep (below boiling point) for 30 minutes. Meanwhile bring remaining 2 quarts water to boiling, remove from heat, add tea, cover, and steep for 10 minutes. Strain both mixtures and combine; while still hot, stir in the sugar until dissolved. Add the juice of the lemons and oranges (strained). If made ahead, refrigerate until needed.

Reheat to serve hot; garnish with a small whole orange, stuck with about 6 whole cloves. Or serve the well-chilled punch over ice in a punch bowl; garnish with the orange slices.

# Sangria

*RED WINE PUNCH*

**MAKES 12 TO 14 SERVINGS**

**CHILL PUNCH BASE AS LONG AS 24 HOURS (REMOVE CITRUS SLICES AND PEEL AFTER 4 TO 6 HOURS)**

| | |
|---|---|
| 1 | whole orange |
| 1 | whole lemon, thinly sliced |
| | Juice of 1 lemon |
| 2 | bottles (4/5 qt. each) Burgundy or Pinot Noir |
| ½ | cup sugar |
| 1 | bottle (1 qt.) sparkling water, chilled |

This popular Spanish punch is made with red wine, orange and lemon juice, and sparkling water.

Cut the outer rind from the orange in a spiral strip, removing as little of the white membrane as possible. Then squeeze orange juice. In a large bowl, mix together the orange spiral, orange juice, lemon slices, and lemon juice. Add the Burgundy and sugar. Stir until the sugar is dissolved. Chill at least 4 hours. Remove the lemon slices and orange peel. Pour into a punch bowl; add sparkling water.

# Ginger Wine Punch

**MAKES 22 TO 24 SERVINGS**

| | |
|---|---|
| 2 | bottles (1 qt. each) ginger ale, chilled |
| 3 | bottles (4/5 qt. each) Sauterne, chilled |
| 3 | sprigs mint |
| 1 | whole lemon, thinly sliced |

Lemon slices and sprigs of mint float on the top of this light amber, sparkling punch, which is shown off at its best in a clear glass bowl.

In a large punch bowl, mix together the chilled ginger ale and chilled wine. Place mint sprigs and lemon slices on the top for garnish. Add a chunk of ice to keep punch chilled. Serve in punch cups.

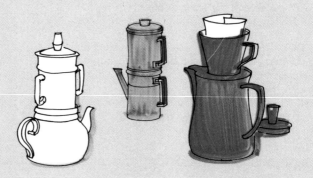

# COFFEES FROM AROUND THE WORLD

Because of the coffee houses which have become popular throughout the West and the frequency of foreign travel, most guests will be familiar with (and appreciative of) any foreign coffee you choose to serve.

**Italian Caffé Espresso.** You need an espresso machine, which forces water and steam under pressure through finely ground, dark, Italian-roast coffee, or you can prepare a reasonable facsimile using an Italian *macchinetta* (sometimes called Neopolitan or *caffettiera*) or a pressurized Domus espresso pot.

Follow the manufacturer's directions. Serve in demitasse cups with sugar (raw or refined)—never with cream!

For *Espresso Romano*, pour coffee into small, stemmed, heat-proof glasses and garnish with a twist of lemon peel. To make *Cappuccino*, combine coffee with an equal amount of milk heated on an espresso steam valve. Or quickly pour coffee into an equal amount of hot milk, and stir until foamy. Serve in slender Cappuccino cups and sprinkle with cinnamon.

**French Café.** In specialty food shops and some supermarkets, you can purchase a tin of French-roast coffee. Make in a drip pot, or by the individual cup with French coffee filters.

The French use two pots to make their *café au lait*. One is filled with a strong, hot French coffee, the other with an equal amount of hot, rich milk. Taking a pot in each hand, you pour from them simultaneously into a cup.

**Turkish Coffee.** Genuine Turkish coffee is made with pulverized coffee, much resembling instant coffee in appearance, which you can buy in cans or jars at specialty food shops.

It's traditionally made in a copper *cezve*, a tapering pot with a handle and open at the top, but you can use a saucepan or uncovered percolator pot instead. Cezves can be purchased in sizes making from 2 to 10 demitasse-sized cups.

To make coffee for 4 people, measure 4 demitasse cups of cold water into a 4-cup-size cezve, a saucepan, or similar container. Add 4 teaspoons sugar and heat. When water is boiling, remove from heat and stir in 4 tablespoons pulverized coffee. Bring to a boil again, allow to froth up, remove from heat for a moment, and pour a little of the froth into each cup. Repeat the frothing-up process two more times. Add a few drops of cold water, without stirring, to settle the grounds. Pour some of the foam into each demitasse cup, then pour in the coffee. (Many Americans prefer Turkish coffee a little milder, frothed up only once or twice, and with more or less sugar.)

**Viennese Coffee.** Brew extra-strength coffee, pour into cups, and top with a drift of sweetened whipped cream. Dust the cream lightly with powdered nutmeg or cinnamon.

**Caffé Borgia.** The Italians probably named this drink after the aristocratic Borgia family of the 15th and 16th centuries. Pour equal parts hot chocolate (made with milk) and double-strength coffee into heated cups. Top with a heaping spoonful of lightly sweetened whipped cream; sprinkle with grated orange peel and shaved bittersweet chocolate.

**Irish Coffee.** Into a warmed table wine glass, place 2 teaspoons of sugar; fill glass about ⅔ full of strong, hot coffee. Stir. Add 2 tablespoons of Irish whiskey, and top with softly whipped cream. Makes 1 serving.

**Syrian Demitasse.** Place 2 or 3 crushed cardamom seeds in each demitasse cup and fill with double-strength coffee. (Use 8 tablespoons coffee with 2 cups water.) Serve with sugar. Turkish Coffee (see recipe in column to left) also is good with cardamom. Add 1 whole crushed pod to each cup.

**Tahitian Coffee with Coconut Milk.** Heat 2 cups milk until a film forms on top. Add 1 can (4 oz.) or 1 cup flaked coconut and 2 tablespoons sugar. Cover and allow to stand in the refrigerator overnight. Strain milk and reheat slowly. Combine milk with 2 cups freshly brewed strong, hot coffee. Serve with a topping of toasted coconut, if desired. Makes 6 coffee-cup servings.

(Note: *This coffee can also be served chilled. Pour into brandy snifters or glass tumblers and serve as an afternoon refreshment.*)

**Russian Coffee.** In the top of a double boiler, melt ½ ounce semisweet chocolate over hot water. Add ¼ cup sugar, ⅛ teaspoon salt, and ¼ cup water. Place over direct heat and simmer for 5 minutes, stirring. Add ½ cup *each* milk and whipping cream (or 1 cup half-and-half) and heat, but do not boil. Add 2 cups hot, strong, freshly made coffee, and 1 teaspoon vanilla. Beat with a rotary beater until foamy and serve immediately. Serves 4.

**Dutch Koffie.** Place a cinnamon stick in each serving cup, fill with freshly brewed black coffee, stir in 1 tablespoon whipping cream, and float a pat of butter on top. Serve with sugar.

**Mexican Coffee.** For this Mexican dessert coffee, spice 1½ cups strong black coffee with ½ teaspoon cinnamon; sweeten to taste and top each demitasse cup with a generous dollop of sweetened and spiced whipped cream. (Use ¼ teaspoon *each* nutmeg and cinnamon with ½ cup whipping cream.) Makes 4 demitasse servings.

**Belgian Coffee.** Beat 2 egg whites until stiff and fold in 2 cups of cream, whipped. Sweeten to taste. Half-fill heated coffee cups with egg white mixture and fill with hot coffee. Serve immediately. Makes about 6 servings.

# White Wine Punch

*MENU FOR TAHITIAN PARTY INCLUDES THIS DRINK—PAGE 49*

**SERVES 12 TO 16 PEOPLE**

**BEGIN PREPARATION 12 HOURS TO A DAY AHEAD**

1 medium-sized pineapple, peeled and cut into fine chunks
½ cup brown sugar, firmly packed
½ whole nutmeg, grated
1 vanilla bean, slit in half lengthwise
  Sections of 2 grapefruit
  Sections of 2 oranges
  Zest (outer peel) of 1 lime
  Juice of 2 limes
1 bottle (4/5 qt.) of chilled dry white wine
6 cups fruit juice (orange, pineapple, grapefruit, or a combination)

Slices of fresh citrus fruits garnish this flavorful Island punch. Start making it a day before the party to let flavors mingle. Leave the split vanilla bean in the punch when you serve it.

The day before the party, place in a large bowl or pitcher the pineapple, brown sugar, nutmeg, and vanilla bean. Mix and cover. Place in a cool place (not in refrigerator), and allow to stand 12 to 24 hours. Add grapefruit and orange sections. Twist strips of lime zest to extract oil and drop into punch. Add lime juice, wine, and fruit juice. Pour over ice in a large punch bowl. Makes about 2½ quarts.

# Champagne Fruit Punch

*MENU FOR ELEGANT CHAMPAGNE PARTY INCLUDES THIS DRINK—PAGE 28*

**MAKES 18 TO 20 SERVINGS**

**CHILL ALL INGREDIENTS**

1 bottle (4/5 qt.) Sauterne, well chilled
1 bottle (4/5 qt.) Champagne, chilled
2 bottles (1 qt. **each**) grapefruit soda, well chilled
2 cups washed, stemmed strawberries

Strawberries garnish this refreshing punch, made with grapefruit soda, Sauterne, and Champagne. Have all ingredients well chilled.

In a punch bowl, mix together until blended the Sauterne, Champagne, and grapefruit soda. Drop in strawberries. Ladle some of the punch into each punch glass or Champagne glass, and add a strawberry to each serving.

# Cider Wassail Bowl

**MAKES 12 SERVINGS**

**BEGIN PREPARATION 20 TO 30 MINUTES BEFORE NEEDED**

3 tablespoons light corn syrup
3 tablespoons sugar
¼ teaspoon cinnamon
8 lady apples (or 5 small red cooking apples)
2 quarts apple cider
1 lemon, thinly sliced
1 stick cinnamon
4 whole cloves

This hot and spicy cider punch has roasted apples bobbing on top, the way they are served on the traditional English wassail of ale or wine.

Heat corn syrup in a small pan; combine 3 tablespoons sugar with ¼ teaspoon cinnamon in a shallow dish. Roll each apple in hot syrup, then in the sugar; arrange on a baking pan, and bake in a 400° oven until partially cooked, about 15 minutes (apples should not lose their shape).

  In a large pan, heat slowly over very low heat to just below boiling point the apple cider, sliced lemon, stick cinnamon, and cloves. Before serving, strain out the spices and add the roasted apples. Serve piping hot. The small lady apples may be served in the punch cups.

# Glögg

*HOT WINE PUNCH*

In American Scandinavian communities, glögg (pronounced "glug") is well known. It's the traditional hot Christmas wine of Sweden. Whole clove-studded baked oranges floating in the punch contribute flavor and also garnish the punchbowl.

Stud each whole orange with 10 to 12 whole cloves. Place on a baking pan and bake in a 300° oven for 2 hours, or until juices start to run. Transfer to a heatproof 2-gallon serving bowl (or copper pan). Pour over warm rum, ignite, and flame. Then pour in hot apple cider and add cinnamon sticks. Keep hot over a warmer during serving time, ladling into small heatproof punch cups. If you wish, stir in additional rum.

**MAKES ABOUT 32 SERVINGS**

**BEGIN BAKING ORANGES 2 HOURS BEFORE SERVING**

6  oranges
    About 6 dozen whole cloves
1  cup warm rum
1  gallon (4 quarts) hot apple cider
3  sticks cinnamon

## COOL TROPICAL DRINKS WITH COCONUT MILK

Start with well-chilled ingredients to make these exotic drinks of coconut milk and fruit juices. Use your blender or stir ingredients together thoroughly to mix. Each recipe makes 2 servings. If you want to include rum in any of these drinks, add about 1 ounce per serving.

You can buy frozen or canned coconut milk in many markets, or make the milk yourself from fresh or packaged coconut (directions follow). Use only fresh lime juice.

**Coconut-Passion Fruit.** Combine 1 cup coconut milk, 1½ cups canned passion fruit nectar, ¼ cup *each* lime juice and sugar. Serve over ice.

**Coconut Frost.** In the blender container, combine ½ cup coconut milk, 2 tablespoons lime juice, 1 tablespoon sugar, and 1½ cups crushed ice; whirl. Pour into chilled glasses.

**Coconut-Lime.** Combine 1½ cups coconut milk, ¾ cup lime juice, and 6 tablespoons sugar. Serve over ice.

**Coconut-Guava.** Combine ½ cup coconut milk, 1½ cups canned guava nectar, 2 tablespoons lime juice, 3 tablespoons sugar, and 1 teaspoon tamarind syrup (optional). Serve at once over ice.

**Planters' Punch.** Combine ¼ cup coconut milk, ¼ cup *each* canned papaya juice, guava nectar, passion fruit nectar, pineapple juice, and fresh or frozen orange juice, 2 tablespoons lime juice, 1 tablespoon sugar, and 1 teaspoon grenadine syrup. Pour over ice to serve.

**Coconut-Pineapple-Papaya.** Mix together 1 cup coconut milk, ½ cup *each* canned pineapple juice and papaya juice, ¼ cup *each* lime juice and sugar. Serve over ice.

**Coconut-Papaya.** Combine 1 cup coconut milk, 1 cup canned papaya juice, ¼ cup lime juice, and 4 tablespoons sugar. Serve immediately over ice.

**Coconut-Pineapple.** Combine 1 cup coconut milk, ½ cup pineapple juice, ¼ cup lime juice, and 4 tablespoons sugar. Serve at once over ice.

**To Make Fresh Coconut Milk in the Blender.** Drain and crack open 1 fresh coconut; taste to make sure it is free from any off flavors. Remove coconut meat and cut in ½-inch cubes. For each cup of cubed coconut meat, add ¾ cup hot liquid (hot water added to liquid drained from coconut) in the blender. Whirl for 20 to 30 seconds, then steep for 30 minutes. Strain through double thickness of cheesecloth, squeezing out liquid. One coconut makes about 2 cups.

**To Make Coconut Milk from Packaged Coconut in the Blender.** Combine 2⅔ cups *each* packaged flaked coconut and cold milk; leave in refrigerator 1 hour. Whirl in blender for about 40 seconds. Strain through double thickness of cheesecloth, squeezing out liquid. Makes at least 2 cups.

**To Make Coconut Milk Without a Blender.** Mix 2 cups shredded coconut (fresh or packaged) with 2 cups half-and-half (light cream). Heat just below simmering point, then remove from heat and steep 30 minutes. Pour through sieve or cheesecloth, pressing or squeezing out all liquid. Chill. Makes 2 cups.

# Index

## A

Abalone
  Parmigiana, 132
  Seviche, appetizer, 59
Accompaniments and Side Dishes, 145–171
Agurkesalat, 27
Aïoli meal, sauce, 25
Alcohol fuel for chafing dishes, 116
Alexander Icicle, 196
Almonds
  Almendrado, pudding, 178
  Chicken with almonds, 37
  Curried, 54
  Finnish Orange Torte Cookies, 192
  Mexican Almond Horchata, 197
  Persian Baklava, 184
Anchovies, Salade Niçoise, 141
Antipasto, 63
  Potato Salad, 87
  Salad, 37
Appetizer Recipes, 51–67
  Dips, Spreads, Tidbits, 52–62
    Abalone Seviche, 59
    Almonds, Curried, 54
    Artichoke Appetizers, Crisp, 53
    Artichoke with Red and Black Caviar, 57
    Asparagus Spears, Chilled, 53
    Avocado Butter, 53
    Avocado Dip with Red and Black Caviar, 57
    Banana Chip Appetizers, 54
    Bean Dip, Refried, 59
    Beef Sticks, Hawaiian, 62
    Carrots, Ginger-Minted, 55
    Caviar with Deviled Eggs, 57
    Cheddar Cheese Spread, 58
    Chicken, Indonesian Broiled, 60
    Chicken Liver Pâté, Molded, 62
    Chorizo Tostadas de Harina, 56
    Cream Cheese Trio, 54
    Crudités, 54
    Cucumber-Cheese Slices, 56
    Edam Cheese Balls, 54
    Fennel and Blue Cheese, 54
    Guacamole, 52
    Liver Pâté, Scandinavian, 26
    Melon with Meat, 54
    Mushroom Caps, Ham-Filled, 60
    Mushrooms, Marinated Raw, 55
    Mushrooms à la Grecque, 54
    Onion-Dill Dip, 52
    Pomegranate Cheese Loaf, 22
    Quiche Lorraine, 58
    Radish Dip, Raw, 52
    Sausage Balls, Sweet-Sour, 62
    Shrimp in Dill Marinade, Iced, 59
    Shrimp Toast Canapés, 60
    Swordfish and Cantaloupe, 55
    Tiropetes, pastries, 56
    Tomatoes, Philippine Shrimp-Stuffed, 55
    Tostadas de Harina, 56
  First-Course Appetizers, 63–67
    Antipasto Platter, 63
    Artichokes, Ham Sauce in, 63
    Artichokes Vinaigrette, 64
    Clam, Stuffed, 65
    Coquilles St. Jacques, 67
    Eggplant, Broiled, 20
    Fettucine, 65
    Melon Appetizer, 65
    Pâté en Croûte, 67
    Shellfish Cocktails, 66
    Shrimp Saganaki, 66
  Simple recipes, 54
  Use of ice in serving, 64
Apples
  Baked, with Orange Cream Sauce, 191
  Cider Wassail Bowl, 202

English Fruit Pudding, 183
Sweet Potatoes and Apples Caramel, 160
Apricot French Toast, 23
Arni Souvlakia, 103
Artichokes
  Basque Artichokes with Eggs, 137
  Crisp-fried appetizers, 53
  Veal Indorato, 97
  Vinaigrette, appetizer, 64
  with caviar, 57
  with ham sauce, 63
Asparagus
  Carrot-Asparagus Platter, 155
  Chilled Spears, appetizer, 53
  Cream of, soup, 75
  Flank steak, mushrooms, and, 92
  Pozharsky, 90
  Tips in Aspic, 151
  with Cashew Butter, 151
Aspic, see Gelatin Salads
Avgolemono sauce
  Chicken with, 119
  Stuffed grape leaves or cabbage with, 94
Avocados
  Bouillon, 71
  Butter, spread, 53
  Dip with caviar, 57
  Grapefruit-Avocado Salad, 78
  Green and Gold Salad, 78
  Guacamole, 52
  San Diego Salad, 141
  Sauce, for Seafood Fondue, 46
  Stuffed, salad, 84
  Vegetable-Filled, salad, 84

## B

Bab Leves, 140
Bacon
  Quiche Lorraine, 58
  Veal Paupiettes, 96
  Veal Roast Orloff, 97
Bagels, Egg, 165
Bake-broil method for steaks, 95
Baked Alaska, Pineapple, 175
Baklava, Persian, 184
Bali, Pork Satés, 109
Bananas
  Baked, with Orange Cream Sauce, 191
  Chips, appetizer, 54
  Condiment Chicken Salad with Avocado, 86
  Fresh Fruit Trays, 191
  Green and Gold Salad, 78
  Ham with, 106
Barbecued Ham Buffet menu, 29
  Ham recipe, 109
Barley bread, Rieska, 167
Basil
  Butter, 149
  Pasta a Pesto, 163
  Pistou for soup, 74
Basque Artichokes with Eggs, 137
Batter bread, 168
Beans
  Dried
    Hungarian Speckled Bean Soup, 140
    Refried Bean Dip, 59
    White Bean Salad, 20
  Garbanzos, Chana Masala, 10
  Green
    Casserole, 149
    Mediterranean Style, 148
    Salad with onions, 81
    Salade Niçoise, 141
    with Water Chestnuts, 148
  Limas and Peas Baked with Herbs, 152
Beef, 90–97, also see Beef, Ground
  Beef Burgundy, 94
  Beef Sticks, appetizer, 62
  Beefsteak Pie, 93
    (Beef and Kidney Pie, 93)
  Chile Verde, 138
  Chinese "Hot Pot," 35
  Corned Beef Hash and Egg Cups, 23

Flank Steak, Mushrooms, and Asparagus, 92
Fondue, 46
Giant Beef-Lobster Kebabs, 93
Javanese Satés, 91
Northern Italy Spaghetti, 134
Petite Marmite, soup, 138
Pozharsky, casserole, 90
Sirloin, Barbecued, with Parsley Herb Butter, 43
Soup stock, 72
Steak, bake-broil cooking, 95
Tongue and Beef Tenderloin, Cold Sliced, 91
Beef, Ground
  Burgundy Burgers, 41
  Danish Meatballs, 27
  Jamaican Stuffed Pumpkin or Squash, 136
  Northern Italy Spaghetti, 134
  Pastitsio, 134
  Stuffed Grape Leaves or Cabbage, 94
Beets
  Soup, Chilled, 71
  with Mustard Butter, 154
Belgian Coffee, 201
Berries, also see individual kinds
  Cantaloupe Stuffed with Berries and Orange Ice, 176
  Fresh Fruit Yogurt Coolers, 197
  Fruit on Ice, 191
  Sour Cream Sauce for, 191
Bhindi Masala, 11
Biscuits, Whipped Cream, 167
Blazer pan with bain Marie, 116
Bombes, 185
Borscht, chilled, 71
Bouillabaisse, Carmel, 139
Braculine, 105
Brandied Carrots, 154
Brandied peach garnish, 92
Brandy, Milk Punch, 198
Brazil nut sauce for ice cream, flaming, 176
Brazilian Baked Trout, 129
Breads, 164–171
  Buttery Pan Rolls, 164
  Cheese Puff Ring, 164
  Cheesy Spoonbread, 167
  Cardamom Tortilla Crisps, 140
  Egg Bagels, 165
  Fancy shapes for dinner rolls, 169
  Finnish Coffee, 171
  French Toast, 23
  Hamburger Buns, 168
  Honey-Pecan Cornbread Sticks, muffin variation, 170
  Pine Nut Sticks, 140
  Pumpernickel Twist, 170
  Rich White Batter, 168
  Rieska, Finnish, 167
  Swedish Flatbread, 140
  Upside-Down Lemon Muffins, 171
  Vörtbröd, Swedish rye, 169
  Wheat Batter Bread, 168
  Whipped Cream Biscuits, 167
Breakfasts for guests, 23
Broccoli
  Cold, with Cashews, 150
  Cream of, soup, 75
Brussels Sprouts with Pecan Butter, 152
Buffet Menus
  Barbecued Ham, 29
  Build-Your-Own Salad, 24
  Cold Salmon, 48
  Greek, 32
  Patio, with lamb, 13
  Scandinavian, 26
  Shellfish on Ice, 33
  Tahitian, 49
  Turkish Meze, 18–20
  Wintertime, 42
Build-Your-Own-Salad Lunch, 24
Bulgur (wheat) pilaf, 161
Buns, Hamburger, 168
Burgundy, Beef, 94
Burgundy Burgers with Roquefort, 41
Butter, fancy shapes, 165
Butter, sweet, 165

Buttermilk
  Lemon Frappé, 196
  Sherbet, 174
Butters, Butter Sauces
  Avocado, 53
  Basil, 149
  Blue Cheese, 46
  Dill, 149
  Fines Herbes, 149
  Maitre d'Hôtel, 149
  Mustard, for beef, 46
  Mustard, for vegetables, 149
  Parsley Herb, 43
  Red Onion, 149
  Toasted Onion, 46

## C

Cabbage
  Carrot, Radish, and Cabbage Salad, 19
  East Indies Salad, 86
  Stuffed, rolls, 94
Caesar Salad, 78
Caffé Borgia, 201
Cakes
  Chocolate-Caramel Torte, 189
  Finnish Old Times, 189
  Four Seasons, 190
  Orange Cheddar Cheesecake, 190
  Punschtorte, 187
  Sultana Raisin, 187
  Sweet Lemon-Yogurt, 192
California wines, 121
Canapés, see Appetizers
Canard à l'Orange, 123
Candle heating units, 116
Candy, taffy, 42
Canned heat for chafing dishes, 116
Cantaloupe, also see Melons
  Appetizer with swordfish, 55
  Stuffed with Berries and Orange Ice, 176
Cappuccino, 201
Cardamom Cookies, Persian, 192
Carmel Bouillabaisse, 139
Carne de Porco con Vinha d'Alhos, 40, 108
Carrots
  Brandied, 154
  Carrot-Asparagus Platter, 155
  Carrot, Radish, and Cabbage Salad, 19
  Ginger-Minted, appetizers, 55
  Shrin Polo, chicken, 112
  Soup, cream, 75
  Sushi, 39
Cashews
  Asparagus with Cashew Butter, 151
  Broccoli, cold, with, 150
  Cashew Chicken, 115
Cassata, 176
Cauliflower, Marinated, 82
Caviar, buying and serving, 57
Celery Parmigiano, 147
Chafing dish cookery, vessels, fuels, 116
Champagne
  Fruit Punch, 202
  Party menu, 28
  Strawberries, Oranges, and Champagne in Orange Shells, 191
Chana Masala, 10
Cheese (cheese guide on page 156)
  Blue
    Appetizer with fennel, 54
    Butter, 46
    Greek Country Salad, 82
    Salad dressing, 76
  Cheddar
    Cheesy Spoonbread, 167
    Orange Cheddar Cheesecake, 190
    Pomegranate Cheese Loaf, 22
    Refried Bean Dip, 59
    Spread, 58
    Tostadas de Harina, 56
  Cream Cheese
    Asparagus cream soup, 75
    Cucumber-Cheese Slices, 56
    Mincemeat-Cheese Pie, 184

Pomegranate Cheese Loaf, 22
Tiropetes, appetizers, 56
Trio, appetizer, 54
Edam balls, appetizer, 54
Feta
 Greek Country Salad, 82
 Tiropetes, appetizers, 56
 Turkish Meze, 19
Fondue, 45
Gruyère
 Danish Chicken and Meatballs
  au Gratin, 113
 Fondue, 45
 Tiropetes, appetizers, 56
 Veal Roast Orloff, 97
Guide to serving and description
 of 65 kinds, 156
Jack
 Cheesy Spoonbread, 167
 Oven Omelet, 137
 San Diego Salad, 141
Parmesan
 Maritata, soup, 73
 Pasta a Pesto, 163
 Potato Soufflé, 158
Pomegranate Loaf snack tray with
 fruit, 22
Sweet County Cheese with Berries,
 182
Swiss
 Cheese Puff Ring, 164
 Cheesy Spoonbread, 167
 Fondue, 45
 French Cheese Soup, 37
 Quiche Lorraine, 58
 Salad, 87
Cheesecake, Orange Cheddar, 190
Chelo, Persian rice, 161
Cherries
 Iced Red Fruits in Wine, 191
 Jubilee, 176
Chestnut-chocolate sauce for ice
 cream, 176
**Chicken,** 111–119
 Broiled Chicken Piquant, 113
 Carrot Soup, 75
 Cashew Chicken, 115
 Chicken-Cucumber Soup, 74
 Circassian, 20
 Coq au Vin with olives, 118
 Curried, Tempura, 117
 Danish, with meatballs au gratin,
  113
 Freezer Chicken Kiev, 111
 Indonesian Broiled, 60
 Kiev, 111
 Livers
  Pâté, Molded, 62
  Petite Marmite, soup, 138
  Sautéed with mushrooms, 136
 Momi, 115
 Paella, 133
 Pilaf-Stuffed Legs, 111
 Salads
  Hot, 143
  San Diego Salad, 141
  Tahitian Condiment with
   Avocado, 86
 Sesame-Soy, 112
 Shrin Polo, 112
 Stuffed Papayas Congo, 118
 Wiener Backhendl, 117
 with Almond Sauce, 37
 with Lemon Sauce, 119
Chile Verde, 138
Chinese
 Cashew Chicken, 115
 Hot Chicken Salad, 143
 "Hot Pot" menu, 34
**Chocolate**
 Chocolate-Caramel Torte, 189
 Chocolate-Macadamia Nut
  Sundaes, 15
 Chocolate-Mint Fizz, 196
 Hot Soufflé, 181
 Ice Cream in Chocolate Cups, 176
 Ice Cream with Chocolate-
  Chestnut Sauce, 176
 Leaves, garnish, 180
 Mexican, 198
 Mocha Cooler, 198

Chorizo Tostadas de Harina, 56
Chutney
 Condiment Chicken Salad, 86
 Podina, onion-mint, 10
 Salad dressing, 78
 Sauce, 46
Cider, apple
 Cider Wassail Bowl, 202
 Glögg, punch, 203
Circassian Chicken, 20
Citrus Cups, garnish, 92
**Clams,** *also see* Seafood
 Bordelaise, 132
 Shellfish Cocktails, 66
 Stuffed, appetizers, 65
Cocktails, shellfish, 66
Coconut
 Coconut milk, making, 203
 Coconut milk drinks, eight kinds,
  203
 Tahitian Coffee, 201
 Tahitian Poë, dessert, 183
Cod, in Caper Cream Sauce, 124
Coffee Bread, Finnish, 171
Coffee Smorgasbord menu, Finnish,
 12
Coffees, foreign, 201
Congo, Baked Papayas, 118
**Cookies**
 Finnish Orange Torte, 192
 Persian Cardamom, 192
 Suspiros, 193
 Three Finnish, 193
Cooking with wine, 104
Coq au Vin, 118
Coquilles St. Jacques, 67
Cornbread sticks, 170
Corned Beef Hash and Egg Cups, 23
**Cornish game hens**
 Buttery Barbecued, 120
 under Glass, 120
Couronnes, 49
Couve con Cebolas, 40
**Crab,** *also see* Seafood
 Freezer Seafood Newburg, 126
 Seafood Soufflés, 124
 Shellfish Cocktails, 66
Cranberries
 Cranberry jelly garnish, 92
 Cranberry-Mint Cocktail, 196
 Fruit Soup, 183
Crème de Menthe Grapes, 22
Crème Royal Viking, 27
Crisp breads for soups and salads, 140
**Cucumbers**
 Agurkesalat, salad, 27
 Cheese-filled appetizer, 56
 Chicken-Cucumber Soup, 74
 Cucumber-Filled Tomatoes, 142
 Greek Country Salad, 82
 Japanese Cucumber Salad, 80
 Mold, salad, 85
 Persian Punch, 199
Curry
 Chicken Tempura, 117
 Curried Almonds, 54
 Indian dinner, 10
 Salad dressing, 142
 Tahitian Prawns, 130

**D**

Danish
 Chicken and Meatballs, 113
 Cucumber salad, 27
 Meatballs, 27
Dessert garnishes, 180
**Desserts,** 173–193, *also see* the
 following listings:
 Cakes
 Cookies
 Frozen Desserts (including ice
  cream and sherbet)
 Fruit Desserts
 Pastry
 Pies
 Puddings
 Soufflés
**Dinner Menus,** *also see* Buffets,
 Outdoor Meals, or Parties
 Chinese "Hot Pot," 34

Duckling, 16
 French Peasant Aïoli, 25
 Indian Curry, 10
 Italian Fritter Meal, 48
 Oriental Meal Cooked at the
  Table, 21
 Portuguese Country, 40
 Spanish Paella, 13
 Supper Beside the Fire, 43
Dinner party tips, 119
Dinner rolls, shaping, 169
Dips, Appetizer
 Avocado, with caviar, 57
 Guacamole, 52
 Onion-Dill, 52
 Raw Radish, 52
 Refried Bean, 59
Dressing Up Green Salads, 76
Dressings, *see* Salad Dressings or
 Stuffings
**Drinks,** 195–203, *also see* Coffees or
 Punches
 Alexander Icicle, 196
 Chocolate-Mint Fizz, 196
 Coconut milk drinks, 203
 Coffees, foreign, 201
 Cranberry-Mint Cocktail, 196
 Double Fruit Soda, 197
 Fresh Fruit Yogurt Coolers, 197
 Kahlua Frost, 198
 Lemon Frappé, 196
 Mexican Almond Horchata, 197
 Mexican Chocolate, 198
 Milk Punch, 198
 Mocha Cooler, 198
 Planters' Punch, 203
Drinks, ways to ice and garnish, 199
Duckling Dinner menu, 16
Duckling with Orange Sauce, 123
Dumplings, Egg-Foam, 162
Dutch Koffie, 201

**E**

East Indies Cabbage Salad, 86
Easy
 Appetizers, 54
 Entrée garnish ideas, 92
 Fresh fruit desserts, 191
 Ice cream desserts, 176
Eggplant
 Moussaka, 102
 Pozharsky, 90
 Ratatouille, 155
 Salad, Broiled, 20
 Veal Indorato, 97
**Eggs**
 Baked in tomato shells, 23
 Baked, with sausages, 23
 Basque Artichokes with, 137
 Caper Stuffed, 142
 Corned Beef Hash and Egg Cups,
  23
 Deviled, with Caviar, 57
 Egg-Foam Dumplings, 162
 Jack Cheese Oven Omelet, 137
 Omelet instructions, 131
 Pimiento Egg Cups, 23
 Scotch, 23
 Souffléed Omelet, 180
 Sushi, 39
 Suspiros, cookies, 193
English
 Beefsteak Pie, 93
 Cider Wassail Bowl, 202
 Fruit Pudding, 183
Entrée garnishes, 92
**Entrées,** 89–143, *also see* individual
 listings for various meats and
 seafood, *plus* Varied Entrées,
 Soups (Main-Dish), or Salads
 (Main-Dish)
Espresso, 201
European wines, 121

**F**

Fennel
 Baked, 147
 Blue cheese appetizer, 54

in ice ring, 28
 Salad dressing, 87
Fettucine, 65
Fiesta Ice Cubes, 199
Figs
 Fresh Fruit Trays, 191
 Honeyed, 22
Fila pastry
 Dough recipe, 98
 Lamp Chops in Pastry Crust, 98
 Persian Baklava, 184
 Tiropetes, appetizers, 56
Finnish
 Coffee Bread, 171
 Coffee Smorgasbord menu, 12
 Cookies, three kinds, 193
 Old Times Cake, 189
 Orange Torte Cookies, 192
 Rieska, bread, 167
Fireplace supper menu, 43
**Fish,** *also see* Seafood and listings
 for individual kinds
 Barbecuing over coals, 128
 Butter-Sautéing, 128
 Oven-Broiling, 128
 Poaching, 128
 Sauces, 128
 Smoked, in Caper Cream Sauce,
  124
Flaming food, flambéing, 116
Flavored butters, 149
Floating Island pudding, 182
Flower-Lei Straws, 199
Folded napkins, 83
Fondue party menus and recipes,
 44–46
Fondue pots, 116
Four Seasons Cake, 190
Frappé, Lemon, 196
**French**
 Aïoli, 25
 Béarnaise Sauce, 95
 Beef Burgundy, 94
 Bombes, 185
 Cheese Soup, 37
 Coffee, 201
 Coq au Vin, 118
 Coquilles St. Jacques, 67
 Crudités, 54
 Dressing with Shallots, 76
 Gateau Sultana, 187
 Gougère, Cheese Puff Ring, 164
 Ham in Pastry, 108
 Les Halles Onion Soup Gratinée, 72
 Omelet, 131
 Parfait, 174
 Pâté en Croûte, 67
 Peas Cooked in Lettuce, 152
 Petite Marmite, 138
 Potatoes Anna, 159
 Quiche Lorraine, 58
 Ratatouille, 155
 Roast Duckling with Orange
  Sauce, 123
 Salade Niçoise, 141
 Soufflés, *see* Soufflé listing
 Soupe au Pistou, 74
 Soupe de Légumes, 76
 Stuffed Provençal Lamb Shoulder,
  100
 Toast, 23
 Veal Paupiettes à la Provençale, 96
 Veal Veronique, 96
 Wines, 121
Fritter meal, Italian, 48
Fritters, Italian, recipe, 97
**Frozen Desserts**
 Bombes, 185
 Cantaloupe Stuffed with Berries
  and Orange Ice, 176
 Cassata, 176
 Cherries Jubilee, 176
 Chocolate-Macadamia Nut
  Sundaes, 15
 Coffee Mold with Flaming Nut
  Sauce, 176
 Ginger Sundaes, 176
 Ice Cream in Chocolate Cups, 176
 Ice Cream with Chocolate-
  Chestnut Sauce, 176
 Maple Parfait, 174

**Frozen Desserts** *(continued)*
  Meringue Shell Glacé, 175
  Orange Shells Glacé, 177
  Pineapple Baked Alaska, 175
  Pumpkin Ice Cream Pie, 186
  Raspberry Torte, 177
  Sherbet, 174
Fruit appetizers on ice, 64
Fruit-cheese snack tray, 22
Fruit garnishes, 92
**Fruit Desserts**
  Baked Apples or Bananas with
    Orange Cream Sauce, 191
  Cantaloupe Stuffed with Berries
    and Orange Ice, 176
  Cherries Jubilee, 176
  Easy Fresh Fruit Desserts, 191
  English Fruit Pudding, 183
  Four Seasons Cake, 190
  Fresh Fruit Trays, 191
  Fruit on Ice, 191
  Fruit with Sour Cream Sauce, 191
  Iced Red Fruits in Wine, 191
  Melon Mélange in Watermelon
    Shell, 191
  Pineapple Baked Alaska, 175
  Pineapple or Pears with Brown
    Sugar Rum Sauce, 191
  Raspberry Torte, 177
  Strawberries, Oranges, and Cham-
    pagne in Orange Shells, 191
  Sweet Country Cheese with
    Berries, 182
  Tahitian Poë, 183
Fruit in salads, 37, 77, 78, 86, 141, 142
Fruit soda, 197
Fruit Soup, Cranberry, 183
Fruit-yogurt drinks, 197

**G**
Garbanzo beans, Indian Chana
  Masala, 10
Garlic Mayonnaise, Aïoli, 25
**Garnishes**
  Appetizer, 64
  Butter, 165
  Dessert, 180
  Drink, 199
  Entrée, 92
  Salad, 76
  Soup, 73
  Vegetable butters, 149
Gateau Sultana, 187
Gazpacho, Pacific, 70
**Gelatin Salads**
  Asparagus in Aspic, 151
  Avocado, Stuffed, 84
  Cucumber Mold, 85
  Sole in Wine Aspic, 143
  Tomato Aspic, 85
German wines, 121
Gingerbread Waffles, 36
Glögg, punch, 203
Gougère, 164
Grape leaves
  Canned, stuffed, 32
  Stuffed, 94
Grapefruit
  Avocado Salad, 78
  Pink Chiffon Pie, 185
Grapes
  Crème de Menthe Grapes, 22
  Veal with grapes in wine, 96
**Greek**
  Arni Souvlakia, shish kebab, 103
  Buffet menu, 32
  Chicken Avgolemono, 119
  Country Salad, 82
  Grape Leaves or Cabbage, Stuffed,
    94
  Lamb Chops in Pastry Crust, 98
  Moussaka, 102
  Pastitsio, 134
  Saganaki, appetizer, 66
  Sweet Lemon-Yogurt Cake, 192
  Swordfish Piraeus, 127
  Tiropetes, appetizers, 56
Green beans, *see* Beans
Green peas, *see* Peas
Green salads, tips for, 76

Greens, Couve Con Cebolas, 40
Guacamole, 52
Guava-coconut drink, 203
Gulab Jamans, 11

**H**
Half-Moons, cookies, 193
**Ham**
  Baked, Jewel Fruit Sauce, 110
  Buffet menu, 29
  Charcoal-Barbecued Honeyed, 109
  Fiesta, cheese-coated, 37
  Ham and Bananas, 106
  Ham in Pastry, 108
  Layered Ham Pancakes, 106
  Mushrooms stuffed with, 60
  Pâté en Croûte, 67
  Sauce in Artichokes, 63
Hamburgers
  Buns, 168
  Burgundy Burgers, 41
  Menu, 41
**Hawaiian**
  Beef Sticks, appetizers, 62
  Chicken Momi, 115
  Kalua pig, 15
  Kauai Fillet of Sole, 129
  Luau menu, 14
  Macadamia Cream Pie, 186
  Pork Roast, 15
  Salad plate, 142
Horchata, 197
Horseradish sauces, 91, 143
Horseshoes, cookies, 193
"Hot Pot" menu, 34, 35
**Hungarian**
  Bean soup, Bab Leves, 140
  Layered Ham Pancakes, 106
  Palacsinta Soup, 72
  Pancakes, Palacsinta, 106

**I**
**Ice**
  Appetizer garnish, 64
  Bowl for dips, 64
  Ring for dips, 64
  Drink icing, 199
    Cones, 199
    Fiesta Ice Cubes, 199
    Iced Bottle, 199
    Orange-Shell Cups, 199
    Ring for punch bowl, 199
    Watermelon Shell Glass Chiller,
      199
Ice cream desserts, *see* Frozen
  Desserts
Ice Cream Drinks
  Alexander Icicle, 196
  Chocolate-Mint Fizz, 196
  Double Fruit Soda, 197
  Kahlua Frost, 198
  Mocha Cooler, 198
Icing, Rum Butter, 187
Indian Curry Dinner menu and
  recipes, 10, 11
Indonesian Broiled Chicken, 60
Irish Coffee, 201
**Italian**
  Antipasto, 63
  Braculine, pork rolls, 105
  Caffé Espresso, 201
  Cappuccino, 201
  Cassata, 176
  Fennel, Baked, 147
  Fettucine, 65
  Fritter meal menu, 48
  Fritters, 97
  Maritata, soup, 73
  Melon with meat, 54
  Minestrone, 24, 139
  Pasta a Pesto, 163
  Pine Nut Sticks, 140
  Risotto, rice, 162
  Spaghetti, Northern Italy, 134
  Spinach Salad with Pine Nut
    Dressing, 81
  Veal Indorato, 97

**J**
Jamaican Stuffed Pumpkin, 136
**Japanese**
  Chicken Tempura, Curried, 117
  Cucumber Salad, 80
  Onigari Yaki, shrimp, 130
  Soup garnishes, 73
  Sushi picnic menu, 38
  Sushi recipe, 39
Javanese Satés, 91
Jewel Fruit Sauce, 110

**K**
Kahlua Frost, 198
Kale with onions, 40
Kauai Fillet of Sole, 129
Kebab Barg, 104
Keema Curry, 11
Kidneys, Beefsteak Pie, 93
Kippered salmon or cod, 124
Kota Avgolemono, 119

**L**
**Lamb**, 98–104
  Arni Souvlakia, kebab, 103
  Chinese "Hot Pot," 35
  Chops in Pastry Crust, 98
  Crown roast, with Pilaf
    Indienne, 100
  Herbed Leg of, 103
  Kebab Barg, Persian, 104
  Keema Curry, 11
  Molded Eggplant Moussaka, 102
  Mustard-Coated Lamb Roll, 98
  Patio Buffet menu, 13
  Stuffed Provençal Lamb
    Shoulder, 100
Leeks, Scalloped, 157
**Lemons**
  Butter Mayonnaise, 66
  Chicken with Lemon Sauce, 119
  Frappé, 196
  Muffins, Upside-Down, 171
  Spicy Citrus Punch, 200
  Yogurt Cake, Sweet, 192
**Lettuce**, in salads
  Greens with Dilled Shrimp, 80
  Hot Chicken Salad, 143
  Marinated Mushroom Salad, 80
  Mixed Vegetables with Sweet-
    breads, 81
  Spinach with Pine Nut Dressing, 81
Lime
  Coconut drink, 203
  Salad Dressing, 76
Liver, *also see* Chicken Livers
  Pâté, Scandinavian, 26
**Lobster**, *also see* Seafood
  Freezer Seafood Newburg, 126
  Giant Beef-Lobster Kebabs, 93
  Imperial, 126
  Shellfish Cocktails, 66
  Turkish Marinated, 20
Lomi-Salmon-Stuffed Tomatoes, 15
Luau menu, 14
**Lunch Menus**, Light Meals
  Build-Your-Own-Salad Lunch, 24
  French Peasant Aïoli, 25
  Nouveau Riche Hamburgers, 41
  Shellfish on Ice, 33

**M**
Macadamia nuts
  Cream Pie, 186
  Sundae, 15
Macaroni, *also see* Noodles or
  Spaghetti
  Pastitsio, 134
  Salad, Scandinavian, 27
Main-Dish Salads, 141–143
Main-Dish Soups, 138–140
Maple Parfait, 174
Maritata, soup, 73
Masa, 31
Mayonnaise, *see* Sauces
**Meat**, *see* listings for individual kinds

Meatballs
  Danish, 27
  Sweet-Sour Sausage Balls, 62
  Veal meatballs, with Danish
    chicken, 113
Melons, *also see* individual kinds
  Appetizer, 65
  Melon Mélange in Watermelon
    Shell, 191
Menu planning, 29
**Menus for Entertaining,** 9–49 (For list
  of menus, see Table of Contents, 6)
Meringue Shell Glacé, 175
Meringue, Suspiros, 193
**Mexican**
  Almendrado, pudding, 178
  Almond Horchata, drink 197
  Asparagus soup, 75
  Chile Verde, 138
  Chocolate, 198
  Coffee, 201
  Guacamole, 52
  Pico de Gallo, salad, 77
  Refried Bean Dip, 59
  Tamalada menu, 30, 31
  Tamales, 30, 31
  Tostadas de Harina, 56
Meze menu, Turkish, 18–20
Milk Punch, 198
Mincemeat
  English Fruit Pudding, 183
  Mincemeat-Cheese Pie, 184
Minestrone, 24, 139
Molded salads, *see* Gelatin Salads
Moussaka, Molded Eggplant, 102
Mousse in orange shells, 177
Muffins
  Honey-Pecan Cornbread, 170
  Upside-Down Lemon, 171
**Mushrooms**
  à la Grecque, 54
  Chicken Livers and, 136
  Coq au Vin, 118
  Flank steak and asparagus with, 92
  Ham in Pastry, 108
  Ham-Filled, appetizer, 60
  Raw, in salad, 80
  Raw, marinated appetizer, 55
  Sausage Pie, 137
  Scalloped, 154
  Sushi, 39
Mustard greens with onions, 40

**N**
Napkins, decorative folding, 83
Natillus with Crunchy Caramel, 182
Niçoise, Salade, 141
Nockerln, dumplings, 162
**Noodles**, *also see* Macaroni or
  Spaghetti
  Fettucine, 65
  Green, with Sour Cream, 162
  Maritata, soup, 73
  Pasta a Pesto, 163
Nouveau Riche Hamburgers menu,
  41
Nuts, *see* individual kinds

**O**
Oeufs à la Neige, 182
Okra, Indian Bhindi Masala, 11
Old Times Cake, Finnish, 189
Olives
  Chicken in wine with, 118
  Turkish, 19, 20
Omelet pan chafing dish, 116
Omelets
  Basic recipe, 131
  Jack Cheese Oven Omelet, 137
  Souffléed Omelet, 180
Onigari Yaki, 130
**Onions**
  Beefsteak tomato salad, 85
  Danish fried, 27
  for hamburgers, 41
  Les Halles Onion Soup Gratinée,
    72
  Onion-Dill Dip, 52
  Potato-Onion Pancakes, 159

Scalloped, 157
Soufflé, 157
Spiced Baked, 157
**Oranges**
Cantaloupe Stuffed with Berries and Orange Ice, 176
Chiffon Soufflé, Chilled, 181
Duckling with Orange Sauce, 123
Fresh Fruit Trays, 191
Glögg, punch, 203
Orange Cheddar Cheesecake, 190
Orange Cream Sauce, 191
Orange-Shell Cups, 199
Orange Shells Glacé, 177
Orange Sponge Waffles, 36
Orange Torte Cookies, 192
Pico de Gallo, salad, 77
San Diego Salad, 141
Spicy Citrus Punch, 200
Strawberries, Oranges, and Champagne in Orange Shells, 191
Oriental Meal Cooked at the Table menu, 21
**Outdoor Meals,** *also see* Picnics
Cold Salmon Buffet, 48
Nouveau Riche Hamburgers, 41
Patio Buffet, 13
Patio Luau, 14
Shellfish on Ice, 33
Tahitian Party, 49
Turkish Meze, 18
**Oysters,** *also see* Seafood
Pan Roast, 130
Shellfish Cocktails, 66
Sole Oyster Roll, 129

**P**

Paella
Dinner menu, 13
Spanish, recipe, 133
Twenty-Minute, 37
Painting chocolate, 180
Palacsinta, Hungarian pancakes, 106
Pancakes
Hungarian Palacsinta, 106
Layered Ham, 106
Potato-Onion, 159
Souffléed Omelet, 180
**Papaya**
Coconut drink, 203
Hawaiian Salad, 142
Pork Loin with Sautéed Papaya, 110
Stuffed Baked Papayas Congo, 118
Tahitian Poë, 183
Parfait, Maple, 174
Parsnips, Honey, 154
**Parties**
Champagne, 28
Dinner party tips, 119
Finnish Coffee Smorgasbord, 12
Fondue, 44
Mexican Tamalada, 30
Patio Luau, 14
Taffy Pull, 42
Tahitian, 49
Waffle, 36
Wine-Tasting, 17
Passion fruit-coconut drink, 203
Pasta a Pesto, 163
**Pastas,** 162–163, *also see* Noodles, Spaghetti, or Macaroni
Pastitsio, 134
**Pastry**
Egg, pie crust, 93
Fila Dough, 98
Gulab Jamans, dessert, 11
Ham in Pastry, 108
Lamb Chops in Pastry Crust, 98
Pâté en Croûte, 67
Persian Baklava, 184
Tiropetes, appetizers, 56
Pâté
en Croûte, ham and veal, 67
Molded Chicken Liver, 62
Scandinavian Liver, 26
Patio Buffet menu, 13
Patio Luau menu, 14
Paupiettes, veal rolls, 96
Peaches, garnish, 92

Peanuts
Nut-Crusted Squash Squares, 160
Pork Satés Bali, 109
Pears with Brown Sugar Rum Sauce, 191
Peas
Chinese Snow (edible pod)
Cashew Chicken, 115
Chinese "Hot Pot," 35
Snow Peas with Sesame Dressing, 84
Green
Baked with limas, 152
Cooked in Lettuce, 152
Salad, in sour cream, 82
Sushi Rice with Vegetable Tidbits, 39
Wheat pilaf with, 161
Pecans
Brussels Sprouts with Pecan Butter, 152
Honey-Pecan Cornbread Sticks, 170
Peppers, bell
Aïoli meal, 25
Ratatouille, 155
Persian
Baklava, pastry, 184
Cardamom Cookies, 192
Chelo, rice, 161
Cucumber Punch, 199
Kebab Barg, lamb, 104
Shrin Polo, chicken, 112
Petite Marmite, 138
Pheasant-in-a-Bag, 123
Philippine Shrimp-Stuffed Tomatoes, 55
**Picnics,** *also see* Outdoor Meals
Japanese Sushi, 38
Patrons of the Arts, Viennese, 47
Pico de Gallo, salad, 77
**Pies, Dessert**
Macadamia Cream, 186
Mincemeat-Cheese, 184
Pink Grapefruit Chiffon, 185
Pumpkin Ice Cream, 186
**Pies, Non-Sweet**
Beefsteak, 93
Mushroom and Sausage, 137
Spinach, 148
Pilaf
Chicken legs stuffed with, 111
Rice, Indienne, 100
Stuffing for turkey, 122
Wheat, with Peas and Lemon, 161
Pimiento Egg Cups, 23
Pine nuts
Braculine, 105
Pine Nut Sticks, 140
Spinach with Pine Nut Dressing, 81
Pineapple
Baked Alaska, 175
Coconut drink, 203
Hawaiian Salad, 142
Pineapple Fingers, Pistachio, 22
Tahitian Poë, 183
with Brown Sugar Rum Sauce, 191
Pistachio nuts
Persian Cardamom Cookies, 192
Pineapple Fingers, 22
Pistou in vegetable soup, 74
Planning the Perfect Menu, 29
Podina Chutney, mint-onion, 10
Poë, Tahitian Fresh Fruit, 183
Poi, 15
**Pork,** 105–110, *also see* Bacon, Ham, or Sausage
Braculine, stuffed rolls, 105
Chicken Momi stuffing, 115
Chile Verde, 138
Chops, Stuffed Smoked, 105
Danish Meatballs, 27
Hawaiian Salad, 142
Loin with Sautéed Papaya, 110
Paella, 133
Roast, Hawaiian-Style, 15
Satés Bali, 109
Spareribs in Garlic Wine, Portuguese, 108
Portuguese
Dinner menu and recipes, 40

Spareribs in Garlic Wine, 108
Suspiros, cookies, 193
**Potatoes**
Brown-Sugar-Glazed, 159
Carrot-Asparagus Platter, 155
Casserole, 158
Pancakes, Potato-Onion, 159
Parmesan Soufflé, 158
Salad, Antipasto, 87
Salade Niçoise, 141
Skillet Potatoes Anna, 159
with Fresh Tomatoes, 158
**Potatoes, Sweet**
and Apples Caramel, 160
Pecan-Topped, 160
Roast Pork, Hawaiian, 15
**Poultry,** 111–123, *also see* Chicken, Cornish Hens, Duckling, Pheasant, or Turkey
Pozharsky, casserole, 90
Praline Lace Crust, 180
Prawns, *see* Shrimp
**Puddings**
Almendrado, 178
Chilled Zabaglione Cream, 178
Cranberry Fruit Soup, 183
Crème Royal Viking, 27
English Fruit, 183
Natillus with Crunchy Caramel, 182
Tahitian Fruit Poë, 183
Pumpkin
Ice Cream Pie, 186
Jamaican Stuffed, 136
Punch bowls, 199
**Punches**
Champagne Fruit, 202
Cider Wassail Bowl, 202
Ginger Wine, 200
Glögg, 203
Milk, 198
Persian Cucumber, 199
Planters', 203
Sangria, 200
Spicy Citrus, 200
White Wine, 202
Punschtorte, 187

**Q**

Quiche Lorraine Appetizers, 58
Quick dinners, 37

**R**

Radishes
Carrot, Radish, and Cabbage Salad, 19
Dip, Raw Radish, 52
Raisins, Sultana Cake, 187
**Raspberries,** *also see* Berries
Cookies, Raspberry Strip, 193
Iced Red Fruits in Wine, 191
Sherbet, 174
Torte, 177
Ratatouille, 155
Refried Bean Dip, 59
**Rice**
Crusty Golden, Chelo, 161
Paella, Spanish, 133
Paella, Twenty-Minute, 37
Pilaf, Indienne, 100
Pilaf-Stuffed Chicken Legs, 111
Pilaf Stuffing for Turkey, 122
Pork chops, stuffing, 105
Risotto, Italian rice, 162
Shrin Polo, chicken, 112
Sushi, with Vegetable Tidbits, 39
Wild, stuffing, 120
Rieska, Finnish bread, 167
Risotto, rice, 162
Rock Cornish game hens, 120
Rolls
Buttery Pan, 164
Fancy shapes for, 169
**Romaine**
Caesar Salad, 78
Greens with Dilled Shrimp, 80
Grapefruit-Avocado Salad, 78
Pico de Gallo, salad, 77
Rose Water Syrup, 184

Rum
Brown Sugar Rum Sauce, 191
Butter Icing, 187
Coconut milk drinks, 203
Glögg, 203
Russian
Coffee, 201
Pozharsky, casserole, 90
Rye bread
Pumpernickel Twist, 170
Rieska, 167
Vörtbröd, 169

**S**

**Salad Dressings**
Blue Cheese, 76
Cardamom, 77
Chutney, 78
Cumin, 141
Curry, 142
Fennel, 87
French, with Shallots, 76
Lime, 76
Mayonnaise, *see* Sauces
Pine Nut, 81
Sesame Seed, 84
Salad ingredient ideas, 76
Salad lunch menus, 24, 25
**Salads,** 77–87, *also see* Salads, Main-Dish
Agurkesalat, cucumber, 27
Antipasto, 37
Antipasto Potato, 87
Asparagus Tips in Aspic, 151
Beefsteak Tomatoes and Onions, 85
Broiled Eggplant, 20
Caesar, 78
Carrot, Radish, and Cabbage, 19
Condiment Chicken, with Avocado, 86
East Indies Cabbage, 86
Fresh Cucumber Mold, 85
Gazpacho, 70
Grapefruit-Avocado, 78
Greek Country, 82
Green and Gold, 78
Green Beans and Onions, 81
Green Peas in Sour Cream, 82
Greens with Dilled Shrimp, 80
Japanese Cucumber, 80
Macaroni, 27
Marinated
Cauliflower, 82
Mushroom, 80
Shrimp or Lobster, 20
Mixed Vegetables with Sweetbreads, 81
Orange and Onion, 37
Pico de Gallo, 77
Salad Tropical, fruit, 77
Snow Peas with Sesame Dressing, 84
Spinach with Pine Nut Dressing, 81
Stuffed Avocado, 84
Swiss Cheese, 87
Tomato Aspic with Vegetables, 85
Tomato, with Mint or Dill, 19
Vegetable-Filled Avocados, 84
White Bean, Turkish, 20
**Salads, Main-Dish,** 141–143
Aïoli meal, 25
Build-Your-Own-Salad Lunch, 24
Hawaiian, 142
Hot Chicken, 143
Main-Dish Caesar, 78
Salade Niçoise, 141
Salmon Cornucopia Platter, 142
San Diego, 141
Sole in Wine Aspic, 143
**Salmon**
Baked, with Tarragon Dressing, 127
Buffet menu, 48
Cornucopia Platter, salad, 142
Lomi-Salmon-Stuffed Tomatoes, 15
Smoked, in Caper Cream Sauce, 124
San Diego Salad, 141
Sangria, 200

Satés
  Bali, pork, 109
  Javanese, beef, 91
Sauces, *also see* Sauces, Dessert, or
    Butters
  Avgolemono, 94
  Avocado, 46
  Béarnaise
    Blender, 95
    Tomato, 93
  Brown Butter Almond, 128
  Chile, for tamales, 31
  Chutney, 46
  Cumberland, for game, 123
  Hollandaise
    Blender, 126
    with Cucumber, 128
    with Shrimp, 128
  Horseradish, 143
  Horseradish, Fluffy, 91
  Jewel Fruit, for ham, 110
  Mayonnaise
    Blender, 54
    Browned Butter, 53
    Garlic, Aïoli, 25
    Green, 66
    Lemon Butter, 66
  Meunière, 128
  Remoulade, 66
  Spicy Cocktail, 66
  Soubise, onion, 97
  Teriyaki, 46
  Tomato, 102
  Tomato, for fish, 128
Sauces, Dessert
  Almond Custard, 178
  Brown Sugar Rum, 191
  Chocolate-Chestnut, 176
  Flaming Nut, 176
  Flaming Strawberry, 175
  Ginger, 176
  Orange Cream, 191
  Soft Custard, 181
  Sour Cream, 191
Sausage
  Baked Eggs and, 23
  Mushroom and Sausage Pie, 137
  Scotch Eggs, 23
  Sweet-Sour Balls, 62
Scallops, *also see* Seafood
  Chafing Dish, 132
  Coquilles St. Jacques, 67
  Cream of, soup, 74
Scandinavian Buffet menu, recipes,
    26
Scotch Eggs, 23
Seafood, 124–132, *also see* Abalone,
    Clams, Crab, Fish, Lobster,
    Oysters, Scallops, or Shrimp
  Aïoli meal, 25
  Carmel Bouillabaisse, 139
  Chinese "Hot Pot," 35
  Fondue, 46
  Freezer Seafood Newburg, 126
  Paella, Spanish, 133
  Paella, Twenty-Minute, 37
  Seafood-dip ice platter, 64
  Shellfish Cocktails, 66
  Shellfish on Ice menu, 33
  Soufflés, Individual, 124
Sesame French Toast, 23
Sesame salad dressing, 84
Shellfish, *see* Seafood and individual
    listings
Shellfish on Ice menu, 33
Sherbet
  Bombes, 185
  Cantaloupe Stuffed with Berries
    and Orange Ice, 176
  Double Fruit Soda, 197
  Lime-Pineapple, 174
  Orange, 174
  Pineapple, 174
  Raspberry, 174
Sherries, types of, 121
Shish kebab, Greek, 103
Shrimp, *also see* Seafood for dishes
    of mixed seafoods
  Canapés, 60
  Cocktails, sauces, 66
  Curried, Tahitian, 130

Greens with Dilled Shrimp, 80
Hawaiian Salad, 142
Iced, in Dill Marinade, 59
Marinated, 20
Newburg, 126
Onigari Yaki, skewered, 130
Philippine Tomatoes, 55
Saganaki, appetizer, 66
Sushi, 39
Shrin Polo, 112
Silver rose dish for butter
  "blossom," 165
Simple appetizers, 54
Smorgasbord, Finnish Coffee, 12
Smorgasbord, Scandinavian, 26
Snack tray, cheese and fruit, 22
Sole
  Kauai Fillet of, 129
  Sole Oyster Roll, 129
  Sole in Wine Aspic, 143
Soufflés
  Chilled Orange Chiffon, 181
  Fresh Tomato, 146
  Hot Chocolate, 181
  Onion, 157
  Potato Parmesan, 158
  Seafood, Individual, 124
  Souffléed Omelet, 180
Soup garnish ideas, 73
Soup stock, beef, 72
Soups, 70–76, *also see* Soups,
    Main-Dish
  Asparagus, Cream of, 75
  Avocado Bouillon, 71
  Beef Stock, 72
  Beet, Chilled, 71
  Broccoli, Cream of, 75
  Carrot, cream, 75
  Cheese, French, 37
  Chicken-Cucumber, 74
  Egg Drop, 37
  Jellied Wine Consommé, 71
  Maritata, 73
  Minestrone, canned, additions to,
    24
  Onion Soup Gratinée, 72
  Pacific Gazpacho, chilled, 70
  Palacsinta, pancake strip, 72
  Scallops, Cream of, 74
  Soupe au Pistou, 74
  Soupe de Légumes, 76
  Tomato, Iced, 70
  Wine Consommé, 71
Soups, Main-Dish, 138–140
  Carmel Bouillabaisse, 139
  Chile Verde, 138
  Hungarian Speckled Bean, 140
  Minestrone, North Beach, 139
  Petite Marmite, 138
Spaghetti, *also see* Noodles or
    Macaroni
  Northern Italy, 134
  Parsley, 163
Spanish
  Natillus, dessert, 182
  Paella dinner menu, 13
  Paella recipe, 133
  Sangria, punch, 200
  Sherries, 121
Spareribs, Portuguese, 108
Spinach
  Green Noodles with Sour Cream,
    162
  Hawaiian Salad, 142
  Pie, 148
  Tomatoes stuffed with, 147
Spoonbread, Cheesy, 167
Squash, *also see* Zucchini
  à la Grecque, crookneck and
    zucchini, 150
  Jamaican Stuffed, Hubbard, 136
  Nut-Crusted Squash Squares,
    Hubbard or banana, 160
Steak cuts and selection, basic
  cooking, sauce, 95. *See* Beef for
  individual recipes.
Strawberries, *also see* Berries
  Champagne Fruit Punch, 202
  Finnish Old Times Cake, 189
  Iced Red Fruits in Wine, 191
  Meringue Shell Glacé, 175

Sweet Country Cheese with, 182
  with Oranges and Champagne in
    Orange Shells, 191
Straws, Flower-Lei, 199
Stuffing
  Rice, for pork chops, 105
  Rice pilaf, for turkey, 122
  Veal and pork, for chicken, 115
  Wild rice, for Cornish hens, 120
Sultana Raisin Cake, 187
Supper Beside the Fire menu, 43
Sushi picnic menu, recipe, 38, 39
Suspiros, cookies, 193
Swedish
  Flatbread, 140
  Glögg, punch, 203
  Vörtbröd, rye bread, 169
Sweet Country Cheese, 182
Sweet Potatoes, *see* Potatoes
Sweetbreads
  Danish Chicken and Meatballs au
    Gratin, 113
  Vegetable salad with, 81
Swiss chard with onions, 40
Swiss Cheese Salad, 87
Swiss Fondue, 45
Swordfish
  Skewered with cantaloupe,
    appetizer, 55
  Piraeus, Greek kebab, 127
Syrian Demitasse, 201

T

Taffy-pull party, recipe, 42
Tagliarini, noodles
  Fettucine, 65
  Pasta a Pesto, 163
Tahitian
  Coffee with Coconut Milk, 201
  Curried Prawns, 130
  Fruit Poë, 183
  Party menu, 49
Tamalada, Mexican, 30, 31
Tamale-making party, recipes, 30, 31
Tempura, Curried Chicken, 117
Tetrazzini, Turkey, 122
Tiropetes, appetizer, 56
Toast, French, 23
Tofu, Chinese "Hot Pot," 35
Tomatoes
  Aspic with Vegetables, 85
  Baked Eggs in Tomato Shells, 23
  Baked Green, 146
  Beefsteak Tomatoes and Onions,
    salad, 85
  Cherry, shrimp-stuffed, 55
  Cucumber-Filled, 142
  Greek Country Salad, 82
  Lomi-Salmon-Stuffed, 15
  Potatoes with, 158
  Ratatouille, 155
  Salad with Mint or Dill, 19
  Sauce, 102, 128
  Shrimp-Stuffed, Philippine, 55
  Soufflé, 146
  Soup, Iced, 70
  Spinach-stuffed, 147
  Tomato Béarnaise sauce, 93
Tongue, Cold Sliced, and Beef
  Tenderloin, 91
Tortes
  Chocolate-Caramel, 189
  Punschtorte, Viennese, 187
  Raspberry, 177
Tortillas
  Cardamom Crisps, 140
  Crisp-fried, with bean dip, 59
  Tostadas de Harina, 56
Tropical drinks, 203
Trout, Brazilian Baked, 129
Tuna, Salade Niçoise, 141
Turkey
  Rice Pilaf Stuffing for, 122
  Schnitzel, 122
  Tamales, 30
  Tetrazzini, 122
Turkish
  Coffee, 201
  Meze menu, recipes, 18–20
  Rice Pilaf Stuffing for Turkey, 122

U

Unexpected guests, quick meals for,
  37

V

Varied Entrées, 133–137
  Basque Artichokes with Eggs, 137
  Chicken Livers and Mushrooms,
    136
  Jack Cheese Oven Omelet, 137
  Jamaican Stuffed Pumpkin or
    Squash, 136
  Mushroom and Sausage Pie, 137
  Northern Italy Spaghetti, 134
  Paella, 133
  Pastitsio, 134
Veal, 96–97
  Chicken Momi, stuffing, 115
  Danish Chicken and Meatballs
    au Gratin, 113
  Indorato, fritters, 97
  Pâté en Croûte, 96
  Paupiettes à la Provençale, 96
  Roast Orloff, 97
  Veronique, with grapes, 96
Vegetable Recipes, 146–160
Vegetables, *also see* name of vegetable
  Aïoli meal, 25
  Chinese "Hot Pot," 35
  Crudités, appetizer, 54
  Onion-Dill Dip for, 52
Viennese
  Coffee, 47, 201
  Egg-Foam Dumplings, 162
  Picnic menu, 47
  Punschtorte, 187
  Wiener Backhendl, 117
Vintage, wine, 163
Vörtbröd, rye bread, 169

W

Waffles
  Gingerbread, 36
  Orange Sponge, 36
  Party menu, 36
Wassail bowl, 202
Water Chestnuts, Green Beans with,
  148
Watermelon-Shell
  Glass Chiller, 199
  Melon Mélange in, 191
Wheat Batter Bread, 168
Wheat Pilaf, 161
Wiener Backhendl, chicken, 117
Wild Rice Stuffing, 120
Wine
  Age, 163
  Appetizer, 101
  California, 121
  Cooking with, 104
  Dessert, 101
  European, 121
  Glasses, 101
  Grape varieties, 121
  Labeling, guide to, 121
  Punches, 200, 202
  Serving rules, 101
  Sherry, 121
  Vintage, 163
  Wine-Tasting, 16, 17
Wintertime Buffet menu, 42

Y

Yeast rolls, shaping, 169
Yogurt
  Fresh Fruit Coolers, 197
  Lemon-Yogurt Cake, 192

Z

Zabaglione Cream, Chilled, 178
Zucchini
  Ratatouille, 155
  Skillet, 150
  Squash à la Grecque, 150
  Veal Indorato, 97
  Zucchini Fans, 150